CHRIST'S
LAST WORDS *to*
HIS CHURCH

Christ's Last Words to His Church
John S. Barnett

Müllerhaus Publishing Arts, Inc.
DBA Müllerhaus Legacy
5200 South Yale Ave, Penthouse | Tulsa, Oklahoma 74135
www.MullerhausLegacy.com

ISBN-13: 978-1-7328044-1-8
LCCN: 2018961765

Cover and Interior Design by Laura Hyde | Müllerhaus Legacy
Index by Nancy Kopper

Printed in Canada.

CHRIST'S
LAST WORDS *to*
HIS CHURCH

Revelation 1-3

DR. JOHN S. BARNETT

müllerhaus
[LEGACY]

TULSA

DEDICATION

This book is dedicated with much gratitude, from their pastor of 2008–2017, to those amazing saints at Calvary Bible Church of Kalamazoo, Michigan. You dear and precious saints loved, supported, encouraged, and prayed me through the twelve months of daily exegetical research, and all the rigors of expository work to complete this explanatory journey through perhaps the three greatest chapters of the Bible. Only here do we see what Jesus Christ, our Lord and Savior, is DOING today. Jesus is still walking around Calvary Bible TODAY as He did the First Church at Ephesus, and Smyrna, and Pergamum, and Thyatira, and Sardis, and Philadelphia, and Laodicea—2,000 years ago!

Jesus Christ wants to bless us (Rev. 1:3) as we read with our minds, hear with our hearts, and choose each day to obediently hold on to the treasures of these verses in the last book of the Bible. May the Lord bless each of you who read, hear, and keep the words Christ has given to us. With much love and gratefulness for your partnership in the Gospel,

John Barnett
Hebrews 13:20–21

Introduction

Today may I lead you through the only chapters exclusively devoted to introducing us to what our Master and Savior, Jesus, is doing RIGHT NOW: in the last book of the Bible, the Revelation of Jesus Christ?

Have you paused yet today to check in with Jesus Christ? The best way to do that is through your Bible, because Jesus Christ is revealed to us as the Word of God. He is the Word, and the Word reveals Him. Each time we open God's Word, we can hear His Voice.

At Creation God the Son, the Creator, spoke and made all things, and through His apostles and prophets, His Word has been given.

As you open to the last book of your Bible, you open to the climactic conclusion of God's Word written down for us.

The first word in the Greek New Testament text of Revelation is the word *apocalupsis*, which can be translated as either "revelation" or "unveiling." The next two words are "Jesus Christ." That means in this last book we are:

Getting to See the Real Jesus

So we are opened to the "revelation of Jesus Christ," or the "taking the cover off of Jesus Christ," or the "disclosure of Jesus Christ," or the "manifestation of Jesus Christ," or the "unveiling of Jesus Christ," the Word of

God. There is so much to think about as we open to these Last Words of Christ, God's Word.

Revelation completes God's revelation of Himself to humanity through Christ.

In Genesis, the Creator, God the Son, walks and talks with Adam and Eve, the first two humans to ever exist, created from the hand of God. But God does not stay walking and talking to them. Because they sinned, He banishes them from the Paradise He made for them. Thus began all the sorrows and woes that have plagued humanity all these thousands of years.

But in the book of Revelation, the Creator explains that He is back, actively walking on Earth again, among His people.

The book of Revelation explains for us that God the Son, Jesus Christ, the Creator, is here on the ground guiding His Church to accomplish His purposes in the world.

Much like a coach on the floor with his team, Jesus Christ is walking around and watching us play the positions He gave us to play. That is perhaps the most arresting truth in all the Bible for us. We are not alone; the Coach Himself, our Creator, is personally wanting to help us get done what He desires us to do.

To begin our look at Christ's Last Words, we need to listen to His Voice, and begin in Revelation 1.

John Barnett
Serving the Next Generation in Asia, Europe & Africa
October, 2018

Foreword
by John MacArthur

No book in Scripture reveals the glory of God and Christ in more splendor than does the book of Revelation. Yet no book has been more misunderstood, misinterpreted, and neglected than this book. At the end of the book, Revelation 22:10 says, "Do not seal up the words of the prophecy of this book, for the time is near." Clearly, God wants His children to know what this book teaches, so that they can appropriate its truth to their lives.

Those who read Revelation and heed its message will be greatly blessed. In fact, it is the only book in the New Testament that begins and ends with a promise of blessing to its readers. In Revelation 1:3, we find, "Blessed is he who reads and those who hear the words of this prophecy, and keep those things which are written in it." And at the end of the book, a similar promise is given: "Blessed is he who heeds the words of the prophecy of this book" (22:7). Those who ignore Revelation deprive themselves of a rich treasure of divine truth, and the promised blessings that come from understanding that truth.

Far from being the mysterious, incomprehensible book many imagine it to be, Revelation's purpose is to reveal truth, not to obscure it. That fact is evident in its title, "The Revelation of Jesus Christ," which primarily refers to our Lord's second-coming glory. The Greek word for *revelation* could also be translated "an uncovering," "an unveiling," or "a disclosure." It is used in the New Testament to speak of the disclosure of spiritual truth

(Romans 16:25; Galatians 1:12; Ephesians 1:17; 3:3), the manifestation of the sons of God (Romans 8:19), and the advent of Christ at both His first (Luke 2:32) and second (2 Thessalonians 1:7; 1 Peter 1:7) comings. In each case, the word *revelation* describes something (or someone) that was formerly hidden, but now has become visible. Thus the book of Revelation unveils truths about Jesus Christ and His final victory, which were alluded to but not fully disclosed in earlier portions of Scripture.

Because this book is first and foremost about Jesus Christ, its focus is inherently devotional. The book depicts Christ as the risen, glorified Son of God ministering among the churches (1:10ff.) as "the faithful witness, the firstborn from the dead, and the ruler over the kings of the earth" (1:5), as "the Alpha and Omega, the Beginning and the End" (1:8), as the One "who is and who was and who is to come, the Almighty" (1:8), as "the First and the Last" (1:11), as "the Son of Man" (1:13), as the One "who is holy [and]... true" (3:7), as "the Amen, the Faithful and True Witness, the Beginning of the creation of God" (3:14), as "the Lion of the tribe of Judah" (5:5), as the Lamb in heaven, with the authority to open the title deed of the earth (6:1ff.), as the Lamb of the throne (7:17), as the Messiah who will reign forever (11:15), as "The Word of God" (19:13), as the majestic King of kings and Lord of lords, returning in glorious splendor to conquer His foes (19:11ff.), and as "the Root and the Offspring of David, the Bright and Morning Star" (22:16). Because of its Christ-centered focus, the book of Revelation fuels worship, motivates holiness, and cultivates hope, which is why its message is so desperately needed today.

In *Christ's Last Words to His Church*, John Barnett has made the book of Revelation accessible to anyone. These chapters will do far more than merely pique your curiosity about the book's remarkable imagery. They will serve to enrich both your worship and your walk by prompting you to focus on the central figure of Revelation, Christ Himself. So dig in on a regular basis to this mighty treasury that exalts the glory of our Lord.

The Book of the Revelation | *1*

THE BOOK OF THE REVELATION IS OFTEN DESCRIBED as one of the most confusing books in all the Bible. For centuries, pastors have avoided preaching on it and Revelation kind of sat on a shelf for all that time. Even the great leaders of the Reformation, Martin Luther and John Calvin, were reluctant to preach on Revelation because it was too hard to understand. And for centuries, the Church has, for the most part, missed out on the blessing of this book.

But there's something special about Revelation. It is the only book of the Bible that makes this promise: "Blessed is he who reads and those who hear the words of this prophecy, and keep those things which are written in it; for the time is near."[1]

We are blessed just by reading this book. We are blessed just by hearing it preached. And most importantly, we are blessed when we obey it. God doesn't just call us to be hearers of His Word, but doers of His Word.[2] When we read and when we hear, what is our response? To obey God's Word and be blessed? Or to set it aside because it's too confusing?

We know that by this time in history, when Revelation was written, the Church already had the Old Testament. They were already reading the four gospels written by Matthew, Mark, Luke, and John. Paul's thirteen

---

1   Revelation 1:3
2   James 1:22–25

letters were circulating among the churches, as were the letters from the other apostles. God could have left it at that. He could have decided, like the Reformers did, that what the Church already had was good enough, that adding anything to it would be unnecessary. But the message of the book of Revelation was so important, God actually delivered it personally.

When John the apostle, exiled to Patmos for the Word of God and the testimony of Jesus Christ, was worshiping God one Sunday morning,[3] he could have been moved by the Holy Spirit as he had been four times before to write God's Words. The Holy Spirit had moved him to write the gospel of John, and three epistles after that. But this time, this last time, something different happened. John heard a voice. And when he turned to see who it was, he saw Jesus Himself, standing on that island with him. And Jesus spoke.

This wasn't a vision or a hallucination. This wasn't John too long alone on that island, sleep-deprived and hungry and everything else. This was a personal visit from God the Son. Every other time God wanted His Words written down, He breathed out the words, through the Holy Spirit, for someone to write, but this time, God sent Jesus Himself to speak the words.

Revelation is the most personal book in all of Scripture. It's the only book hand-delivered by Jesus Christ. It contains the only epistles He personally dictated. The words in the Book of the Revelation are the last words of Christ to His Church.

The Grand Unveiling

The key to understanding Revelation is not to have a chart sitting beside your Bible telling you exactly what the dragon is and listing in order the seven bowls, and telling you which nations are in the End Times. The key to understanding Revelation is to know what God says about it. He knows we get confused. He knows we don't understand everything right away, so the Author Himself stops to explain exactly what we'll be reading so we don't miss it.

Right at the beginning, in Revelation 1:1, God gives this book a divine title. He didn't leave it to us to guess what this book is about. He calls it, "The

---

3 Revelation 1:9–10

Revelation of Jesus Christ." Now, He could have called it, "The Prophecies of the End Times," or "The Warnings about the Future," but He didn't. This is the "Revelation of Jesus Christ."

The first thing we need to know about Revelation is that this book, all twenty-two chapters and 404 verses of it, is about revealing Jesus Christ. If we can understand that, then everything else starts to fall into place.

But God goes even further. He doesn't stop at giving us the title. He gives us a divine outline. He did that before in the book of Acts: "And you shall be witnesses to Me in Jerusalem, and in all Judea and Samaria, and to the end of the earth."[4] And the whole book of Acts follows this outline exactly as the gospel spreads first to Jerusalem, then Judea, Samaria, and to the ends of the earth.

God does the same thing for us in Revelation 1:19. Jesus says to John, "Write the things which you have seen, and the things which are, and the things which will take place after this." God divides Revelation neatly into three parts. Part 1: the things that John sees. Part 2: the things that are, present day, that Jesus dictates to John. And part 3: the things that will take place later. And Revelation follows this outline perfectly.

God gives us a title, an outline, and in Revelation 1:1–8, He describes Himself, the Author, and gives us the purpose of this revelation, why He took the time to hand-deliver it, and why it's so important.

Revelation 1:1–8

The Revelation of Jesus Christ, which God gave Him to show His servants—things that must shortly take place. And He sent and signified it by His angel to His servant John, who bore witness to the Word of God, and the testimony of Jesus Christ, to all things that he saw. Blessed is he who reads and those who hear the words of this prophecy, and keep those things which are written in it; for the time is near.

John, to the seven churches which are in Asia: Grace to you and peace from Him who is and who was and who is to come, and from the seven Spirits who are before His throne, and from Jesus Christ, the faithful witness, the firstborn from the dead, and the ruler over the kings of the earth.

To Him who loved us and washed us from our sins in His own blood, and has made us kings and priests to His God and Father, to Him be glory and dominion forever and ever. Amen.

Behold, He is coming with clouds, and every eye will see Him, even they who pierced Him. And all the tribes of the earth will mourn because of Him. Even so, Amen.

"I am the Alpha and the Omega, the Beginning and the End," says the Lord, "who is and who was and who is to come, the Almighty."

Getting to See the Real Jesus

The first word of the Book of the Revelation is the Greek word *apocalupsis.* You've heard the English words "apocalypse" or "apocalyptic." But here, this word translates as "revelation" or "unveiling." It means to disclose, to uncover, to take the lid off, to reveal. Like the unveiling of next year's model in the showroom of a car dealership, *apocalupsis* means "to pull back the curtain." If it was once covered, it is now uncovered. If it was once hidden, it can now be fully seen.

Every chapter of Revelation is dedicated to unveiling Jesus Christ. Chapters 4–22, the last part of God's revelation to John, reveals to us Jesus Christ, coming in the clouds. We see Jesus, the fulfillment of all His promises, the completion of every prophecy. We see the conclusion of His perfect plan for this planet. And we see Him perfectly reigning on earth and in heaven for all eternity.

Chapters 2 and 3 of Revelation reveal what Jesus' priority is, right now, as He walks among us. He dictates letters to John for seven local churches, warning them of the challenges they face, telling them how to be pleasing to God. Here is revealed for us, for the first time, Jesus' current, present-day, number-one priority.

But chapter 1, "the things you've seen"[5] on God's divine outline, is the moment of Jesus' grand unveiling. God pulls the curtain back, not on the four horsemen, or the tribulation period, or the millennial kingdom, but on Jesus Christ.

Up until this moment, Jesus has been partially hidden to us. We

---

5   Revelation 1:19

caught our first glimpse of Him as Creator in the Garden of Eden, walking and talking with Adam and Eve. He spoke to them face-to-face, He walked with them as friends, but when they were tempted and fell into sin, their communication with God was cut off. He hid His face, and throughout the Old Testament, there was a curtain between Jesus Christ the Creator and His people.

If you read the Old Testament carefully, you will catch brief glimpses of Jesus showing up as the Angel of the Lord, but He never stays for very long. In the New Testament, we finally get what we've been waiting for, Jesus Christ, God in human flesh, come to live among us, but entire decades go by where the Bible tells us nothing about His life. We see Him most clearly during His brief three-year ministry, but just as those closest to Him on earth were beginning to see Him for who He really is, He leaves again.

But in Revelation, God takes the lid off, pulls back the curtain, and opens our eyes to see the Risen Christ like we've never seen Him before. We're given a perfect set of seven descriptions of Jesus, the only place in all the Bible where we're told what He looks like right now. And every description beautifully pictures for us what Jesus is doing today.

Revelation is the only book of the Bible exclusively devoted to revealing what Jesus Christ is doing right now. This isn't what He looked like in the Garden of Eden. This isn't what He was doing 2,000 years ago. This is Jesus now, live-and-in-person. This is what He looks like today, what He's doing today, what is important to Him today.

Revelation is not an afterthought. It is the climactic conclusion to God's Word, the completion of His revelation to us. This is where God takes threads from the Old Testament, the New Testament, the apostles, and the prophets, and finally ties them together. This is where the Old and New Testaments meet, where God's plans for His people, the nation Israel, and His plans for the Church come together. Like a divine switchboard, Revelation is where every other part of Scripture merges together and fits together perfectly. Revelation is the marvelous explanation of things God only hints at in the rest of Scripture, and after millennia of Jesus being partially hidden, this is His grand unveiling.

The Last Words of Jesus Christ

When God gave this last revelation to John, He concluded it by saying there was nothing left to add.[6] By God's own admission, these were Christ's last words to His Church. Jesus hasn't been dictating more epistles through the centuries, delivering more revelation as the times change. This was His final message, His last words.

Nothing spells out more clearly what is important to a human being than their last words on this earth. When they're on oxygen and struggling to breathe, and they manage to utter one last message to their loved ones, those words are treasured more than anything else they've said. In that moment, everything trivial is forgotten. Everything they wasted their life doing is unimportant. What is it they have to say if it's the last thing they'll ever say? And if those are the words of someone you love, they're words you never forget.

The book of Revelation is Christ's last words to us. What are His last words? What is most important to Him? What stands out against everything else He could have said, the last thing He gets to tell His people before He returns?

If you have a red-letter edition of the Bible and you were to flip through it to focus just on the words that came from the mouth of Jesus, you'd find the seven letters to the churches blocked out in red. But going further, to the very end, the last words spoken by Jesus and recorded in Scripture are found in Revelation 22:20: "Surely I am coming quickly."

This is the same promise Jesus gave His disciples when He was about to leave them at the end of His earthly ministry: "Let not your heart be troubled; you believe in God, believe also in Me. In My Father's house are many [rooms]; if it were not so, I would have told you. I go to prepare a place for you. And if I go and prepare a place for you, I will come again and receive you to Myself; that where I am, there you may be also."[7]

This promise would have been familiar to the disciples. It was the same promise every young man gave his bride when they got engaged. As soon as the deal was made, the young man would return to his father's house. And

---

6   Revelation 22:18
7   John 14:1–3

while he was there, he would build a place for his bride to come and live. In fact, if you travel to Israel today, you can still see the remains of houses built like this, one onto the side of another, generation after generation.

Why would Jesus paint us this picture of heaven? And what was the bride doing this whole time? Did you know that until the man returned for his bride, she was not allowed to see him? She went back to her father's house, to her own town, and waited. And while she was waiting, she was preparing everything she'd need for her own house someday, so that the day that her bridegroom would come triumphantly into town and everyone would see him coming, and she'd run out of her house to see if it was really him, she would be ready.

Are we ready for Jesus to come back? Have we been packing our bags, sending our things ahead, investing in heaven so that when He comes we'll be ready?

If you want a test of how much you love Jesus, how much do you long to hear His voice? When two people are in love, they can't get enough of each other. If they can't see each other, they call each other. If they can't call each other, they write letters. If they can't get new letters, they read and reread the ones they have until they're worn out. Have you worn out Jesus' last letter to you? Because this is our communication with Him, the One who loves us completely. This is our connection to Him. This is how we hear His voice. And this is where we see the picture Jesus paints of Himself for us.

Jesus' Top Priority

Chapters 2–3 of Revelation, "The things that are," were personally dictated by Jesus as seven letters to seven local churches. And these local churches are representative of every church. We struggle with the same distractions they did. We face the same challenges. The same thing that kept those seven churches from being useful to God, hinder us from being useful, too. So when Jesus wrote to them, He wrote to everyone who would hear His Words, including us.[8]

Not all things are equally important to Jesus. For His last revelation, He doesn't give a three-day sermon on everything we could possibly ever

8   Revelation 2:7, 11, 17, 29; 3:6, 13, 22

want to know. In the only book that Jesus hand-delivered, the only letters He personally dictated, Jesus spells out for us His top priority.

Jesus could have written about anything. He could have reminded us of all He did for us. He could have reminded us of all His promises. He could have given us a detailed explanation of every End Time prophecy, but when Jesus uttered His last words to His Church, He focused on one thing: what His churches do that pleases Him and what His churches do that doesn't.

John saw Jesus "in the midst of the seven lampstands,"[9] which are the seven churches He's writing to.[10] These are "the things that are."[11] Not the things that were, or that will be someday, but what is happening right now. And right now, Jesus is walking among us, His Church. He's checking to see that we are being what He called us to be and doing what He called us to do.

Of all the things that Jesus could be doing today, His priority is gathering with His local churches. The assembly of the believers is so important to Jesus that He never misses it. And every time we gather as believers, Jesus is here with us. What is it that He sees?

When Jesus came back from His tour of the seven churches, from walking with the believers of Ephesus, Smyrna, Pergamos, Thyatira, Sardis, Philadelphia, and Laodicea, He found some things that pleased Him. Some churches were rooting out the false teachers and suffering for Christ without wavering and standing faithful to the end, and Jesus says He knows their works, and He's pleased. But some churches were allowing distractions to pull them away from their first love, allowing wickedness and false teaching into their churches and forgetting what Jesus left them on earth to do. And Jesus says that He knows their works, too. And He warns them, so that they can repent and become useful again.

Notice these are not unbelievers. These are believers. These are the ones Jesus bought and died for, the ones He owns. The ones who have already been getting letters from the apostles for years now. And some of them are living their lives in a way that displeases God. And Jesus

9   Revelation 1:13
10   Revelation 1:20
11   Revelation 1:19

warns them, telling them to repent so they don't fail the Master who bought them.

Today, Jesus' highest priority is to gather with His local churches, to walk among His people, checking that we are being what He made us to be and doing what He called us to do.

And we don't have to guess what that is. We don't have to somehow divine what God's will for our lives is. It's not some blurry, unclear concept that we can never really nail down for sure. No. Jesus tells us in plain English what pleases Him in chapters 2 and 3, so that when He comes for His bride, we will be found being what we're called to be and doing what we're called to do.

The End of Days

The last section of Revelation, chapters 4–22, describe for us the End of Days. Jesus gives us a picture of what the world will look like when He returns. But what's interesting about this is that when the book of Revelation was given to these seven assemblies, when it was passed around and read by the first-century church, it never divided people. The believers in the churches at Ephesus and Smyrna and Pergamos and everywhere else did not divide themselves into camps, saying, "I believe in a pre-tribulation rapture," or "I believe it happens after the millennium," or "I don't believe in a millennium at all." No. When they read this book, it united them. They rallied around a longing for the return of Christ.

Did you know that there is a crown in heaven for those who long for His return?[12] When God promises a blessing with this book, He doesn't promise it to those who get all the charts and graphs and timelines figured out. He gives it to those who obey. So what did the first-century church do with Revelation? They longed for Jesus' coming. They eagerly waited for Him to come back. When Jesus in Revelation 22:20 said, "Surely I am coming quickly," the response was a unanimous, "Amen. Even so, come, Lord Jesus!" And that should be our response. We should be eagerly waiting for our Lord and Savior to come back, to finish what He started. And He warns us it's going to happen quickly.

---

12 2 Timothy 4:8

God's Tornado Watch

The church I used to pastor in Oklahoma was in a part of the country where, every spring, we'd have to watch out for tornados. So when the weather got bad, we'd turn on the TV or radio and listen for a tornado watch. The meteorologists would look at all the data and see where this front met that front and where the high pressure systems were going to be, and when everything lined up just so, they knew the conditions were right for a tornado. That's a tornado watch.

So we'd hear that and start pulling our lawn furniture inside. Call all the kids from the neighbors' yards, make sure the cars were in the garage. We'd pull out all the candles in case the electricity went out and make sure we had backup batteries for the radio so we'd be able to hear when it was upgraded to a tornado warning.

And all that time, there still wasn't a funnel cloud. A tornado hadn't touched down yet, but the meteorologist saw something we didn't, that all the conditions were right and we could have a tornado any minute.

In the book of Revelation, Jesus gives us a tornado watch for the End Times to tell us when the conditions are right for His return. God gave us the book of Revelation "to show His servants—things which must shortly take place."[13] And Jesus told John to write in verse 19, "the things which will take place after this." In Revelation 4–22 Jesus paints for us a picture of what the world will look like when He returns. He gives us the weather conditions to look for, the signs, and when they appear, we'll know it's soon. And every time Jesus describes the signs of the End of Times, He says the same thing: They're very easy to spot.

The disciples were just as curious about the End Times as we are, and when they asked Jesus to give them signs, He described a world where everything from travel, to communication, to commerce had become global. He tells us the whole world will watch events simultaneously, that a quarter of the earth's population will be wiped off the planet in a staggeringly short amount of time.

Before the invention of airplanes, computers, satellites, television, smartphones, and weapons of mass destruction, the events Jesus described

---

13   Revelation 1:1

weren't even possible. No wonder theologians have had trouble under-standing this book for centuries. To a people whose fastest method of travel was wooden ships and months at sea, global travel must have been unimag-inable. And when God describes the nation Israel as actively participating in global events, how could the Reformers have made sense of that when from the destruction of Jerusalem by the Romans all the way until 1948, there was no nation Israel?

Jesus gives us a picture of the End of Days that only now, in our gen-eration, is beginning to come into clearer and clearer focus. This should inspire confidence in a God who predicted what for centuries was impos-sible to even imagine and is bringing everything together exactly how He said it would be.

When God says these things must "shortly" take place in Revelation 1:1, the word "shortly" is translated from the Greek word *taxos*, meaning "quickly." Once it starts happening, it will happen irrecoverably fast. When Jesus told John in verse 19 to write "the things which will take place after this," He described a world that looks more and more like what we see out-side our windows and on our televisions every day. When the End of Days begins, the world will be so startled by it, the world will never recover. But God wants His servants to know what's coming. Jesus is going to keep His promise: He's coming back.

God's divine tornado watch has warned us that the conditions are right for Christ's return. Jesus tells us, "So you also, when you see all these things, know that it is near—at the doors! Assuredly, I say to you, this gen-eration will by no means pass away till all these things take place,"[14] and "Now when these things begin to happen, look up and lift up your heads, because your redemption draws near."[15] For centuries, theologians have tried to make the signs of the End Times fit with what they saw around them, but they never could until now. That's why Revelation has been sit-ting on a shelf for so long, because only now, in our generation, are we see-ing all the signs that Jesus warned about start to take shape. All the weather conditions are lining up, and we need to be ready.

---

14   Matthew 24:33–34
15   Luke 21:28

Words to Live By

In view of Christ's soon return, how well do our priorities line up with His priority? Revelation unveils for us Jesus as He really is. His work in us is not finished until His very last words are fulfilled and He comes back for His bride. Until then, what is our priority? Is it His? If Jesus came back tomorrow, would He find us doing what He called us to do and being what He called us to be? Will He find that we've ignored the tornado watch and are caught without candles or batteries and our radio turned off?

Will He find us polluted with worldliness like the Thyatirans? Will He find that we've left our first love like the believers at Ephesus? Will He find us so distracted by the things of this world like the Laodiceans that He wants to spit us out of His mouth, or will He find us eagerly looking out our windows for Him, bags packed and ready, ready and waiting for our bridegroom?

The book of Revelation contains the last words of "Him who loved us and washed us from our sins in His own blood."[16] Jesus went to the cross for us. He gives eternal life to us. He walks among us, and He will one day soon return for us. If this same Jesus has hand-delivered the Book of the Revelation as His personally dictated letter to His people, then what will we do with Christ's last words to His Church? We could let this book sit on a shelf for another few centuries because it's too difficult to understand. Or will we claim the blessing that comes from reading this book and live our lives being what He called us to be and doing what He called us to do? If there were ever words to live by, let us make those words Christ's last words to His Church.

---

16 Revelation 1:5

RESPOND to Truth

What does the apostle Paul say the book of Revelation is good for?
(2 Timothy 3:16–17)

How does the apostle John say we want to react when He returns?
(1 John 2:28)

What does Jesus say the world will look like when He returns?
(Matthew 24:3–14)

How does that compare to what I see in the news this week?

If Jesus returned today, how would I react? Why?

What can I do today so that on the day of Christ's return, I will be confident and unashamed?

PART I

The Risen Christ

2 | Unwrapping Jesus Christ

The first word of the Book of the Revelation, *apocalupsis*, to uncover or unveil, is a promise. When God opens the book with this word, He's giving us a promise that we're about to see something spectacular.

God has given us a gift, all wrapped up, sitting on our kitchen table, and we've been looking at it for so long. We know it's special, know it's going to be amazing, but we never see exactly what's inside.

We've been catching glimpses since the Garden of Eden of what God promises to uncover for us, Jesus Christ. But until now, we've never fully seen Him. Harry Ironside used to say that God puts all the truths of the Bible like cookies on the bottom shelf. The Book of the Revelation isn't written to theologians. It's not written to intellectual types who have spent their entire lives studying eschatology. It's written to ordinary people like you and me who need to have simple truths unwrapped for us.

That's what Revelation 1 is. God Himself, the very intentional, purposeful God who knows exactly what we need, has hand-delivered to us a gift, and now He's about to unwrap it. The Jesus we've been seeing bits and pieces of since the Garden of Eden is now standing before us, live and in person. This is His Grand Unveiling.

Jesus' Favorite Word for Himself

When the apostle John received the Book of the Revelation on that Lord's

Day, he was living in what we would call hard times. He was living in exile, cut off from his family and friends. He was living in a prison colony on an island reserved for the worst enemies of Rome, on an inescapable island, unable to reach the mainland without drowning or being eaten by sharks. And the whole time, John was going through all the normal hardships of old age, and it is not a stretch to say that at this point, John was simply waiting to die.

By this time in history, the apostle Paul was already dead. That great apostle, who planted so many churches, who had suffered for Christ and preached on, had already gone to Rome and been beheaded. The apostle Peter, a childhood friend of John's, whom he went fishing with all those years ago, had been hunted down and crucified. Even John's own brother, James, who sat beside him as they listened to Jesus, who, like John, was sent out by Jesus to preach the gospel, had been arrested and executed for his faith. Every other apostle had been hunted down and murdered, and John was the only one left.

Imagine being on a list of twelve, the twelve men known as the leaders of this movement called The Way, and the Roman Empire, the greatest empire in the world, wants every person on that list dead. And one by one, each person on that list was slowly being exterminated. Eleven of the twelve were already dead, and killing the apostle John was now at the top of their to-do list.

That is where John is on the Lord's Day when God Himself stops to hand-deliver a message.

REVELATION 1:9–13

I, John, both your brother and companion in the tribulation and kingdom and patience of Jesus Christ, was on the island that is called Patmos for the word of God and for the testimony of Jesus Christ. I was in the Spirit on the Lord's Day, and I heard behind me a loud voice, as of a trumpet, saying, "I am the Alpha and the Omega, the First and the Last," and, "What you see, write in a book and send it to the seven churches which are in Asia: to Ephesus, to

*Smyrna, to Pergamos, to Thyatira, to Sardis, to Philadelphia, and
to Laodicea."*

*Then I turned to see the voice that spoke with me. And hav-
ing turned I saw seven golden lampstands, and in the midst of the
seven lampstands One like the Son of Man, clothed with a garment
down to the feet and girded about the chest with a golden band.*

In Revelation 1:9, John describes for us exactly what the Christian life
is like. *Flipsis*, "tribulation." This is the word for being squashed. He was
doing what he was supposed to do, preaching the Word of God like he was
called to, and because of that, he was in trouble. *Flipsis*, squashed, can't
hold up the weight any longer.

John's readers were going through the exact same thing. They were
meeting in secret to avoid being fed to lions. They were suffering for their
faith. They were constantly surrounded with so much immorality that they
faced temptation just walking down the street, and they, with us, and with
John, need what God is about to unwrap for them.

When John uses the word "patience" in verse 9, he's using the word for
God telling us to hold on even when it hurts. Paul described the Christian
life as *sumagonizumai*, "with agony." Christians are, according to Paul,
"with agonizers."[17] We struggle together, we are squashed, and God calls us
to hold on even when it hurts.

When God gave the book of Revelation to John, He was speaking to
suffering people. And when God comes to squashed, agonizing people
who are barely holding on, we see His gift to us in one glorious moment,
when God Himself rips away the wrapping paper and we get to see the real,
present-day Jesus Christ.

Yesterday, Today, and Forever

When the box opens and John first sees inside, he isn't shocked by the sight
of something he can't describe. No. In the exact moment in verse 13 when
the wrapping paper comes off, John recognizes someone.

He sees a figure and immediately calls Him "One like the Son of Man."

---

17   Colossians 1:29; 1 Timothy 6:12; 2 Timothy 4:7

Did you know this is Jesus' favorite word for Himself? In all the Bible, He calls Himself "Son of Man" more than anything else. And when He reintroduces Himself to us, the first thing He wants us to see is that He is "One like the Son of Man." He could have been "Son of God," or "Messiah," or "King of the Jews," or "the Lamb of God who takes away the sin of the world," but when Jesus walked on this earth, His favorite word for Himself, more than anything else, was "Son of Man." And that is what we see here more than half a century later.

But wait. This is the Risen Christ, the One who cast out demons and raised the dead and who disappeared up into the clouds, gone to His Father's side, and now, here He is. But He's not something unrecognizable. He's not completely obscured in glorious light so that John had no idea what he was seeing. No. This is someone he recognizes. Someone he knows.

This Jesus is the same. The same One he went fishing with, who got hurt, who got tired, and thirsty. This is the One who called Himself the Son of Man.

When God unwraps Jesus, He could have reintroduced Him, first and foremost, as God, the perfectly divine, all-powerful Creator. He could appear as the Judge, riding on a white horse, returning to earth with a conquering army. But when the wrapping paper comes off, the very first thing we see about Jesus isn't His divinity. It's His humanity.

This would have been an easy thing for John to forget. After all, how many humans are beaten to a pulp, nailed to a cross, wrapped up, buried, sealed in a tomb, and then come back to life? Not many humans can do that. And then He walked through walls, disappeared right in front of people, rose up and vanished into the clouds, and now, when John sees Him, the first thing he needs to be reminded of is that Jesus is 100 percent human.

He's not 99 percent. And He's not some kind of half-god, half-man, super sort-of human. Jesus was 100 percent human. That is what John sees when he sees the Son of Man. Not a stranger, not some unrecognizable, god-like something. He sees the Jesus who never changes, the one who Hebrews says is the same, "yesterday, today, and forever."

Yesterday, when Jesus walked the dusty trails of Galilee with John; today, when He's standing on Patmos, speaking with a voice like a trumpet;

and forever, here with us now and for all eternity, Jesus never changes. The same Jesus who fell asleep in John's fishing boat all those years ago is the same One God unwraps for us, the unchanging, perfectly recognizable, 100 percent human Jesus.

One Like the Son of Man

Do you want to understand what Jesus meant when He calls Himself the Son of Man? Do you want to know why this is His favorite way to describe Himself to us? To understand what we see in Revelation 1:13, we need to look first at the book of Hebrews.

Remember that what John sees isn't new. He sees someone he recognizes. What God does in the book of Revelation is take truth He's already given us and bring it into sharp focus.

Hebrews 2:14–15 tells us, "Inasmuch then as the children have partaken of flesh and blood, He Himself likewise shared in the same."

This is where God explains the purpose of the 100 percent humanity of Christ. The ancients used to say it this way: The Son of God became a Son of Man so that the sons of men might become sons of God.

Because we are human, flesh and blood, according to Hebrews 2:14, Jesus had to become a human. Why? "That through death He might destroy him who had the power of death, that is the devil, and release those who through fear of death were all their lifetime subject to bondage."[18]

This is why Jesus Christ had to come, wrap Himself in human flesh, and become weak, and hungry, and tired, and tempted, and everything else human. Jesus had to be completely human. Only by dying as a human being could He defeat the one with the power of death, and by doing that, free those who were subject to bondage.

So when John sees One like the Son of Man, what exactly does he see? The One who was human, who suffered, who felt pain, whose body was broken and bleeding, who died as one of us to bring us to God.

But that's not all. Hebrews 4:15 gives us another reason for Christ's humanity. Only in His humanity could Jesus Christ truly sympathize with us.

---

18   Hebrews 2:14–15

When you're struggling, how many times does someone come up and say to you, "I know what you're going through," when they have everything they need, and they've never lost the things you've lost, and they've never been through what you're going through? But they claim to know what you're going through.

When Jesus claims to know what you're going through, He says He "sympathizes"[19] with us. The English word "sympathy" is transliterated from the Greek *sumpatheo*, literally, *sum*, "with," *patheo*, "to feel." When Jesus says He sympathizes, He literally feels with us.

Jesus isn't just aware intellectually of our sufferings. He doesn't just sit up there, on His throne in heaven, imagining what it must be like to suffer like we suffer. No. When Jesus says He feels what we feel, He isn't giving us a greeting card message of sympathy. He knows what it is to be hungry because He was hungry. He knows what it was like to be tired because He was tired. He knows what it was like to lose a loved one because He lost people He loved.

He grieved as we grieve. He suffered unbearable loneliness in those hours on the cross as even His own Father turned away from Him. He was despised and rejected. Isaiah calls Him a "Man of sorrows, acquainted with grief."[20] Every aching need we as humans feel, Jesus feels with us.

He wrapped Himself in frail humanness. He had a human body that got hungry and thirsty, that needed sleep, whose feet got sore, who needed time alone, who had to work to provide for His family. He was tempted, lonely, misunderstood, and through all that, He learned what it was like to feel with us.

The One riding a white horse, leading a conquering army, the King of the Jews, the Judge, if that's all He was, could never have claimed to "sympathize" with us humans. Only as the Son of Man could Jesus feel our needs completely.

But do you know what is perhaps the most amazing thing about Jesus' humanness? He didn't just sympathize with our weaknesses. He understands our temptations.

---

19   Hebrews 4:15
20   Isaiah 53:3

Jesus was, according to Hebrews 4:15, "in all points tempted as we are, yet without sin." Jesus never sinned. He never gave in to temptation, but as the Son of Man, He faced the same temptations that you and I face every day. The same struggles, the same choices, the same difficulties that you and I wrestle with, Jesus wrestled with.

How incredible is it to know that someone knows exactly what we're going through? But even more powerful than that is to know why Jesus chose to go through all this with us. It's so that He could come to our aid when we are tempted, when we are weak and lonely, and human, because He's already been there.[21]

If someone we love suffers a loss, we send flowers, or a casserole, or a card that says they have our sympathy. But when Jesus sympathizes, it isn't just to feel bad for us or even to feel with us. He became human so that He could bring us aid. We couldn't go to a holy, infinite, perfect God, so God became the Son of Man and came to us.

We don't have to face temptation alone. We don't have to go through life believing no one understands. The Son of Man has already gone through it. No one understands like Jesus. Are you afraid to share what you're going through with the people around you because you're afraid they won't understand, or that they'll judge you for it? We already have One who knows everything we feel, everything we struggle with, every secret in our hearts, and instead of looking on us with frustration, or annoyance, or judgment, or anger, Jesus, the Son of Man, looks on us with compassion.

There is compassion, and then there is the kind of compassion Jesus has. The word *splanchnoi,* literally refers to the feeling you have when your intestines move. This is not disappointment or feeling your heart sink when you know someone is hurting. It's deeper, down in your gut.

Did you know that every time the verb translated as "having or showing compassion" is used in the whole Bible, it's used for Jesus? This is the gut-wrenching, deep-down compassion, and Jesus corners the market on it. Nobody has compassion like Jesus does, and it moves Him to respond.

During the entire ministry of Christ, all three and a half years, if ever Jesus was going to ignore human suffering, it would have been in Matthew 20:18.

---

21   Hebrews 2:18

Jesus is going up to Jerusalem, and He is on His way to die. He knows this is His last trip. He knows exactly what's going to happen. He's already told His disciples He'll be betrayed, condemned, tortured, and crucified.

If ever there was a time Jesus would be wrapped up in His own problems, it was now. On the one hand, the mother of two of His disciples is there, asking Him to give her sons the best place of honor in heaven, and on the other hand, He had a whole crowd of people pressing in on Him, all fighting for His attention, never giving Him a moment to Himself.

But through all that, Jesus hears the feeble cry of those who need Him. Two blind men, sitting by the side of the road, cry out for mercy, and Jesus hears them.[22] Immediately, the crowd tries to keep them quiet, to usher Jesus on past, and He could easily have gone right on by. After all, Jesus had more important things to do. He was facing the darkest hour of His life, when even His Father would turn away from Him, but instead of being annoyed or impatient or too busy, Jesus is moved with compassion. *Splanchnoi.* His intestines move, He touches their eyes, and they see.

Surrounded by a multitude of people who needed Him, on His way to the cross, Jesus stopped for something as inconsequential as the physical needs of two beggars. But when Jesus appears as the Son of Man, we see the One who feels our every need, and none of them is inconsequential.

In His compassion, Jesus sees a great multitude in Mark 6:34. He sees that they are lost, like sheep without a shepherd, and He teaches them. He sees next that they are hungry, He feels their need, and He multiplies the bread and fish to feed them.

Jesus could have been annoyed with the crowds for following Him for so many days without thinking to bring along a lunch. When a sick woman stops Him in the road on His way to heal a dying girl, He could have responded with impatience. When His disciples ask, "Who sinned, this man or his parents, that he was born blind?"[23] Jesus could have responded with, "they're all sinners, and they really had it coming." But He doesn't.

He touches the eyes of the blind, and they see. He touches the place where leprosy has eaten away at the flesh, and the flesh is healed. He touches

22   Matthew 20:30
23   John 9:2

the legs of the lame and they walk. Instead of responding with anger or impatience or frustration or lack of concern because He's simply too busy running the universe, Jesus stops, He is gut-wrenchingly moved, and He touches our place of greatest need.

This is the Son of Man unwrapped for us in Revelation 1:13.

Jesus, Our Great High Priest

But what is the next thing John sees? He recognizes the Son of Man, but when the lid comes off Jesus Christ, he also notices what Jesus is wearing. Now, these aren't the clothes He's wearing in all the Hollywood portrayals of Him. The picture God gives us here of "a garment down to His feet and girded about the chest with a golden band"[24] is very specific.

To twenty-first-century Christians, this means very little. But when John saw what Jesus was wearing, he would have known immediately what it was. John had seen them all his life, running around the temple, wearing this outfit. These were the clothes of a priest.

You see, the Old Testament is all about a God who couldn't be approached, but wanted to be. That's what the priests were there for, to go between God and His people and continually make sacrifices for their sins.

For centuries, to have access to God, you had to go through a priest. And the priest had to go through the tabernacle, perfectly designed, every piece of furniture, every ceremony, every sacrifice, to be a picture of Jesus Christ.[25]

But when the Son of God became the Son of Man, everything changed. All of a sudden, the God who couldn't be approached was walking around on earth and He couldn't get away from people. If you read in the Gospels, Jesus was mobbed everywhere He went. He didn't have a secret service detail keeping people at a respectful distance. His disciples couldn't keep the people back. The unclean, the sick, the infirmed, and all the people who could never have direct access to God were now able to see Him in person. They could speak to Him, they could touch Him. That's what makes Christmastime so important. He became the Immanuel, God with us.

---

24 Revelation 1:13
25 Hebrews 9

"I am the way, the truth, and the life," Jesus said. "No one comes to the Father except through Me."[26] Even in the Old Testament, the only way to God was through the priests and the tabernacle, all pictures of Jesus, but now, the real thing is here, accessible, approachable. Jesus in the flesh, human, able to sympathize with our weaknesses, able to understand our struggles, has put on the clothing of our High Priest.

We couldn't go to God, so God came to us.

Jesus' Greatest Miracle and Our Greatest Need

Jesus performed miracle after miracle during His time on earth, but one miracle stands out as greater than all the rest. He healed lepers, fed the hungry, calmed the storms, and even raised the dead, but none of these compares to Jesus' greatest miracle. He didn't come to impress people. He didn't come in order to feed the hungry or heal lepers or manipulate the weather. In fact, all the other miracles He did were to point to this one.

In Mark 2:1–5, Jesus is preaching, and as usual, the crowd is so large there's no more room in the house. But a man is there, a man who is paralyzed, in need of the compassion only Jesus could give, and his four friends are so desperate to get him to Jesus that they dig a hole down through the ceiling and lower him down on a stretcher right in front of Jesus.

So, of course, we're all expecting Jesus to reach out, touch his broken body, and heal him. But what does Jesus do instead? "Son, your sins are forgiven you."[27] In that moment, He doesn't cure him, He doesn't straighten out his twisted body. He forgives.

When Jesus has compassion, He reaches out and touches our place of greatest need. And what is the greatest need that we as human beings have? It isn't wealth, money for the next car payment or to pay off our mortgage. It's not health, a cure for cancer or a miracle drug for whatever's plaguing us. Our greatest need isn't happiness. It's forgiveness.

And what was that man's greatest need in Mark 2? To walk again? To be able to pick up the pallet he was lying on? No. His greatest need wasn't healing for a twisted body. It was healing for a twisted soul.

26   John 14:6
27   Mark 2:5

The most compassionate act of Christ, the greatest miracle He ever performed, the reason He came to earth in the first place, the reason the Pharisees wanted to kill Him, the miracle He died for, is forgiveness.[28]

Every other miracle Jesus performed was temporary. When the wine ran out, He turned the water into wine, but that ran out, too, eventually. He fed a crowd of thousands, and they were satisfied. For about a day. He healed the sick, but eventually their bodies weakened, they aged, and they died.

Now, Jesus did heal this man's body. That man just picked up his mat and walked right out of there, but how long before the effects of old age twisted him up again? Even those Jesus raised from the dead died again just like everybody else.

But when Jesus forgives, that can't be undone. It doesn't wear off, it can't be taken away. It's a lifetime warranty, no fine print at the bottom of the page that says it only lasts as long as you don't do something stupid to mess it up. When Jesus forgives, it's absolute.

When Jesus puts on the robe of a high priest, He does something no other priest could do. The Old Covenant provided a temporary forgiveness for sins. Day after day, year after year, priest after priest, when they died, another took their place and continually offered sacrifices for sins. But when Jesus, the Risen Christ, the Son of Man, takes on the role of a high priest, He does something that no one else could do.

"Also there were many priests," Hebrews 7:23–25 says, "because they were prevented by death from continuing. But He, because He continues forever, has an unchangeable priesthood. Therefore He is also able to save to the uttermost those who come to God through Him, since He always lives to make intercession for them."

When we begin to see the unwrapped Jesus, we see a God who is not just intellectually familiar with the kinds of sufferings that we go through, but a God who chose to become like us, to share in our sufferings, to feel what we feel, to intimately know our weaknesses, and to be tempted in all the same things we are.[29] "In all things He had to be made like His brethren, that He might be a merciful and faithful High Priest," Hebrews 2:17 says.

---

28 Mark 2:5–7; John 10:31–33; Mark 14:64
29 Hebrews 4:15

God has come to us, made Himself approachable, the Son of Man, and takes on the role of our High Priest. And instead of offering sacrifices year after year, He offered Himself to God just once, so that He forever intercedes for us.[30]

We are not temporarily saved. We are not mostly saved. Our sin is not almost always atoned for. Do you know what Jesus says about sin? All sins are forgivable. That's what Jesus says in Mark 3:28.[31] There's not one too many or one too big or one too far. We are saved to the uttermost.

Do you know what human forgiveness is like? It's like deleting an email. You can't see it in your inbox, but, oh, there it is again in your trash folder. So you delete it from the trash folder, but if someone really wanted to find it, they could, because it'll always be out there on some server somewhere or floating around on the cloud.

But when God forgives, there's no record of it. Colossians tells us that the record of our sins, spelled out in black and white, was nailed to the cross the moment Jesus, our High Priest, offered Himself to God. When Jesus died, our sins were taken away, nailed to the cross, and they no longer have the power to condemn us.[32]

God's Reminder to Us

Revelation is a book of reminders. Nothing God says in this book is only said here, just here, for the first time. By some counts of some who have spent their whole lives studying this book, there are over eight hundred allusions to the rest of Scripture in Revelation's 404 verses. The prophecies here make clear and tie together what Ezekiel, Daniel, Joel, Zechariah, and Jesus Himself already said about the End Times. When Jesus tells His churches what pleases Him and what doesn't, He's not giving a brand-new list of sins or great new ways to please God that no one had ever heard of before. He's just reminding them of what Paul already said, and what Peter and John already wrote to them. And when God reveals Jesus in chapter 1, John sees the same Jesus he'd walked with and known and loved for years.

---

30   Hebrews 7:27
31   Mark 3:28
32   Colossians 2:14

But it had been sixty years since he'd last seen Jesus, since he'd last walked and talked with his best friend. Of all the disciples, John was the one who was closest to Jesus. He was called the disciple whom Jesus loved. But now six decades have passed and John is dying in exile, and if anyone ever needed to be reminded of who Jesus really is, it's John. It is not a stretch to think that the apostle John, like so many of us, felt distant from Jesus. It had been so long since he'd walked with Him, since he'd seen Him face-to-face, and at the very least, the purpose and plan of God that used to seem so clear now felt like a distant memory. But what God says we need isn't some new truth; we just need to be reminded of the old ones.

God never promises we won't have troubles. "In the world you will have tribulation,"[33] Jesus says. You will be squashed. You will hang on till it hurts. You will agonize together. John, the apostle Paul, and Jesus Himself all say the same thing: The Christian life is hard.

But God gives us the same message He's been giving to suffering people for centuries.

When Job lost his children, when his wealth was stolen, when he was so sick he couldn't do anything but scrape himself with broken pots, his wife told him to just give up, curse God, and die, and his friends spent all day every day trying to convince him he somehow deserved what he got, all Job wanted to do was to speak to God face-to-face, to hear an answer, to present his case and get an explanation for his suffering.

And if anyone deserved an explanation from God, it was Job. If you read what God says about Job, it's one of the most glowing recommendations in all the Bible. God calls him "a blameless and upright man, one who fears God and shuns evil," and that "there is none like him on the earth."[34] This is a man who loved God. This is a man who hated evil. This is a man who lived his whole life to please God. But when God finally speaks to Job in his suffering, He never explains why.

God could have explained what was going on in heaven with Satan. He could have spelled out exactly how He planned to reward Job by

33   John 16:33
34   Job 1:8

replacing all he'd lost. He could have given Job a list of reasons bad things happen. Instead, God paints Job a picture. He spends four chapters describing His greatness, the scope of His power, the expanse of the universe He holds in His hands, and it leaves Job speechless.

And what, finally, is Job's response? "I have uttered what I did not understand, things too wonderful for me, which I did not know. I have heard of You by the hearing of the ear, but now my eye sees You."[35]

This is the *El Shaddai*, the God who is enough, the same yesterday, today, and forever. In Revelation, He calls Himself "the Almighty," in the Old Testament, the *El Shaddai*—both meaning the exact same thing. God's message to suffering people? I am the God who is enough.

God could have included a long list of comforting verses in His Revelation 1 message. He could have given us words to memorize, to pull out every time we're struggling, but instead, He gives us something worth a thousand words, a picture of the Risen Christ, the Son of Man, the Great High Priest, Jesus Christ.

We have heard of Jesus, His miracles, His compassion, His forgiveness, but now our eyes have seen Him, and, like Job, we are left speechless.

Peter, a simple fisherman from a small town, climbed out of his boat and followed Jesus onto the waves. In his humanness, Peter got distracted by the wind whipping all around him, by the waves threatening to sink their small fishing boat. He saw the lightning and the thunder, he focused on the storm, and in his fear, he began to sink. But in that moment, he cried out to Jesus, and immediately, he stopped sinking.[36]

The waves still crashed over the boat, the wind still churned up the water, but Peter didn't sink. When, overwhelmed by the storm and afraid of drowning, Peter stopped looking at his circumstances and lifted his eyes to Jesus, Matthew 14:31 says "immediately" he stopped sinking. That's how powerful keeping our eyes on Jesus is.

Jesus is the One who wants to calm your fear, who wants to permanently delete your sins, who wants to aid you when you're tempted. He is the One who sees everything you're struggling with and says, "Neither do I

35 Job 42:3, 5
36 Matthew 14:28–32

condemn you,"[37] and then He gives us the power to leave behind that defilement, to leave behind that sin.

Hebrews 7:25 tells us Jesus "always lives to make intercession for [us]." When Satan goes before God to accuse us, Jesus is there, dressed as John describes Him in Revelation 1, saying to God, "I paid for that."

Are you weak? He understands, and looks on you with compassion. Are you afraid? He is acquainted with all we face, and knows our fears. Are you alone? He faced the loneliness of the Garden of Gethsemane, the wilderness temptation, and the long hours on the cross. He knows what it is to be alone. Do you feel defiled? He alone can forgive and cleanse. Do you feel the fear of future judgment? He can take away that penalty you deserve forever.

This is the message that God, the all-knowing, all-powerful, perfectly intentional God-who-is-enough chose to give suffering people. We don't need some lightning flash of brand-new revelation. We just need to rip off the wrapping paper, pull the cover back, open the lid, and see what we already have. And every time we feel alone or afraid or ashamed, every time we are plagued by guilt or doubt or anxiety, we can look at Jesus, who loved us and gave Himself for us,[38] and like Peter, we stop sinking.

Maybe you don't know if you are forgiven. You don't know if Jesus has met your greatest need. If you've never, like the paralytic in Mark 2, come to the place where you know you have a need that only Jesus can meet, then, right now, ask Jesus to save you. Ask Jesus to be your High Priest, to save you to the uttermost, to take away your guilt, to perform His greatest miracle and forgive you. If that is your prayer, then you have a High Priest in heaven who says, constantly, on your behalf, "I paid for that." And your sins are remembered no more.

And if you are suffering, and you feel alone, and feel like no one understands, then make it your goal to look to Jesus, who feels with you, who hurts with you, who has compassion on you. Let us never forget, and always remember the One who died to meet our greatest need, and lives to meet our every need.

---

37 John 8:11
38 Ephesians 5:2

Heavenly Father, we thank You for unwrapping this beautiful picture of Your Son, Jesus Christ. And we pray that when the stuff of this world distracts us and disappoints us and discourages us, that we will remember Your Word, Your reminder to us to keep our eyes on Jesus. Let us never forget what You've done for us. Amen.

The gift God already gave us is sitting there, waiting to be opened. We already know who it's from, that it's going to be exactly what we need to see, something so incredibly special, but with all the hints, shaking it and picking it up to see how heavy it is, we've never fully seen inside.

Until now.

Jesus Christ, unwrapped for us, is exactly what we need. In His humanity, the Son of Man feels with us. In His compassion, He touches our place of greatest need. And as our High Priest, He forever intercedes for us. Today, more than anything else, we need to experience Jesus as He is in Revelation 1:13, the never-changing Christ, the same, yesterday, today, and forever.

RESPOND to Truth

How am I struggling right now? How does Jesus feel about that? (Matthew 9:36; 14:14; 15:32; 20:34; Mark 1:41; 6:34; 8:2; Luke 7:13)

How does Jesus know what it is to feel what I feel? (Feel abandoned?—Matthew 26:31. Feel betrayed?—Luke 22:47–48. Feel dread?—Matthew 26:38; Luke 22:44. Feel exploited?—John 6:26, 41. Feel grief?—Isaiah 53:3–4. Feel guilt?—Isaiah 53:11–12. Feel lonely?—Psalm 22:1–8. Feel misunderstood?—Matthew 13:54–58. Feel tempted?—Matthew 4:1–11; Hebrews 4:15. Feel shame?—Hebrews 6:6; 12:2. Feel sorrow?—Isaiah 53:3–4.)

What is my favorite name for Jesus? Why?

How does Jesus' favorite name for Himself change how I see Him?

When I am suffering, what is the first thing I usually look at?

What steps can I take today to keep my eyes on Jesus?

Seen with Eyes of Fire | 3

The Book of the Revelation was written to help God's people. Verse 1 says, "to show His servants—things which must shortly take place." God wanted His people to be prepared, to understand His plan, to be ready for whatever was about to happen.

I've often thought about what I'd have written to people who were suffering, who were facing persecution, who were going into a time when Christianity itself would nearly go extinct. And the more I read Revelation 1, the more I think I would have stopped at verse 13.

Verse 13 gives us Jesus with His arms held wide, inviting and comforting His people. This is the Jesus who died for us, who lives for us, who intercedes for us, and if it stopped there, we'd be happy. But from verse 14 on, we see a very different side of Jesus.

On that Lord's Day when John was in the Spirit, he first sees that gentle Son of Man he knew, the One who would never condemn. And he sees the High Priest, the One who always intercedes. But as Jesus comes more clearly into sight, John begins to see a very different picture.

Beginning in Revelation 1:14, we are no longer given a comforting, arms-open-wide picture of Jesus. We're confronted with a set of seven descriptions that gives us a very sobering picture of Jesus.

The Unstoppable, All-Powerful Ancient of Days

REVELATION 1:12–14

Then I turned to see the voice that spoke with me. And having turned I saw seven golden lampstands, and in the midst of the seven lampstands One like the Son of Man, clothed with a garment down to the feet and girded about the chest with a golden band.

And then verse 14:

His head and His hair were white like wool, as white as snow, and His eyes like a flame of fire.

When John sees His head and His hair this pure, radiant white, he doesn't see Jesus as He was sixty years before when He walked on this earth, but as He appeared centuries before to the prophet Daniel. When Daniel caught a glimpse of Jesus, he wrote, "I watched till thrones were put in place, and the Ancient of Days was seated; His garment was white as snow, and the hair of His head was like pure wool. His throne was a fiery flame, its wheels a burning fire; a fiery stream issued and came forth from before Him."[39] Daniel and John both describe the Ancient of Days the same way: with the color white like wool or snow, and surrounded by fire. Not nearly as comforting as the Jesus with kids on His lap.

John sees Jesus' white head and hair, indicating the great age of the never-changing, ageless Ancient of Days of Daniel. But this color also speaks of incredible purity. This isn't a dull white or a kind of salt-and-pepper gray. This is the color of purity, the same brilliant searchlight white that John saw once before on the Mount of Transfiguration. Matthew 17:2 describes it as shining like the sun, as white as light. And this picture of blinding holiness hasn't changed for centuries.

The second description in verse 14 is just as compelling: "His eyes were like a flame of fire." This isn't how we would say, "his eyes lit up," or "his

---

39   Daniel 7:9–10

eyes burned into you." This is not a quiet burning like coals in a fireplace. This is a *whoosh* like a flamethrower, speaking of a blazing, piercing, penetrating gaze.

When John saw the fiery eyes of Jesus, he was brought to his knees by the awesome power that fire represents. He would have known of the consuming power of fire from when Rome invaded Jerusalem. The greatest engineering marvel Herod ever erected was an eighty- or ninety-foot stone arch, connecting to the temple and suspended out into space. But when the Romans invaded, they decided to prove that Herod's great, indestructible archway was really very weak, so they set a fire under it. That fire burned so hot it expanded the air inside the cracks of the limestone and the entire stone archway, the one Herod meant to last forever, crumbled. That is the consuming power of fire, and that is the picture God gives us of His holiness.

Secondly, we see the purifying work of fire. Fires that are allowed to burn hot enough can refine, and purifying metals such as silver, gold, brass, and iron, and all the dross, all the impurities, float up to the surface. The eyes as a flame of fire speak of both power and purity. We see portrayed both the purifying work of fire as well as the unquenchable power of fire. When fire's powerful flames are combined with the idea of Christ's eyes, it speaks of an unstoppable, all-powerful, purifying gaze.

When Jesus looks at us, He sees with those blazing eyes and nothing is hidden from Him. His laser-like eyes see past the smiles and the closed doors. And when Jesus looks with those flaming eyes into our hearts, He's looking to see what parts of our lives are surrendered to Him, and what parts aren't.

The Pentagon is constantly keeping track of which areas overseas are under control. They look to see which parts are already secured by the military, and which parts are under the control of the enemy. But when Jesus turns His piercing gaze on us, He is looking for which areas of our lives are under the Spirit's control, and which areas are given over to the enemy. He's looking to see what parts of our lives are being controlled by sin and lust and when He finds large portions of our lives that are surrendered to sin, His eyes blaze, not like gently glowing coals, but with a *whoosh* like a flamethrower.

This looks nothing like the kind, compassionate, loving Jesus we saw in verse 13. Is this the same Jesus who felt compassion and reached out to heal the ones who were hurting? This is a terrifying Jesus, pure white head and hair, with holy, blazing eyes, who cannot tolerate sin in the lives of believers. No wonder John fell at His feet like a dead man in verse 17.

God's Only Three-Fold Name

When God says something, it's important. Every word of God matters, and if it mattered enough for God to say it, to inspire someone to write it down or to carve it into stone with His finger, then it must be something He wants us to know. So if God says something, it's important.

If something is really important to God, He repeats it. When we see Jesus repeating Himself, "truly, *truly*, I say to you…"[40] it must be really important. That's why Revelation is a book of reminders, because we need to be told again and again or we'll forget, and these are things we can't afford to forget.

But if something is of utmost importance, if its importance can't be overstated, God says it in threes.

You know something is really important if you're filling out paperwork and they make you do it in triplicate. You know, there's one copy for you, one for them, one for somebody else even higher up, just so there's no confusion, no chance of misplacing it.

So when God says something in triplicate, we should sit up and take notice. And there is only one name of God that is said in threes.

When God is worshiped in heaven, the angels are echoing His three-fold name over and over. But the angels are not saying, "sovereign, sovereign, sovereign." They're not saying, "love, love, love." They're saying, "holy, holy, holy."

The only three-fold description of God is one of never-changing, all-consuming holiness. In Revelation 4:8, we see another reminder that He never changes: "who was and is and is to come." Again, He's called the "Lord God *Almighty*," the *El Shaddai*, the God who is enough. But it is His holiness that He emphasizes three times.

---

40   For example, John 3:3, 5 NASB

PART I | 37

This is the name that forever rings out in heaven, the name God surrounds Himself with, the name the angels are constantly praising before the throne. This is the name Isaiah heard in heaven and John records for us in Revelation.[41] This is the name we'll be praising forever.

All throughout the Old Testament, the holiness of God kept people at arms' length. The Israelites were kept back from even touching the base of the mountain of God because His holiness was so powerful they would be consumed.

God's holiness is a serious thing. It demanded that Adam and Eve leave the Garden. It separated God from His people, putting a tabernacle, a priesthood, and a thick curtain between them. It demanded the blood of animals year after year, and it ultimately cost Him His Son. Jesus didn't die to buy us back from Satan or as an act of love just to catch our attention. He did it to satisfy a holy God.

I have a dear friend who was recently firing up the outdoor grill to make steaks for the first time in the spring. And he hadn't used the propane tank for a while, so the top was stuck, and as he was trying to get it to open, all of a sudden, a fireball burst out from the tank and knocked him backward. The fire was only there for a second, like a camera flash, and then it was gone, but the hair on his arms, his eyelashes, his eyebrows, and the hair on his head were all singed and burned away, just from that brief, millisecond of exposure to that fire.

That's what the holiness of God is like. He isn't sitting up in heaven looking for unrepentant sinners so He can throw down lightning and smite them. He is a consuming fire, and when we get too close, anything that's flammable, anything that's impure or sinful, is simply engulfed in flames.

God's holiness is unstoppable. It is all-powerful. And it must be satisfied. God's justice is absolute. He cannot allow impurities, sin, into His presence, otherwise the sin and the sinner are burned up. And only by His perfect, blameless, innocent Son becoming man and dying in place of sinners could God's holiness ever be satisfied.

Holiness is very serious to God. It isn't just something He *has*. It's who He *is*. And was. And will always be.

---

41   Isaiah 6:3; Revelation 4:8

The Never-Changing Christ

This is not a comforting picture. I see why John was afraid. How do I know he was scared? Because Jesus had to reach out His hand and say, "Do not be afraid."[42] I'm so glad this isn't the first thing we see.

Remember, the first thing God reveals to us when He lifts the lid on Jesus Christ is His humanity, His compassion for us. When we think of Jesus, God wants us to think of Him first with His arms outstretched, inviting us to come to Him just as we are. We can bring our sinfulness and our weaknesses. We can bring our needs, because He understands and looks on us with compassion.

Jesus' outstretched arms of compassion and love are never more clearly seen than when He stretched them out on the cross for us, when He opened His arms and paid for our sin. And now, as our High Priest, He stands interceding for us.

We like to, as Christians, put God into a neat little box, to define exactly who we think He is. So we've drawn a line down the middle of God's Word between the fiery, wrathful God of the Old Testament and the New Testament sappy, weak Jesus, as if somewhere in that four hundred years of silence between Malachi and Matthew, God changed.

So we have, on the one hand, the Old Testament God of wrath and power. He's opening up the ground to swallow people, He's drowning the Egyptians in the Red Sea. He's turning back and crushing whole armies. And on the other hand, we have Jesus. He turned the other cheek, preached forgiveness, refused to throw stones when someone was caught in the act of adultery, and gave His life to save sinners.

But God was always a God of love. In the Old Testament, we see clearly His all-consuming holiness, but it was always "through the Lord's mercies" that "we are not consumed, because His compassions fail not. They are new every morning."[43] It's His love that kept His people at arms length, that protected them from His all-consuming holiness, and it was His love that provided us with a solution for our sin.

All throughout the Old Testament, we see God showing us our need of Him. He gave us the Law so we would see our sin so clearly we would

---

42   Revelation 1:17
43   Lamentations 3:22–23

understand our need for a Savior. And when Jesus came, He didn't just throw out the Old Testament Law. He fulfilled it. The loving, healing, saving Jesus is the same One who had been showing His power for centuries, so that all the world would know which God saves, which God heals. He's been putting signposts up all along the way so that when He came, we'd know it was Him, the same God of love He's always been.

"Mercy and truth have met together," Psalm 85:10 says. "Righteousness and peace have kissed."

Jesus is where mercy and truth meet. His truth and His holiness of the Old Testament demand satisfaction. His mercy and compassion provided it when He offered Himself to God as a sacrifice for sin.

But there's another side to that, another truth we need to understand. The same Jesus who was always loving is still the holy, awesome God who can't allow sin in His presence.

Somehow we've gotten this idea that when Jesus fulfilled the Law, everything that used to be an abomination to God is somehow okay now. Maybe it used to grieve Him and cause Him to pour out His wrath, but somewhere along the way, He must have gotten over it. After all, we're not under the Law. And now, everything that used to make God sick is no big deal. It's all okay because we're under grace.

But sin is still a serious thing to Jesus. Long before He was seen healing the blind and feeding the hungry, He was seen as the Ancient of Days sitting on a throne of fire. And when He looks on us with those fiery eyes and sees sin in His Church, He is just as offended now as He's always been.

If God hated something before the Law, and if He calls it an abomination in the Old Testament, and if He still hates it when He finds it in the first-century church, then He still hates it today. Jesus is the same yesterday, today, and forever. Sin is no less serious to God than it was when He poured down fire from heaven.

The same Jesus who stretched out His arms and took on our sin to redeem us is the same Jesus who looks on us with eyes of fire to purify us. This picture of Jesus in Revelation 1 tells us that He's still a holy God. He still sees with eyes of fire.

LED BY THE SPIRIT

Blameless and Holy

When Jesus died for us, He completed a legal transaction, trading our sin for His righteousness. Now when God looks at us, He doesn't see our sin. He sees Jesus. That's justification. It can't be reversed, it can't be undone, and when Jesus, our High Priest, exchanged our sin for His righteousness, He saved us to the uttermost.

But as long as we're still sinners, and as long as we still live in a sinful world, we will struggle. We will still be tempted, we will still wrestle with our sin, but God never commands something He doesn't give us grace to accomplish.

At the exact moment of salvation, a process begins. Jesus, who is holy and who still hates sin, begins to make us more holy. Jesus gives us this command: "Be perfect, just as your Father in heaven is perfect,"[44] and "Be holy, for I am holy."[45] Sound impossible? That's because it is—without help.

So Jesus sent us a Helper.

The Holy Spirit's Fire

Two of my daughters live and work in the jungles of Honduras, and in Honduras, they have an ant problem. Now, these aren't the nice little ants we have here. These are the big ones. They come into the house in a thick, black line, looking for food. And then they're like a river, coming in and carrying everything out.

So my daughters tell me that when you move into a house down there, you have to mark out your ownership, lay down a line of poison all around the house. Then you have to scrub away and clean all the ants out of the house. That way, when the ants try to come back in, they reach that line of poison and find that something's different. There's no access into the house anymore.

Sanctification means that the Holy Spirit comes in and takes ownership of the house. The Helper that Jesus promised in John 14 takes up residence in my life and marks out His ownership. He cuts off all the supply

---

44 Matthew 5:48
45 1 Peter 1:16

lines so that the old sins, the old habits that displease the Owner of the house, can't find a way back in. They find that there's something different. They're not getting fed anymore, they're not allowed access, and they no longer have free rein in my life.

When the apostle Paul planted a church in the city of Thessalonica, he found that they had a major ant problem. Worse than that, Thessalonica had an infestation.

Thessalonica was one of the great hubs of the ancient world. It was the place where the largest highway that stretched from India to Britain crossed with one of the most strategic ports of the Mediterranean. Imagine the glitz and flesh of Las Vegas combined with the party-flaunting attitude of New Orleans at Mardi Gras, and put that in the worst, slummy, seedy, downtown red light district and you have Thessalonica. And in a place where people are constantly coming and going, a city crops up where the things you'd never do if you had to live there became commonplace. Whatever happens in Thessalonica, stays in Thessalonica. Needless to say, the sin level was high.

The apostle Paul planted a church right in the slums of the red light district, and in three short weeks, a whole bunch of people got saved. But even though the Lord had come to clean out their house, the ants were used to attacking it. In less than three weeks, where intercontinental caravans met at the docks of a huge seaport, a group of drunkards, sex addicts, greedy and dishonest businesspeople, and all the normal, well-adjusted, lost pagans had come to Christ. All the lusts and entanglements and the chains of sin kept trying to get a foothold, so what did Paul say they needed? The same thing we need: to learn sanctification.

This is God's sanctification plan: "Now may the God of peace Himself sanctify you completely; and may your whole spirit, soul, and body be preserved blameless at the coming of our Lord Jesus Christ."[46]

When the Holy Spirit takes ownership of me, I am, as John the Baptist said, "baptized with the Holy Spirit and with fire." That fire is the same we see in Jesus' eyes in Revelation 1 and coming from the throne of the Ancient of Days in Daniel 7. It's a purifying fire, a cleansing one, and, like the *whoosh* of a flamethrower, it sanctifies.

46 1 Thessalonians 5:23

God's Plan for My Sanctification

As we are sanctified, more and more areas of our lives are brought under the Spirit's control until, in heaven, God's sanctifying work is complete and we forever reflect and magnify the holiness of Christ.

What does that look like? Paul says to the Corinthians, "But we all, with unveiled face, beholding as in a mirror the glory of the Lord, are being transformed into the same image from glory to glory, just as by the Spirit of the Lord."[47] "Unveiled face" means that our eyes our opened, we are paying attention. We see in God's Word the glory of the Lord, and we begin to reflect that glory. Our lives are under new ownership, and we begin to look different.

Galatians tells us that if we walk in the Spirit, we will not fulfill the desires of the flesh.[48] Instead, we will see our words, our responses, our attitudes, and our actions more and more lining up with Christ's. If someone walked around with me for twenty-four hours, they should be able to measure my sanctification. If I am surrendered to the Holy Spirit, they should be able to see an increasing frequency of my response to the Spirit, and a decreasing frequency of my response to my flesh. If they don't see that in my life, then I'm either resisting the Spirit's work in my life, or I'm not saved.

Sanctification is an increase in my response to Christ's holiness, and it isn't automatic. God plans for my sanctification, but the power of the Holy Spirit in my life must be unleashed by participation.

When John says in Revelation 1:10 that he was "in the Spirit on the Lord's Day," he doesn't mean "in the Spirit" saved, but "in the Spirit" surrendered. We are sealed with the Holy Spirit at salvation, but it is a lifelong process of surrender to His control in our lives that makes us sanctified.

Throughout Scripture we are warned not to ignore the Holy Spirit's leading. The apostle Paul warns the Christians at Ephesus, "And do not grieve the Holy Spirit of God, by whom you were sealed for the day of redemption."[49] He tells the Thessalonian church not to "quench the Spirit,"[50] and he warns the Corinthians not to defile themselves because they are the temple of the Holy Spirit.[51]

---

47 2 Corinthians 3:18
48 Galatians 5:16
49 Ephesians 4:30
50 1 Thessalonians 5:19
51 1 Corinthians 6:19–20

The Holy Spirit never forces me to obey Him. All throughout Scripture we see the Spirit of God blessing or withholding blessing based on whether events pleased Him or displeased Him. When the children of Israel obeyed God, He allowed them to win incredible battles with only a handful of soldiers. But when they fell into sin, a handful could defeat them. Either way, the victory or defeat was ultimately in the hand of God, and He blessed or withheld His blessing based on their responses.

My choices can either please the Holy Spirit, unleashing His further work in my life, or they can grieve and offend Him, and He withholds the blessing He was prepared to pour out on my life.

This is my Personal Surrender Plan, and it's how I make the choice every day to surrender to the Holy Spirit's work in my life.

MY PERSONAL SURRENDER PLAN

Number One: Read God's Word

Number one on my personal surrender plan is that I want to listen to God daily through His Word. Job 23:12 says, "I have treasured the words of His mouth more than my necessary food." Only by looking into the mirror of God's Word do I see what in my life is pleasing to God and what isn't.

God's Word is the only place we can go and see ourselves exactly as we are. If you look back on the last week, did you check your email every day? Did you check in with God's Word? Do you have to have the latest updates on social media, the latest sports scores, the up-to-the-minute weather report on an app on your phone? Do you crave God's Word that much? If you feel jittery without your morning cup of coffee or if you're offline for more than a few hours at a time, but can go days or weeks without checking in with God's Word to see the up-to-the-minute report on how His sanctification plan is progressing in your life, then how important is holiness to you?

It's very important to Jesus.

So the first step in my personal surrender plan is to listen to God daily through His Word. But it can't stop there.

Number Two: Respond to God Through Prayer

James 1:22–25 says that if we look into the mirror of God's Word, see all the things that don't line up with His plan for us, and then go away without changing anything, we are like a man who looks at his face in an actual mirror, goes away, and immediately forget what he looks like.

As soon as I see something in God's Word that my life doesn't align with, I want to, number two, respond to God throughout the day in prayer.

I want to ask Him to reveal to me what in my life doesn't match up with His Word, what in my life needs to be brought more under the Spirit's control. I want to go to the Great High Priest who is interceding for me, who knows my weaknesses and my temptations, and ask for help to overcome them.

I want to make sacred vows to obey. I want to say, "Lord, I'm going to read Your Word first. Lord, I'm going to try to memorize a verse about my constant struggle with this or that. Lord, what choices can I make so that when You look at me, You see more and more of my life reflecting Your ownership?"

Number Three: Reach Out to Other Believers

After I've read God's Word and responded to Him through prayer, I want to share my plans with another believer so they can encourage me in my walk. And if I am going to surrender to the Spirit's work in my life, I want to partner with other believers so that they will hold me accountable.

If I get out of bed, and my hair's a mess, I have a pimple right in the middle of my forehead, but I go on with my day anyway, I would hope that a good friend would pull me aside before I got too far. I would hope they would point out that I still have breakfast on my face and say, "Did you see a mirror this morning?"—maybe offer me a napkin and a comb.

And if we are the body of Christ, we should do the same thing with a fellow believer who is ruled by the same temper that ruled them five years ago, or someone who's just as anxious and fearful as they were thirty years ago.

We're not to be marbles in a vase. If I had a glass vase full of marbles, they would appear so close together, but the moment I tipped the vase over, the marbles would scatter as far from one another as they could get, because nothing connects them. The modern-day church has become like that. The pastor says, "and now, in conclusion," and the marbles start rolling out the doors.

Do you know why the first-century church had so much power? They didn't scatter like marbles. They were a body, all connected to one another. When one hurt, the others hurt. When one rejoiced, the others rejoiced.

So my Personal Surrender Plan is to look into the mirror of God's Word, pray over what I see that isn't as it should be, make vows to God to do something about it, and share my struggles with other believers so that they can hold me accountable.

When the unstoppable, all-powerful Ancient of Days looks at you with eyes of fire, what is your response? Do you have a personal surrender plan, or are you hoping the work of the Spirit will happen automatically?

We could simply close our Bibles and choose to remember the loving, compassionate Jesus. After all, that is the first picture God gives us. We could prefer to remember His arms of compassion and love open wide to us, accepting us. The fire-and-brimstone God was just for the Old Testament, after all. Right?

But the Truth pictured so clearly in the Old Testament meets Mercy in Jesus Christ. His welcoming, cleansing, forgiving arms of compassion are open wide to us, but the white hair and fiery eyes of the Ancient of Days remind us that He will not tolerate sin unchecked in our lives. When we choose to ignore His holiness, we grieve and quench the Holy Spirit living inside us, and we offend the One who died to justify us.

We can respond with indifference and apathy, or we can make a personal vow of surrender today. Let us choose to align our lives with the One who surrounds Himself with the name, "holy, holy, holy," with the One who has always hated sin, and who always will.

Heavenly Father, we want to respond to Your holiness today. When You look at us with eyes of fire, we want You to see more and more areas of our lives under Your control. Let us choose to give You first place in our lives. Let us choose to devote time daily to Your

Word, to respond to You in prayer and make vows to obey. May we find other believers to hold us accountable, to encourage us, and may we encourage others as we strive together to live in a way that pleases You. Thank You for Your arms of compassion. Thank You for the Holy Spirit's sanctifying work in our lives. May we ever live to reflect Your ownership. In Your Son's holy name, we pray. Amen.

RESPOND to Truth

How does Isaiah's description of purity in Isaiah 1:18 compare to John's description of Jesus in Revelation 1:14?

How did Peter, James, and John react to Christ's purity in Matthew 17:1–7?

When Christ looks at me with eyes of fire, what areas of my life are under His control?

What areas aren't?

What is my personal surrender plan?

What steps can I take to put it into practice today?

4 | A Sobering Portrait of the Real Jesus

"*Who do you say that I am?*"[52] Jesus asked His disciples the most important question they could ever answer. And it's the most important question we can answer.

There are a lot of possible answers. The crowds of Jesus' day were saying that He was Elijah, or maybe a prophet. Herod thought He was John the Baptist, back from the dead. The Pharisees said His power was demonic, that He was casting out demons by the ruler of demons.[53] Peter said He was the Christ, the Son of God. And everyone today has some idea of who Jesus is. Maybe a good teacher, maybe some kind of prophet, maybe just a really good man. But what I want to know is, who does Jesus say He is?

In Revelation 1, God begins to unwrap Jesus Christ and we are given twin descriptions of Him. He is the Son of Man, and He is our Great High Priest. But in the next words, we see a perfect set of seven descriptions telling us, not just who Jesus is, but exactly what He looks like. No other passage in Scripture gives us a physical description of Christ. But in each of these seven descriptions of Christ, we also get to see what Jesus is doing today.

We all have a picture in our head of what God is like. We think we know what He would or wouldn't do, what He would or wouldn't allow,

---

52   Matthew 16:15
53   Matthew 12:24; 14:1–2

and who Jesus really is. We wear little rubber bracelets asking, "What would Jesus do?" and we wonder if Jesus were walking among us today, what would He be thinking? If He were here among us, what would He be saying? What would He be doing?

Well, we do have Jesus walking among us today. And if we want to know what Jesus would do, we need to know who He is, not who people say He is, but who *He* says He is. And that is what we find in Revelation chapter 1.

REVELATION 1:12–17

Then I turned to see the voice that spoke with me. And having turned I saw seven golden lampstands, and in the midst of the seven lampstands One like the Son of Man, clothed with a garment down to the feet and girded about the chest with a golden band. His head and hair were white like wool, as white as snow, and His eyes like a flame of fire; His feet were like fine brass, as if refined in a furnace, and His voice as the sound of many waters; He had in His right hand seven stars, out of His mouth went a sharp, two-edged sword, and His countenance was like the sun shining in its strength. And when I saw Him, I fell at His feet as dead. But He laid His right hand on me, saying to me, "Do not be afraid; I am the First and the Last."

Divine, Corrective, and Sobering

The description of Jesus in Revelation 1:12–17 is unlike any other single passage in all of God's Word. In these verses we see Jesus as He is right now, and what we see here isn't what we usually think of when we picture Jesus. That's why God gave us this portrait.

Firstly, it is a divine portrait. God promised to unveil, to reveal, to uncover the Risen Christ. And when Jesus is revealed to us, we know that this isn't John's impression of who Jesus is, or Paul's idea, or Peter's. This is a divine portrait, given to us by God. This is the way God wants every person in the Church to see the Jesus we know and love.

When someone we love moves away or our kids are grown and gone, we still have all those early pictures of them when they were little, but what is important to us is to have a current picture of them so that we recognize them as they are. We want to see what they look like now, what they're doing now.

John had a wonderful picture of Jesus. He had the picture of Jesus in the gospels, Jesus feeding the five thousand, and Jesus with the kids on His lap. But now God gives him a current picture. This isn't a blurry photo of what Jesus might have looked like two thousand years ago. This is who Jesus is today.

When God describes Jesus, He gives us the full picture. Yes, He is the compassionate, loving, gentle Jesus with kids on His lap. And yes, He is also the fiery preacher with zero tolerance for unrepentant sin, warning of hellfire and endless doom, who takes on the hypocrites mercilessly. Both are the real Jesus, and God sent us a divine portrait so we would never forget.

Secondly, we see a corrective portrait of Jesus. He's just come back from walking among the lampstands, the churches, and He's found things that need to change.

The churches by the end of the first century had grown lax in those decades following Christ's death, burial, and resurrection. They had slowly moved away from the writings of James, Peter, Paul, and John that emphasized holy living, consecrated lives, and Spirit-prompted walks. Believers seemed to be abandoning lifestyles that reflected Christ's ownership of them as His servants individually, and collectively as Christ's purchased Church.

In just sixty short years, the first edition of Christ's Church had drifted away from what God called them to be. They had drifted away from Christ as their first priority. He was still important, but so were other things, like work, and their plans for the future. They had allowed sin to make inroads into their lives so they no longer lived like the holy, Christ-owned people they actually were. They were making friendships with the world that limited their effectiveness to Christ, and they were beginning to look so much like the unbelievers around them that it was getting hard to tell the difference.

We in the twenty-first century need to see the same corrective portrait of Jesus that God painted for the believers two thousand years ago. There are often times when we seem to have drifted away from the passion we had for Christ when we were first saved. If you talk to many believers, you'll find that there was a time in most of their lives when they felt closer to God than they do now. There was a time when they couldn't be stopped, when they'd share Jesus with anyone who would listen. They were constantly hungry for God's Word. They couldn't get enough of it, couldn't memorize enough. And every time the doors were open, they were at church.

But now, in spite of all the books and music, the tools we have to help us in our Christian walk, we all have times when we drift away from what we're called to be and do and arrive at a place where we feel distant from God.

So God gives us a corrective portrait of Jesus to get us back on track.

And lastly, the portrait of Jesus in Revelation 1 is a sobering portrait, as we see Jesus' response to sin in His Church. When Jesus walks among His Church, He looks like He does in verse 15: "His feet were like fine brass, as if refined in a furnace, and His voice as the sound of many waters."

Those feet, glowing red like they'd just come out of a furnace, speak of Jesus' chastening work in His Church, the work that He would perform until repentance was produced.

John says His voice is loud like a trumpet in verse 10, and like the sound of many waters in verse 15. This is not the still, small voice we think of with Jesus. He is not quietly suggesting that maybe we think about changing how we are living. He is adamant. He calls us to repent.

When John comes face-to-face with the real Jesus, He falls to the ground like a dead man. It isn't that he's old or weak or overcome by emotion. He is confronted with a side of Jesus that we usually reserve for the fire-and-brimstone God of the Old Testament. But nowhere is the intolerance Jesus has for sin more clearly seen than in this sobering portrait of the real Jesus in Revelation 1.

Cleansing the Temple

John sees Almighty God the Son, Jesus Christ, and He is displeased with His Church. I used to think that John falls to his face in verse 17 because he couldn't believe he was seeing Jesus again after all this time, or because he was shocked at the sight of God standing in front of him. But the more

I see Jesus' sobering portrait in Revelation 1:12–17, the more I believe John was knocked down by how Jesus looks when He finds sin in His Church.

Jesus demands purity. He demands obedience. And He demands submission to Him as Lord of the Church. That's not a message we hear very often. We hear that Jesus wants us to be happy, successful, that He wants to bless us. Yes—if we repent. But the divine, corrective, sobering portrait God gives us of the real Jesus doesn't send John merrily on his way. It knocks him to the ground.

John saw His eyes like a flame of fire. He saw His feet like refined bronze. He heard His voice like the sound of many waters. He saw the sword of His mouth, and knew instantly: He'd seen this look before.

Near the beginning of Jesus' ministry, when His disciples had just recently left their fishing nets to follow Him, John caught a glimpse of this side of Jesus. "Now the Passover of the Jews was at hand, and Jesus went up to Jerusalem."[54] Now, this was Jesus, but it was also about one million Jews, all there for the Passover. And they were crowding into a city that was meant to hold about one hundred thousand. It was standing room only.

Picture this in your mind. Jesus came up to Jerusalem with, literally, hundreds of thousands of people, for the Passover. He would have come from the south side of Jerusalem, up the southern steps that Herod carved into solid rock. Remember that because of the holiness of God, the Jews couldn't enter the temple if they were unclean. So they had these huge pools, called *mikvaot,* at the top of Herod's staircase that they'd walk into, all the way down until the water would come over their heads, then they'd walk up the steps on the other side and come out ceremonially clean so they wouldn't defile the temple of God.

This is why all these people were in town, to get to God's house, where God lives. These people had come from all over just to be here for the Passover, and now they were squeezing in to get to the place where God was.

This is the picture we see in John 2: Jesus comes in with swelling crowds of people, up that south staircase, down into the *mikvaot* just like

54 John 2:13

everybody else did. He comes out on the other side, ceremonially clean with thousands of other Jews, ready to enter the holy temple of God, and that's when He sees it:

A parking lot-sized flea market.

Does He see a house of prayer, a holy place for sacrifices? No. He sees a forty-acre "house of merchandise"[55] large enough for hundreds of thousands of people to come through. It was just like a farmer's market. There were cattle, all sorts of animals, boxes of birds, and the money changers.

The poor would come up to Jerusalem with the few coins they had to buy a sacrifice, and the money changers would take their money and tell them they couldn't use that coin at the temple because it was unclean. It had pictures of Roman gods on it. But they could trade ten, or even forty, of their unclean Roman coins for a temple coin, and they could buy sacrifices with that.

So Jesus came into what should have been His Father's house, a place of worship and prayer, and found it defiled by what He called a "den of thieves."[56] Those who should have been taking care of God's house were trampling down the poor so they couldn't even buy a sacrificial lamb.

And Jesus doesn't take it well.

The House of the Living God

In the Sunday school pictures, we see a few people are standing around, maybe a cow or two, and a table that Jesus kind of bumps and knocks over. But this was no small thing. What we see in God's Word is Jesus driving out scores, if not hundreds, of people from His temple with a whip. He grabs up these cords, ties them together to make a whip, turns over tables, and with His loud voice so that all could hear, says, "Do not make my Father's house a house of merchandise!"

This is when John saw those eyes. This is the same anger, the same determination, the same power and strength John recognizes in Revelation 1. This would be like when you're little and you see your father get angry. Everyone kind of goes really still and slides out of the room as quietly as they can. You

---

55 John 2:16
56 Matthew 21:13

just get out of the way, because if something makes Daddy angry, then you don't want to be anywhere near it.

Wait a minute. *This* is what makes Jesus upset? A building? Of all the things He could be angry about, why this? Because when Jesus enters this building, He's going "into the temple of God."[57] See, it's not just a building. This is where God lives, His holy dwelling place, the only one there was.

When God designed His house, He fashioned it to be a picture of Him on earth. All those chapters in Exodus and Leviticus that we tend to skip over because they describe in painstaking detail every bowl and pillar of the temple, God spelled out specifically. It wasn't left up to the temple builders' imagination to build what they thought would look good. Every piece of furniture, every color, the layout, and even the building materials used were all designed to point people to something, and that something is Jesus Christ. He is the Way, the Truth, and the Life, the only way to the Father.[58]

If you wanted to meet with God, you had to go to the temple. This is where His presence, the pillar of cloud and fire that led Israel for all those years in the wilderness, had come to rest. This was the Most Holy Place, the Holy of Holies, the physical representation of the living God for all the nations to see.

But when Israel fell into sin and Solomon's temple became defiled, God allowed His perfectly designed dwelling place to be destroyed by the Babylonians. Later, Zerubbabel rebuilt the temple, but, once again, it failed to represent God's holiness the way He demanded, and it, too, was torn down. Herod built a magnificent temple, marble and stone, and that thing was supposed to last forever, but Jesus had to clean it out, and eventually, the Romans destroyed it too.

Jesus says, "My house shall be called a house of prayer for all nations."[59] The temple was supposed to be the place where anyone in the world who wanted to know the true and living God could come and meet Him, and the only way the temple could do its job was if it was kept clean, no worldly trappings of greed, or materialism, or any other defiling sin. But when God, who surrounds Himself in heaven with the name, "holy, holy, holy," walked

---

57   Matthew 21:12
58   Hebrews 9; John 14:6
59   Mark 11:17; Isaiah 56:7

into His house in John 2, He found it defiled. So He, with the strength of Samson, cleans out everything that dishonors God. Can you blame Him?

Well, after that, things calmed down. The meek and mild Jesus was back again, feeding the crowds and healing the sick. And He began to teach of another temple, this time one that's not made by human hands. He spoke of a time when the worship of God wouldn't be confined to a building, but God's people would worship Him in spirit and truth.[60] But that time wasn't here yet.

Three years go by, and Jesus once again walks into His Father's house. And that's when John sees it a second time. With blazing eyes, feet like bronze, and a voice like many waters, Jesus marches in and cleans out His house.[61]

And now John sees this side of Jesus for the third time.

First Corinthians 6:19–20 tells us the time has come: God has a new temple. Now, as believers, our "body is temple of the Holy Spirit." When the Holy Spirit whom Jesus promised came to live in us, we became the living temple of God, and guess what? We have the same job as the old temple did.

When the world wants to see God, it doesn't look to a building in Jerusalem anymore. The world looks to us. The old temple was supposed to be like a lighthouse, leading people to the God who saves, but now, Jesus says to us, "You are the light of the world. Let your light so shine before men, that they may see your good works and glorify your Father in heaven."[62] The old temple, every piece of furniture and every detail, was designed to point people to Jesus Christ. When the world looks at us, we are designed, every word and every action, to do the exact same thing.

Do you know what you're actually saying when you tell someone, "I'm a Christian"? In the first century, the word "Christian" was meant as a joke, an insult. It means, "little Christ." There goes a "little Christ." They're all thinking like Him. They're all acting like Him. They're always talking like Him.

Is that what we are? Is that how people know us? When we call ourselves a Christian, are we really acting like a "little Christ"? In today's world, one of the highest compliments is that someone is true to themselves. We take time off to go "find ourselves." We tell our kids, "Just be yourself." But

60   John 4:23; Acts 7:48
61   Luke 19:45–46
62   Matthew 5:14, 16

is that what we're supposed to be? Are we supposed to be ourselves, or are we supposed to be like Christ?

First Peter 2 says, "You also, as living stones, are being built up a spiritual house, a holy priesthood, to offer up spiritual sacrifices acceptable to God through Jesus Christ." We are a "chosen generation, a royal priesthood, a holy nation, His own special people, that [we] may proclaim the praises of Him who called [us] out of darkness into His marvelous light." When the world looks at us, they should see the God we represent. We are to reflect God's glory, the holiness of Christ, and when someone looks at us, they should see that our responses are more Christ-like today than they were yesterday, and if we are surrendered to the Holy Spirit, we will be more Christ-like tomorrow than we are today.

Jesus walks among us with His strong feet and loud voice. And when we begin to misrepresent Him, when He finds sin in the living representatives of God on earth, He does what He's always done with His temple: He cleans house.

BOUGHT WITH A PRICE:
WHAT JESUS EXPECTS FROM HIS CHURCH

Jesus' Inspection Tour

The first time John saw Jesus angry, it must have shocked him. John was fresh off the fishing boat, a newbie disciple. They'd just come from a nice wedding where Jesus did His first miracle, and they were supposed to all be celebrating the Passover together, when all of a sudden, Jesus clears the temple with a whip.

The second time, John had three years of experience under his belt, three years of Jesus teaching them to turn the other cheek, to love their enemies, and he sees once again, something so uncharacteristic of Jesus, it must have caught him off-guard.

But the third time, John falls to the ground as if dead, because he knows what this look means. After all, if Jesus got that upset about the temple building in Jerusalem, how must He feel about the living temple that He purchased with His own blood?

In chapter 1 of Revelation, Jesus has just come back from His inspection tour of His Church. Chapters 2–3 tell us what He found.

Did Jesus have a moment of déjà vu? He comes into the city, through the gate, up the steps, ready to enter the holy temple of God, and that's when He sees it: His Church, the light for all the nations, the physical representation of God on earth, the living temples He loved and gave His life for…

And they look just like a forty-acre flea market.

The church at Ephesus had become so busy with other things that they forgot that Jesus was supposed to occupy first place in their lives.

The Pergamite believers had become so comfortable with sin that there was no discernible difference between them and the pagans around them.

Thyatira was tolerating false teachers and false doctrine, which Jesus says He hates.

Sardis had a reputation for being alive, but they were like walking corpses, acting, thinking, and walking like all those dead-in-their-sins lost people around them.

And when Jesus finally arrived at Laodicea, He found them so apathetic and distracted by materialism that He wants to vomit them out of His mouth.

Jesus walks through His new temple, made up of all the redeemed saints He bought with His own blood and He finds that the new temple has gotten almost as bad as the old one. No wonder John collapsed.

Jesus inspected His Church and gave a 70 percent disapproval rating. Five out of seven churches had drifted so far from God's purpose for His living temple that they faced stern reprimands and warnings to repent, or else. Jesus warns that if they don't repent, He will remove their church from its lampstand. He would rather have no church in that city than a church that misrepresents Him.

The temple of God needed a major cleansing. And with His strong feet of chastisement and loud voice of rebuke, that's exactly what Jesus is about to do.

The Grace of God That Brings Salvation

When God showed to us the compassionate Son of Man, He unwrapped the One who sacrificed His life, not just to save us, but to sanctify us. "For you were bought with a price; therefore glorify God in your body and in your spirit, which are God's."[63] There's a reason God unwrapped the comforting Son of Man, Great High Priest first. The price Jesus paid for us is too high to ignore.

Jesus didn't become human and die so that we could wallow in our sin. First Corinthians 6:19 says, "Or do you not know that your body is the temple of the Holy Spirit who is in you, whom you have from God, and you are not your own?"

We have been saved for a purpose, and that purpose is not health, wealth, or happiness. It's to glorify God. We are to glorify God with our bodies—where we put them, what we do with them, where they go, and what they do—and with our spirits—all the invisible things that no one else sees.

Jesus died to cleanse us, to purify us, inside and out, and the life I live doesn't belong to me anymore. I am owned by the unstoppable, all-powerful Ancient of Days, and His holiness demands holiness in me. He is walking among the congregations of the Redeemed, and with His strong feet and loud voice, He is cleansing His temple wherever He finds sin.

"Who do you say that I am?" There is no more important question than that.

Titus 2:11–12 gives Jesus one of the most beautiful names in all of Scripture: "the Grace of God that brings salvation." Isn't that wonderful? It's the first picture God gave us, Son of Man, Great High Priest, compassionate and loving.

We don't have a problem with that. Grace is something we can get onboard with. When we ignore the Holy Spirit's warnings in our lives, we fall back on grace. After all, we're saved by grace, not by works, and we are irrevocably justified, blameless in the sight of God. We have our fire insurance. So why not simply live our lives rejoicing in our freedom and falling back on grace every time we go our own way?

Because grace brings salvation, and salvation means that I was bought—at no cost to me, at all cost to God. I had no contribution. He paid it all. I was bought, and I'm no longer my own. Sometimes we get so amazed by the grace of God that we neglect His holiness. But the Grace of

63 1 Corinthians 6:20

God does two things. Yes, it brings salvation, but it also is "instructing us to deny ungodliness and worldly desires and to live sensibly, righteously and godly in this present age."[64]

This is His second picture, the less comfortable one. This is the Ancient of Days, the One whose eyes are like a flame of fire. This is Jesus, walking among us with strong feet and loud voice, intolerant of sin, cleansing His temple. This is the vision of Jesus that laid John out on his face.

Jesus didn't give His life so that we could live ours however we want. He died to make us holy as He is holy. The Grace of God that brings salvation was never intended as an excuse or a license to do whatever we like. "Or do you think lightly of the riches of His kindness and tolerance and patience, not knowing that the kindness of God leads you to repentance?"[65] God didn't give us grace so we can feel good about our sin. Grace teaches us to say "no" to sin. We were not saved so we could be happy. We were saved so we could be holy.

Who does Jesus say He is? The Son of Man, the Great High Priest, the Ancient of Days, the Grace of God. He brings salvation, and He teaches us to deny ungodliness. He saves, and He sanctifies. And He will not tolerate sin in His Church.

John Newton was a slave trader who was stopped in his tracks by the amazing grace of God, and he put it this way; "Twas' grace that taught my heart to fear and grace my fear relieved." By God's grace, we see our need for a Savior. By grace we are justified and made righteous in His sight. And by His grace we are taught to deny ungodliness and live our lives in such a way that, more and more, we reflect the holiness of Christ.

The report Jesus asked John to send to His churches was not good, but the situation wasn't hopeless. All that was needed was repentance: a change of mind that would lead to a change in behavior.

We can hold on to our fire insurance, boasting in our freedom, and just be ourselves, or we can, in every word and action, point people to the true and living God. We can use God's magnificent grace as an excuse to allow sin to make inroads into our lives, or we can be like the apostle Paul,

64   Titus 2:11–12 NASB
65   Romans 2:4 NASB

and say, "May it never be!"[66] When we see the sobering portrait of the real Jesus, we can respond with indifference, treating lightly the kindness of God, or, like John, we can fall on our faces and repent. When we come face-to-face with the Grace of God, there are only two choices. What will yours be today?

RESPOND to Truth

Who do I say that Jesus is? Does that match up with the Jesus of Revelation 1:15?

How does Ezekiel's description of the God of Judgment in Ezekiel 8:2 compare to John's description of Jesus in Revelation 1:14–15?

How does God react to finding corruption in His temple at Jerusalem? (2 Kings 21:11–13; 2 Kings 23:26–27; Ezekiel 7:20–22; Ezekiel 8–9)

---

66 Romans 6:1 NASB

What should be going on in the living temple of God?
(Psalm 5:7; 27:4; 29:9, Matthew 21:13; 2 Corinthians 6:16)

When Jesus walks through the living temple of His Church, and when He sees the living temple of my body, what does He find going on here?

What can I drive out of my life to make my body the holy temple of God that it was designed to be?

5 | When Jesus Finds Sin in His Church

Most of us have been there before. We're sitting in the waiting room, a friend or family member is in with the doctor, and we're waiting. We're wondering if everything is going to be okay. And when the doctor finally finishes his examination and comes out to deliver the news, we know. We know what he's going to say before he says it just by the look on his face.

And the doctor sits us down together and says, "I have good news and I have bad news. The bad news is you have cancer. The good news is you're going to live." And then he starts to explain what we have to do to get healthy again.

What we see in Revelation chapter 1 is John sitting in the waiting room. And Jesus has just come out of the examination room. He's come back from giving each of His seven churches a checkup, and the moment John sees His face, he knows the news isn't going to be good. In fact, when John sees the look on the face of the Great Physician, he faints with fear.

But Jesus also has good news. The bad news is that His Church has cancer. But the good news is that it doesn't have to be terminal. Jesus has a Cancer Treatment Plan that can't fail, and while the surgery, the chemotherapy, and the radiation treatments may be painful at the time, our Great Physician will do anything and everything necessary to get His Church healthy again.

In the Waiting Room of the Great Physician

Revelation is a book of sevens. Seven bowls, seven seals, seven trumpets, seven angels of seven churches. But the first set of seven is the most sobering: a seven-fold description of Jesus Christ. Each description begins with the same word: "His." We've looked at His head and hair, His eyes, His feet, and His voice, and now we'll look at the last three.

But Revelation 1 isn't giving us seven separate pictures of Christ. No. Each description gives us yet another facet of the same Jesus, and when all seven are put together, we see Him as the Great Physician, the One who saves, the One who heals, and the One who will not tolerate malignant sin in His Church.

REVELATION 1:12–17

His head and hair were white like wool, as white as snow, and His eyes like a flame of fire; His feet were like fine brass, as if refined in a furnace, and His voice as the sound of many waters; He had in His right hand seven stars, out of His mouth went a sharp two-edged sword, and His countenance was like the sun shining in its strength. And when I saw Him, I fell at His feet as dead. But He laid His right hand on me, saying to me, "Do not be afraid; I am the First and the Last."

This is the picture God gives us of our Great Physician. We don't see Him as some young, just-out-of-medical-school doctor, but as the Ancient of Days, a wise old Physician who was practicing medicine, healing disease, and rooting out cancer long before we were born. His fiery eyes tell us that He can see exactly what He's going for. He has the x-rays, the MRI, He sees every part of us and knows exactly what's going on. And like we saw when He cleaned out His temple, His strong feet and loud voice tell us He is committed to our health. This is not a timid doctor who might make a suggestion or, better yet, send us elsewhere for a second opinion. He knows exactly what's going on, He knows exactly what needs to happen, and He speaks with absolute authority.

The Scalpel of His Mouth

Some people know something's wrong with their body, but they avoid going to the doctor because they're afraid to find out what it is. Life is mostly good. The symptoms are manageable, and they don't want a cancer diagnosis to interrupt the way they're living their lives.

But sin doesn't get better on its own. It doesn't go away because we ignore it, and it will spread until it becomes debilitating.

The good news is that no matter what He finds wrong with us, Jesus has the cure. Look at verse 16: "He had in His right hand seven stars, out of His mouth came a sharp two-edged sword, and His countenance was like the sun shining in its strength." Imagine coming out of a dark place, a place you've been for so long your eyes are adjusted to almost total darkness, and coming out to the overwhelming, knock-you-over brightness of the sun. That's what Jesus' countenance is like. There's no doubt He knows what He's doing.

But not only that. John also describes the scalpel of His mouth. Do you notice that? What comes out of Jesus' mouth, the Word of God, is described as a scalpel. A sharp two-edged sword. Hebrews 4:12 says, "For the Word of God is living and powerful, and sharper than any two-edged sword, piercing even to the division of soul and spirit, and of joints and marrow."

The Word of God is not a prescription of juicing the right vegetables or a daily supplement of some herb that is "not intended to treat, diagnose, cure, or prevent any disease," but might possibly be beneficial to your overall health. No. The Word of God, the sword of His mouth, is a scalpel, and the Great Physician is ready and willing to cut away any diseased, dead, or cancerous tissue that prevents His Body from being useful to Him. No matter how close it is to the brain stem, His scalpel that's sharper than a two-edged sword can cut it out. No matter how far it's spread, the radiation of hearing His voice can eradicate it.

Jesus holds in His right hand seven stars. Revelation 1:20 tells us those are the messengers to the seven churches. Jesus tells John to write down His diagnosis, His prognosis, and give it to messengers for the seven churches: Ephesus, Smyrna, Pergamos, Thyatira, Sardis, Philadelphia, and Laodicea. He's taken each of them into the examination room. His feet like bronze have walked among them. His fiery eyes have seen inside them. With the wisdom that comes from age, a voice of great authority, and a blazing countenance that can't be ignored, He's about to give His diagnostic report.

And that's when John falls at Jesus' feet as if dead.

But Jesus reaches out a comforting hand to him and says, "Do not be afraid; I am the First and the Last."[67] God promises us that "He who has begun a good work in [us] will complete it until the day of Jesus Christ."[68] Jesus is the "author and finisher of our faith," and He "has sat down at the right hand of the throne of God."[69] That means the work Jesus did is complete, it's done. When He said, "It is finished,"[70] He meant it.

We are saved to the uttermost, and no sin, no matter how malignant, no matter how far spread, no matter how debilitating, can destroy what Christ died to save. Our Great Physician will not let the cancer of sin beat us. These are not a doctor's best efforts. These are God's promised results, and Jesus has a 100 percent patient survival rate. He is the First and the Last, and what He started, He will finish.

Jesus already performed on us His most miraculous medical procedure. Ephesians 2 tells us that when He found us, we weren't sick. We weren't on life support. We weren't dying. We were dead. Flatlined, brain-dead, no pulse, absolutely lifeless.

But God made us alive. This isn't a coat of whitewash or a simple cosmetic surgery. We have been fundamentally altered. At the moment of salvation, we were given a heart transplant: "I will give you a new heart and put a new spirit within you; I will take the heart of stone out of your flesh and give you a heart of flesh."[71] We have a new operating system. We are new creations.

But sometimes that new heart starts behaving an awful lot like the old, dead one. So Jesus, our Great Physician, gives us constant checkups to ensure that the new heart is functioning properly. And if it isn't, He does something about it.

Jesus holds in His hand His written diagnoses, His prescribed treatment, and we would be fools to ignore Him.

---

67 Revelation 1:17
68 Philippians 1:6
69 Hebrews 12:2
70 John 19:30
71 Ezekiel 36:26

CHRIST'S DIAGNOSTIC REPORT

Ephesus' Spiritual Heart Condition

Jesus comes out of the examination room and writes John a diagnostic report as well as the prescribed treatment plan. He roots out what's wrong in His Church, and tells His people exactly how to fix it.

The first stop on Jesus' medical inspection tour is Ephesus. And it doesn't take long for Him to find a serious spiritual heart condition. But you wouldn't know it to look at them.

Ephesus appeared to be thriving. It was easily the largest church in Asia Minor. Paul had pastored there for three years, explaining the Scriptures daily, answering their questions and teaching them to live sanctified lives. When Paul moved on from Ephesus, he left Timothy behind, his spiritual son in the faith. And just before being exiled to Patmos, John lived and ministered in Ephesus, and he had Mary, Jesus' mother, living with him.

More Scripture was written directly to Ephesus than to any other city. This letter Jesus dictates to John is epistle number four written specifically for this church, and yet when Jesus examines Ephesus, He finds a major heart problem.

At first glance, Ephesus appeared healthy. If you read the diagnostic report found in Revelation 2:1–7, Jesus' initial observations appear to be a glowing report on the health of His largest and most influential local church. "I know your works," He says. "Your labor, your patience, and that you cannot bear those who are evil. And you have tested those who say they are apostles and are not, and have found them liars; and you have persevered and have patience, and have labored for My name's sake and have not become weary." Sounds like a healthy heart to me.

But Jesus found something wrong. Their blood pressure was up, their arteries were clogged. Their hearts had experienced a gradual buildup of other things so that Jesus was no longer holding the position of first place in their hearts. He wasn't first in their schedules, in their concentration, and all that signaled that He was no longer the supreme ruler of their hearts and lives.

In ancient math, when you added up a column of numbers, the sum went at the top. Jesus started adding everything up, all of Ephesus' great works, but what He found was that the sum total of their lives did not add up to Him. They had "left their first love." Jesus wasn't at the top. He was part of the equation, part of the calculations. He was important, He just wasn't the *most* important. He wasn't the sum total of their lives.

In modern, American math, the total goes at the bottom. So when someone asks you what the bottom line is, they're not asking for an explanation of everything that went into the calculations. The Ephesians were overflowing with good works. They labored. They were patient. They wouldn't tolerate evil. They rooted out false prophets. They persevered. But bottom line? Jesus didn't take first place in their lives.

Their heart didn't belong solely to Him. Their spiritual arteries were clogged with so many other things that they were in danger of a spiritual heart attack. And while Ephesus may have felt fine on the outside, Jesus warns them of the seriousness of their heart condition and tells them to deal with it before it became fatal.

The prognosis was simple: repent.

Pergamos' Spiritual Immunity Problems

So Jesus moves on. He travels on to Pergamos, and examines the church there. But if He was hoping for a better diagnosis than Ephesus had, He would have been disappointed.

The church at Pergamos was sitting right on top of a nuclear sin reactor, "where Satan's throne is."[72] This would be like living in the twenty-kilometer radius zone around a nuclear reactor. And Satan's throne was just pumping out wave after wave of all this marrow-shriveling radiation for the soul.

So Pergamos had developed spiritual immunity problems. They had been doing really well for a while. They held fast to Jesus' name, even when one of their great leaders was martyred. But by the time Jesus examines the church at Pergamos, His people were falling for one of the oldest tricks in the book.

In the book of Numbers, the prophet Balaam, paid by a wicked king, taught Israel to sin so that God would come against them and destroy them. And when Jesus examines Pergamos, He finds them holding to the doctrine of Balaam.

Pergamos started out so strong, just how we imagine the first-century church to be: strong, witnessing, persecuted, but remaining faithful to Christ. And we wish we in modern-day America could be like them. But they were as susceptible to sin as we are today, and as susceptible as the Israelites were in Numbers.

No amount of vitamin C can keep you from catching a cold if you're constantly bombarded with every germ and virus there is. Eventually, your immunity will wear down and you'll get sick.

Spiritual immunity is compromised when believers, God's own people, are constantly around what God hates. They hang around with it. They handle it. They touch it. They get it on their hands, they bring it into their homes, and somehow, they think their immune system is strong enough not to be affected by it.

But in Numbers, "the anger of the Lord was aroused against Israel," and He sent a plague that wiped out twenty-four thousand of His own people.[73] In Revelation, He finds His bought-and-paid-for Church going the same way and says, "Repent, or else I will come to you quickly and will fight against them with the sword of My mouth."

And today, when what God hates finds its way into our Netflix queue, into our internet search history, into the magazines we buy, when we flirt with it, touch it, get it on our hands, and bring it into our homes, how do you think Jesus feels? His anger was aroused in the Old Testament, He says, "repent or else" in the New Testament, and when sin comes right into our camp and we do nothing to stamp it out, Jesus says our spiritual immunity is compromised no matter how impervious we think we are.

And Jesus says, "Repent."

Thyatira: The Raging Infection of Sin

When Jesus says, "Repent or else" to Pergamos, we sometimes imagine the parent who's fed up with their child's behavior and keeps threatening to do something but never does. But when Jesus says, "Repent or else," it's not an idle threat. He isn't hoping His disobedient child will

---

73   Numbers 25:3, 9

get the message and change all on his own. He gives us time to repent, and then He takes action. And that's what we see in Thyatira.

Jesus' next ailing patient is already well past spiritual immunity problems. Thyatira is dealing with a raging infection. God says He has two things against them: "You allow that woman, Jezebel," number one, "to teach," and, number two, to "seduce My servants."

Thyatira was a go-getter church. They were growing, their ministry was expanding, and they had a great pastor. Unfortunately, she was teaching lies.

Notice what Jesus has against the believers at Thyatira. He didn't say that *they* *we*re teaching falsehood and seducing His servants. They were *allowing* it. In their church, from their pulpit. They were tolerant.

But tolerance sounds so nice. We shouldn't throw stones, shouldn't judge. We leave the God of judgment to the Old Testament and sing about our wonderful New Testament God of love. After all, Jesus preached tolerance. Didn't He?

Not to Thyatira, He didn't. They were tolerating a false teacher, and He holds that against them.

Jesus has already said, "Repent, or else." Now we get to see what "or else" looks like. "And I gave her time to repent of her sexual immorality, and she did not repent." It's already too late. Jesus gave her time. What she's teaching is wrong, she knows it's wrong, and she will not repent. So, like a good parent, Jesus follows through and says, "Indeed I will cast her into a sickbed, and those who commit adultery with her into great tribulation."[74]

This isn't "I might if she doesn't stop soon." This is Jesus fresh out of the examination room, scalpel in His hand. Sign the release forms, put on the gown, you're going in for surgery. Jesus cannot let this go any further.

So He's going to make this woman physically sick. "Sickbed" is not a metaphor. It's real, and it's taught all the way through Scripture. The church in Corinth had the same problem. They were coming straight to communion from living like pagans all week, acting like everything was fine even though it wasn't, and Jesus says, "For this reason many are weak and sick among you, and many sleep."[75]

74 Revelation 2:22
75 1 Corinthians 11:30

First John 5:16 says there is a sin that leads to death. Not spiritual death. Remember, this is talking to believers here. But actual, physical death. When believers persist in unrepentant sin, like the false teacher Jezebel, and like those who are following her in Thyatira, Jesus will make them weak, and then make them sick, and if He has to, He will make them dead.

Jesus says the same thing in Revelation 2:23: "And I will kill her children with death." Just in case we're unclear, it's not just "kill," it's "kill with death." No confusion. This is a serious sin, and it's infecting the rest of the church. Jezebel's students have gotten worse than the teacher, and Jesus is going to raise the temperature and burn out the infection to save the body.

The way the churches in America are going today, you can be living in sin, sleeping with your boyfriend, and singing on stage, and nobody does anything about it because we preach tolerance. We're all about love. But Jesus is all about holiness. And in His love, He won't allow His body, the Church, to destroy itself.

The God of love doesn't give me an aspirin for the symptoms. He goes after the disease. And when we tolerate disease running rampant in our local church, the intolerant Jesus does the only loving thing and burns it out.

The Walking Dead of Sardis

Jesus originally found Sardis, and Ephesus, and Pergamos, and Thyatira, and Laodicea, dead in a ditch. Every person was spiritually dead, exactly like every other unsaved person in town. But Jesus performed a miracle. This was the kind of transformation no doctor could explain. He took people who were dead and made them alive.

Nobody but God could do this, and Jesus didn't just make the church at Sardis alive. He made them abundantly alive. But when the Great Physician comes to give Sardis a checkup, He finds that something is very wrong.

They're lying in a ditch again, no pulse, not breathing, flatlined. The ones He saved, brought to life, fundamentally altered, and made alive were behaving like they were dead. Sardis was in spiritual cardiac arrest.

They looked alive. Jesus even comments that they have a reputation for being alive, but when He examines them, He finds that they are not. No pulse. The church of Sardis was full of the walking dead. They walked like, talked like, and acted like all the dead-in-their-trespasses-and-sins unbeliev-ers around them, and however good a front they put up to everyone else, Jesus could see right through it.

To Jesus, Sardis looked like death warmed over. And when He finds His Church in a state of cardiac arrest, flat-lining in a ditch, no measure is too drastic to shock His Church back into usefulness to Him. The power their new heart once possessed is still available if only Sardis will repent of her corpse-like condition and return to God's prescribed plan for her health. Once again, Jesus prescribes radical repentance. They needed to stop just going through the motions of being a Christian and get His power at work in them again. They needed to repent.

Laodicea's Materialism-Induced Blindness

Perhaps the most frustrating condition of all was what Jesus found in Laodicea. They weren't living near Satan's throne, struggling with martyrdom, or being led astray by false teachers. Their condition was completely self-induced.

The Laodiceans were rich, well fed, well dressed, and had every advantage. And they knew it. They boasted that they had "need of nothing."[76] But God's Word had been taken for granted. Forgotten. Swallowed up with all the other information and gadgets and material possessions that demand attention.

Laodicea had gotten distracted. Yes, they had His Word, but they also had everything else. There was just so much to capture their attention that God's Word had kind of gotten lost in the shuffle.

When I preach overseas in third world places, I'm always amazed at how little they have. In places like rural Russia, they'll have a church service that goes from eight in the morning to noon, have a short lunch, and then they'll ask me to preach again. Even if I don't have anything else prepared, they're willing to hear the same message over again because they have nothing else going on. They have nothing else going in life but God.

But when you're rich and increased in goods, you become like Laodicea. Laodicea had so much going on, they'd been so overexposed to the distrac-tions of having too much stuff, that they had become spiritually blind. Like those creatures that live for years in caves with no exposure to sunlight,

76 Revelation 3:17

Laodicea had gone for so long without proper exposure to the Light of God's Word that they had become blind.

But they weren't just blind. Laodicea was so distracted by everything else that they'd become bland and useless to God. Jesus says that rather than being hot, on fire for Christ, or cold, like a refreshing drink of water to those who are perishing, the church at Laodicea had become lukewarm and useless. And Jesus wanted to vomit them out of His mouth. God's solution? As always, repent.

They had neglected for so long what they needed for their spiritual souls, because they were so distracted by their materialistic pursuits of pleasure that they had become un-needing of Christ. And Jesus says they've allowed themselves to become blind and miserable and putrid. He wanted to spit them out of His mouth, like a sickening taste, or a spoiled piece of food—that's what the church had become. Jesus reports that what is needed is for them to repent of their apathy for Him and start sacrificially giving whatever time it took to get their eyesight restored. The Laodiceans had every advantage, but they were so focused on everything that didn't matter, they could no longer see the one thing that did matter.

Jesus doesn't differentiate between those who are meant to be on fire for Him and those who are simply expected to live a life of mediocrity. Not hot, not cold, just lukewarm, going along avoiding the really big sins and living the American dream. We are called to something higher. He calls all of us to be set apart for Him, to be on fire, to refresh the world like a cool drink of water, and if we're not, Jesus says, "be zealous and repent."[77] "Repent or else." There is no middle ground with Him.

Jesus' Cure for Cancer

Between surgeries, one Christian physician spent His free time studying the Bible. And this is what he wrote about the cancer of sin in the Body of Christ:

> *Sometimes a dreaded thing occurs in the body—mutiny, resulting in*
> *a tumor. A tumor is called benign if its effect is fairly localized and*
> *it stays within membrane boundaries. But the most traumatizing*

---

77   Revelation 3:19

condition in the body occurs when cancer cells defy inhibition. They multiply without any checks on growth, spreading rapidly through-out the body, choking out normal cells.

White cells, armed against foreign invaders, will not attack the body's own mutinous cancer cells. Physicians fear no other malfunc-tion more deeply than cancer. For still mysterious reasons, these cells—and they may be cells from the brain, liver, kidney, bone, blood, skin, or other tissues—grow wild, out of control. Each is a healthy, functioning cell, but disloyal, no longer acting in regard to the rest of the body.

Even the white cells, the dependable palace guard, can destroy the body through rebellion. Sometimes they recklessly reproduce, clogging the bloodstream, overloading the lymph system, strangling the body's normal functions—such is leukemia.

In His warnings to the church, Jesus Christ showed no concern about the shocks and bruises His Body would meet from external forces. "The gates of hell shall not prevail against my church," He said flatly (Matthew 16:18). He moved easily, unthreatened, among sinners and criminals. But He cried out against the kind of danger that comes from within. Few doctrines are more important than the Church.

Because of the constant attack, we need to be good students of the subject. Because disease can diminish the effectiveness of the Body, we must maintain habits of health. Furthermore, a regular checkup by the Great Physician is a must. Not once a year but at least, once a week. And be prepared for the cost of that visit.[78]

"Benign" Sin

Cancer is so terrifying because it comes from within. The body's own defenses don't recognize it as a threat, and it begins attacking the rest of the body. Cancer patients often say, "My own body turned on me," and that is the threat Jesus warns against in Revelation 2–3.

When Jesus visited Smyrna and Philadelphia, two of His seven churches, He found no such cancer within them. Smyrna was facing serious persecu-tion. Jesus says many of them will be thrown into prison, and some will

---

78 Adapted and quoted from Brand and Yancey, *Fearfully and Wonderfully Made.*

even be killed for their faith in Christ, but He only tells them not to be afraid. Philadelphia was faithful, they were witnessing, and His only warning to them is not to be disqualified. Threats from outside, He had covered. It was the threats from within the church that concerned God.

Nothing is more dangerous to the health of the Church than sin spreading through it like a cancer, and no treatment plan is too radical to get rid of it. Jesus won't allow the new heart He gave us to start behaving like the old one, and when it does, Jesus will take whatever measures are necessary to shock that heart back into usefulness to Him.

Christ's diagnostic report on the seven churches is pretty harsh. He could have spent more time on what they were doing right and glossed over those small problems. After all, no one's perfect.

With all Ephesus had done to serve Christ, all their patience, their labor, their good works, why couldn't Jesus just be a team player and sign off on a clean bill of health? In light of all the persecution Pergamos was facing, having a few minor false doctrines shouldn't have been that big of a deal. Doesn't their behavior matter more than what they believe anyway? And the Thyatirans were doing more good works than they had been doing at the beginning. Surely a woman teacher can't be that bad if their ministry was growing. Sardis had such a good reputation that if they had asked for a second opinion, another doctor would have pronounced them healthy, and Laodicea wasn't hurting anybody. If they were okay with poor eyesight, shouldn't that be their business?

Let's just leave Revelation to the theologians and go back to Jesus in the gospels. It would be so much easier to just forget all this negative stuff and talk about the grace of God.

Okay. Let's talk about the Grace of God. The Grace of God that brings salvation is a package deal. The Grace of God that brings salvation teaches us to deny ungodliness and worldly desires.[79] If you're not taught to deny ungodliness and worldly desires, then you didn't get the right kind of grace, because that's the kind God gives.

Jesus has found a potentially terminal condition in His Church. He has the cure in His hands, and no matter how painful or unpleasant the

---

79   Titus 2:11–12 NASB

treatment plan is, the worst thing He can do when He finds sin in His Church is to do nothing. Do you want to go to the doctor with a potentially lethal condition and hear him say, "You're good to go. Keep doing what you're doing"? That's not grace. That's not love.

Some say the standard God demands from His Church is unrealistic. Some say His chastening work in our lives is the cruel act of an intolerant God. Sometimes the pain of the shock to our heart or the cutting away of some sin in our lives makes us think God doesn't love us. But only a God of love could look at the state His bought-and-paid-for people had gotten themselves into and go to whatever lengths it takes to bring them back to health.

The cancer of sin has only one cure. Repentance. The Great Physician, with flaming eyes, blazing countenance, and a scalpel poised and ready, gives the same message to all five unhealthy churches: "Repent, or else."[80]

Nothing is more important to Jesus than the health of His Church. He is still walking among us, still examining His Body to see if it is healthy, checking new hearts to be sure they're still functioning as they should.

When He examines my life, will He find a spiritual heart condition, the silent killer that only the Great Physician would notice? Do I look fine on the outside, serving, sharing, coming to church with a smile on my face, but I'm doing it all for selfish reasons? When He adds up everything in my life, is the sum total, the bottom line, Jesus Christ, or is it something else?

Will He find my spiritual immunity compromised? Will He find that I've become so comfortable with the sin around me that it's gotten all over my hands and into my house? If He walked into my house today, would I want to hide the books I read, the TV shows I watch, the DVDs in my drawer, because I am entertained by what He hates?

Will He find a raging sin infection in my life? Am I tolerating sin in my own life, seeing it, excusing it, and claiming God's grace to cover it? Will He have to raise the temperature just to burn out what I've allowed to infect my life?

Or will He find me in spiritual cardiac arrest? Am I behaving so much like the unsaved person I was before that when Jesus looks at me, He

---

80   Revelation 2:5, 16, 22; 3:3, 19

pronounces me dead? If He lined me up with all the still-dead-in-their-sins people around me, would anyone even be able to pick me out as different?

Or will He check my eyes and find me blind? Have I allowed the stuff of this world to so crowd my vision that I've become blind to the things of God? Am I stagnating, neither hot nor cold, comfortable and increased in goods with no real urgency about pleasing God?

No wonder we as Christians have such a hard time reading God's Word regularly. We want a pat on the back and a clean bill of health; no such luck with Jesus.

There's no such thing as benign sin. There is no such thing as a little white lie, a harmless little private sin that, as long as it stays behind closed doors and doesn't hurt anybody, is okay. No sin stays inside the boundaries of its own membranes. Every sin is malignant, and sin, by its very nature, will spread.

Jesus has found five potentially fatal conditions in His bought-and-paid-for Church, and He prescribes a radical treatment plan for each: absolute, no-holds-barred repentance. If you're looking for a pat on the back and a clean bill of health, the Sword of His Mouth, the Word of God, probably isn't the Book for you. But this Book is the only one that saves, that heals, that gives the abundant life we were meant to live.

The moment the Great Physician first found us dead in a ditch and made us alive, we were fundamentally altered. And Jesus will keep working in us until we start living like it.

I have some good news and some bad news. The bad news is you have cancer. The good news is you're going to live.

RESPOND to Truth

What benign sin have I been tolerating in my life?

How have I been treating the Grace of God?

If Jesus were to diagnose me today, what would He find in my life?
(Spiritual heart condition?—Revelation 2:4. Spiritual immunity problems?—
Revelation 2:14–15. Spiritual infection?—Revelation 2:20. Spiritual cardiac
arrest?—Revelation 3:2. Or spiritual blindness—Revelation 3:16–17.)

What would Jesus' prognosis be? (Revelation 2:5, 16, 22; 3:3, 18–19)

What steps do I need to take toward spiritual health today?

What does repentance look like in actions I can take today?

Seven Lessons from Revelation 1 | 6

The Book of the Revelation

Revelation is God's book of reminders. In His Word, He has given us everything we need for life and godliness, and Revelation begins with seven reminders that set the stage, seven lessons that get us ready for Christ's dictated message to His Church.

REVELATION 1:18–20

"I am He who lives, and was dead, and behold, I am alive forevermore. Amen. And I have the Keys of Hades and of Death. Write the things which you have seen, and the things which are, and the things which will take place after this. The mystery of the seven stars which you saw in My right hand, and the seven golden lampstands: The seven stars are the angels of the seven churches, and the seven lampstands which you saw are the seven churches."

The last verses of Revelation 1 bring us full circle, back around to the Author and Subject of the book, Jesus Christ. When He hand-delivers Revelation to John, He addresses the envelope as from the Risen Christ, "He who lives, and was dead," and is "alive forevermore." He stamps the envelope with the equivalent of "Top Priority—Open Immediately." The envelope contains what John saw, the sobering portrait of the real Jesus. It tells us the things that are, what really matters to Jesus, and it contains God's revealed plan for the future, when Jesus comes back for His bride.

That's who this letter is addressed to, the bride of Christ. These are Jesus' last words to me. His last words to you. And only by understanding these seven lessons from chapter 1 will you and I be ready to hear His last words to us.

Lesson 1: Revelation is about Jesus (Revelation 1:1).

Revelation is not about the apocalypse. It's about the *apocalupsis,* the Grand Unveiling of Jesus Christ. The very first word is God's first reminder to us: keep your eyes on Jesus. Jesus, the Amen, the completion of everything God has ever said is the final word. And Jesus is at the forefront of every page in between.

These are not God's afterthoughts. This is His presentation of His Son. This is the capstone of His Word, the culmination of everything He's ever said. His closing pitch, the final chapter, the completion of what He started in Eden. These are Christ's last words to His Church, and there are no more important words to live by.

Lesson 2: We are slaves of God (Revelation 1:1).

Revelation 1:1 tells us what this book is about. The next words tell us who it's for: "which God gave Him to show His servants—things which must shortly take place." When Jesus delivered Revelation, He didn't just deliver it to John. He delivered it to "His servants."

Throughout Scripture, in both the Old and New Testaments, there is one term that consistently describes the people of God.

A servant is what we see in Matthew 18. Jesus tells a story about a land-owner who goes out and hires day laborers to work his field. They could choose to work for the wages offered or turn down the job if they wanted to. If the money wasn't good enough or they wanted to work somewhere else that day, that was their choice. A servant can take it or leave it.

That is not what we are.

We are not independent contractors. We don't exchange obedience for blessings on a take-it-or-leave-it basis. The Greek word in Revelation 1:1 is *douloi*, and it does not mean "servant." All 127 times this word is found in Scripture, it means a bought-and-paid-for, no-rights-of-his-own slave.

This is why the majority of the people who followed Jesus throughout His ministry stopped following Him after a while. In John 6, after He fed five thousand men and their families, He started talking about what it really means to follow Him, and almost all of them left because it was just too hard. They didn't want to be His slaves. They wanted to be fed.

But we aren't just coming to God on an as-needed basis, getting fed when we're hungry and going our own way when we're full. We have been bought. We are owned. We belong to Jesus Christ.

In John's day, a slave was known by his master's name. He was known as Nero's slave or Cornelius's slave, but a slave did not have an identity of his own. We don't get to have our own identity, and then hire out to God when we want something. We are "little Christs." We are known by His name.

A slave had no possessions of his own. Any possessions he had belonged to his master, and they were only temporarily entrusted to him so he could invest them for his master. Our money, our houses, our cars, our families, our lives do not belong to us. We, and everything in our temporary possession, belong to God, and all of it is His to do with as He pleases.

Also, a slave had no plans outside of His master's. He had no agenda, no plans for the future that his master didn't give him. We aren't here to further our own agendas. We are here to follow God's plan for our lives. But don't worry. It's not a secret. He tells us exactly what it is.

Lesson 3: We are called to keep God's Word (Revelation 1:3).
God didn't give us the Book of the Revelation so we could add another chart to our studies of End Times prophecy. He gave us Revelation so we could keep His Words.

Revelation 1:3 says, "Blessed is he who reads and those who hear the words of this prophecy, and keep those things which are written in it; for the time is near."

In light of Jesus' soon return, we aren't to be hoarding canned food in our bomb shelters. We're to be hoarding His Word so we aren't deceived.

The Greek word, *tereo*, "to keep," means exactly what we'd think it does. Jesus uses the same word in Matthew 28:20 when He says to teach people to "observe" His commands. He uses it again in John 15:10 when He says we are to "keep" His commands. But it also means to hold on to, to treasure, to cling to, to not lose track of. These are choices we make. A conscious decision to hold fast to something. When Paul says that he has finished the race, he has "kept" the faith,[81] it is a decision he made so he wouldn't be disqualified.

But the most interesting use of this word is in Acts, first when Peter and John are "put in custody," and later when the Roman guards are commanded to "keep" Paul during his trial.[82]

In Peter, John, and Paul's day, if a guard or a jailer lost a prisoner, they were executed in that prisoner's place. So when they were charged to *tereo*, "to keep" a prisoner, it was a matter of life or death. So they would guard. They would watch. They would keep their eyes on, pay attention to, and "keep" what they were charged with guarding as if their lives depended on it. And that's the same word Jesus uses when He tells us what to do with His last words.

THE PRESENT-DAY JESUS

Lesson 4: Sunday is the Lord's Day (Revelation 1:10).

When John was "in the Spirit on the Lord's Day," he was not observing the Sabbath day. The Sabbath is Saturday. It's always been Saturday, and we don't observe a Sabbath day anymore. Colossians 1:17 says that the Sabbath was "a shadow of things to come, but the substance is in Christ."

We don't observe the shadow. We worship the substance; that's Jesus. He didn't rise from the dead on a Saturday, or a Friday, or a Monday. He rose on the first day of the week, and that's what we've celebrated ever since.

When Jesus rose from the dead, He fulfilled the Law. He completed it.

---

81   2 Timothy 4:7
82   Acts 4:3; 24:23

No longer do we carry around a tablet carved with a list of rules we have to keep or be stoned for breaking the Law. We answer to a higher law, the Risen Christ.

The day He rose from the dead, Jesus announced His victory over sin and death and the Law. The Word of God isn't just written on stone or parchment anymore. The Word was made flesh,[83] and you and I have the living, breathing Word of God walking among us.

Lesson 5: Revelation is for Christ's Church (Revelation 1:11).

If you were to make a word map of Revelation 1–3, where the computer blows up the key words out of a text, one word would stand out from all the others. Nowhere in Scripture can we find a more concentrated treatment of one of Jesus' favorite subjects: the Church. In just three chapters, Jesus refers to His Church nineteen times. Revelation is the longest letter written to any church, it's the only letter personally addressed by Christ to His Church, and nowhere else do we see Jesus as focused on the character and conduct of His Church than we do here.

When we as believers gather together, we become the visible manifestation of Christ's Church here on earth. We come together to form the living temple of God. God expects us to gather regularly for worship and instruction. And every time we gather, Jesus gathers with us.

When He wrote His last words to His Church, Jesus addressed it to seven local, geographic gatherings of believers. But He didn't just write each letter to one church in one place at one time in history. He is writing to every church at every place at every time in history.

He says to Ephesus, "He who has an ear, let him hear what the Spirit says to the churches." Notice He doesn't say "church," singular, but "churches," plural. Jesus wanted Ephesus to hear and to keep what He said to every church. And He wanted every church to hear and to keep what He said to Ephesus.

Jesus said the same thing to all the churches.[84] These aren't just a cross-section of all believers and all churches of the first century, but a

---

83   John 1:14
84   Revelation 2:7, 11, 17, 29; 3:6, 13, 22

cross-section of all churches of every century. What they struggled with, we struggle with. What distracted them from following God distracts us today. What pleased God then pleases God now. And what He hated in the first century, He hates in the twenty-first. Christ's last words aren't just for seven local churches, but for every church and every believer.

Lesson 6: Christ's attention is on His church (Revelation 1:13). Jesus could be anywhere, doing anything, but He stands in the midst of the lampstands, with His churches. His attention is on His people, and He is doing one thing: making sure our character and conduct lines up with His Word.

Jesus says that we have a responsibility to hear God speak through His Word. And we have a responsibility to obey what we hear. Whether you know what the speed limit is, when you're pulled over going ninety on the highway, you're going to get a ticket. It doesn't matter if you were unaware of the speed limit, you are responsible to know the laws of the road. And whether we know God's expectations of His people or are blissfully unaware of them, God holds us responsible for whether our character and conduct are pleasing to Him or not.

We don't have any excuses for not knowing God's Word. We don't live in ancient Israel, when a city would have a single scroll containing a part of God's Word they could only hear when the scribes read from it. We don't live in the Middle Ages, when the Bible was only read in a language no one spoke. You and I have His Word available to us. We have no excuses for not knowing what it says, for not knowing what God expects of us.

There's no guessing. There's no confusion. God gives us in His Word all that we need for life and godliness, and here in Revelation, the culmination of every word of God, everything we need to know is distilled down to two things.

Yes. Just two. Christ's last words to every church of all time, to the abundantly wealthy of Laodicea and the dirt poor of Smyrna, to the mega church at Ephesus and the tiny gathering of believers at Philadelphia, to every culture of every person living in the cosmopolitan city of Pergamos, and those who were still living by the ancient Jewish laws, to every socioeconomic level, every culture, and every time period, Christ's last words to His Church come down to two things:

Number 1: These are the things that please God.

Jesus says to the churches, "I know your works." He lists all their works that are pleasing to Him. This is what He loves. This is what He approves of. This is what He wants to see when He gathers with us. And then He notes something else.

Number 2: These are the things that don't please God.

"But I have this against you," He says. To each church that had allowed sin to creep into their congregation, Jesus lists, not in general terms, but in specifics, with names and doctrines and actions, what does not please Him. This grieves Him. This disappoints Him. This dishonors Him. This is what He hates.

God's will isn't unknowable. Jesus tells us exactly what pleases Him, what's always pleased Him, and how we are to live because of it.

THE CHURCH IN ALL HER GLORY

Lesson 7: Jesus' top priority is the health of His Church (Revelation 1:14–16).

When we are saved, the Holy Spirit takes up residence and begins to systematically burn out everything that doesn't reflect His ownership. The same Jesus who cleaned out the temple is walking through His living temple, and when He finds it misrepresenting God, He takes a scourge of cords and cleans house. And when the Great Physician finds cancer in His body, the Church, He goes after it with the scalpel of His mouth.

When a believer starts acting like an unbeliever, God steps in. This is called the doctrine of chastening, and it's one of the most neglected doctrines in all of Scripture. "Repent or else," the simplest definition of chastening there is, doesn't play well in church. It's not politically correct. It doesn't make us feel good about ourselves or comfort us like we think a God of love should, but this is the real Jesus.

This is what's important to Him. In all the universe, this is where His attention is, where He spends His time. And when He finds believers acting like unbelievers, He spanks us until we stop. Repent or else.

"If you endure chastening, God deals with you as with sons."[85] This isn't the wrath of a hateful God. This is the warning of a loving Father. God is not that permissive parent who excuses His child, saying, "Well, that's just the way he is." God says, "No. That's not the way you are. You have been changed, fundamentally altered, and you can't act the way you used to anymore." He won't allow it.

We are something new. Whoever says, "You're just born that way," whatever habitual sins we used to fall into, whatever parts of our personality are simply not pleasing to God, we have been changed. Our old, stony heart has been taken out, and we have been given a new heart. And the Holy Spirit inside us gives us the power to say no to sin. To act like the child of God we are. And when we don't, God spanks us until we stop.

"Now no chastening seems to be joyful for the present, but painful; nevertheless, afterward it yields the peaceable fruit of righteousness to those who have been trained by it."[86]

Chastening is how God trains us for righteousness, and Hebrews 12:5–6 uses three key words to describe the process of correction in a believer's life.

The first step in God's discipline is rebuke. "My son, do not despise the chastening of the Lord, nor be discouraged when you are rebuked by Him."

Rebuke may be a prick of our conscience, a verse we read, a message we hear from a pastor, conviction from the Holy Spirit, or a timely word from another person. David was rebuked when He sinned with Bathsheba. His servants confronted him, but he chose to ignore them. And if we belong to God, we will hear His rebuke in our lives, whether we choose to respond to it or not.

But if we ignore God's rebuke, He will increase the pressure to what He calls chastening. *Chastening* is often used in God's Word interchangeably with the word *discipline*, but specifically here, it's a more serious degree of discipline. "For whom the Lord loves, He chastens." That's the second key word. This isn't just the prick of a conscience or a gentle conviction when we read God's Word.

Chastening is something you feel as emotional anxiety or distress. What used to bring you joy now doesn't. Pressures increase in your work,

---

85 Hebrews 12:7
86 Hebrews 12:11

and home, in your health, or your finances. Many Christians bump along at this chastening level of discipline yet fail to read the signs. They feel unfulfilled at church. They feel critical of their Christian friends, and they feel "on the outs" with God. When they pick up their Bible, it feels like a lead weight instead of a welcome relief. Their relationship with the Lord is seemingly blighted by lethargy or sadness.

Chastening is when God removes from us the joy of our salvation. If any of these symptoms sound familiar, you don't need to go to church more; you don't need to read your Bible with a better attitude. You need to look for any ongoing sin in your life and repent.

But if we don't, if we ignore His rebuke, if we grieve the Holy Spirit by refusing to respond to His chastening, then Jesus has to go to stage three. "And [He] scourges every son whom He receives."

This is the same word used in the gospels for what the Romans did to Jesus before they nailed Him to the cross. It means to punish, to inflict excruciating pain.

Why does Jesus, our loving, compassionate Savior, do that to us? It's not out of anger or frustration. He has a purpose, and a plan, and nothing is more important to Jesus than the health of His Church.

Jesus' Plan for His Church

We know that Jesus is, right now, preparing a place in heaven for us. He's gone to His Father's house, and the day that dwelling place is ready, the Father will send Jesus to go get His bride.

But Jesus isn't just preparing a heavenly dwelling place for His bride. He's also preparing His bride for her heavenly dwelling place. This process began the day we were saved.

Ephesians 5:25–27 says that "[Christ] loved the church and gave Himself for her." This was His work on the cross. We were redeemed, justified, saved. It is finished. But Part 2 of Jesus' plan is a process that He began the day we were saved and that won't be finished until He takes us home. "That He might sanctify and cleanse her with the washing of water by the word."

God doesn't see two classes of Christians. We're not all on one big plane heading to heaven, some in first class, living fruitfully and pleasing to God, and the rest of us back in coach, just coasting but ultimately going to the same place. Sanctification isn't optional. Holiness isn't a bonus that some Christians manage to achieve. Jesus is working in all of us to produce holiness. Why?

"That He might present her to Himself a glorious church, not having spot or wrinkle or any such thing, but that she should be holy and without blemish." That's Part 3, the Church in all her glory, a pure bride on her wedding day, home where she belongs in the place Jesus has been preparing for her since the day He left.

Jesus died to save His bride, and one day He will return, sweep her off her feet, and take her home to His Father's house. But in the meantime, He has a plan for us, and we don't get to skip step two.

You can't get to heaven unless you've been sanctified. And you can't be sanctified unless you've first been justified. Hebrews 12 tells us God only disciplines His children. If Jesus isn't sanctifying you, if you're living like an unbeliever and God isn't spanking you until you stop, Hebrews 12:8 says, "then you are illegitimate and not sons." Unbelievers can act like unbelievers all they want. As a friend of mine says, they're just doing their job description. But if you are God's child, He will not tolerate that in you. If you're not being sanctified, then you're no son of His. You haven't been justified.

So let me ask you this: Have you met the real Jesus? Have you met the One who became a Son of Man and died for you? Only the Great High Priest could satisfy the holiness of God and trade your sin for His righteousness. Because of what Jesus did, God can look at you and see you as if you're already holy and blameless, but only if you have put your faith in Jesus Christ, in the work He did on the cross.

The Christian life isn't fire insurance. It's absolute slavery to God. It's belonging to Him, being identified by Jesus' name, allowing Him to make the plans. And when He commands us to hang on to His words like our life depends on it, it's not because we'll be condemned if we fail, but because our life depends on God holding on to us. First Peter 1:4 says our salvation is secure. God is reserving my spot in heaven with the same word, *tereo*. That's what my life depends on, not on the exact words I prayed when I was five or the aisle I walked, but on Him.

We aren't following a list of rules; we're following the Risen Christ. His words aren't outdated or a take-it-or-leave-it proposition. They're His marching orders to the Church He bought with His own blood, and His highest priority should be our highest priority.

If you belong to Jesus, then He wants you to know two things: These are the things that please Him. These are the things that don't please Him. Whether you read on or not, you are responsible for whether or not your life is pleasing to God. Whether you're aware of what pleases God and what doesn't, Jesus will chasten you as His child until you are in line with His Word. We are responsible to hear God speak through His Word. We are responsible to obey it. No excuses, no exemptions.

We're about to dive into Christ's messages to the seven churches, His rebukes, His chastening, and the scourging He inflicts when His people ignore His warnings. We will see what God loves in His people, and we'll see what He hates. This isn't a take-it-or-leave-it proposition. This is the Christian life, and no one gets to skip Part 2 of Jesus' plan. He will perfect us until we are pure and spotless, ready to present to Him in heaven.

Are you ready?

Precious Jesus, there is nothing more important to us than to live a life that is pleasing to You. We look forward to the day when You return for Your bride, when we are finally presented spotless and wrinkle-free, but until that day, let us heed Your gentle word of rebuke when You speak to us as sons, and, like You told the Ephesians, the Pergamites, the Thyatirans, and the believers at Sardis and Laodicea, let us repent immediately and live as Your slaves. May we be known by Your name. May we hold our possessions with open hands knowing they belong to You, and may we set aside our own plans in favor of Yours. Thank You for Your Word. Thank You for Your Holy Spirit. In Your precious name, we pray. Amen.

RESPOND to Truth

What are the two kinds of people on earth, according to the apostle Paul? (Romans 6:16–23). Which one am I?

Is my identity my own, or Christ's? Am I treating my possessions like they're mine or like they're God's? Am I following His plans or my own?

How does the apostle Paul describe a life that belongs to God? How does he describe a life that doesn't? (Romans 8:5–14)

When was the last time I felt God's chastening in my life? How did I respond/how am I responding?

What would a true slave do with his possessions? (Matthew 25:14–27). How can I please God with my possessions today?

What would a true slave do with his time? (1 Corinthians 10:31; Matthew 24:46; Colossians 3:22–24). How can I please God with my time today?

PART II

Christ's Letters to His Bride

EPHESUS

7 | The Three Secrets of a Powerful Church

EPHESUS: JESUS' MOST SUCCESSFUL CHURCH

The first of the seven churches Jesus writes to is Ephesus, the largest church, and the most successful. No church received more commendations than Ephesus.

The church at Ephesus was in top spiritual condition, in optimal health except for a spiritual heart problem. And when Jesus warns them to repent, He says to return to the works they did at the beginning. That's where we get to see what loving Jesus most looks like.

The Third Wonder of the Ancient World

Jesus writes a list of commendations, one serious warning, and a promise, and sends it by messenger to the port of Ephesus. And the moment this messenger walked into the city, holding this letter from Jesus, the first thing he would have seen would not have been the bustling harbor teeming with boats, or the roads lined with exotic goods from all the trade routes to the east, but the largest building in the ancient world.

Standing ten stories high and taking up an entire city block, the temple of Diana (or Artemis, in Greek) was completely covered and overlaid with pure gold. It stood gleaming in the sun directly in the center of the city, and it became one of the seven wonders of the ancient world.

In and around Diana's temple, prostitutes, both men and women, lured people in for unbridled immorality in worship to Diana, a goddess of sex and fertility. Hundreds of temple prostitutes were always on the grounds to promote this unrestrained indulgence of the flesh. Ephesus was a magnet for not just the sexually enslaved, but it was also the center of the black arts, witchcraft, superstition, and all the powers of Satan.

This third wonder of the ancient world was the center of everything that went on in the city, and standing for all to see was the huge, pornographic statue of Diana carved out of black stone. All of this fostered a culture of evil that promoted materialism, pride, occultism, and sensuality. With the demon worship going on in Ephesus, the "spiritual hosts of wickedness," were out in full force, shamelessly advertising everything that God hates.

And this is where God chose to plant His most successful church.

City on a Hill

God planted His church to be a city on a hill, a light in a very dark place, but also in a very strategic place. Ephesus wasn't just a major seaport on the Mediterranean. It was also known as the gateway to the entire continent of Asia. It was a city where four major trade routes crossed. Rome, the largest city in the Roman Empire, traded directly with the second-largest city, Ephesus, through the seaport, and from here, all of Asia was accessible. What better place could Jesus place His lamp, His Church, to shine the light of the gospel into all the world?

Ephesus quickly became the major publishing house of the ancient world. Every letter circulating among the churches came through Ephesus first. Missionaries were sent from here. Pastors got their start here. From Ephesus, everyone who passed through and heard the gospel could take the truth of Jesus Christ with them across the world. Acts 19:10 tells us that from here, all the province of Asia heard the gospel proclaimed, and it's very possible that the other six churches of Revelation 2–3 were products of the ministry started in Ephesus.

This church had the most powerful founding of all the seven churches. The saints at Ephesus were heirs to the apostle Paul's longest and most powerful ministry. He stayed here longer than any other city, and when he left, he passed the pastoring of the church down to his spiritual son, Timothy, and sent back not one, but three letters (Ephesians, 1 Timothy, and 2 Timothy) to continue to instruct the Ephesians in the faith.

This is where Jesus' mother, Mary, lived and died. It was from Ephesus that John was arrested by Domitian and exiled to Patmos. Notable Christian leaders such as Apollo, Tychicus, Priscilla and Aquila, and others all ministered here, and Timothy pastored the church here until he was martyred by a mob for preaching Christ. And at its largest, the church at Ephesus numbered 50,000 people.

The saints of Ephesus overcame the same pressures facing us as believers today: a pleasure-seeking culture, a mind-assaulting media, and a materialism-dominated way of life. For forty years, Ephesus had stood as a beacon of Christ in one of the darkest places in the Roman Empire. And this is Jesus' most powerful church.

BIOGRAPHY OF A POWERFUL CHURCH

Many notable authors have written books about what makes a successful church. But if God were to write a manual on how to make a church successful, what would He say the secret is?

Acts 19 is the authorized biography of the powerful church at Ephesus, the biography that God wrote. And in this chapter we find the timeless keys of what makes a church that God can use greatly. Throughout history, in every culture, no matter what century it is, what does a powerful, successful church look like to God?

Number 1: God's Son Is Magnified

In a materialism-dominated, pleasure-seeking culture like Ephesus, religious opportunism abounded. But when the apostle Paul arrived, he refused to become just another religious peddler. Instead of living off the hardworking people of Ephesus, Paul found a way to support himself, taking a job as a leatherworker.

Paul wanted nothing to stand in the way of his message, so he labored day and night with his own hands and taught the word of Christ to any who would listen during the citywide afternoon siesta, and again on the weekends.

Leatherworkers always had two things on them when they were working: the thick apron to protect them from the sharp tools they used, and a sweat-rag so they wouldn't drip sweat and stain the leather. Now look what God did with the tools of Paul's trade: "Now God worked unusual miracles by the hands of Paul, so that even handkerchiefs or aprons were brought from his body to the sick, and the diseases left them and the evil spirits went out of them."[87]

This is unlike any other time in Paul's ministry. God didn't do miracles like this all the time. But here, in Ephesus, because Paul's only goal was to magnify Christ, because he didn't care about magnifying his own ministry, his own name, his own status, God especially blessed Paul's ministry like at no other time in his life.

But, like always, the power of God attracted counterfeits. A clever group of opportunists wanted to get in on the action, so they started selling God's power. Notably, the seven sons of a man named Sceva. They were peddling the power to exorcise demons, but when they ordered one demon out in the name of Jesus and the name of Paul, the demon didn't recognize them. He said, "Jesus I know, and Paul I know, but who are you?" And the seven sons of Sceva barely got away with their lives. "This became known both to all Jews and Greeks dwelling in Ephesus; and fear fell on them all, and the name of the Lord Jesus was magnified."[88]

The first secret of a powerful church is that God's Son is magnified. There is power in Jesus that can't be faked, that can't be counterfeited. No matter how much money is in the offering plate or how many people are in the Sunday morning service, the church has no power if they don't magnify Christ.

A powerful church is one that magnifies Jesus, not the facilities, not the programs, not the teachers. Paul purposefully supported himself so no one could accuse him of being in it for the profit, and when the greedy opportunists came in to profit from the power of God, they were discredited, and Jesus was magnified.

---

87 Acts 19:11–12
88 Acts 19:17

The lesson? God looks for men and women to use who are willing to work unhindered by the sacrifice, laboring with an undivided heart, proclaiming an undiluted message, investing even in a humble occupation—all to make the gospel of Christ known.

We are to love God more than anything else. That should prompt why we serve Him, that should prompt why we read His Word, that should prompt why we want to sacrifice for Him. The Ephesians didn't do what they did because their church was the biggest. They didn't do it to earn a name for themselves. They simply did it because they loved Jesus Christ. Christ needs to be the focus, the goal, the desire. And when He is, God's Son is magnified, and the church has power that makes demons run.

Number 2: God's People Are Consecrated.

When Paul originally began spreading the gospel in Ephesus, he was not talking to commendable, God-honoring saints. They "walked according to the course of this world, according to the prince of the power of the air." Paul says, "We all once conducted ourselves in the lusts of our flesh, fulfilling the desires of the flesh and of the mind, and were by nature children of wrath, just as the others."[89]

These were Diana-worshiping, sex-addicted, materialism-controlled, occult-practicing sinners we're talking about here. This is who God saved. But He doesn't just leave them there. Paul began to teach about what pleases God and what doesn't please God, and all of a sudden, these recently dead, made-alive-in-Christ saints heard God's rebuke. This is where chastening comes in. Their eyes were opened, they saw all the things in their lives that didn't glorify God, and they started cleaning house.

Acts 19:18–19 says, "And many who had believed came confessing and telling their deeds. Also, many of those who had practiced magic brought their books together and burned them in the sight of all."

This is what consecrated living looks like. They had been living in the lusts of their flesh, so when they felt the rebuke of the Lord, they went through their homes and found everything that promoted sensuality, that promoted the lusts of the flesh, and they cleaned it out. They used to walk

---

89 Ephesians 2:2–3

according to the course of the world, according to the materialistic pursuits so big in Ephesus, so they cleaned out everything that promoted materialism. If it made them want to indulge in the desires of the mind, in their own pride, they got rid of it. This is what they were saved from, and they chose not to live in it anymore.

Everything God's enemies, the evil one and his angels, were promoting in Ephesus, the saints at Ephesus decided they wouldn't be ruled by those things anymore. They chose not to give Satan a foothold in their lives by getting rid of every occult object and book that they owned. That's why Paul tells the Ephesians they aren't fighting against flesh and blood, but against the "spiritual hosts of wickedness in the heavenly places." And so in order to put on the armor of God, to shield themselves against all the temptations and the flaming arrows of the evil one, they chose not to put temptations before their eyes. And they didn't just close it all up in a drawer. They dragged it all out onto their front lawns and set it on fire.

God's church is always strongest when it's purest. The level of their desire to repent and follow the Lord was seen in this costly choice to rid their lives of anything that displeased Him. Their example recorded by God in His Word should stir us to ask, "Have we likewise carefully purged out of our lives anything that displeases the Lord?"

One of the biggest reasons people refuse to come to church is because of all the hypocrisy. But when God's people are consecrated, when, as Acts 19:18–20 says, they take out their secret sins and burn them on the front lawn for all to see, unbelievers are attracted to the powerful holiness of God's people. When God's people are consecrated, the church has power that the whole world can see.

Number 3: God's Word Prevails.

Secret number three of a powerful church: God's Word prevails. Here, in Ephesus, Paul didn't just plant a church and move on. He began teaching daily in the synagogue, "reasoning and persuading concerning the things of God." But after three months, some people began speaking out against him, so he moved into the lecture hall, the school of Tyrannus. And that's when word really began to spread.

For two years, every single day, Paul came from his leatherwork shop on his lunch break and explained the Scriptures. The word is *dialogizumi*. It's where we get the word "dialogue." It means to talk through or reason through. He didn't just read the Word. He explained it.

For two years, every single day, when the whole city was taking an afternoon siesta, people would gather to hear Paul preach. Counting the time he had on Sundays, every day for two years, Paul preached a total of 3,000 hours to this one church. That's the equivalent of attending Sunday morning services, Sunday evening service, and a Wednesday night service for thirty years. The Ephesians received a lifetime of learning in just two years. When God's Word prevails, the church has power that lasts for generations.

LOVING WHAT GOD LOVES; HATING WHAT GOD HATES

Forty years later, after Paul had moved on, after Timothy had pastored there, after John was exiled, Ephesus was still the largest church in Asia Minor. It was still Jesus' most successful church, and Jesus commends them.

REVELATION 2:1–7

To the angel of the church of Ephesus write,

"These things says He who holds the seven stars in His right hand, who walks in the midst of the seven golden lampstands: 'I know your works, your labor, your patience, and that you cannot bear those who are evil. And you have tested those who say they are apostles and are not, and have found them liars; and you have persevered and have patience, and have not become weary. Nevertheless I have this against you, that you have left your first love. Remember therefore from where you have fallen; repent and do the first works, or else I will come to you quickly and remove your lampstand from its place—unless you repent. But this you have, that you hate the deeds of the Nicolaitans, which I also hate.

He who has an ear, let him hear what the Spirit says to the churches. To him who overcomes I will give to eat from the tree of life, which is in the midst of the Paradise of God.'"

God's Stamp of Approval

What God sees Ephesus doing right boils down to two things: They loved the things that God loves, and they hated the things that God hates. Jesus gives Ephesus an unparalleled stamp of approval, pointing out ten areas that are marvelous in His sight.

First, "I know your works." We're not just supposed to be saved. We're supposed to serve, and Ephesus was serving God. They didn't just say all the right things. They did what was right. They had good works. And God approved.

Second, "your labor." This is the word *kopos*, which means toiling to the point of physical exhaustion. These people weren't just doing token good works. They were laboring until they were exhausted, and they kept going.

Third, "your patience." There are two Greek words for patience. The first is passive, like a table that holds up while you keep piling things on it. But Jesus uses the word for active patience, for actively lifting and bearing, moving forward even under ongoing pressure.

In verse 3, Jesus repeats the list. "You have persevered and have patience. You have labored for My name's sake and have not become weary." They had remained faithful to the Lord and to His Word. They had labored for the Lord through the difficulty, through the persecution, in the face of a culture of evil permeating every aspect of Ephesian life, and they stood as a light in one of the darkest places on the planet. They loved what Jesus loves.

But the one thing that Jesus commends, not twice, but three times, is perhaps the most surprising. Ephesus hates what God hates, and He commends it three different ways.

First, He says, "you cannot bear those who are evil." They were living in purity in the midst of wickedness and perversion all around them, in the shadow of the magnificent temple to gross immorality, and they were persevering. They didn't let sin into their homes, they were not entertained by it, and when they found it in their own homes, they cleaned house.

Second, God says, "You have tested those who say they are apostles and are not, and have found them liars." They were orthodox, they were strong. They were exercising spiritual discernment. First Thessalonians 5:22 says, "Test all things; hold fast what is good." They were to check the credentials of those who claimed to speak for God, to check that they were who they said they were, and to test what they said against the Word.

So they were testing. Everyone coming through the port or coming in on one of the many highways, if they claimed to be an apostle, the Ephesians tested them, comparing what they taught to the teachings of Paul and Peter and John, and when they found something that didn't line up with Scripture, they rejected it immediately. They refused to fall prey to it. And they didn't hesitate to call them liars.

"But this you have," Jesus says, "that you hate the deeds of the Nicolaitans, which I also hate."

As twenty-first-century Christians, we're politically influenced to be "correct." We're not supposed to hate anybody or anything someone else believes. They have the right to their opinion. But for the third time in seven verses, Jesus commends Ephesus, not on loving what He loves, but on hating what He hates.

This was an identifiable group of people, teaching a specific doctrine, exerting influence over many believers. In fact, Jesus points this out in Pergamos, because they didn't hate the doctrine of the Nicolaitans. They accepted it, they taught it, they held to it, and Jesus says, "repent or else."

But Ephesus did it right. As the publishing center of the ancient world, Ephesus had access to all of Paul's letters, not just the letters written to this church. So they had the truth of God's Word to test everything against, and when they compared the teachings of the Nicolaitans to what Paul had said, and what Peter said, and what John said, they found that it didn't match up. They tested Nicolas, the leader of this group of people, and they found him to be teaching lies.

There is something to be said for confronting the evils, the errors, and the error-promoters in our culture. It's not popular to name names and to point out error, but Jesus honored Ephesus for knowing what pleases Him and what doesn't, and for standing against what He hates.

The Secret of a Powerful Life

Ephesus was the most powerful church. They had a powerful founding, a godly nurturing, a tremendous history. God gifted Ephesus with more incredible pastors than any other church, He sent more of His Word directly to this church than any other, and Ephesus was His first stop when He walked among His lampstands. But something happened. Their spiritual arteries got clogged, and Jesus' most successful church was in danger. Other things crowded in and demanded their attention and Jesus Christ no longer took first place in their lives.

Jesus is calling you and me to the same level of commitment He demanded from the Ephesians. It wasn't enough that they were doing all the right things. He wanted them doing them for the right reasons. He had one thing against them, just one, after ten commendations for the things that pleased Him. This is what didn't: They had left their first love.

When everything was added together, all ten wonderful God-honoring areas of their lives couldn't stack up against the one area that didn't. The bottom line was this: Their lives did not add up to Jesus Christ. He commanded them to go back to the way they were at first, when God's Son was magnified, when God's people were consecrated, and when God's Word prevailed.

Jesus' admonition to Ephesus is to love God most. A life that loves God most magnifies God's Son. "He who has an ear, let him hear," Jesus says. This isn't just for Ephesus. This is His desire for us, that we live a life that gives Him first place, that magnifies, not our particular church, not our group, or ourselves, but Jesus Christ.

My life is only powerful when it is consecrated to God. If I am hoarding in my home, in my daily schedule, in my priorities, in my plans, something that promotes materialism, or pride, or sensuality, or the occult, then I am choosing to love what God hates.

I discovered recently that the bushes around my house were growing up against the walls, and I know they're not supposed to grow up against the house like that, so I had to mercilessly cut them back. I never intended them to encroach on the house, but I had allowed them to grow that way without even realizing it. And when we aren't systematically, mercilessly, cutting back what displeases God in our lives, it will slowly grow and cut God out of His first place in our lives. It will encroach on the space that should be reserved for God. So we must be like the Ephesians and cut back anything that robs God of His rightful place. One pastor in Chicago put it this way:

> *What would be burned today if the Spirit's conviction swept this church? I think some DVDs, magazines, and videos would be quietly removed from out-of-the-way desk drawers or certain novels from the family bookshelves.*
>
> *Perhaps some television shows, movies, web sites, radio stations, and video games would be boycotted. Some people would ask others to pray that they would be set free from whatever is dragging them down. And many would come to Christ for forgiveness of sin and deliverance from the eternal wrath of God.*[90]

Acts tells us that when God's people were consecrated, the result is that God's Word "grew mightily and prevailed." People tell me that I preach an awful lot about daily reading God's Word, but that's because we don't do it. It's hard. It takes time. And there are so many things that crowd in and demand our attention. But God's Word can't prevail from the bottom of the pile on our nightstand. It can't prevail sitting on our shelves gathering dust.

But when God's Word is treasured, kept, held on to like our lives depend on it, the things of this world grow strangely dim. When God's Son is magnified, what He hates becomes detestable to us and we, whether literally or figuratively, push it out of our lives and set it on fire. And when God's people are consecrated, then there's nothing left to rob God of His first place in our lives.

When God's Son is magnified, God's people are consecrated, and God's Word prevails, the sum total, the bottom line, is a life that loves God most.

90 Hughes, R. Kent, *Preaching the Word: Ephesians—The Mystery of the Body of Christ* (Wheaton, IL: Crossway Books), 1997.

The power of the early Church was simply genuine holiness. Energized by grace they magnified Christ, God's Word prevailed in them, and they lived consecrated lives. The Spirit of God moved unhindered, flowed unquenched, and God got all the glory. No one competed for the credit, no one sought to be in control. God reigned, the Spirit moved, and Christ was magnified.

When the Church cleans house, when believers renounce hidden sins, when there is a banishment of all hypocrisy and pretense, and genuine holiness begins to permeate Christ's Church, unbelievers become attracted to this new way of life.

The success of a church isn't measured by the money in the offering plate, the size of its building, or the number of people in its seats, but in how much its people love God. The secret to a powerful life is simple: Love God most. There is no life more powerful than a consecrated, Christ-magnifying, Word-filled life. The choice is ours.

RESPOND to Truth

What did God do for the people of Ephesus? (Ephesians 1:1–2:10).
What did He do for me?

What did God expect from the Ephesians? (Ephesians 4:1, 17–32).
What does He expect from me?

How did Ephesus become a powerful church in a wicked city?
(Acts 19:8–41)

What am I working to magnify in my life?

If Jesus walked through my house, what would He find to burn on my front lawn?

What in my life is prevailing over the Word of God? How can I take steps to change that today?

Rekindle Your First Love | 8

When two people are in love, they just can't get enough of each other. They can't spend enough time together, they can't see each other often enough, and they can't wait to see each other again when they're apart.

One test of how much we love Jesus Christ is how much we want to spend time with Him. Ephesus was a church that was, at one time, known for their love for Christ. He was first, He was best, He was loved the most, but somehow, after a while, they'd drifted away from that, and He was no longer their first love. So Jesus writes to them to get them back to where they're supposed to be.

FIRST LOVE: THEN AND NOW

How Jesus Speaks to His Church

The first rule of textual interpretation is what did the text mean to the people it was written to. When we read Scripture, we're reading something that was originally written to real people with real problems in a real place and time, and when Jesus says, "You have left your first love," it meant something to them.

But this epistle, this letter from Jesus, wasn't just written to Ephesus. He is writing to every Christian of every century in every church. All Scripture is inspired by God, and all Scripture is profitable for doctrine, reproof, correction, and training in righteousness. So after we've seen what God was saying to the Ephesians, we need to look and see what He's saying to us, how we can be trained in righteousness by Jesus' words in Revelation 2.

REVELATION 2:1–7

To the angel of the church of Ephesus write,

"These things says He who holds the seven stars in His right hand, who walks in the midst of the seven golden lampstands: 'I know your works, your labor, your patience, and that you cannot bear those who are evil. And you have tested those who say they are apostles and are not, and have found them liars; and you have persevered and have patience, and have labored for My name's sake and have not become weary. Nevertheless I have this against you, that you have left your first love. Remember therefore from where you have fallen; repent and do the first works, or else I will come to you quickly and remove your lampstand from its place— unless you repent. But this you have, that you hate the deeds of the Nicolaitans, which I also hate.

'He who has an ear, let him hear what the Spirit says to the churches. To him who overcomes I will give to eat from the tree of life, which is in the midst of the Paradise of God.'"

Notice how Jesus addresses His church. First, He addresses them personally. This isn't a form letter. He knows these people. He knows their works, their labor, their patience. And He sent it to someone specific.

The word is translated "angel," but it literally means "messenger." This is a human being, a man whom God entrusted with His church. This is probably an elder or a pastor who was leading the church of Ephesus at the time, and Jesus addresses him and this church personally. He knows them, what they're struggling with, and He knows exactly what they most need to hear.

Secondly, Jesus addresses them with authority. He calls Himself, "He who holds the seven stars in His right hand, who walks in the midst of the seven golden lampstands." He isn't the one who "walked," past tense.

Jesus is still walking among them. He's still walking among us. And He holds the leader of this church in His right hand. They are His, and He has certain expectations.

For the most part, Ephesus was meeting those expectations. Jesus addresses them, thirdly, with approval. He lists ten areas that please Him, ten commendations. This is more than any other church, a more glowing report than any other church received. Why?

Because of their works.

Since the Reformation, and the emphasis on grace alone, we've started leaning away from good works like they're somehow the opposite of grace. Like if we preach good works or spend our lives doing good works, we're somehow nullifying the grace of God. But remember that the Grace of God teaches us to be different. It teaches us to put away the old self and how we used to live, and to put on something new.

The Ephesians knew this. They'd been living like this for forty years. They had received a letter decades earlier, and they understood how grace worked. "For by grace you have been saved through faith, and that not of yourselves; it is the gift of God, not of works, lest anyone should boast." But what did the believers in Ephesus read in Paul's very next words? "For we are His workmanship, created in Christ Jesus for good works, which God prepared beforehand that we should walk in them."[91] We're not saved *by* good works, but we are saved *for* good works.

Jesus didn't commend them on their marvelous heart attitude. He commended them on their works. For forty years, Jesus had been seeing a church that truly loved Him, and more importantly, that they loved Him first. They were living like they were supposed to, walking in the good works He prepared for them. Why did God commend Ephesus so much? Because they were the book of Ephesians in action. This was their "first love."

The Right Things for the Wrong Reasons

If only He stopped there.

"Nevertheless I have this against you," He says. As much as He approves of the church at Ephesus, Jesus cannot tolerate this one thing. They had

---

91   Ephesians 2:8–10

lost their first love. Ephesus was no longer doing good works solely for the approval of Jesus. They were no longer serving Him just because. They had started caring about status, about the approval of men. They had started getting busy with other things, all the other important things in life that demanded their time and attention, and somewhere along the way, Jesus had lost His first place. Ephesus was doing all the right things, but He warns them to beware of doing all the right things for the wrong reasons.

You can tell when someone is doing something simply for Jesus. It doesn't matter who sees them or if no one ever does. They never need to be thanked, they never need to be noticed. They serve tirelessly for Jesus Christ. Ephesus used to be that way. They used to do everything for God's glory. But somehow they had lost that, and Jesus admonishes them.

"Repent and do the first works," Jesus says. He doesn't just ask for a change in heart attitude. He asks for actions. He asks for works. "Repent and go back to the works you used to do, for the reason you used to do them, because those works were pleasing to Me."

Jesus' next words are a very serious warning: "or else I will come to you quickly and remove your lampstand from its place—unless you repent."

Remember how Jesus cleaned out the temple in John 2? That wasn't the first time He cleaned it out. He had allowed it to be destroyed by pagan nations more than once. Every time His temple on earth stopped representing Him the way it was supposed to, He cleaned house, and He warns that He'll do the same thing here if this church doesn't repent.

Did you know that if you visit Turkey today, what we used to call Asia Minor, and get on a bus at the Port of Mercer and drive from Ephesus to Smyrna to Pergamos and all around these seven cities, you will find that, by and large, these seven churches have gone extinct? The cities are still there, but the churches are gone. When Jesus said He'd remove the church from Ephesus, He meant it.

His warning is serious because the spiritual heart condition of Ephesus is serious. When a heart no longer beats only for Him, when the spiritual arteries are clogged with other things, when Jesus no longer occupies first place, that isn't just an unfortunate condition. It's a potentially deadly one. Ephesus was the most strategic, most influential, second-largest city in the greatest empire on earth, but Jesus would rather have no church there at all than to have a wealthy, 50,000-strong mega church that gives Him second place.

THIS I HAVE AGAINST YOU

You Have Left...

The word "left" is the Greek word *aphiami*. This word is usually translated "forgiveness." It's the idea of something being pulled off of something else. Like a predator on the back of its prey, choking the life out of it, and something comes and lifts it up off of, detaches it, and removes it completely. When Jesus removes our sin, He completely detaches the thing that is choking the life out of us.

But the way *aphiami* is used here is more like how it's used in 1 Corinthians 7:11–13. It's the same idea of being pulled apart, being separated from, being detached and removed, this time used for when a wife "departs" from her husband, or a husband "divorces" his wife.

Jesus has always had one desire for His Church: "That He might sanctify and cleanse her with the washing of water by the word." Why? "That He might present her to Himself a glorious church, not having spot or wrinkle or any such thing, but that she should be holy and without blemish."

Jesus wants to present the Church like a pure bride. The Church is betrothed to Him, and in Hebrew culture, being betrothed to someone was like already being married, and if you were unfaithful, you were stoned for adultery. But what did Jesus find in Ephesus? "Adulterers and adulteresses! Do you not know that friendship with the world is enmity with God? Whoever therefore wants to be a friend of the world makes himself an enemy of God. Or do you think that the Scripture says in vain, 'The Spirit who dwells in us yearns jealously'?"[92]

Our bridegroom isn't just a loving husband "who loved [us] and gave Himself for [us]."[93] He is jealous for us. Jesus is making ready a place for His bride. He's preparing a place in His Father's house. But what did Jesus find when He came to see His bride?

92   James 4:4–5
93   Ephesians 5:25–27

In forty short years, the Church had become friends with the world. Her eyes were wandering. She forgot her first love. Jesus had left to go prepare a place for her and she had drifted so far away from what He left her to do that He was forced to send her a letter, telling her to repent immediately.

...Your First Love...

"First" is the word *protos*. It means in front of, above, and before. Jesus wasn't just the first person they loved. He was the person they loved in front of everything else. Above everything else. Before everything else. First love. It's a superlative. It's not good. It's not better. It's best. Not some, or more, but most.

Whatever we love *protos* comes foremost in time. If we have a block of time, it comes at the front end of the time. Like when news reporters put something at the top of the hour. It's the most important thing. If something runs long, if the news report gets cut off, if something unexpected happens, at least the most important thing made it at the top of the hour.

First love comes foremost in place. In a big area, this comes at the leading edge, at the front. If you're packing a U-Haul truck and you might run out of room, this goes in first. It's clearly the most important. This is the one thing you can't leave out.

First love is foremost on any list. If you have a to-do list, Jesus should be at the top of it. Bible reading, service, whatever it is that glorifies Jesus, should be more important than anything else on the list. He comes first.

First love comes foremost in order of importance. It moves to the front of the line. It's the top priority. Other things might matter, but nothing else matters as much.

We were going through airport security this week, and this happened to us. We were getting everything out of our pockets, taking off our shoes, and waiting for the people in front of us, when all of a sudden, an airport employee came through and everyone else had to wait for them to go through first. They had priority. They were the most important. The plane couldn't take off if the pilot wasn't on it. It was important that I was on the plane, too, at least it was important to me. But the pilot had priority, so he went to the front of the line.

First love is the best and the chiefest. It is simply first of all. And Jesus said all that with one little word: *protos*. That's what He wants to be in our lives. And that's what Ephesus had forgotten.

They didn't stop loving God. They didn't stop serving Him. They didn't stop going to church. They just stopped loving God *first*. They stopped serving *only* for Him. They didn't go to church *simply* to worship God. He was no longer first.

John sums it up this way: "Little children, keep yourselves from idols."[94] An idol doesn't have to be a city block–sized golden temple topped with a carved image of a goddess that supposedly fell from heaven. It doesn't have to be occult books on your bookshelves that need to be taken out and burned on the lawn. An idol is anything that makes us not want God, anything that robs Him of first place.

If you only hang on to one truth from the epistle to Ephesus, understand what it means to leave your first love. If it seems like a minor thing to put God as number two on my to-do list, to move Him to the end of my free time instead of the beginning, to give Him a place at the end of the line, then look at what Jesus says in Matthew 22:37–38:

> 'You shall love the Lord your God with all your heart, with all your soul, and with all your mind.' This is the first and great commandment.

This is the "first" commandment, the *protos*. This wasn't just another command in a list of commands. A lawyer came to Jesus wanting to know the very most important thing, the one law that sums up all the other laws. And Jesus said to love God most.

Jesus uses this word again in Matthew 6:33. "But seek first [*protos*] the kingdom of God and His righteousness, and all these things shall be added to you." If there's something we love most, then it never gets left out. It never gets forgotten. It goes in first. I hear so many people say, "Well, I'm just not a morning person." They watched the news report, listened to a talk show on the radio, did their hair and makeup,

---

94   1 John 5:21

and got to work on time, but they didn't read their Bibles because they're not a morning person. And then at night, they're just too tired, so they'll try to do better tomorrow. But whatever our first love is never gets left out. It never gets forgotten. It goes in first. And that's what Jesus is supposed to be.

How many of us have made a New Year's resolution to read the Bible through in a year, but some time around March we realize we're so far behind, we just can't find enough time, that it's never going to happen? We might as well scratch that off the to-do list altogether. But the average American, and I would suggest that Christians are average here, spends 150 hours a month, five hours a day, watching TV. That is how much time it takes to read the entire Bible all the way through, out loud, twice a month. If you and I have enough time in our schedules to read the Bible through twenty-four times a year and can't even get through it once because we've spent that time watching TV instead, then what is our first love really? It's not Jesus.

THREE DAILY HABITS OF LOVING GOD MOST

Jesus says, put Me first. If you seek first, *protos*, His kingdom and His righteousness, then all the other important things that demand our attention either all fit in around it, or we realize they weren't all that important to begin with. Jesus doesn't want to take second place. And He won't let us get away with giving away the love that should belong to Him.

So what does "first love" look like? Well, we know what it looks like because Ephesus used to be doing it. They were living out the book of Ephesians in three daily God-loving habits.

Habit 1: Grace-Prompted Shedding

Paul spent three years in Ephesus, teaching the truth of Jesus. And this is what they learned: "that you put off, concerning your former conduct, the old man which grows corrupt according to the deceitful lusts."[95] This is the habit of grace-prompted shedding. To take off, to put off, the old self with our former conduct.

---

95 Ephesians 4:22

But wait, didn't Jesus take all that off of us already? Isn't forgiveness, *aphiami*, taking off our sins? Yes. In God's sight, we are as if we've never sinned, but we've gotten used to wearing those sins. We've gotten used to all the old habits, the former conduct, the old man, and we have to daily, habitually, shed those old sins.

We already know what it is to "put off." We put off our homework, our housework, mowing the lawn, reading our Bibles, our exercising, everything we don't really want to do. We make excuses to do something else instead. We keep putting other things first. In our time, in place, on our lists, in importance. And somehow the things we "put off" get squeezed out altogether.

We are to put off our old self, our former conduct, the way we used to act. This is how God's people are consecrated. We find excuses not to feed our lusts. We find ways to avoid our old habits. We jump at the opportunity to fill our time with something else. The Ephesians did this by burning their old possessions, the trappings of their old lives that reminded them of how they used to live. Because God was first, it didn't matter how valuable their ungodly possessions were. If God hated it, so did they. No excuses.

The Ephesians didn't excuse their behavior because of their culture. They didn't excuse it because it was just who they were. They were still wearing the old man, the person they used to be, and because they hated what God hated, they began to systematically, daily, put off the old man and let God make them someone new. How?

Habit 2: Grace-Prompted Thinking

We need to make it a habit to let God renew our minds, to change our thinking. Ephesians 4:23 tell us, "and be renewed in the spirit of your mind." When we think godly, we behave godly; when we believe right, we behave right. The ruts in our mind determine the direction our actions go, so if we're going to change our actions, and not fall into the old habits again, we need to cultivate the habit of grace-prompted thinking.

God's plan for our minds always starts with us personally reading and studying His Word. Then from that flows our personal request to God's Spirit, asking Him to renew our minds. As we prayerfully read, we have in our minds God's thoughts. As we submit to God's desires through His

Word, He infuses His mind into ours. Paul said that we can have the mind of Christ by this constant renewal process. A grace-energized mind comes as believers regularly—daily, I hope—get God's Word into their hearts and minds.

A simple goal would be to listen to God's voice all the way through His Word once each year. If we watch an average amount of TV, we have twenty-four times as much free time as we actually need to make this happen. But whether we make this our specific goal or not, reading the Bible expectantly and asking God to speak to us through His Spirit in His Word is an imperative.

Habit 3: Grace-Prompted Wearing

And what does grace-prompted thinking lead to? "And that you put on the new man which was created according to God, in true righteousness and holiness."[96]

God makes it clear that it is not enough to merely put off old fleshly habits. They must be replaced with the newness of Christ in wearing His love, wearing His peace, etc.[97] If I lose my temper with my wife or children, and repent and put it off, that is not enough unless I also put on Christ's love and patience.

God is at work in us His children, and energized by His grace we must work at living out this new life.[98] Our daily task is getting dressed in our divine clothes. Spiritually speaking, clothes do make the man. These are the good works, the labor, the patience, the right things for the right reasons. This is what Ephesus had been doing so well for so long. The new man puts God first, in time, in place, on every list, in importance. He is best and chiefest. He is simply number one. Nothing else compares.

Our sanctification is not just something that is done to us. It is something we participate in. If we struggle with anger, anger must be shed daily. If we struggle with pride, pride must be shed daily. If we struggle with lust, with fear, with anything that characterized the old man, then it is a daily habit, a daily decision to put that off.

96   Ephesians 4:24
97   Galatians 5:22
98   Philippians 2:12–13

We must daily strip off any return of the rotting garments of the old life. We must personally reject any hint of sensuality, selfishness, pride, materialism, and bitterness in our lives. We must consume God's Word and ask for renewed minds by His Spirit. We must work out our own salvation as Philippians 2:12 says by choosing to do the disciplines that will develop a biblical mind. We must put on and wear our new, shining garments of light each day, and live like the new us we became in Christ.

Jesus is returning, and He's returning soon. He is a jealous husband, coming for His bride, and by God's grace, it is my goal to love Him more today than I did yesterday, to love Him more tomorrow than I do today, so that on the day He returns, He will find me eagerly waiting at the window with eyes only for Him.

It's not enough to love God. We are to love God most. When the Philistines captured the Ark of the Covenant, the place where God's glory came to rest on earth, they knew the power of the God of Israel, and gave Him a place of high honor in their great temple, right beside their god, Dagon.

But God doesn't share with anybody.

"I am the Lord, and there is no other. And My glory I will not give to another."[99] And Dagon fell over and broke in pieces.

God is a jealous God, and He won't tolerate second place. If the sum of my life isn't Jesus Christ, if whatever I eat or drink or whatever I do isn't done to the glory of God, then I have broken God's greatest commandment. He doesn't ask me to love Him with part of my heart, soul, mind, and strength. He isn't content with most of my heart, soul, mind, and strength. I am to love Him with all, with everything, to love Him first.

Father in heaven, thank You for this church. What an example Ephesus was. I pray that we will labor and toil and test everything against Your Word. And Lord, I pray that we will not lose that first love that You long for in our lives. Let us decide that we're not going to coast, that we're not going to live on our past accomplishments, that we won't glory in all of our activity, but that we would repent of all but loving You with all of our heart, pleasing You with all of our

---

99 Isaiah 45:5; 42:8

being, responding to You as Your slaves. Conquer us with the sword of Your Word. Break down and destroy anything that has taken Your first place in our lives. I pray that You will find in us ears to hear and hearts to obey. In Jesus' precious name, I pray Amen.

RESPOND to Truth

What choices did David make to love God most? (Psalm 101)

What does a grace-prompted God-lover put off? (Galatians 5:19–21, 26)

What old habits am I wearing that grace prompts me to shed?

What does grace-prompted God-lover choose to wear instead?
(Galatians 5:22–23)

Which of these fruits of the Spirit does grace prompt me to put on today?
What specific steps can I take do that?

Have I established the habit of daily renewing my mind with the Word of
God? What can I get rid of that's getting in the way?

SMYRNA

9 | Life Is Camping; Heaven Is Home

THE NEAR-EXTINCTION OF CHRISTIANITY

The early Church faced three major waves of persecution. The first came when Nero needed someone to blame for all his failings as a leader, and he chose the movement called "The Way," the ones who called themselves followers of Jesus. This wave of persecution was limited mostly to Rome, but we know from Church history that at least two major Church leaders, Peter and Paul, who were both arrested and executed, got swept up in Nero's persecution.

A more widespread persecution came when Domitian became emperor of Rome. It was during this time that John was arrested and exiled to the maximum-security prison colony on Patmos.

But the closest Christianity ever came to being wiped out was during the reign of the emperor Diocletian. He administratively went through the empire and found an anomaly, a group of people that didn't behave the way they were supposed to. They didn't worship the emperor like everyone else, they didn't visit the pagan temples and engage in sexual immorality, and they didn't sacrifice to the Greek pantheon of gods that so dominated the way of life. They were anomalies, and so Diocletian decided to get rid of them.

First, he went through and found the meeting places, anywhere the Church gathered together, and tore them down. Then he went in and arrested the Christian leaders, killing every one of them he could find. Then he searched out and destroyed every copy of the Scriptures he could get his hands on so that not a single, complete copy of the Scriptures survived from before the fourth century. Diocletian came closer to exterminating Christianity than any other emperor, and there were at least thirty of them who tried.

This was just beginning at the time that John was writing down the Revelation of Jesus Christ, and in the midst of this persecution, the struggling believers at Smyrna receive a letter from Jesus.

REVELATION 2:8–11

To the angel of the church in Smyrna write,

"These things says the First and the Last, who was dead, and came to life: "I know your works, tribulation, and poverty (but you are rich); and I know the blasphemy of those who say they are Jews and are not, but are a synagogue of Satan. Do not fear any of those things which you are about to suffer. Indeed, the devil is about to throw some of you into prison, that you may be tested, and you will have tribulation ten days. Be faithful until death, and I will give you the crown of life.

"He who has an ear, let him hear what the Spirit says to the churches. He who overcomes shall not be hurt by the second death."

When the Lord of the Church inspected His people at Smyrna, He finds nothing to condemn, and from this shortest letter Jesus wrote, we can learn some of the greatest lessons on how to please God in an ungodly world. While Jesus found the world raging against Smyrna, they stood fast, and this church is for us an example of how to please God in the midst of terrible suffering.

FIVE LESSONS FROM SUFFERING SMYRNA

When John falls to his face in fear in Revelation 1:17, Jesus comforts him by saying, "I am the First and the Last," and this is the name He gives Himself now, to the people of Smyrna. Yes, they will suffer, but as the First and the Last, He's already been there. He knew what they had already faced. He knew what they were facing right then, and He knew everything they'd face in the future. No one could be better qualified than the Alpha and the Omega, the Beginning and the End, the First and the Last to tell Smyrna exactly what they needed to hear in the midst of their suffering. And through Smyrna, you and I can learn how to serve God in suffering, and how to do it without fear.

Lesson 1: We share in Christ's sufferings.

The first lesson we can learn from Smyrna is that we are called to share in Christ's sufferings. Jesus said to John, "And to the angel of the church in Smyrna write, 'These things says the First and the Last, who was dead, and came to life.'"

Jesus is writing to a town whose name, *Smyrna*, is the Greek word for myrrh, and that was the town's one major industry. They would take a machete-type blade and hack, cut, slice, and injure the bark of the thorny trees around Smyrna, and where the sap would run and scab over the wounds, they would gather the sap and refine it into myrrh.

Myrrh always has to do with suffering in Scripture. At Jesus' birth, He was given three gifts: gold for the King of the Jews, frankincense that spoke of His priesthood, and myrrh for His suffering. When Jesus hung on the cross, He was offered wine mixed with myrrh to dull the pain. And at His burial, He was wrapped with myrrh.

Jesus' life is characterized by the most potent picture of suffering a citizen of Smyrna could imagine. Jesus' first lesson to Smyrna, and to us, is that we are called to share in His sufferings. They would suffer. They would have tribulation. They would even die, but Jesus also offers a reassurance.

Jesus introduces Himself as the One who was dead. His death was foreshadowed by the gift He received at birth, He refused to dull His pain on the cross and instead suffered the full wrath of God for sin, and He was wrapped in myrrh at His burial. Yes, He suffered. Yes, He died. He is the One "who was dead." But He's also the One who came to life. And so, to this church known for its suffering, its poverty, its tribulations, whose name,

Smyrna, means "myrrh" in Greek, Jesus writes a letter reminding them who He is: "the First and the Last, who was dead, and who came to life."[100]

At Christ's return, He will be given gifts of gold and frankincense, but not myrrh.[101] At His return, He will no longer suffer. And one day, the One who was dead and came to life, who received myrrh at His birth, His death, and His burial, but never again, will one day return for His people, and "there shall be no more death, nor sorrow, nor crying. There shall be no more pain, for the former things have passed away."

Smyrna was called to share in the sufferings of Christ, but also in His life. And we have been called with the same high calling. When Peter and the other apostles were imprisoned in Acts 5:41, they "departed from the presence of the council, rejoicing that they were counted worthy to suffer shame for His name." "For to this you were called," Peter says, "because Christ also suffered for us, leaving us an example, that you should follow His steps."[102] To suffer for Christ is a privilege, and to share in His sufferings is a calling. That's the first lesson from Smyrna.

Lesson 2: Persecution is inevitable.

The next thing Jesus says to Smyrna is this: "I know your works, tribulation, and poverty (but you are rich); and I know the blasphemy of those who say they are Jews and are not, but are a synagogue of Satan."

Not only does Jesus know their suffering, He is not surprised by it. Decades before this letter arrived at Smyrna, Jesus was speaking to His disciples, and He said, "Blessed are you when they revile and persecute you, and say all kinds of evil against you falsely for My sake. Rejoice and be exceedingly glad, for great is your reward in heaven, for so they persecuted the prophets who were before you."[103] And at the same time Jesus was speaking these words to His disciples, the first stirrings of persecution began in Smyrna.

In the last days of Jesus' life, in the little town called Smyrna, the Emperor Tiberius built an altar to himself. Year after year, he asked the

100 Revelation 2:8
101 Isaiah 60:6
102 1 Peter 2:21
103 Matthew 5:11–12

people to reaffirm their allegiance to him, and it was pretty simple. You didn't have to say anything out loud. The crowd couldn't really see what you were doing. You just had to put a tiny bit of incense on the altar, and that was all it took.

Picture it. The whole city is lined up. One by one they come through the archway leading into the forum area. Soldiers stand guard, the city clerk sits with the registry of names, his pen, and a bowl of incense in front of him. The stream of citizens walk by, take a pinch of the powder, drop it onto the coal fire burning in the censor, and walk out into another year of peace and security.

To stay a happy part of the empire, all you had to do was stop by the temple and take a pinch of incense and put it on the fire. Then a certificate was given, like our auto license renewal stickers. That event, and the paper, called a libelli, verified that you had passed. It was an annual homage to the emperor that became the one action that unified the masses of people in the Roman Empire.

If you just go with the flow, your children, wife, husband, friends, job, and home are all secure. But if you refuse, if you believe that only Jesus is Lord, if you say that Caesar is not God, then the slow grind of that efficient machine called Rome will begin to hunt you down and either force you to recant, or take your life.

By the time this letter arrived at Smyrna, they had already been seeing persecution grow for decades, and Jesus' second lesson to them is that persecution is inevitable, and it's a lesson that all the first-century churches learned.

Timothy, killed by a mob in his own city, received these words from the apostle Paul: "Yes, and all who desire to live godly in Christ Jesus will suffer persecution."[104]

Notice who will suffer persecution. Not some. Not first-century believers or middle-ages Christians or third-world-country converts. No. Paul doesn't say "some." He says all. All who desire to live godly will suffer persecution.

Even today, in China, they spend more money on policing their own people than on their entire defense budget and warfare because they're so intent on controlling Christianity. At the underground house churches

---

104 2 Timothy 3:12

in China, they take away all the cell phones and put them in a box in a closet so that no one can activate your cell phone and find out where everybody's meeting and what they're saying. Even today, when we visit Russia, we meet with believers who, their whole lives, were unable to advance in their careers because they were known to be Christians. Even today, in the Middle East, believers are being beheaded for the testimony of Jesus Christ. Jesus said persecution is inevitable.

Sooner or later, it's going to get out that we're intolerant, because we believe the Word of God, because we believe in Christ alone, because we have a home outside this world, and we believe God says this is sin and sin is wrong, and eventually, they'll administratively go through and find us to be an anomaly, a group of people that doesn't behave like the rest, and we will be asked to get our little auto license renewal slip that says we're with the program. Persecution is inevitable. Jesus said it's inevitable.

Lesson 3: God uses persecution for His purposes.

How, then, should we respond? With anger? With the demand for our rights? Marching with signs for our freedom of speech or freedom of religion? Jesus only gives one command to Smyrna, and it's not new. In fact, He gives Smyrna the most-often-repeated command in the whole Bible: fear not.

"Do not fear any of those things which you are about to suffer," Jesus says. "Indeed, the devil is about to throw some of you into prison, that you may be tested, and you will have tribulation ten days."[105]

The devil has a plan, but God has a greater one, and God always uses persecution to accomplish His purposes. Even during the reign of Diocletian, when Christianity came so close to extinction, the emperor was fighting a losing battle. He was losing soldiers, not because the Christians were killing them, but because the soldiers were being converted. They would lead the Christians into the arena, lay down their armor, and die with them. They'd lead Christians to the stake, put down the colors of Rome, and walk into the flames with them. When ten thousand Christians were taken to a cliff and told to recant or they'd be thrown off, for every one that died, people were coming to Christ because of the testimony of the faithful.

---

105 Revelation 2:10

One Roman governor in Asia Minor was so puzzled about the Christians who were brought before him for trial that he wrote a famous letter to the Emperor Trajan asking for his advice. When a Christian was brought before the governor, the governor tried to threaten him.

"I will banish you," he said.

"You cannot," said the Christian, "for all the world is my Father's house."

"Then I will slay you," he said.

"You cannot," answered the Christian, "for my life is hid with Christ in God."

"I will take away your possessions."

"You cannot, for my treasure is in heaven."

"I will drive you away from man and you will have no friend left," was the final threat.

And the calm reply once more was, "You cannot, for I have an unseen Friend, from whom you are not able to separate me." What was a poor, harassed Roman governor, with all the powers of life and death, torture, and the stake at his disposal to do with people like that?

Throughout history, God has used the persecution of His Church to advance the gospel, by scattering His people to go to the unsaved world, and by using it to show the world what true Christlikeness looks like. When Jesus visited His persecuted church, He told them not to fear, to be faithful unto death, and He would reward them richly.

Peter, who was crucified for following Jesus, says, "In this you greatly rejoice, though now for a little while, if need be, you have been grieved by various trials, that the genuineness of your faith, being much more precious than gold that perishes, though it is tested by fire, may be found to praise, honor, and glory at the revelation of Jesus Christ."[106]

God doesn't give us a spirit of fear.[107] The world does. Our flesh does. Satan does. But God doesn't. His message to Smyrna, and to us, no matter what we're facing in our daily lives, our health, our careers, our finances, the message is simply to fear not. The Church shines brightest as a light for Christ when we fear not even in the face of persecution and martyrdom.

---

106 1 Peter 1:7
107 Romans 8:15

Lesson 4: God promises treasures to the persecuted.

All throughout Scripture, God promises rewards to the persecuted, treasures that only they will receive.

Hebrews says, "Others were tortured, not accepting deliverance, that they might obtain a better resurrection. Still others had trial of mockings and scourgings, yes, and of chains and imprisonment. They were stoned, they were sawn in two, were tempted, were slain with the sword. They wandered about in sheepskins and goatskins, being destitute, afflicted, tormented—of whom the world was not worthy. They wandered in deserts and mountains, in dens and caves of the earth. And all these, having obtained a good testimony through faith, did not receive the promise, God having provided something better for us."[108]

All the Old Testament saints endured persecution, persevering, not giving up, because they were trusting in the promised rewards of God, and God has promised something even better for us, Jesus Christ, the proof of all of God's promises.

Peter says, "Blessed is a man who perseveres under trial; for once he has been approved, he will receive the crown of life which the Lord has promised to those who love Him."[109] "Be faithful until death," Jesus says to Smyrna, "and I will give you the crown of life."[110]

Whether we are suffering for the name of Jesus or suffering from the ravages of old age or from a debilitating disease, Paul says, "the sufferings of this present time are not worthy to be compared with the glory which shall be revealed in us." The treasures God has in store for us are beyond our comprehension, and it's this promise that Jesus gave Smyrna to hold on to when they're suffering.

Lesson 5: To die in Christ is to die triumphantly.

It was during the time of the public games; the city was crowded; and the crowds were excited. The Jews in Smyrna were violently opposed to Christ's Church and were blaspheming and persecuting the Christians. Suddenly the shout went up: "Let Polycarp be searched for." Polycarp was, as far as

108 Hebrews 11:35–40
109 James 1:12 NASB
110 Revelation 2:10

we know, the last person on earth to have known one of the apostles personally, and he was the pastor of Smyrna.

They came to arrest him, but not even the police captain wished to see Polycarp die. On the brief journey to the altar of Tiberius the officer pled with the old man, "What harm is it to say, 'Caesar is Lord' and to offer sacrifice to be saved?"

But Polycarp was adamant that for him only Jesus Christ was Lord. When he entered the arena, the proconsul gave him the choice of cursing the name of Christ and making sacrifice to Caesar or death. "Eighty and six years have I served Him," said Polycarp, "and He has done me no wrong. How can I blaspheme my King who saved me?"

So the crowds came flocking with burning coals from the workshops and from the baths, and the Jews, even though they were breaking the Sabbath law by carrying such burdens, were foremost in bringing wood for the fire.

The soldiers were going to bind Polycarp to the stake, but he said, "Leave me as I am, for He who gives me power to endure the fire, will grant me to remain in the flames unmoved even without the security you will give by the nails." So they left him loosely bound in the flames, and Pastor Polycarp faithfully died for Christ.[111]

In Jesus' letter to Smyrna, He doesn't promise they'll escape with their lives. He doesn't promise to blind the eyes of those hunting them. He doesn't promise their careers will be safe, their homes will be safe. He never says their friends and family will be safe. He says, "Be faithful until death, and I will give you the crown of life. He who overcomes will not be hurt by the second death."

Persecution has power. It refines God's people, it magnifies the name of Jesus, and it stands as a witness to those who see it as the purest expression of love for God. Jesus' last lesson for Smyrna and for us is that to die in Christ is to die triumphantly. And there is no greater witness for Christ than remaining faithful till death.

---

111 MacArthur, *Church in Prophetic Prospective;* and William Barclay, *The Revelation of John*, vol. 1 [Philadelphia: The Westminster Press 1976] pp. 76–77.

HOW TO DIE TRIUMPHANTLY

We aren't ready to live until we are prepared to die, and one of the most important choices we can make is how we choose to leave this world. Instead of worrying about who's going to get our stuff, and who's going to pay the bill, and whether we have the absolute best doctor on the planet, we can choose to die triumphantly.

For the past twenty-eight years, I have read the Bible through at a rate of twice through the Old Testament and three times through the New Testament each year. In these repetitive readings I have always looked for something, and one of the areas that has fascinated me over the years is the way the Lord records the end of the earthly lives of His beloved saints. And each death is an example to us of how we could choose to die.

We could choose to die like Jacob, who died trusting in the promises of God. As he lay dying in Genesis 47, he told his sons not to bury him in Egypt. He was looking forward instead to the Promised Land, and even though they might be in Egypt for a while, he trusted the promises of God.

We could choose to die like Joseph, pointing to the faithfulness of God. He knew he was about to die, but even though he wouldn't see God bring them out of Egypt, Joseph knew that God is faithful. What God promised to do, He will do.

David died exhorting his family to follow the Lord. He spent his life loving and serving the Lord and spent his last breath exhorting his family to do the same.

Jesus died pointing the way for someone else to come to God. As He hung on the cross, struggling to breathe, He told the man dying beside Him, "Assuredly, I say to you, today you will be with Me in Paradise."[112]

Stephen died praising God. He was being murdered, stoned by his own countrymen for the testimony of Jesus Christ, and instead of responding with anger or hatred or even pain, Stephen died forgiving his persecutors and praising the name of Jesus.

His testimony was so powerful that even the Church's greatest enemy saw it. The same man who hunted them and persecuted them and murdered

---

112 Luke 23:43

them, who went from town to town to wipe out the followers of Jesus, saw how Stephen died, and God got a hold of him.

We could choose to die like Stephen's murderer did, finishing the plan God laid out for him. He said, "For I am already being poured out as a drink offering, and the time of my departure is at hand. I have fought the good fight, I have finished the race, I have kept the faith."[113] What matters isn't how we start the race, but how we finish it, and the apostle Paul finished well.

And lastly, we could choose to die like Peter did, reminding the saints of the words of God: "I will not be negligent to remind you always of these things. I will be careful to ensure that you always have a reminder of these things after my decease."[114] He had spent his life preaching the Word of God, he was about to die for the Word of God, and his last act was to leave behind a legacy, reminding the saints of the Word of God.

We live best when we know what counts when we die, and this is what counts: Believers always find that we have nothing in life to hold on to at the end except for Jesus. Everything else can be taken away. Jesus is all we have, and by faith, we remain faithful to Him no matter the price.

Some of the last recorded words of Peter before he was martyred are recorded in his last epistle: "I live in the tent of this body, because I know that I will soon put it aside."[115] Life is camping. Heaven is home. The older we get, the more God is loosening our tent pegs, getting us ready to, as Peter said, lay aside our tent and move into the heavenly home Jesus is preparing for us.

Peter lived the way Abraham did, as an alien and stranger in a land that was not his home. Abraham never built anything in this world but altars to God. He never bought anything but a place to bury his wife. He looked ahead. Paul says, "Our citizenship is in heaven,"[116] and the old hymn echoes that thought: "This life is not my home, I'm just passing through." Life is camping. Heaven is home.

How do we die triumphantly? Trusting in God's promises, pointing to His faithfulness, exhorting our families to follow God, pointing others to Christ, praising God, finishing the plan, reminding the saints of God's

113   2 Timothy 4:6–7
114   2 Peter 1:12, 15
115   2 Peter 1:13–14 NIV
116   Philippians 3:20

words… We die triumphantly when we die leaving behind our tent and looking toward heaven. There is no more powerful witness for Christ than dying triumphantly, faithful unto death.

If It Really Came Down to It

If there's two things we learn from Smyrna, it's how to handle persecution, and how to die well. But what about those of us who aren't on our deathbed? Many Christians, especially in America, are so far removed from persecution and martyrdom that the best we can do is wonder if we would be so bold for Christ to die for His name.

So perhaps the more relevant question isn't whether Jesus is worth dying for, but whether He is worth living for. Jacob and Joseph, who lived their lives on the Promised Land they inherited by the faithfulness of God also died looking forward to that same Promised Land, still trusting in the same faithfulness of God. David, who spent his life in obedience to God, died exhorting his family to do the same. The same people who, on their deathbeds, are calling for their charge nurse, their doctor, their unsaved family members to share Christ with them one last time are the same people who spent their lives sharing Jesus with everyone around them. How can we expect to die like Stephen, in forgiveness and praise, if we live our lives refusing to forgive those who wronged us, characterized by complaining, and not by praise? We can't, like Paul, die finishing the plan if we aren't today, every day, making the choice to run the race to win the prize. And we can only die like Peter, reminding people of God's Word if it's something we've hidden in our own hearts.

A death died for Christ comes from a life lived for Christ. And we can't claim Christ is worth dying for if we act like He's not worth living for. If we live for ourselves, if we live for our own gain, our bank account, our agenda, our goals, our way of life, then we will finish with regret, wishing for more time. But if we live for Christ, then death is gain, not a loss. Paul said that it was his "earnest expectation and hope that in nothing I shall be ashamed, but with all boldness, as always, so now also Christ will be magnified in my body, whether by life or by death. For to me, to live is Christ, and to die is gain."[117]

---

117 Philippians 1:19–20

How we live and how we die go hand in hand. To die triumphantly, for death to be gain, then we must live for Christ. "For if we live, we live to the Lord; and if we die, we die to the Lord. Therefore, whether we live or die, we are the Lord's."[118]

Do we look at sufferings as a blessing, a cause for rejoicing, a high calling, and an opportunity to glorify Christ, who suffered first in our place? Or are we known for complaining, for self-pity, for trying to escape the refining fire as quickly as we can?

If persecution is inevitable, will they find me an anomaly in culture? Someone who sticks out as different, a problem, whose commitment to holiness is unacceptable and whose passion for Christ is a serious problem that needs to be stamped out? Or will persecution pass me over because I'm disguised as the world?

If God uses persecution for His purposes, then am I willing to stand for my faith at work, at school, and let God do His work in me, or do I keep silent so everything suits my own purposes and I don't rock the boat?

Am I so concerned about earthly treasures that I'll sacrifice the heavenly treasures persecution brings so that I can keep what I'm storing up on earth? Or am I willing to be poor in this world and rich in faith?

Am I hoping one day to die triumphantly but living my life in defeat? Am I hoping that if it came to it, I'd die for Jesus, but my choices each day betray my lack of commitment to the cause of Christ? Do my words say Jesus is worth dying for but my actions say He's hardly worth living for?

The choice to finish well begins today, and how well we stand the test of inevitable persecution is determined by the character we establish today. Jesus' message to Smyrna, and to everyone with an ear to hear is this: Trust Me to the end. In death, in life, and in every decision of every day.

Persecution is inevitable, but we have been called to suffer with Christ. He is our example, our hope, and through His suffering, we will never be hurt by the second death. He promises treasures to those who suffer in persecution, and He uses persecution for His purposes, to magnify the name of Jesus to the glory of God.

---

118 Romans 14:8

By His grace, we can choose to die triumphantly, whether we're put to death for the name of Jesus, whether we die at the age of ninety-five surrounded by loved ones, or if we're hit by a bus tomorrow. And we can choose to live with that same triumphant hope that characterized the church at Smyrna. Let us make it our prayer today to finish well, and to be faithful to Jesus Christ with our lives, with our death, and with the choices we make every day.

Dear heavenly Father, we thank You for the beautiful examples of saints who died triumphantly for Your name, pointing others to Christ. Let us remember not just to honor You with our last moments, but to honor You with every day of our lives as if each day could be our last. Let us be emboldened by the examples of Christians who lost their lives for You, and who, as Jesus said, whoever loses his life for My sake will find it. Let us find our lives in You by daily dying to the things of this world and living crucified with Christ. And whether we die a martyr's death or just a normal, weardown, wear-out-and-everything-fail death, we want to be faithful to You to the end. In the precious name of Jesus, we pray. Amen.

RESPOND to Truth

How did Abraham (Hebrews 11:13–16) and Moses (Hebrews 11:24–27) endure loss, homelessness, and persecution?

What treasures does God promise to those who suffer for Christ? (Isaiah 57:2; 2 Thessalonians 1:6–7; James 1:3–4; 1 Peter 1:7; Hebrews 11:39–40)

What inspired epitaph does God give to the man after His own heart? (Acts 13:36). What would God write on my headstone if I died today?

What does the apostle Paul say he would give up everything to have? (Philippians 3:8–10). What would I give up for Christ?

What am I holding on to that won't matter on the day I die? How can I let go of that today?

What refining fire am I trying to escape? How could I instead use it as an opportunity to live triumphantly for Christ?

PERGAMOS

10 | Where Satan's Throne Is

SATAN'S CONSPIRACY

Jesus begins His letter to Pergamos with a sobering statement: "I know your works, and where you dwell, where Satan's throne is." Satan has been sitting enthroned in the hearts of men since he first conspired to thwart the ways of God, but this is the only city God ever equates with the throne and rule of Satan. God calls Pergamos the place "where Satan dwells,"[119] and here, in Pergamos, we see him sitting as king.

The Ultimate Counterfeiting Scheme

Satan's name means Adversary, the one who stands against God and His people. He's not a metaphor or a figment of the imaginations of the religiously delusional. He's real. He's powerful. And he's leading a global rebellion against God.

The plan that he enacted in Genesis comes to a head in Pergamum, and in Revelation 17 Satan's conspiracy rules the whole earth. This is what I call the Pergamos Connection, the thread throughout human history from Eden, to Babel, to Pergamos and the doctrine of Balaam, to Satan's 1.2 billion followers in the world today, to the beast in Revelation 17. In every language, every people group, across cultures, and throughout the

119 Revelation 2:13

world, we see it: our Adversary, the devil, offering the same alternative to the ways of God.

In six thousand years of human history, Satan always has the same plan. He fell from heaven for wanting to be like God, and ever since, he's presented mankind with an alternative to God's way of doing things: idolatry.

Idolatry is putting anything in the place of God. Anything. It can be a car, it can be a girl, it can be a job, it can be a substance. But here's God, who's supposed to reign supreme, and idolatry is putting something other than God in that place where God's supposed to be.

The Scriptures talk about two forms of idolatry, the idolatry of materialism, substituting God for things, and the idolatry of religion, substituting the worship of God His way for the worship of God my way.

Jesus described the End of Days this way: "For false christs and false prophets will rise and show great signs and wonders to deceive, if possible, even the elect."[120] Jesus gives ten signs of the End of Days, but the most prevalent description, the one He repeated more than any other, is religious deception.

If I tried to pass off a two-foot-wide, bright pink hundred-dollar bill, no one would be taken in by it. But if I tried to pass off one of the North Korean counterfeits, a nearly perfect copy, most of us wouldn't be able to tell the difference. That's what Satan does. Satan always counterfeits God's plan. He doesn't invent something completely ludicrous and try to lure people into it. He counterfeits. He fakes. He imitates God's plan, God's way, the worship of God, and that's what we call religion. That's what Jesus warns against.

"But I have a few things against you," Jesus says to Pergamos. "Because you have there those who hold the doctrine of Balaam." In Jude 11, God makes an interesting connection between the doctrine of Balaam and something else much earlier in human history. "Woe to them! For they have gone in the way of Cain, have run greedily in the error of Balaam."

Until Cain, there was only one way. Adam and Eve sinned, but they repented and followed God's prescribed remedy for sin, His way. But with Cain, Satan made his first convert.

---

120 Matthew 24:24

"And in the process of time it came to pass that Cain brought an offering of the fruit of the ground to the Lord."[121] Notice who Cain brought it to. He didn't sacrifice to Satan. He didn't put materialistic things in place of God. He just decided to bring God what he thought was best.

I can just imagine him, carrying a gargantuan, milk-fed pumpkin, big smile on his face. And his brother Abel, killing a bloody sacrifice, making a mess. But Abel was following God's example of a substitutionary sacrifice, and Cain was doing what Cain thought was best. "And the Lord respected Abel and his offering, but He did not respect Cain and his offering. And Cain was very angry, and his countenance fell."[122]

Now we don't see God in Genesis 4 explaining exactly what He wants to Cain and Abel, but we do have God's inspired commentary on what happened. "Not as Cain who was of the wicked one and murdered his brother. And why did he murder him? Because his works were evil and his brother's righteous."

God said Cain's works were evil. Not misguided. Not pretty close. Evil. Disobedient. Wrong.

The Way of Cain

Throughout history, there have only been two types of people, two roads, two choices. The way that pleases God, and the way that doesn't. The way of Abel, and the way of Cain. Abel's choices show us what God's followers look like. Cain's choices show us what Satan's followers look like.

Cain and Abel were both born outside of Eden. They were both sinners and fallen. Both were lost and guilty of the individual sins they'd personally committed. Neither were innocent, but starting in Genesis 4:3, they start down two separate paths, the way of righteous Abel, and the way of Cain.

Cain, number one, neglected God's example of a bloody substitute. God wouldn't accept the leaves Adam and Eve covered themselves with when they sinned. He killed an animal to cover them. But Cain brought of the "fruit of the ground." Literally, leafy things. It could have been a dozen roses, it could have been a giant ear of corn, it could have been any sort

---

121 Genesis 4:3
122 Genesis 4:4–5

of produce, but it was not what Cain knew God asked for. He neglected God's example of a bloody substitute and covering for sin, and God won't accept that.

Cain, number two, portrays a salvation based on merits. He brought the best he could come up with. He looked to himself for help to please God. He is a picture of the natural, self-sufficient, self-righteous lost person.

And because of this, Cain, number three, was rejected and cursed by God.

There are only two choices: what God's demands, what God desires, what He expects, what He says in His Word that He wants... or everything else. Religion is mankind offering any kind of worship to God other than what God's Word has prescribed. Anything other than Spirit-prompted offering in strict obedience to God's Word is a self-styled, human-based worship, and that's what the whole world is filled with, all of human history—self-styled, human-invented worship of God. Doing it my way. Going to God the way I think He should be approached, rather than submitting to what He said He wants. That's religion.

Satan has two choices. He can get people to worship something other than God (materialism), or he can get people to worship God in a way other than the way God says we're supposed to (religion). And Satan's first convert, Cain, didn't go after false gods. He went after God his way.

IF YOU CAN'T BEAT IT, JOIN IT: THE DOCTRINE OF BALAAM

Religion: The Deadliest Evil

Continuing the work he began with Cain, Satan presented the great-grandchildren of righteous Noah with an alternative to the way of God. When God offered a way for mankind to come back to Him after they sinned in the garden, Satan saw what God in His plan was going to do, and he made a fake. Satan found a way to make a counterfeit of God's promised deliverer, and he's been promoting it ever since.

First, he led humanity to believe they could get to God if they just built a tall enough tower. The deadliest evil Satan ever introduced into this world was religion, and the first object ever worshiped in human history was the tower they built in the city called Babel. And while humanity was building their tower, their monument to human achievement, using the work of their hands to reach God, Satan began a pagan religion that every religion in the world is derived from.

Satan knew of God's promise in Genesis 3 of a future Savior, God's Son, who would be born of a woman, so he put out a fake. Nimrod, the founder of Babel, married a woman named Semerimis, who was evil and demonic. She brazenly claimed to be the fulfillment of God's promise, saying that she was hit by a sunbeam sent from the gods and became pregnant. But her supposedly virgin-born son, Tammuz, died. He was killed by a wild animal one day while out hunting, so his mother, Semerimis, wept over him for forty days, and he allegedly came back to life. It was Satan's effort to delude mankind with an imitation so like the truth of God that they would not know the true Seed of the woman, promised in Genesis 3:15, when He came in the fullness of time. And it worked.

Remember what God did at Babel? He confused their languages and scattered them throughout the world. But all of these people groups still worshiped Semerimis and her son, Tammuz, only now, because of the different languages, they were worshiped by different names. In Syria, they were known as Ishtar and Tammuz. The group that settled in Egypt called them Isis and Horus. The Phoenicians worshiped them as Ashterah and her son Baal. The Greeks called them Aphrodite and her son Eros. And the Romans called them Venus and Cupid. But they're all the same. The same pagan religion started by Satan at the tower of Babel, the worship of mother and son, is the oldest form of idolatry on the planet.[123]

And what does God do when He finds His people buying this cheap imitation of His Son? This is what Abraham was called out of, the idolatry of Ur of the Chaldeans who were the original followers of Satan's counterfeit gospel. Moses was commanded to kill those who, after being saved from

---

123 Joseph Campbell, *Oriental Mythology: The Masks of God*, pp 39–40. Adapted from Two Babylons quoted by MacArthur in Acts and 1 Corinthians. (For a discussion of the relationship of the pagan mother-child cults to Roman Catholic teachings about Mary, see Alexander Hislop, *The Two Babylons* [Neptune, N.J.: Loizeaux, 1959].) William James Durant (November 5, 1885–November 7, 1981) was a prolific American writer, historian, and philosopher. He is best known for *The Story of Civilization*, 11 volumes written in collaboration with his wife, Ariel Durant, and published between 1935 and 1975. *The Story of Civilization*, Vol. IV, page 73. Hislop, *The Two Babylon's*, page 241.

slavery in Egypt, returned to serving Isis and Horus of Egypt under their new names. When the children of Israel followed after Baal and Ashterah of the Phoenicians, God Himself wipes out thousands of His own people. Elijah set up a test, God versus Baal, power for power, and when Baal was proved to be false, Elijah killed 950 prophets of Baal and his mother, Ashterah. Jeremiah sees God's people worshiping Semerimis and weeps over it because of God's coming judgment. Ezekiel protests the worship of Tammuz, God calls it an abomination, and when this same Satanic idolatry moves into God's holy temple, God Himself sends the Babylonians to destroy the temple and carry His own people into captivity.[124]

But when Artemis, the newest incarnation of Semerimis, sets up shop in Ephesus, when her prostitution and evil permeates the city, God commends the Ephesians for hating those sins, for rejecting idol worship and immorality. When Rome, with their goddess Venus and her son, Cupid, began persecuting Smyrna to the point of death, God's people were faithful unto death, refusing to renounce Christ. And that presented Satan with a problem—a problem he solved in Pergamos.

Constantine: Persecution versus Pragmatism

For centuries, Satan tried to persecute Christ's followers to extinction. He fed them to wild animals in the arena. He pushed them off cliffs by the thousands. He set them on fire to light the emperors' parties. But still they thrived. The centurions and guards who were supposed to be fighting the Christians began joining them. The truth of the gospel in all its purity, refined by persecution, continued to spread. So something had to change.

Satan had waged a frontal assault against Christ's followers for hundreds of years, but here, in the letter to Pergamos, we see him changing tactics. After failing with Diocletian to exterminate Christianity, Satan, through the emperor Constantine, changed strategies. This is what God calls the doctrine of Balaam.

When the Old Testament prophet Balaam was hired by a pagan king to destroy the nation Israel, he too tried a frontal assault. He sacrificed to pagan gods and stood up on a hill and opened his mouth to curse Israel,

---

124 Joshua 24:2–3; Numbers 25:4, 9; 1 Kings 18:19, 40; Jeremiah 44; Ezekiel 7:20–22; 8:14–15

but God stopped him. When the king was finally so frustrated he said he wouldn't pay Balaam, Balaam told him there was no way to destroy God's people head-on. But he did have an idea, and this was it, this is the doctrine of Balaam: If you can't beat it, join it and defile it, and God will judge it.

Because God is holy and can't tolerate sin in His camp, all the king really had to do was to lure Israel into sin and the worship of false gods, and he wouldn't have to lift a finger. God would destroy His own people.

It worked so well in Numbers 22–25 that Satan tried it again. The Emperor Constantine was a pragmatist. He realized that persecution wasn't working, so he figured if you can't beat it, join it. In order to unite his fractured army, to get those who were dividing over Christ back with the program, he made Christianity the official religion of the Roman Empire. He put crosses on their flags, walked his whole army through a river and called it baptism, and said God gave him a dream that if they did that, they'd win their next battle. And they did.

So Constantine took the Church and merged it with all the religious rites of paganism. Have you ever wondered where the Roman Catholic Church came from? *Catholic* means the truth, the orthodox church, the one Christ founded. Romanism, paganism, got added in when Constantine made it the official religion of Rome. Everything God hates, the counterfeit of His Son, the demon worship, and the immorality, got added in. And Satan didn't have to lift a finger.

Repackaging Paganism for the Church

From the beginning, Satan presented mankind with an alternative, a self-styled, human-invented worship of God, the deadliest evil on earth. God told Cain and Abel He wanted a bloody sacrifice. God says salvation is by divine grace. God says we need help outside ourselves to please Him. But Cain chose a different sacrifice. He chose to earn his salvation by works. And he looked to himself to please God.

After desperately trying to destroy the Church from the outside for so long, the devil changed tactics, walked the aisle, applied for membership, and joined the Church. And almost immediately, the Church began to neglect God's example of a bloody substitute, portraying a salvation based on merits, and when they stand before God some day, they will find themselves rejected and cursed by God just like Cain was.

See if any of this sounds familiar: Semerimis called herself the Queen of Heaven, the doorway to heaven, the way to the true and living God. Semerimis wept over her dead, virgin-born son for forty days and then he came to life. And if her followers didn't offer wafers and mourn with her for forty days every year leading up to the day the son is resurrected, then they were sent to a sort of halfway house to purge their sins before entering the afterlife, a place called purgatory.

If Satan can't get God's people to light candles, burn incense, and pay homage to a pantheon of gods, then he'll just get them to light candles, burn incense, and pay homage to a pantheon of saints. If he can't get them to worship the emperor, then he'll just take clothes, the headdress, the title Pontifex Maximus, and everything else associated with emperor worship and hand it off to the bishop of Rome. If he can't get them to go into Aphrodite's temple and pray to her to influence heaven on their behalf, then just make Mary the next Queen of Heaven and they'll pray to her for the exact same thing.

Close enough? It has Ben Franklin on it. It says "100" in the corner. It's green and the right size and shape. Children's play money might have "not real currency" stamped across it, but Satan isn't playing a child's game. He doesn't warn you that what you're holding is a counterfeit.

The Father of Lies has long since stopped announcing himself. Second Corinthians 11:14–15 says, "Satan himself transforms himself into an angel of light. Therefore it is no great thing if his ministers also transform themselves into ministers of righteousness, whose end will be according to their deeds."

This is what God called Abraham out of. This is what Moses killed people for. This is who Elijah slaughtered on Mount Carmel. This is why God wiped out 24,000 of His own people with a plague. And this is what He says to His Church: "Because you have there those who hold the doctrine of Balaam, repent, or else I will come to you quickly and will fight against them with the sword of My mouth."

Jesus says to His disciples, "Take heed that no one deceives you. For many will come in My name, saying 'I am the Christ,' and will deceive many."[125] For centuries, Tammuz, Horus, Baal, Eros, and Cupid have been claiming to be the virgin-born Son of God, the Deliverer, the One God promised in Genesis 3, and with them came pagan practices, rites, and a religion that is found nowhere in the Word of God. With the pragmatism of Constantine, paganism entered the Church.

When Satan repackages heresy, error, and condemnation for the Church, don't be deceived. Babel's religion moved to Babylon when God confused their languages. When Babylon fell, the priests fled with all their paganism to Pergamos. And when the line of Pergamite kings died off, the high priest of Babylon took his title of Pontifex Maximus and moved from Pergamos to Rome.

Don't be deceived. Revelation 17 describes Satan's one-world religion going to war against God. And on that day, Satan's religion won't be limited to Babel or Babylon or Pergamos or Rome. It's going to be ruling the world.

SEVEN REASONS I'M NOT A ROMAN CATHOLIC

When facing the End of Days, the greatest danger to the Church isn't persecution or the evil of an unbelieving world. The greatest danger, the thing Jesus warned about more than anything else, is religious deception. Over a billion people on this planet have been deceived by the repackaged paganism that Satan's been promoting for thousands of years, but you and I have the best weapon against it: the Word of God. How do we keep from being deceived? By taking a good look at what we've been told is true, and comparing it to the Word of God.

Years ago at the Master's Seminary, I entitled a paper, "Seven Reasons I'm Not a Roman Catholic," and these seven reasons aren't based on my own opinions or even my years of studying history, but on the Word of God. This is my testimony to you from a whole lifetime of studying Scripture, of reading through the Bible four dozen times and looking intently for what the Bible teaches about salvation, about the Church, about the nature of redemption, about the atonement, and about the God we love. So these are seven biblical reasons, not just why I'm not a Roman Catholic, but why I cannot associate with, promote, recommend, or even consider the Roman Catholic Church.

---

125 Matthew 24:5

Reason 1: The lie of the Mass

The Roman Catholic Church says, "In this sacrifice [the wafer at Mass] is contained the same Christ, now offering Himself by the ministry of priests not only for the sins of the faithful who are living, but also for those departed in Christ but not yet fully purified."

God says, "We have been sanctified through the offering of the body of Jesus Christ once for all. And every priest stands ministering daily and offering repeatedly the same sacrifices, which can never take away sins. But this Man, after He had offered one sacrifice for sins forever, sat down at the right hand of God. For by one offering He has perfected forever those who are being sanctified."[126]

The Roman Catholic Church says Jesus has to die over and over. God says He died once, and that was enough. The Roman Catholic Church says we are not fully purified until after purgatory. God says Jesus, by His finished work on the cross, perfected us forever.

Reason 2: The lie of the role of Mary

The Roman Catholic Church says, "Mary is co-redemptrix of the human race because with Christ she ransomed mankind from the power of Satan. Jesus redeemed us with the blood of His body, Mary with the agonies of her heart. You, O Mary, together with Jesus Christ, redeemed us. God has ordained that no grace will be granted to us except through Mary. No one will be saved or obtain mercy except through you, O Heavenly Lady. No one will enter heaven without passing through Mary as one would pass through a door. O Mary, our salvation is in your hands."

Jesus says, "I am the door. If anyone enters by Me, he will be saved. I am the way, the truth, and the life. No one comes to the Father except through Me."[127] God says, "I am the Lord, that is My name; and My glory I will not give to another."[128] "Therefore God has highly exalted Him and given Him the name which is above every name, that at the name of Jesus every knee should bow, of those in heaven, and of those on earth, and of those under the earth, and that every tongue should confess that Jesus Christ is Lord, to the glory of God the Father."

126 Hebrews 10:10–14
127 John 10:9; 14:6
128 Isaiah 42:8

The Roman Catholic Church says Mary is our redeemer. God says Jesus alone is our Redeemer. The Roman Catholic Church says Mary is the way to heaven. God says Jesus is. Period.

Reason 3: The lie of tradition over Scripture

The Roman Catholic Church has penance, indulgences, confessions to priests, orders of monks, nuns, robes, candles, rosaries, masses, holy days, relics, and Lent. And guess what? None of that is in the Bible.

Now there's nothing wrong with tradition that isn't found in the Bible. Sunday school isn't in the Bible, but we do it. The problem comes when the tradition trumps the Bible and we begin ignoring the Word of God.

What does the Bible say? "For laying aside the commandment of God, you hold the tradition of men... making the word of God of no effect through your tradition which you have handed down."

Tradition says the pope is infallible and has absolute authority, that we should pray to Mary, and that Mary was immaculately conceived and her body ascended to heaven. Tradition says that if you are devoted to reciting the rosary, Mary will sanctify you, keep you from perishing eternally, make you worthy of eternal life, deliver you from purgatory, give you a high degree in heaven, and give you all you ask for by faith. Not only are none of these traditions found in Scripture, the Bible says every bit of that is wrong.

Why do you think the Roman Catholic Church burnt at the stake those who tried to translate the Bible into the common language? Why do you think those who passed out Bibles were killed by the church? Because God's Word and Roman Catholic tradition cannot coexist. And if anything is elevated above the level of Scripture, I can't be a part of it.

Reason 4: The lie of veneration or worship of images

The Roman Catholic Church says, "Likewise that the saints reigning together with Christ are to be honored and invoked, that they offer prayers to God for us, and that their relics are to be venerated."

Aside from the fact that added together, the Roman Catholic Church has enough relics (pieces of the saints' bodies or items they used) to make up four bodies for each of the apostles and at least two for each saint, plus enough wood from Christ's cross to build a large building—aside from that—God says, "You shall not make for yourself a carved image—any likeness of anything that is in heaven above, or that is in the earth beneath, or that is in the water under the earth; you shall not bow down to them or serve them. For I, the Lord your God, am a jealous God."

The Roman Catholic Church encourages people to take crucifixes, images of Mary, images of the saints, and pray to them, seeking their help. That is blatant, unmitigated idolatry. That's not Christianity. That's paganism, and that is error.

If no one else will say it, then we ought to say it and believe it. Not to criticize, but to explain why Romanism is wrong. They shouldn't have those statues on their dashboards, they shouldn't have them around their neck, they shouldn't have them in their house, and they shouldn't use them as aids to prayer. Those things aren't aids to worship. If someone is a born-again Christian, then they ought to know the truth and turn from their images because it's wrong. You're reducing the inscrutable, unfathomable God down to a picture. That is the very definition of idolatry.

Reason 5: The lie of the false sacraments

The Roman Catholic Church calls the sacraments, "the chief means of our salvation." Infant baptism is "the means by which men and women are freed from their sins, are reborn as children of God." It is "necessary for salvation, cleanses us from original sins, makes us Christians." And in the sacrament of Mass, "the work of redemption is continually accomplished."

The Bible says, "With His own blood [Jesus] entered the Most Holy Place once for all, having obtained eternal redemption,"[129] and "whoever calls on the name of the Lord shall be saved."[130]

The Roman Catholic Church says, "If anyone says the sacraments of the new law are not necessary for salvation, let him be anathema [eternally condemned, accursed]."

The apostle Paul says, "If anyone preaches any other gospel to you than what you have received, let him be accursed [anathema]."[131]

---

129 Hebrews 9:12
130 Romans 10:13
131 Galatians 1:9

You've heard people say, "It's a matter of semantics"? That is not this. This is not a wording issue. It's not a cosmetic difference in how we choose to say the same thing. This is the gospel we're talking about here. Either salvation is through Jesus Christ alone or it's not.

Reason 6: The lie of paganism

When Constantine blended the paganism of Rome together with the orthodox beliefs of Christianity, the pagans came over with incense in their hands, holy water under their arms, and rosary beads on their shoulders. All the pagan worship and holidays celebrating false gods were renamed for the Roman Catholic calendar and given Christian names. Indulgences, the idea of paying the church for your salvation, prayers for the dead, and the hierarchy of priests didn't come from God's Word. It came from pagan worship.

The best way to counterfeit the things of God is not to call it Satanism. It's to call it Christianity. And the closer Satan can get his false religion to the real thing, by changing the names and slapping on Christian titles, the more people will buy into it. Satan doesn't care if we miss the mark by an inch or a mile. It's still missing the mark. Cain only missed by a little bit. He still went to hell.

Reason 7: The lie of purgatory

The Roman Catholic Church says, "Sins must be expiated through the sorrows, miseries, and trials of this life; otherwise, in the next life through fire and torments. In purgatory, the souls of those who die in the charity of God, truly repentant, are cleansed after death with the punishments designed to purge away their death."

The Bible says, "When He had by Himself purged our sins, sat down at the right hand of the Majesty on high. For by one offering He has perfected forever those who are being sanctified."[132]

This is where the rubber meets the road. The Bible says, "Believe on the Lord Jesus Christ and you will be saved." The Roman Catholic Church says to cooperate with the grace of God infused by the sacraments, and maybe after 30,000 years in purgatory you'll get to heaven. Either Jesus cleanses you

---

132 Hebrews 1:3, 10:14

from your sins, or purgatory does. One is glorious news. One is terrible news. One is the gospel (literally, "good news"). One is not good news at all.

These are not trivial differences. These are not fine points of theology. And these aren't obscure beliefs that your average Roman Catholic has never heard of. This is the way to heaven. Jesus, or not Jesus.

One thing is for sure: They can't both be right. You can't worship God and idols. You can't get into heaven through the only door, Jesus Christ, and through Mary, the only Doorway to Heaven. You can't be saved by grace alone and by a list of sacraments. You can't have your sins 100 percent paid for by Christ and pay for them yourself in purgatory. It's one or the other.

There are some people in the Catholic Church who have met Jesus Christ. I have their books—Martin Luther, John Huss, John Calvin—and there have been many others since then who have come to faith in Christ alone, but they had to do it circumventing their own theology. And so we don't attack individuals, Catholics. We say that Romanism is ungodly, unbiblical, pagan, and false.

If it looks like a real hundred-dollar bill, test it. Check it against what you know is real. Hold it up to the light. If you accept counterfeit currency, you're in trouble. If you accept a counterfeit gospel, you're in a lot worse than trouble.

The apostle Paul says, "I marvel that you are turning away so soon from Him who called you in the grace of Christ, to a different gospel, which is not another; but there are some who trouble you and want to pervert the gospel of Christ. But even if we, or an angel from heaven, preach any other gospel to you than what we have preached to you, let him be accursed."[133]

I can't be a Roman Catholic because they preach the same false gospel Satan has been propagating since Babel, and what Jesus said in Revelation 2, His message to us, is don't get as close to it as you can get and rename all the pagan stuff. Come out from among it and be separate. You don't have to destroy it, don't attack people, but don't have anything to do with idolatry and paganism and false worship. And don't call

---

133 Galatians 1:6–8

those people good brothers in Christ. At the best, they're disobedient. At the worst, they're not saved. That's what Christ told the church at Pergamos.

Don't be deceived. There are only two roads: the one leading to heaven, and the one leading to hell, and Satan puts up signs all along his way saying, "this is the way to God," but don't be fooled. When Satan offers his alternative, test it. Check it against what you know to be true. Hold it up to the light. That's the way of righteous Abel, Christ's call to Pergamos, and His message to us today.

> *Father, I pray that Your Word would find a place in our hearts, that we will have nothing to do with idols. That we will heed John's words, "Keep yourselves from idols," Paul's words, "What agreement do we have with idols," and that we will come out and be separate. Do not let us be deceived by the cleverly packaged lies of the evil one. Let us hide Your truth in our hearts that we might not sin against You. And I pray that You will help us with clean hands and pure hearts to worship You, how You ask us to, in spirit and in truth. In the precious name of Jesus, we pray. Amen.*

RESPOND to Truth

How does Jesus' condemnation of the scribes and Pharisees in Matthew 23 compare to the actions and traditions of the Roman Catholic Church?

How does Paul say I should treat everything I hear in church?
(Acts 17:10–11)

Knowing what the Roman Catholic Church teaches, how should I interact with my Roman Catholic friends?

What other traditions, practices, or philosophies have we put Christian terms to that are dishonoring to God?

What does idolatry look like to God? (Romans 1:22–25)

Are there any idols in my life that I've put in the place that should be reserved for God? What can I do to give God back His rightful place today?

11 | When Believers Compromise

Church history tells us of the pastor of Pergamos, a man named Antipas, who was martyred for his faith. Part of the pagan worship in Pergamos was the worship of bulls, and one of their rituals was to stand under a grate and slit a bull's throat up above so that the blood would run down and you would be "washed in the blood." It was called "being born again," and the bull god, Mithros, was yet another version of the false deliverer from Babel, the so-called son of the true and living God, the one who died and rose again.

Antipas was dragged through the city, brought to the altar, and told to renounce Christ, but Antipas wouldn't bow to a god who could save you by his blood, who died and rose again, who makes you born again because that god wasn't Jesus Christ. He knew the difference, and for that, he was thrown inside a hollow, metal bull, a fire was lit under it, and Antipas was cooked alive. Antipas was faced with false teaching, he wasn't fooled, and the church held fast.

For a little while.

REVELATION 2:13–17

And to the angel of the church in Pergamos write,
"These things says He who has the sharp two-edged sword: 'I know your works, and where you dwell, where Satan's throne is.

And you hold fast to My name, and did not deny My faith even in the days in which Antipas was My faithful martyr, who was killed among you, where Satan dwells. But I have a few things against you, because you have there those who hold the doctrine of Balaam, who taught Balak to put a stumbling block before the children of Israel, to eat things sacrificed to idols, and to commit sexual immorality. Thus you also have those who hold the doctrine of the Nicolaitans, which thing I hate. Repent, or else I will come to you quickly and will fight against you with the sword of My mouth.

'He who has an ear, let him hear what the Spirit says to the churches. To him who overcomes I will give some of the hidden manna to eat. And I will give him a white stone, and on the stone a new name written which no one knows except him who receives it.'''

When Jesus warned Smyrna of coming persecution, He told them to hold fast even to death. But when He arrives at Pergamos, He finds that this church already passed that test. In the days when their pastor, Antipas, was a martyr, they stood strong. Even living in a cesspool of evil, surrounded by immorality, they held fast to Jesus' name, they did not deny the faith. Pergamos started out strong, but something happened, and Jesus discovers that His church has been compromised.

Believers are compromised when they are no longer acting, living, walking, believing, and following Christlikeness. And when Jesus arrives at Pergamos, He finds Satan firmly enthroned. They had blended right into the activities, entertainments, and habits of the lost world and were living lives that displeased God. Pergamos had compromised what they believed, and now they were compromising how they behaved, and by the time Jesus visits their church, they were living just like all the pagans around them and were no longer distinctively Christlike. So what happened between the time of Antipas and the time Jesus writes this letter to Pergamos?

HOW PERGAMOS FELL

Pergamos seemed like such a strong church at the beginning, built on the foundation of the Word of God. Even when the pagan worship of Mithros was whitewashed over with Christian words, Pergamos held fast, but by the time Jesus arrived, they were crumbling. So what happened?

Revelation 2:13 tells us that there is someone behind the scenes, someone who seeks to thwart, to confuse, and to overthrow the plans of God. The Bible calls him the Adversary, and he's the declared enemy of God and mankind.

Satan pulled the wool over the church's eyes, and they let him rule instead of Jesus Christ. He deceived Pergamos the same way he's always sought to deceive God's people. He doesn't attack the building. He attacks the foundation.

The Doctrine of Balaam

The first crack in the godly foundation of Pergamos is found in verse 14: "But I have a few things against you, because you have there those who hold the doctrine of Balaam, who taught Balak to put a stumbling block before the children of Israel, to eat things sacrificed to idols, and to commit sexual immorality."

Israel had just conquered two of the greatest pagan kings in the land of Canaan. The victories were so great that the defeat of these two kings, Sihon, king of the Amorites, and Og, king of Bashan, are repeatedly mentioned throughout the Psalms in praise of God. Israel was on a spiritual high. They were conquering the land and all the pagan nations knew that Israel's God was a God to fear.

So Balak, king of Moab, was afraid he'd be next. And he knew the God of Israel was too great for him, so he hired outside help. He sent for an Israelite named Balaam, who was supposed to be a prophet of God. Balak said he'd give Balaam anything he wanted if he'd curse Israel.

But Balaam couldn't do it. He tried and tried, but no matter what animals he sacrificed or what mountain he stood on, he couldn't speak a word against the people of God. So Balak got frustrated, and in his anger he fired

Balaam, but Balaam gave him a little tip on the way out. If Balak would just put his pagan idolatry at the edge of the Israelite camp, if he'd just get some of the Moabite women to seduce some of the Israelite men, then Israel would invite paganism and immorality right into their camp, and God would destroy Israel.

So, "they invited the people to the sacrifices of their gods, and the people ate and bowed down to their gods. So Israel joined to Baal of Peor, and the anger of the Lord was aroused against Israel."[134] God saw His people going after false gods, believing the deceptions of Balaam, tripping over, as Revelation 2:14 says, the stumbling block he put in front of them, and God was displeased.

Israel—strong, set-apart, consecrated, chosen-by-God Israel—got interested in the altar of Baal at the edge of their camp. They were lured into the pagan parties thrown by the Moabite women, and it wasn't long before they had invited the sin of the pagan nations right into their camp. And Balaam was exactly right. Balak didn't have to send his army after Israel. God did the work for him and sent a plague that killed 24,000 of His own people.

The Deeds of the Nicolaitans

"Thus you also have those who hold the doctrine of the Nicolaitans, which thing I hate."

Church history tells us Nicolas was one of the original seven deacons chosen by the apostles in the book of Acts. Like Balaam, he had the credentials of someone the church should have been able to trust. But Ephesus knew better. Remember, they hated the deeds of the Nicolaitans. They tested those who said they were apostles and found them liars. But Pergamos listened. They were interested. And they started living the way they were being taught.

Nicolas and his followers perverted the grace of God and exchanged liberty for license. Do you know what liberty does? Liberty frees us to live under the holiness of God. Liberty, the freedom we have in Christ, Jesus says, frees us from sin so that we can be slaves of God.

---

134 Numbers 25:2–3

There are two types of people in the world: slaves of sin, and slaves of God. And liberty is never to be used as an excuse to live however we want. Paul says, "You, brethren, have been called to liberty; only do not use liberty as an opportunity for the flesh, but through love serve one another."[135]

But Nicolas taught a perverted grace. He gathered followers, and he deceived the people of Pergamos. His name, *Nike-laos,* means "conqueror of people." Throughout history, people have lorded it over the Church, leading people astray, holding the rod of iron over the Church that Jesus is supposed to hold, and that's what Nicolas was doing.

Pergamos fell for two reasons: They fell prey to the doctrine of Balaam, and they were doing the deeds of the Nicolaitans. The doctrine of Balaam is when sin and false practices are brought into the church, and Pergamos fell prey to this when they allowed paganism to dilute the truth of the gospel. But once the lies of Satan make their way into the camp, it's only a matter of time before the behavior follows suit.

Taking advantage of the grace of God, the saints at Pergamum had gotten too close to the wickedness of the idol worship around them. They had slowly gotten comfortable going back to the old haunts of those idols they had been saved out of and away from. Then, overcome by the temptations and lusts of the flesh, they gave in to sinful practices.

You and I don't live in Pergamos. We don't follow after Balaam or Nicolas. So what lesson is God trying to teach us? The message is the same. If Satan can get strong, persecuted, faithful Pergamos to fall, he can get to us the same way.

PERGAMITE AMERICA

The first thing Satan did in the Garden of Eden was not to tempt Eve to sin. He just asked a question, "Did God really say?"[136] Sounds harmless enough. He made Eve question if God said what she thought He said. Then he offered her an alternative explanation of what God really meant:

135 Galatians 5:13
136 Genesis 3:1 NIV

"For God knows that in the day you eat of it your eyes will be opened, and you will be like God, knowing good and evil."

He didn't tell her to rebel against God. He didn't even tell her what to think. He just told her to think for herself. So Eve thought about it, she looked at the fruit, and she decided for herself. "So when the woman saw that the tree was good for food, that it was pleasant to the eyes, and a tree desirable to make one wise, she took of its fruit and ate."[137]

God says that sin starts, not with our actions, how we behave, but with our minds, what we believe. So Satan doesn't go straight for our actions. He goes for our minds. He presents us with a choice, an alternative. God gives us a command, tells us exactly what He wants, but Satan wants us to have a choice, an alternative, another option. And Eve chose door number two.

A Compromised Foundation

The only absolutely trustworthy and accurate account of the earliest days of both the universe and the human race is found in the inspired words from God in Genesis. The only one. Every other account, if it doesn't line up with God's Word, is wrong.

God says that He created the world. He says He did it in six days. He says that man didn't evolve from something else, man was created with the hands of God from dust. So Satan asks us, "Did God really say?" Well, we know what God said, but did He really mean it?

Let's think for ourselves here.

Maybe God meant "ages," not "days." Maybe He meant "evolved from lower life forms," not "formed from the dust of the ground." Maybe when God said, "in the day you eat of it, you will surely die," He meant, "Things have been dying and making layers of fossils for billions of years, but it's still a good idea to avoid that one tree."

The alternative is reasonable. It doesn't really affect anything critical, like the gospel, or how we behave. Like Satan told Eve, God doesn't want us to be wise, so He gave us a version of the truth, not the literal, absolute, God-inspired-in-every-word completely inerrant truth. Just a metaphoric version of it.

---

137 Genesis 3:5–6

Does it seem foolish to believe God's version of things? Eve thought so too—right before she took a bite.

God's version of history also says the world was covered with a global flood. Does that sound reasonable? All those animals on one boat? Sounds almost as ridiculous as eating a nice piece of fruit being deadly. Did God really say? Maybe He meant a flood so large it seemed global, or it covered the face of the whole earth only from Noah's perspective.

Here's the problem: The gospel boils down to this. We have a problem (sin), and God has the solution (grace). Romans 6:23 says, "The wages of sin is death, but the gift of God is eternal life through Jesus Christ our Lord." That's the gospel. Death or life, sin or grace, hell or heaven. That's the gospel.

But the first time sin turns up is not Romans 6:23, or 3:23, or anywhere else in the New Testament. It's when Eve took a piece of fruit, handed it to Adam, and they ate.

When the apostle Paul presents the gospel, he says on one hand that death comes from sin, and sin comes from Adam, and on the other hand, life comes from grace and grace comes from Jesus.[138] That's how sin works. That's how death works—this is our problem. And grace works the same way—that's our solution, how we get saved.

But if we think for ourselves, we realize that can't be right. Death and fossils were in the world millennia before Adam, so either sin came before Adam or death came before sin… Paul must have gotten it confused.

Maybe Peter got it right. Paul wasn't the only person to explain the gospel. So let's look at Peter's gospel presentation. Peter says Noah's ark was the only way to escape the flood, and "corresponding to that," we are baptized with the Holy Spirit through the resurrection of Jesus Christ, and we are saved.[139]

Oops. The first place we see grace isn't when "God so loved the world that He gave His only begotten Son."[140] It's when "Noah found grace in the eyes of the Lord."[141] The ark was covered in pitch, which is the Hebrew word for atonement. The ark only had one door, picturing Jesus as the only way

138 Romans 5:12–19
139 1 Peter 3:20 NASB; 2 Peter 2:5
140 John 3:16
141 Genesis 6:8

to God. God Himself closes the door and brings all of them safely through the flood—that's eternal security. And everyone who wasn't in the ark died.

But if the flood was local, there were lots of ways to be saved, like to be somewhere else on earth other than the Middle East at the time. But Peter thought the flood was global, so he also thought Jesus was the only way to heaven.

Even if Peter was wrong, Jesus still saves, doesn't He? We're still sealed with the Holy Spirit, and there's still only one way to heaven, and we're still sure we can't lose our salvation, aren't we? Even if Paul was wrong about how sin works, surely he was right about how grace works. It still comes from Jesus, and it still gives life...

Did God really say?

For centuries, Satan has been asking us that question, and we've promised ourselves we won't compromise—not how we behave, not about the gospel—but we've allowed that question to grow like a weed into the foundation of the Word of God and our foundation has started to crack. Satan doesn't have to tear down everything we believe to compromise our behavior. All he has to do is put a crack in the foundation and the building will fall all on its own.

What we believe determines how we behave. When we read the Word or hear it preached, taught, expounded upon and explained, we are hearing God declare what His desires are for us as His people. But when we start to question if what God said is what God meant, when we use our own judgment to see that what God says is bad is actually good, then like Eve, like Israel, and like Pergamos, we sin.

We are living in the most biblically illiterate age since before the Bible was written. The Bible sits on our shelves and gathers dust in our hotel nightstands and is available to us along with a thousand commentaries and Bible study tools on the internet and on our iPhones, but we fail to hide God's Word in our hearts.

The list of what we can know for sure, what we can trust, has been growing to include scientific theory, man's wisdom and logic, man's experience and emotion, what we hear on TV, what we hear from qualified doctors or psychiatrists, and a host of other authorities, but the ultimate authority has been moved to the pile of books full of outdated moral guidelines or the shelf for children's fairy tales, allegories, and myths.

Satan has been whispering to rational, intelligent, hard-to-deceive people, "did God really say?" for so long that, like Pergamos, we have become a people characterized by compromise. According to Barnum and Gallop, there's no statistical difference between Christians and non-Christians in America. There's no discernible difference in the divorce rate, the viewing habits, or the level of sexual immorality—there are just as many unmarried Christians living together in sexual sin as there are non-Christians.

If Jesus were to walk among us today, He'd find a very Pergamite church—wed to the world, focused on money, car, and job, only doing what's socially acceptable. We are country club Christians with no standards, compromising Scripture's absolutes, and more concerned about fashion than holiness. We have lost our distinctive Christlikeness.

And God says to us what He says to Pergamos, "Repent, or else I will come to you quickly and will fight against them with the sword of My mouth."[142]

Come Out and Be Separate

The city of Pergamos was ripe for Satan's rule. It was the capital of the Roman province of Asia, the zenith of Rome's influence and power. There are more Roman ruins in this area than there are in Italy, more biblical sites than in the Holy Land, more Greek temples than in Greece. This was the epicenter of the Roman world, and Pergamos was its capitol.

This is where Satan sat enthroned. The book of Job says that Satan is "going to and fro on the earth,"[143] but his home base was Pergamos. From the center of the known world, Satan could run his global rebellion against God.

Behind every idol, every false god, is a demon warrior, part of Satan's rebellion. And here in Pergamos, the king of the gods, Zeus, and his accompanying demon had an enormous altar. It was the largest wonder of the ancient world, even larger than the temple of Artemis, and it dominated the culture in Pergamos. The god of healing, Asclepios, with real demons and Satan's very real power behind him, counterfeited of God's miracles by

142 Revelation 2:16
143 Job 1:7

healing people of all their diseases with snakes and incantations. Dionysius (Bacchus), the god of drunkenness and orgies, headquartered in Pergamos as well, promoting a culture of abandon and sexual immorality that enslaved all who fell into Satan's trap. And this was the first city to have an entire temple dedicated to Caesar as god.

These were intellectual people. This was a university town, a place of learning. The library at Pergamos was the chief rival of the library of Alexandria, constantly trying to up their volume of 200,000 books so they could call themselves the greatest. These people should have been harder to deceive than most, but Satan got to them. The Pergamite believers were intimidated by the altars and temples to all the false gods, confused by the false miracles and healing, and tempted by the debauchery and pleasure-driven society around them, and they compromised.

Satan is always trying to derail believers from following God. And in this city, they faced the greatest temptations, the most alluring sins, the worst, overpowering evil. This town had more outlets for neutralizing believers' distinct Christlikeness than anywhere around. In a place where people came from all over to be healed by the power of Asclepios, at the center of worship for the king of the pantheon of gods, in the number-one tourist destination for all who want to engage in debauchery and drunkenness, Satan sets up shop. His priests, the ones who fled from Babylon when it fell, came here, and Satan just continued on with his plan for world domination without a hitch.

And Jesus expects his Church to separate from sin—here.

God did not call the believers of Pergamos to build a tower and live inside it and eat food sent in through a slot and never have contact with anything associated with sin or sinners. Paul says to avoid all contact with sinners, "you would need to go out of the world."[144] God doesn't ask them to do that.

God doesn't call them to tear down the altar of Zeus or go to war against the followers of Dionysius. They were supposed to be a city on a hill, a lamp in a dark place, so that others would see their good works and glorify God. They weren't supposed to burn down the unbelievers in their temples.

---

144 1 Corinthians 5:10

But what God does call them to do is to divide, to separate, to judge between truth and lies, between righteousness and unrighteousness, and to separate themselves from sin.

Sin and error mixed with righteousness and truth makes a church that is structurally compromised, and Jesus has only one remedy for the compromised church: repentance. The word is *metanoia*, "a change of mind." When God calls us to separate from sin, He is calling for repentance—a change of behavior, yes, but it starts with a change of mind. And that starts with believing what's right.

What Pergamos did wrong, Ephesus did right. And Ephesus practiced the daily habit of grace-prompted thinking. They stopped listening to false doctrine. They put false teachers out of their life. They put off conduct that invites the wrath of God. And they listened instead to the truth of God's Word.

Jesus says, "Therefore whoever hears these sayings of Mine, and does them, I will liken him to a wise man who built his house on the rock: and the rain descended, the floods came, and the winds blew and beat on that house; and it did not fall, for it was founded on the rock.

"But everyone who hears these sayings of Mine, and does not do them, will be like a foolish man who built his house on the sand: and the rain descended, the floods came, and the winds blew and beat on that house; and it fell. And great was its fall."[145]

SEVEN REASONS I BELIEVE THE BIBLE

Pergamos fell because they built their house on the sand. They heard God's Word, but they also heard everything else, from the culture around them, from false teachers introducing error, and from Satan telling them to question God's words.

When the rain falls and the floods come and the winds blow, the only way to stand firm is to be built on a strong foundation, and I choose God's Word as my foundation for seven reasons.

---

145 Matthew 7:24–27

Reason 7: I believe the Bible because of its endurance through the ages.

Diocletian destroyed every copy of God's Word that he could find, but Scripture says that God watches over His Word to perform it.[146] Despite being the target of empires, armies, and the declared enemies of God, the Bible has endured through the ages. No other manuscript in history can claim anything close to that.

Reason 6: I believe the Bible because of its archeological verification.

For nineteen centuries, many of the cities Paul visited on his missionary journeys were missing, no ruins to be found, so a British archeologist named William Ramsay set out from Britain intending to prove the Scriptures to be false. Ramsay took his Bible, and walked the three days Paul walked in the direction Paul walked from the port Paul landed at, and started digging for the mythical city of Pisidian Antioch. And the first thing that he found was a stone etched with the words, "This is the city of Antioch in the region of Pisidia." He then went all throughout Asia Minor excavating all the previously undiscovered cities and at the end of his mission to disprove Scripture, he became a Bible-believing follower of Christ.

Reason 5: I believe the Bible because of its scientific accuracy.

Science has never found or observed or discovered one thing that is incongruent to the Scriptures. No matter how much science discovers, it all fits in the cosmological framework of the Scriptures. We call a lot of un-scientific things "science," but true science, the verifiable, proven-with-the-scientific-method science has never disagreed with Scripture, and it never will.

Reason 4: I believe the Bible because of its fulfilled prophecy.

No other holy book in the world can claim fulfilled prophecy like the Bible can. Not the Koran, the Hindu Vedas, the Bhagavad-Gita, the Book of Mormon, the sayings of Buddha, or the writings of Mary Baker Eddy (Christian Science). But the Bible is almost one-third prophecy, and a

146 Jeremiah 1:12 NASB

staggering amount of it has already been fulfilled down to the smallest detail centuries after it was first spoken.

Reason 3: I believe the Bible because of its incredible unity.

From over forty men from three continents, over a span of 1,600 years, sixty generations, comes one unified message. Written from prisons and palaces, deserts and dungeons, hillsides and holy places, there is one common denominator, one shared theme, one system of ethics, one rule of faith, and one plan of salvation.

Reason 2: I believe the Bible because the apostles and prophets did.

The apostles declared that the Old Testament was Scripture, quoting from it or referring to it over three hundred times. They affirmed that each others' writings were from God. Peter says, "For we did not follow cunningly devised fables when we made known to you the power and coming of our Lord Jesus Christ, but were eyewitnesses of His majesty."[147] Thousands of times, over and over, they declared that these were not their words. There is a harmony of conviction among the forty-plus authors of Scripture—most of whom never met each other—that the words they spoke came from God.

Reason 1: I believe the Bible because Jesus did.

Jesus believed every "word" of God. Not the thoughts behind the words or the general concepts, but that every word was breathed out by God, specifically chosen to communicate what He wanted to His people.[148]

Jesus believed in a literal Adam and Eve, a literal Abel, a literal Noah, a literal Abraham, Isaac, and Jacob, and a literal Moses. He believed that David, Solomon, Jonah (including the fish he was swallowed by), Elijah and Elisha all really lived, and all really did what the Old Testament said they did. He spent His childhood memorizing the Old Testament, spent His ministry quoting and preaching it, and spent His life fulfilling it. Jesus believed the Bible, and because He did, so do I.

---

147 2 Peter 1:16
148 Matthew 5:18

If we are believers in Jesus, Reason 1 should be enough for us. It shouldn't matter what some church officially declares to be metaphor or myth. It shouldn't matter what they teach in science class or English class or history class. It shouldn't matter what 99 percent of the world believes. It should matter what Jesus said.

God didn't give us the Bible as a veiled, metaphoric version of what He actually meant. God says what He means and means what He says, and every time we take God's Word with a grain of salt, we elevate something else above Scripture, or we claim something else is more applicable, more relevant, or more certain, we treat God's Word with the same disregard that Satan used in his temptation of Eve.

If Satan asks, "Did God really say," then find out. If he tells us to think for ourselves, then let us practice the daily habit of grace-prompted thinking. Grace-prompted thinking and grace-prompted shedding go hand in hand. If God asks us to separate from sin, then we must, like the apostle Paul says, "not be conformed to [squeezed into the mold of] the world, but be transformed by the renewing of [our] mind."[149]

Pergamos' bad behavior didn't show up over night. They had been compromising their beliefs long before that. Satan presented them with a logical, far more socially acceptable alternative, not just to God's prescribed rule of behavior, but to God's plan of salvation, and they, like the Israelites before them and so many after them, accepted it as truth.

Satan likes to twist God's Word to suit his own purposes, just like he did in his temptation of Jesus when he quoted Scripture in an attempt to get Jesus to sin, but don't be deceived. The doctrine of Balaam is still Satan's favorite deception. Like putting a lobster in a slowly boiling pot of water, Satan slowly adds error to the church until the church looks like the world and we, like the Pergamites, accept lies as the truth, error as gospel, and heresy for the Word of God.

Don't be deceived. Whenever we compromise what we believe, how we behave won't be far behind. Let us not build our house on the sand. Let us refuse to stand on a shaky foundation. Instead, let us build our

---

149 Romans 12:2

lives, our beliefs, our behavior on the rock of the Word of God, and when Jesus walks among us, He will find us, like Antipas, faithful.

Heavenly Father, we want to repent today of contamination by the world and draw near to You. Renew our minds so that we will not be squeezed into the mold of the world. We want to be distinctly Christlike. We pray that we would hate the deeds of the Nicolaitans, of anyone who would try to lure Your people into taking Your grace and making it a cloak for sin. That we would repent of listening to false teachers and engaging in behavior that does not line up with Your Word. I ask that Your Spirit would do Your work in our lives. We have such a high calling, as Your living temple, as Your dwelling place, and You call us Your sons and daughters. I pray that we would live up to the name of Your Son, Jesus Christ, the name "Christian" by which we are called. We repent of all things that dilute and defile our distinctly Christlike lives. We pray that we would be used for Your glory, in Jesus' precious name, Amen.

RESPOND to Truth

What parts of God's Word do I dismiss as non-literal or irrelevant to me? Why do I think that, and what did Jesus think about that part of Scripture? (Matthew 5:18; 24:35; John 10:35; 17:17; 2 Timothy 3:16–17)

How literally did Jesus take the Old Testament? (Matthew 12:3, 40–42; 19:3–9; 23:34–35; 24:15; 37–39; Mark 12:26; Luke 4:25–27; John 8:56–58)

Satan likes to use people with the credentials of a prophet (like Balaam) or a leader of the church (like Nicolas) to get God's Church to compromise. What have I heard from popular Christian leaders or in popular Christian music that lowers God's standard of holiness according to His Word?

When has Satan asked me, "Did God really say?" What does God actually say on the subject?

How does Leviticus 26 apply to Pergamite America today? How seriously does God take compromise?

How have I compromised what I believe? Has it changed how I behave? What steps can I take to change that today?

THYATIRA

12 | When the Church Makes Friends with the World

EYES THAT SEE; FEET THAT JUDGE

When Jesus concludes His inspection of His fourth church, Thyatira, He finds a thriving church. He finds works, faith, patience, and unlike Ephesus, who was told to repent and do the works they used to do, Thyatira's last works were more than the first. Their ministry was expanding, their church was growing, and their works were increasing. You would think that we're about to read a letter of glowing commendations like the letter to Ephesus, maybe with just one or two things to fix tacked on at the end. But after only a few good things, Jesus says the word you never want to hear when He's saying good things: "nevertheless."

REVELATION 2:18–29

And to the angel of the church in Thyatira write,
"These things says the Son of God, who has eyes like a flame of fire, and His feet like fine brass: 'I know your works, love, service, faith, and your patience; and as for your works, the last are more than the first. Nevertheless I have a few things against you, because you allow that woman Jezebel, who calls herself a prophetess, to teach and seduce My servants to commit sexual immorality and eat

things sacrificed to idols. And I gave her time to repent of her sexual immorality, and she did not repent. Indeed I will cast her into a sick-bed, and those who commit adultery with her into great tribulation, unless they repent of their deeds. I will kill her children with death, and all the churches shall know that I am He who searches the minds and hearts. And I will give to each one of you according to your works.

"'Now to you I say, and to the rest in Thyatira, as many as do not have this doctrine, who have not known the depths of Satan, as they say, I will put on you no other burden. But hold fast what you have till I come. And he who overcomes, and keeps My works until the end, to him I will give power over the nations—"He shall rule them with a rod of iron; they shall be dashed to pieces like the potter's vessels"—I also have received from My Father; and I will give him the morning star.

"'He who has an ear, let him hear what the Spirit says to the churches.'"

Sir William Ramsay, the nineteenth-century British archeologist, systematically excavated the biblical cities of Asia Minor, and this is what he discovered about the worldly culture of Thyatira: "Revelry, license, and intoxication marked these pagan religious societies. Lounging on dining couches, surrounded by troupes of unclothed, dancing and singing slaves would be fatal to all self-restraining spirits."

Even nineteen centuries later, the buried ruins of Thyatira testified to the sinfulness that permeated the culture. Thyatira was a titan of industry in the ancient world, a very worldly place to live and work. Daily life in Thyatira was dominated by a system of trade and labor guilds that controlled everything. Every worker industry, all the potters, all the dyers, all the bakers, all the metal-workers, all the textile-makers, and the bronze-smiths, and the slave-dealers, and all the rest had a guild in this town, and guild membership was mandatory.

Thyatiran guilds were a lot like our labor unions. They'd encourage their members and set prices for goods and labor, but they had what we would call here in America a "closed shop." It didn't matter if you were the best bronze smith in the empire, if you weren't a member of the guild, you couldn't practice in Thyatira. It didn't matter what your education was, how good you were, if you weren't a member of your particular guild, you could be, at best, a poor day-laborer.

But the guilds were very pagan. Every guild in Thyatira had a patron god or goddess, and because believers in Thyatira, if they wanted to work, were forced to be members of guilds, they were also forced to join the pagan worship ceremonies. At every monthly meeting, before the business got underway, they'd stop and offer an offering to the patron god of whatever industry they were in. Some wanted incense, some wanted a sacrifice, some wanted flowers, some wanted you to bow, but every guild meeting started with worship to a pagan god.

Guilds were also pleasure-dominated. If, somehow, you managed to go to the guild meetings and avoid the idol worship, after the business was concluded, there would be a huge feast, the most sumptuous, extravagant food available, and you'd lie on the couch surrounded by unclothed entertainers putting on a strip show. Every month. All you could eat, all you could drink, and all you could want of every sensual pleasure.

Imagine the level of talk among coworkers the morning after a guild meeting. But believers in Thyatira didn't just face temptation at work. They didn't have bathrooms in their homes, so they had to go to the bathhouse to bathe and take care of other needs. It was almost obligatory to go to the bathhouse or you'd be ostracized by the rest of society, and prostitution was so prominent in those places, that you were considered unhealthy if you didn't participate. And even if you managed to survive as a day laborer, avoiding the public bathhouse and all that went with it, such an emphasis was placed on the human body that nearly every sport was practiced and competed completely nude.

If you became a believer in Thyatira, you had to kiss your career good-bye. If you didn't bow to the patron god or goddess of the arts, or sports, or the industry you were in, you were out. Poor, unable to advance in your careers, and your children were out as well.

That's a high price to pay. What were the saints at Thyatira supposed to do?

Christ's Call to Holiness

The popular view of salvation is that if you pray the right words, Jesus has to save you, and then no matter what you do or how you live, everything's good. The unpopular view is that if you are saved, you're given a new life, a new operating system. You can't go on acting like the unbeliever you used to be. Something's going to change. Jesus has never been big on what's popular.

The letter to Thyatira is Jesus' longest, harshest, and most pointed letter. As the middle letter in a set of seven, it's also the pinnacle of Jesus' last words to His church, and here we find the clearest description of what God does to a believer who's acting like the world.

This church had been called from darkness to light, from the power of Satan unto God. Jesus said He came to set them free, and when you come to Christ, you're free indeed. And that's what the power of God had done to that church. These saints had been transformed from the kingdom of Satan into the kingdom of God's dear Son. They were a triumph on earth that was a praise to God in heaven.

But when Jesus came on His inspection trip, He saw something ominous. The saints at Thyatira were slipping. When the church at Thyatira was first saved, they were distinctively Christlike. But somewhere along the way, they became friends with the world and they lost their distinctiveness. They were no longer like Christ. They started acting like pagans again. They needed to say no to the allurements, the temptations, the draw of Thyatira's culture. And God says what is needed for them is to repent of friendship with the world and to draw near to God.

Thyatira had gotten so comfortable around the error and wickedness around them that they began to be squeezed into the mold of the world. They had been, as the apostle Paul says, "conformed to the world." They had a choice: compromise and prosperity or Christ and poverty, but no one can serve two masters. The believers today have the same choice to make, to either follow Christ or the world.

"I, the Lord, search the heart, I test the mind, even to give every man according to his ways, according to the fruit of his doing."[150] Hebrews 4:13

---

150 Jeremiah 17:10

says, "There is no creature hidden from His sight, but all things are naked and open to the eyes of Him to whom we must give account."

This time, when Jesus introduces Himself to His church, He's introducing Himself to a church corrupted from the inside out, and He no longer presents Himself like the gentle Son of Man. This time, He comes as the "Son of God." This is the risen and glorified Lord Jesus Christ, with the fullness of divine power. He has the all-seeing, penetrating, discerning, assessing eyes of fire, and no matter how Christian we look, Jesus knows us underneath. This time, He claims the authority of God's Son.

"Who has eyes like a flame of fire." He sees. He sees their culture, He sees what struggles they face on a daily basis, and He sees that they have allowed the evil that permeates their city to permeate their church, and He judges it. God's people are called to too high of a standard for Jesus to allow friendship with the world to destroy the church's usefulness to God.

"And His feet like fine brass." John 5 says God has given all authority to judge to the Son. It's Jesus' voice that will call the dead from their graves to stand before Him. It's Jesus who will judge each one according to his works. Jesus comes to Thyatira as the One with feet like fine brass, or fine bronze, which always symbolizes judgment. As He says to Thyatira, "I am He who searches the minds and hearts. And I will give to each one of you according to your works."

Instead of subscribing to the popular view of salvation, Jesus demands a change in their behavior, and tells them exactly what He expects from His church. Asia Minor, more than anywhere else, was permeated by everything contrary to God, and that's why this area got more letters from Christ and His apostles than anywhere else. And it's also why Jesus holds Thyatira to such a high standard. They knew better.

That Woman Jezebel

Before Jesus came, the people of Israel lived under the Law. But after Jesus, the Jews were telling the Gentiles that they had to keep all the ceremonial law of the Old Testament or they weren't really saved. So at the Council of Jerusalem in Acts 15, Jesus' brother James and the other apostles got together, and determined that since Jesus fulfilled the law and we live under grace, there were only two things that the Gentile believers had to concern themselves with. Just two. Of the whole law, all those dietary restrictions and the feasts and the regulations on how to farm and cook and everything else, just two things.

1. Abstain from sexual immorality.

2. Don't eat things sacrificed to idols.

Sound like a Thyatiran guild meeting? Pagan worship, a feast, and sexual indulgence, all wrapped up into one.

"Nevertheless, I have a few things against you, because you allow that woman Jezebel, who calls herself a prophetess, to teach and seduce My Servants to commit sexual immorality and eat things sacrificed to idols."

Wait a second. Weren't those the two things they weren't supposed to do? The only two things from the whole Law of the Old Testament that they were still supposed to keep? They should have known better. But the believers at Thyatira were tolerating false doctrine, and even worse, it was being declared to the assembly.

Now there will always be people out there who believe things that aren't true, but Jesus says don't ever allow anyone to come in and take the official capacity of a teacher and proclaim error, false doctrine. He didn't stand up on a soapbox and preach fire and brimstone against what was going on around the church of Thyatira, in the sports and bathhouses and guild meetings and pagan temples. He condemned what was going on inside the church.

Whether Thyatira's false teacher was actually named Jezebel, or if Jesus was just comparing her to the seductive, evil queen of Israel from the Old Testament, either way, the people of Thyatira knew exactly who He was talking about. She called herself a prophetess, which means whoever she was, she was teaching from their pulpit. And she was teaching lies.

The Old Testament was a lot more direct about false teachers. The original Jezebel was leading an entire nation after false gods, and God had had enough, so He sent a man to kill her. So as he pulled up to the city in his chariot, he asked the few godly people left in the city to throw Jezebel out the window. And they did. Then he ran her over with his chariot and fed her to the dogs. Second Kings 9:35–37 says there wasn't even enough of her left to point to and say, "here lies Jezebel."

Jesus doesn't ask His church to throw their lady pastor to the dogs, but His condemnation of her and her followers is no less serious. "And I gave her time to repent of her sexual immorality, and she did not repent. Indeed I will cast her into a sickbed, and those who commit adultery with her into great tribulation, unless they repent of their deeds. I will kill her children with death, and all the churches shall know that I am He who searches the minds and hearts. And I will give to each one of you according to your deeds."[151]

Why is this so serious to God? If church growth is the measure of what's pleasing to God, then Jesus should have been happy. Thyatira was a go-getter church. They were growing, their ministry was expanding, and they had a great pastor. Sure, she was a woman, but how bad can she be if the ministry was expanding?

Jesus measures a church by its holiness, not by its size. God said women are not to teach the church. They can teach *in* the church, but they can't teach the church. Whether we like it or not, whether it's socially acceptable or not, whether it's politically correct or not, God designed a system. From cover to cover, from the Garden of Eden, through to the end of His Word, God spells out gender specific roles for the home and for the church. And God doesn't allow women to lead a church.[152] But Thyatira did, and she was leading them astray with the exact two things they should have gotten as far away from as possible.

Jezebel blurred the dividing line between God's people and the pagans around them, and seduced them with lust for the things of this world. Instead of refusing to participate in the paganism around them, the Thyatiran believers were blending in to their culture. God called His people to holiness, to be separate and distinct from the pagans around them—that's never changed. Old and New Testaments, first-century church and twenty-first century. God wants us to be holy, separate, consecrated, distinct, but they were allowing themselves to be seduced by the world. They were tolerating a sinful teacher and her sinful teaching. She might have been an incredibly eloquent pastor, but she was a woman and she was teaching lies, and the Thyatiran believers had allowed the church to be infected with

---

151 Revelation 2:21–23
152 1 Corinthians 14:34; 1 Timothy 2:12

false doctrine and sinful conduct, and Jesus said it was starting to permeate their church.

Of all the things she could have tempted them with, it was those two things, sexual immorality and eating meat sacrificed to idols, the two most prevalent aspects of pagan worship. Those were the two most distinctly pagan practices, the two things most grievous to a Holy God, the two things His apostles determined summed up holiness from the whole of the Old Testament, and she had them running headlong into it. Nothing would have put them more firmly in the camp of the world than what Jezebel taught them to do.

HOW TO MAKE THE WORLD YOUR FRIEND AND GOD YOUR ENEMY

The believers at Thyatira had followed the false teacher, Jezebel right into a state of friendship with the world, but Jesus knows friends of the world by another name. "Do you not know that friendship with the world is enmity with God? Whoever therefore wants to be a friend of the world makes himself," useless to God? Disappointing to the Lord who bought us? A sorry excuse for a bought-and-paid-for slave of God? No. "An enemy of God."[153]

The most dangerous place in the world to stand is in opposition to the God of the universe. If Romans 8:31 says, "If God is for us, who can be against us?" then imagine if God is against us.

Before we were saved, Romans 5:10 says, we were God's enemies. And He was ours. The only thing that stopped Him from utterly destroying us was Jesus Christ. For, "when we were enemies we were reconciled to God through the death of His Son."

Standing between God's righteous anger and a helpless bunch of sinners, Jesus took the full brunt of God's wrath. And because of the horrific death of God's own Son, we went from being God's enemies to being His family. But when Jesus checks on His family, His bought-and-paid-for children, He finds them getting all too friendly with His enemies, blending in with the pagan practices, fitting right in, comfortable and thriving in a cesspool of sin.

153 James 4:4

In choosing to align with the world, Thyatira had set herself firmly against God. Friendship with the world is when we, saved from God's wrath and welcomed into the family by Jesus' incredible sacrifice, go over and join the enemy. Jesus paid too high a price to lose His people to the world. It's something He can't tolerate, and He actively intervenes with whatever measures are necessary to bring us back to where we belong.

Is that us? Have we become comfortable with the world, made light of the sacrifice of Christ, and gone over and joined the enemy? "Whoever therefore wants to be a friend of the world makes himself an enemy of God," and according to God's Word, there are three sure-fire ways to make the world your friend and God your enemy.

1) Yoke Yourself to an Unbeliever

Many people come to Christ after they're married to an unbeliever, and 1 Peter talks about how to witness to an unbelieving spouse, but God's Word is very clear about whom believers should marry.

Nearly every time God's people Israel fell into sin, it began with what the apostle Paul calls being "unequally yoked." This clear command found throughout the Old Testament (don't marry a pagan, don't marry a pagan, don't marry a pagan)[154] is repeated for us in the New Testament. Paul says, "Do not be unequally yoked together with unbelievers. For what fellowship has righteousness with lawlessness? And what communion has light with darkness? And what accord has Christ with Belial? Or what part has a believer with an unbeliever? And what agreement has the temple of God with idols?"[155]

God says you may not marry an unbelieving, idolatrous pagan. Why? Because what communion has light with darkness? What fellowship has God with the devil? Remember that unsaved people, their father is the devil. They might look pretty, they might smell pretty, they might act pretty, but their father is the devil till they're born again.

By the way, if you shouldn't be married to an unbeliever, you shouldn't be engaged to one, and if you shouldn't be engaged to one, you shouldn't

---

154 Deuteronomy 7:1–4
155 2 Corinthians 6:14–16

date one. Ask any of the sweet, Christian ladies married to unbelieving husbands: Evangelistic dating doesn't work.

No believer is to merge their life with someone who is unregenerate. It makes you a friend of the world, and by denying God's authority in who you should spend your life with, it puts you at odds with a Holy God.

2) Stand in the Path of Sinners

The second way to make the world your friend is to walk in the council of the ungodly, to stand in the path of sinners, to sit in the seat of the scornful.[156] You want a good way to be God's enemy? Choose as your closest, most intimate friends those who are walking in opposition to God.

Jesus came to save sinners, to bring them into God's family, to die for them, to redeem them, but what about when it came to His friends? Jesus says those closest to Him are the people who do the will of His Father in heaven.[157]

"Do not be deceived. 'Evil company corrupts good habits.'"[158] Remember, we're supposed to establish habits of loving God most. We're supposed to separate from sin. But how can we do that if our habits are corrupted by the company we keep? How can we love God most if our closest friends are pulling us in the opposite direction? "Can two walk together unless they are agreed?"[159] For two people with different destinations to walk the same direction, one has to compromise, and it's usually the Christian. If your best friend isn't being transformed into the image of Christ, then you're being squeezed into the mold of the world, just like Thyatira.

3) Love the World and the Things in It

Satan likes to wrap ugly things in pretty packages, to couch something good in something defiling so that we compromise ourselves to get it. It might be the compromising or defiling lyrics of a popular musician or the God-dishonoring message of a violent or sensual video game, or the

---

156 Psalm 1:1
157 Matthew 12:50
158 1 Corinthians 15:33
159 Amos 3:3

Spirit-grieving scenes in a movie, or the disobedient direction of an ungodly friendship, but all too often, we compromise with the world and dirty our hands just to get something we think of as good.

We can't hide away in our churches and never go out to share Christ. We can't avoid associating with sinners, because to do that, Paul says, "you would need to go out of the world."[160] We can't help what our eyes happen to see on a billboard as we're driving to work, or what our ears happen to hear in passing. But when we choose to set what is unclean before our eyes, to be entertained by what grieves the Holy Spirit, to love the world and the things in it, to stand in the path of sinners, to put ourselves firmly on the side of those who deny God, to make them our friends, to date, to marry, to spend our lives with those who live in opposition to God, then we haven't just made friends with the world, we've made an enemy of God. And Jesus says that condition is lethal, "unless you repent."

HE WHO SEARCHES THE MINDS AND HEARTS

Thyatira had made herself friends with God's enemies, and Jesus called for His church to make a choice: Him or the world. And in a place like Thyatira, where belonging to God was a death sentence to your career, your social standing, and your future, it was a constant battle, a daily decision whether to make the hard choice and follow Christ, or the easy one and follow the world.

But Paul taught in the epistle to Galatia that the battle has already been won by Jesus Christ. The world, our flesh, and the devil were all defeated at the cross—we just need to believe and act upon that truth.

"I have been crucified with Christ." That is a past event, justification, and it was accomplished by Jesus Christ. "It is no longer I who live, but Christ lives in me." In the present, the life I live is being sanctified. The old self is being put to death daily, being put off daily because of what Jesus did on the cross. "And the life which I now live in the flesh I live by faith in the Son of God." Flesh can't defeat flesh. Resolves, promises, fighting and striving in our own power only leads to further defeat. The only power we have is the power of the cross, by faith in the Son of God "who loved me and gave Himself for me."[161]

---

160 1 Corinthians 5:10
161 Galatians 2:20

The life that can withstand the pressures and temptations of a culture like Thyatira is a life surrounded by justification that prompts the present tense sanctification. Galatians 2:20 begins with justification, teaches sanctification, and finishes by reminding us of justification again. Because of Jesus' justifying work surrounding my life, I can live sanctified. The life I live in the present is based on the work Jesus did in the past.

"What agreement has the temple of God with idols? For you are the temple of the living God. 'Come out from among them and be separate,' says the Lord. Therefore, having these promises, beloved, let us cleanse ourselves from all filthiness of the flesh and spirit, perfecting holiness in the fear of God."[162]

Christ's call to holiness has never changed. It doesn't matter what culture you're in, what temptations you face on a daily basis, what pressures you're struggling under. God says that friends of the world are His enemies, and we were not saved to be God's enemies.

We aren't just any temple, but the temple of the living God, and as such, our hearts should belong solely to Him. This is where Ephesus failed. Their hearts had wandered from their first love, they'd allowed Jesus to slip from first place in their lives, their hearts didn't beat solely for Him.

"Therefore," God says, we are to come out and be separate. And this is where Pergamos slipped up. They allowed their minds to be deceived, they mixed the truth of God with the lies coming from Satan's throne, and instead of separating from sin, they got sucked in.

Paul's last command is to perfect holiness in the fear of God, and this is where Thyatira fell short. Instead of holiness, consecration, set-apartness, they didn't just touch what was unclean, they welcomed it into their church and listened to it from their pulpit.

"I am He who searches the minds and hearts," Jesus says to Thyatira. "And I will give to each one of you according to your works."

What Jesus sees in our minds and hearts comes out in our works. If, like Ephesus, we leave our first love, like Pergamos, we fix our minds on error and lies, then like Thyatira, our works will betray a friendship with the world and God will be our enemy. But if our hearts belong solely to God

---

162 2 Corinthians 6:16–7:1

and our minds are fixed on the truth, then our works will be evidence of a consecrated life, a separated life, and we will be found pleasing to God.

It's time to make a choice. Jesus says if you're not with Him, you're against Him. God says if you're friends with His enemies, you make yourself His enemy as well. We can either consciously, deliberately align ourselves with God, or passively be squeezed into the mold of the world and find ourselves aligned against Him. The last thing in the world we want to be is God's enemy. Let us make the choice today, and every day, to sever our friendship with the world, to divide between truth and error, sin and righteousness, and perfect holiness in the fear of God.

Father in heaven, I thank You for the privilege of hearing Your voice, and may these verses, by the work of the Spirit, pierce through to divide asunder, and may Your Spirit work in our hearts in the areas we need to repent of, the areas we need to change our minds about, and allow You to transform our behavior because of it. Speak to us, we pray. In the name of Jesus, we pray. Amen.

RESPOND to Truth

Where did Paul get his admonition to the Corinthians in 2 Corinthians 6:16–18? (See Leviticus 26:12; Jeremiah 32:38; and Ezekiel 37:27.)

How has Christ's call to holiness changed since the Old Testament?

Am I or is someone I know yoked to an unbeliever? How does God say to handle that? (1 Peter 3:1–7)

Who are my closest friends? Are they pulling me in the direction of the world, or in the direction of God?

God considers anything that makes me not want Him to be an idol. What worldly idols am I loving?

To whom have I given authority in my life (on TV, radio, the advice of friends) that God would disapprove of? What can I do today to replace those voices with godly influences or the Word of God?

13 | How to Suffer Loss and Arrive in Heaven Empty-Handed

There's a deficient gospel that's been preached for generations that salvation is like fire insurance. You just try Jesus, get Him, go to heaven, and everything's great. No one mentions the fact that Jesus bought us for a purpose, and we are to respond to Him and live for Him because we are His purchased slaves.

Jesus told many stories about those who called themselves His servants but weren't, and He said they weren't real. And those who are His but who don't behave like slaves, the Scriptures says He does something about it.

I've raised eight children, and I'm quite aware that I'm an imperfect parent. There have been times I was the threat-repeating parent, saying, "If you do that one more time, if you do that one more time." There were times I was the passive parent, waiting too long to do something.

But God is the perfect parent. Hebrews 12 says that every child in God's family, He chastens, scourges. That is the ultimate spanking. And it's for whenever we choose to not obey the One who bought us, owns us, and lives within us.

Thyatira is the longest of Christ's seven letters to the seven churches and it also has within it the clearest warning Jesus has for those who do not choose to live a consecrated life. So what happens in the life of a person who doesn't live consecrated? Who doesn't respond to His Word? That's what the epistle Christ wrote to Thyatira is all about.

SAMSON: BIOGRAPHY OF A COMPROMISED LIFE

In the book of Judges, we have a Holy-Spirit-inspired, God's-eye-view, written-down-for-us biography of a compromised life. Oftentimes, we have a hard time connecting what God says to a church 2,000 years ago with our lives today, but that's why God gives us biographies, as an example to us either of what we should do, or what we shouldn't do. And the truths of the epistle to Thyatira are perfectly illustrated in Judges 13–16 in the life of Samson.

Samson's is one of the most incredible biographies in Scripture. Of the 2,938 people mentioned in the Bible, Samson is one of four whose birth was announced by angels.

An angel announced the miraculous birth of Abraham's promised son, Isaac. John the Baptist was heralded by angels as one who would make ready a people prepared for the Lord. And the Lord Jesus Himself was announced by angels, to Mary, to Joseph, and to the shepherds. And then there's Samson.

Not only that, Samson was born into a family of incredibly godly parents. Judges 7:8 tells us that Samson's parents went to God to ask how they were to raise their son. Can you imagine that? To take a parenting class given by God? Samson grew up in a godly home, raised by parents who were following God's parenting manual.

Then, there are a few people in Scripture, people like Samuel, like Jeremiah, like John the Baptist, like Paul, who were chosen by God from birth, and Samson was one of those, too. That puts Samson in the top tenth of one percent of all the people mentioned in the Bible. Not only was he announced by an angel and raised by incredibly godly parents, he was chosen by God, set apart, and consecrated from the day he was born.

Consecration means set-apart-ness. To be holy to the Lord. Samson was called to be a Nazarite, a "separated one." A Nazarite was someone who could never touch alcohol, who was supposed to avoid anything dead, and as an outward symbol of his consecration to the Lord, he was never to cut his hair. Those three things. And Samson grew up to be one of the great judges of the nation Israel with incredible physical strength and a calling by God to deliver his people from the Philistines.

Samson was set up for spiritual success. He had everything going for him. But with all his godly upbringing and every spiritual advantage, Samson started down a road of compromise with sin that ending up costing him everything.

Honey in the Carcass of Worldliness

If you remember the end of the story, then you know how Samson ended up. With everything Samson had going for him, one of the unlikeliest places he could have ended up is living as a slave of his enemies, blinded and mocked, with God's mighty hand removed from him. But Samson didn't destroy himself overnight. He went down a path that led to his own destruction, the road of compromise.

Judges 14:1 says, "Now Samson went down to Timnah, and saw a woman in Timnah, a daughter of the Philistines."

The phrase "now Samson went down," is the first clue that something's wrong. The people of Israel lived in the hill country. And the land of the Philistines, the territory of the enemies of God, was always "down," in the coastal plain, by the sea. So when Samson went down, he was going to where God's enemies lived.

When a good Israelite wanted to get married, he went to the hill country to look for a wife among God's covenant people, but Samson went looking elsewhere. He would have known what God said about pagan wives. He didn't have the whole Bible that Thyatira had when God warned them about spiritual compromise, but Samson did have the first five books of the Old Testament. And his godly parents, the ones who asked God how to raise their son, would have taught him God's admonition from Genesis 24: don't take a pagan wife. Exodus 34, beware of pagan wives. Deuteronomy 7:3, don't marry a pagan.

Samson was given supernatural strength from God, the ability to lead, and the upbringing to back it up, but experiencing great blessing and strength in one area of our lives does not make up for neglect and weakness in another area of our lives. Samson chose an ungodly direction, away from the things and people of God, and took the first compromising step by wandering from his godly heritage.

Secondly, Samson denied His godly authority. He disobeyed his parents, who would have told him who to marry. Judges 14:2 says, "He went up and told his father and mother, saying, 'I have seen a woman. Get her for me.'" His parents said no, telling him he should marry an Israelite instead, and he refuses to listen to their godly advice, and says again, "Get her for me, for she pleases me well."[163]

Samson might have known the presence of God in his life, but that didn't automatically overwhelm his will. He still had to choose to obey or disobey, and Samson made the wrong decision. He disobeyed God's Word, his parents' instruction, and God's calling. It didn't bother Samson that what he was doing displeased his godly parents. A truly godly person would have never have ignored a scriptural admonition given by godly parents who obey God's Word.

Thirdly, Samson compromised his life. As he was going down to Timnah to get himself a wife, he was attacked by a lion and killed it, and later, as he was returning that same way, he saw what was left of the lion's carcass, and bees had built a honeycomb in there. So "he took some of it in his hands and went along, eating."

Oops. Remember that as a Nazarite, as one who was holy to the Lord, Samson was never to associate with or touch anything dead. But he saw that sweet honey, he wanted it, and he reached right into that dead carcass to get it. He didn't care that he was defiling himself in the sight of God, he just wanted what he wanted. And he never told his parents what he'd done or where the honey came from.

Next, Samson ignored God's warnings. Each time Samson had victory over the Philistines, there was God's subtle warning that he was going the wrong way. And when his feats of great strength left him tired, thirsty, and weak, Samson prayed to God for something to drink, but as soon as God provided water, Samson once again ploughed ahead in his own strength.

163 Judges 14:3

Instead of heeding God's warning and repenting of his self-indulgent lifestyle, Samson disregarded the fact that his strength came from God. First Corinthians 10:12 says, "Let him who thinks he stands take heed lest he fall," but Samson heeded not the repeated warnings of God, and he was headed for a fall.

Lastly, Samson played with sin. He was tempted by the wicked Delilah, whose name has become synonymous with lust, deceit, betrayal, and ruin, and instead of running in the opposite direction, he toyed with her. She was a Philistine, an enemy of God, but Samson became her friend. Even knowing she was trying to destroy him, Samson was having too much fun.

Three times Delilah seduced him to get him to tell her how he could be defeated, and three times he toyed with her. All three times, she set him up to be captured and killed by the Philistines, but he kept playing the game. He was convinced he was so strong he could never be captured, never be defeated, never be killed. But toying with sin is always deadly to believers, and Samson was finally destroyed when he lost the game. When you play with sin, the house always wins.

The Tragic End of Compromise

In Samson's biography, we see a life characterized, not by consecration, but by compromise. Samson became a friend of the worldly Philistines. He married into them, he hung around with them, he spent his time with them, and he ended up defeated by them. Like Thyatira, he became a friend of the world.

First John 2:16 tells us what friendship with the world looks like: "For all that is in the world—the lust of the flesh, the lust of the eyes, and the pride of life—is not of the Father but is of the world."

Samson lived according to the lust of his flesh. He could kill attacking lions, but he couldn't put to death his own flesh. He could set enemy fields on fire but he couldn't control the fire of his own lust. He could break any chain that was put on him, but he couldn't break the shackles of sin he had put on himself. He could rip a eight-thousand-pound gate off its hinges and carry it for miles—they excavated the city and found the gate—but he couldn't overcome his own weakness for the wiles of a deceitful woman.

Seven times in Scripture it says that Samson saw a woman. That word "saw" actually translates that the woman was "in his eyes." She had captivated his thoughts. He had an image of her imprinted in his mind, in his eyes, and he couldn't get her out of his mind. He demanded that his parents go get a woman for him. If Samson saw something he wanted, he took it. He saw something sweet in the carcass of a lion and took it regardless of the consequences. He lived by the lust of his eyes.

Samson also let himself be ruled by the pride of life. When David saw a Philistine mocking God and His people, he went out to defend the honor of the true and living God. But Samson fights for a different reason. Judges says Samson fights against the Philistines first because he's upset about losing a bet, later because his wife leaves him, and then out of anger and revenge.

If at any point he had called out to God, saying he was tempted by the worldly women he lusted after, if he had cried out to God for help, imagine what a great hero of Israel he could have been. He was a one-man army. He could have defeated the Philistines once and for all. But because he walked in the flesh, not in the Spirit, he lost everything.

Samson lost his outward sign of consecration to God, his hair, and then his strength. When he was captured by his enemies, he lost his sight, his freedom, and his usefulness to the Lord as he spent his days grinding corn for God's enemies instead of defeating them.

What a picture of sin. Sin blinds us, then it binds us with shackles, and then it becomes a grind. Ask anyone who has been habituated into sin that they used to love. They find that it takes more and more of that sin to get less and less pleasure from it. What started out as a thrill ends up as a horrible, aching corrosion.

Samson went from representing the all-powerful God to being a mockery in the temple of Dagon. He lost his testimony, and ultimately his life, all because he started down a road of compromise with sin.

THE SIN THAT LEADS TO DEATH

Saved by the Skin of Your Teeth

Scripture repeatedly says that if you're justified, you will be sanctified, and if you persistently act like an unbeliever, maybe it's because you are one. So the question is, was Samson even saved? Samson lived most of his life like an unbeliever. He fed his lusts, he grieved the Holy Spirit, he lived for himself, he acted out of pride, and finally, God had had enough. Samson sinned out the patience of God, and God killed him. Did he sin once too often?

Many believers are worried that there's a sin too great, or they can commit one sin too many and God won't forgive them. Jesus talks in the gospels about the unpardonable sin. Is that what happened to Samson? Was Samson like one of those counterfeit Christians who never knew God? Because without God's inspired commentary, it's hard to tell.

Hebrews 11 is what we call the Hall of Faith, a list of the great heroes of the faith. But look who's listed in verse 32: "For the time would fail me to tell of Gideon and Barak and *Samson*..." Samson's listed with all the great heroes of the faith in heaven. So how did someone like Samson make it into heaven at all?

First of all, Jesus said that there is no sin that's unforgivable.[164] The only way to commit the unpardonable sin is to persist in rejecting Jesus to the end. The unpardonable sin in the gospels was when someone would look at Jesus Christ in the flesh, performing miracles, healing those with leprosy, doing things only God could do, and they'd look at God in the face and say, "You are not God, You're using the power of the devil." That's the unpardonable sin in the gospels. We can't commit that anymore, because Jesus isn't walking around in the flesh anymore. The *only* thing God won't forgive us for today is lifelong, persistent rejection of Jesus Christ.

That's not Samson.

Samson was saved, as Job 19:20 says, "by the skin of [his] teeth." Paul says in 1 Corinthians 3:15, "If anyone's work is burned, he will suffer loss." He calls it being "saved, yet so as by fire." Samson was, as 1 Corinthians 9:27 says, "disqualified," a "castaway." He ran outside his lane, disobeyed the

---

164 Mark 3:28

rules of the race, and it didn't matter how fast he ran because he was disqualified, and so he missed out on getting the reward. Samson was saved. But all the works that could have been done for God, he did instead for revenge, out of anger, for his own pride, and all of those works burned up. He was saved, yet so as by fire.

The Impact of Chastening on a Compromised Life

In the biography of Samson, we see the impact that God's chastening has on a compromised life, and there is much we can learn about God's chastening work by examining the life of Samson.

Like Samson, all believers are consecrated. "For the temple of God is holy [set apart, consecrated], which temple you are."[165] We're not just God's temple, we're the holy of holies. We are bought with a price, we belong to God, we are called to holiness, and to separate from sin. All New Testament believers are consecrated, "separated ones," not with uncut hair or any other outward symbol, but with a life that follows God's direction, separate from sin, not a friend of this world.

Like Samson, we are answerable. We will all answer to God for what we did with our body. "Therefore we make it our aim to be pleasing to Him. For we must all appear before the judgment seat of Christ, that each one may receive the things done in the body, according to what he has done, whether good or bad."[166] Did you know this is something everyone gets to see? We'll all be lined up before the judgment seat of Christ watching Him give out rewards, and when it's Samson's turn, he'll be welcomed into heaven, but his works are going to burn up. And we, like him, are going to answer to God for how we lived our lives.

We are also warned when we're living in sin. Samson was warned over and over. Hebrews 12:5 says, "My son, do not despise the chastening of the Lord, nor be discouraged when you are rebuked by Him." This is something every believer experiences. If we start down the road of compromise, we will be warned. Samson was warned first by his godly parents, and then by his heavenly Father, who gave him opportunity after opportunity to repent.

---

165 1 Corinthians 3:17
166 2 Corinthians 5:9–10

But if we refuse to repent, like with Samson, God gets involved. He will not stand idly by as we sin. God isn't the permissive parent. He doesn't just shrug and say, "you'll be sorry... it'll ruin your life..." He actively intervenes. "For whom the Lord loves He chastens, and scourges every son whom He receives... for our profit, that we may be partakers of His holiness."[167]

Like Samson, you and I can go too far. As 1 John 5:16 says, going too far too often with sin will be deadly for believers. We are confronted when we're living in unrepentant sin, but if we, like Samson, ignore it, then we're in real trouble.

God kills believers who don't repent in time. Jesus says to the church in Thyatira, "I gave her [Jezebel] time to repent, and she did not repent. Indeed I will cast her into a sickbed, and those who commit adultery with her into great tribulation, unless they repent of their deeds. I will kill her children with death." God gives us time to turn back, but Samson found out the hard way that there is a time in a believer's life when God says that's enough.

Chastening is one of the strongest proofs of salvation. God says He only chastens His own children. If you can live like an unbeliever, disregarding all the clear commands of God, wallowing in unrepentant sin, and sail through life happy as a clam, then you're sailing to hell. But if you are consecrated, answerable, warned, and still living in sin, then God will get involved, confront in the strongest terms the believer who's going too far too often with sin, and if they don't repent in time, God will say, that's enough.

When God Kills His Own

REVELATION 2:20–23

"Nevertheless, I have this against you, because you allow that woman Jezebel, who calls herself a prophetess, to teach and seduce my servants to commit sexual immorality and eat things sacrificed to idols. And I gave her time to repent of her sexual immorality, and she did not repent. Indeed I will cast her into a sickbed, and those who commit adultery with her into great tribulation, unless

167 Hebrews 12:6, 10

they repent of their deeds. I will kill her children with death, and all the churches shall know that I am He who searches the minds and hearts. And I will give to each one of you according to your works."

To say that God literally made Jezebel sick doesn't sound much like our God of love, does it. And to kill His servants, "her children," with death, literally? That certainly doesn't sound much like the longsuffering God we sing about. But I'm not pushing my own interpretation into these verses. This doctrine is found all throughout Scripture.

First John 5:16 says, "there is a sin leading to death." Paul tells the Corinthians who were approaching the Lord's Supper in an irreverent way, "for this reason many are weak and sick among you, and many sleep."[168] And that's what happened to Samson. God's protection, His strength, His power was removed, and we read in Judges 16:20 the saddest words in Samson's whole biography: "And she said, 'the Philistines are upon you, Samson!' So he awoke from his sleep, and said, 'I will go out as before, at other times, and shake myself free!'" And here's the worst part: "But he did not know that the Lord had departed from him."

Samson had gone too far with sin too often, and while Jesus says all sins are forgivable, God will not tolerate His children acting like their father the devil. Samson sinned the sin that leads to death, so God's power departed from him, Samson was captured, blinded, enslaved, and he died.

FIVE STEPS TO GOING TOO FAR AND LOSING THE REWARD

Henry Ford, after he'd made his fortune selling cars, was interviewing chauffeurs to drive for him, and he took them to the edge of a cliff and asked how close each could drive to the edge without going over. The first got pretty close to the edge. The second got even closer. But the third drove down the opposite side of the road, as far from the edge as he could get, and Henry Ford said, "You're hired."

Many Christians "fall into sin," because they've lived their life like Samson did, getting as close to the edge as they possibly could, confident

168 1 Corinthians 11:30

they wouldn't go over. James 1:14–16 is God's explanation of how sin works. "But each one is tempted when he is drawn away by his own desires and enticed. Then, when desire has conceived, it gives birth to sin; and sin, when it is full-grown, brings forth death."

Samson was drawn down into the enemy camp by his own desires. He was enticed by the woman in his eyes. The desire for honey gave birth to the sin of compromising God's holy calling on his life, and that sin grew throughout Samson's life until it brought forth death.

Samson walked throughout his life as close to the edge as he could get, saying to himself, "I will go out before, at other times, and shake myself free." And he did not know that the Lord had departed from him until it was too late. What was the result of Samson's life? He will stand at the judgment seat of Christ, redeemed, saved by grace, but suffering loss. Samson went too far. He grieved God for too long, ignored the chastening of the Holy Spirit to the point that God said that's enough. And all the works that Samson did in his flesh, for his pride, are going to burn.

How do we go too far and lose the reward?

Step 1: Wander from your godly heritage.

All of us in Christ's Church have been called from darkness to light at salvation. We have been saved from the power of Satan, we are being transformed into saints of God by sanctification, and that whole process is consecration, that we are increasingly responding to God. That's just the gospel. That's just what the Lord expects from us.

But the saints at Thyatira were letting their consecrated lives slip. They were living lives of compromise with sin. And in this letter to Thyatira, we see how far God is willing to go to get His children back in step with Him.

The first step to going too far and losing our heavenly reward is to, like Samson, be drawn away from our godly heritage by our own desires. Samson became a friend of the worldly Philistines and it cost him everything. Thyatira also became friends with the world, and it would cost them everything if they didn't repent. And we will lose everything if we persist down the same road Samson traveled.

Step 2: Deny your godly authority.

Samson became his own authority, made his own decisions, and not only did he ignore godly advice from his parents, he ignored God's rules. We take that second step when we reject the godly authority God has set over us. When we look at a clear command of God and say that it applies to someone else, not to me, we do the same thing Samson did. Thyatira had God's commands about women teachers, but either it didn't seem like a big deal, or they'd neglected God's Word for so long it had been forgotten. And they were so displeasing to God that they were in danger of the ultimate consequence of sin for a believer: when God has to resort to killing His people to stop them.

When we dismiss God's Word as irrelevant or no longer applicable to real life, we're rejecting God as the ultimate authority. When we start listening to other voices, including our own, over the voice of God through His Word, then we've taken the second step down the road to spiritual loss. Our desires have drawn us away, and now we're enticed.

Step 3: Compromise with sin.

John's admonition, "Do not love the world or the things in the world"[169] could also be said, "Do not love the carcass or the honey in the carcass." When, in order to reach something that looks good and sweet, we touch something dead, something of the world, something sinful, then we've taken the same step of compromise that led Samson to ruin. When we compromise, then lust has given birth to sin.

Step 4: Ignore God's warnings.

God's chastening begins when we're living like our friend, the world. When we look like an unbeliever, when like Samson, we're getting our hands so defiled by death that no one would know we're supposed to be set apart, God will warn us. Beware of ignoring God's warnings. They start as a gentle rebuke, but God does not hesitate to scourge the children He loves. Sin grows when God's warnings are ignored, and when you start ignoring the warnings of God in your life, you're getting close to going too far and losing the reward.

169 1 John 2:15

Step 5: Toy with sin.

The last step Samson took was to toy with sin, and it destroyed him. He lost everything, used up his last chance, and came to the end of God's patience. The end of the road of compromise leads nowhere good, and it is always deadly to our spiritual lives to toy with sin. We're not strong enough to handle it, we're not promised that we can just "shake it off as [we] did every time before." Eventually it will be too late. Full grown sin brings forth death. Every time. There are no exceptions for exceptionally strong believers. If ever there was someone strong enough to handle toying with sin, it was the heralded by angels, raised according to God's parenting manual, consecrated from birth, one-man army. No one is strong enough to toy with sin. Don't follow the same road Samson did.

Samson is an enduring example, not just of the destructive power of sin, but also of the restoring power of God's grace. Samson's last act on this earth was to sever his friendship with the world. He was blind, a slave, grinding corn for the Philistines, but he asked one of the servants which pillars held up the palace, and as his enemies were mocking God, Samson asked God for strength one more time, and brought down the house.

Remember how God's power went out of Samson? Psalm 66:18 says, "If I regard iniquity in my heart, the Lord will not hear." But God did hear Samson. Samson no longer regarded iniquity in his heart, and in his repentance, he cried out to God, and God heard him. Though he descended into the depths of a lustfilled life, wandered far from his calling, and neglected his consecration, the Lord never let go of him.

God never gave up on Samson. He kept chastening His child until He produced the sanctifying fruit of repentance in his life, but it cost Samson everything. Instead of responding to God's gentle rebuke, Samson's lustful eyes had to be carved out by the Philistines with hot spoons before he would stop living by the lust of those eyes. The pride of life that drove his every action was broken when he became a slave to be mocked and ridiculed by the people God raised him up to defeat. The lust of Samson's flesh wasn't put to death until in his desperation, he stopped relying on himself for strength, and called out to the God who had given him the strength in the first place.

Samson could have been remembered for all that he built, but instead he's remembered only for what he destroyed. He destroyed lions and foxes and fields and gates and soldiers and women's purity and he destroyed his own life and ministry. He could have led the nation, but he preferred to live for himself, and he had no permanent victory or reward. And God says to the church in Thyatira, don't you do that too.

Samson arrived in heaven, saved, but with his hands empty of every eternal reward he forfeited for the fleeting pleasure of the world. We could be like Samson and lose our reward. We could wait until it's too late, until we've gone too far and God is forced to end our sinful lifestyle the hard way. Or we could choose to heed the chastening work of God in our lives and repent of friendship with the world.

Father in heaven, we bow before You in the name of Jesus, who came to save us from the power of sin. And I pray for those believers who are playing with sin, that are secretly feeding sin in their lives, and for those who, not so secretly, are just blatantly following after disobedience. They're going into enemy territory, and they're compromising the Spirit of God of holiness that lives within them. I pray that they would be smitten in their heart with conviction, and that today, they would come back to You. That they would ask You to purge them of all filthiness of the flesh and of the spirit, and that they could draw near to You with full assurance of faith, knowing they're forgiven, and asking for Your new beginning. Do a work in each heart that's listening to Your voice today. In Jesus name Amen.

RESPOND to Truth

How do Samson's choices compare to Lot's?
(Genesis 13:8–13; 14:8–16; 19:12–38)

How do Samson's choices compare to David's?
(Judges 14:1–3; 16:4–20 with 2 Samuel 11:1–17; 12:1–13; Psalm 51; Acts 13:22)

What is the Timnah, the enemy territory, in my life, and how often do I venture into it? How close to the edge is safe? Is there a way I could get further from it?

Are there any areas of my life I'm compromising in order to enjoy the honey in the carcass of worldliness? Is it worth the price?

Is there a godly warning in my life I'm not heeding? What can I do to get off the road of compromise and back in line with God's Word?

Is there someone in my life going the way of Samson? What would God want me to do as their friend?

SARDIS

14 | When the Great Physician Declares You Dead

MEET THE REAL JESUS AND HIS STRONGEST CONDEMNATION

All across this country, you can drive past mega-churches, hustling, bustling, busy places that are just humming. They are crowded, they are full of people, full of life—at least on the outside. And if you had been riding in a caravan passing through Sardis in the first century, you would have passed by that church and not perceived anything wrong with it. It was just humming, crowded, and apparently full of life.

But when Jesus writes to Sardis, He writes as the all-knowing One, the only One with the vantage point that He could see into their hearts and know their motives. Even though they had a thriving reputation, a name that they were alive, Jesus saw the inside, He held their very existence in His hands. If they didn't repent, He would come upon them unawares and snatch their lampstand away. He was right there in Sardis as they gathered to read His letter to the assembly, and He wasn't pleased.

Jesus introduces Himself in Revelation 1 as the High Priest, but when He comes to Sardis, He takes on one of the most important roles of the High Priest, the role of Chief Health Inspector. In the Old Testament, one job a priest had was to be the Center for Disease Control for the whole nation Israel. The priest was the one who looked at what the people ate, looked at where they lived, checked the condition of their skin, and declared them healthy or not. And when Jesus, the Health Inspector and Great Physician, comes to Sardis, He finds the worst spiritual health of any of His churches so far.

And to the angel of the church in Sardis write,

"These things says He who has the seven Spirits of God and the seven stars: 'I know your works, that you have a name that you are alive, but you are dead. Be watchful, and strengthen the things which remain, that are ready to die, for I have not found your works perfect before God. Remember therefore how you have received and heard; hold fast and repent. Therefore if you will not watch, I will come upon you as a thief, and you will not know what hour I will come upon you. You have a few names even in Sardis who have not defiled their garments, and they shall walk with me in white, for they are worthy. He who overcomes shall be clothed in white garments, and I will not blot out his name from the Book of Life; but I will confess his name before My Father and before His angels.

"'He who has an ear, let him hear what the Spirit says to the churches.'"

It had been just two generations since Pentecost, since the gospel had spread out from Jerusalem and founded this once-great church. But in just two generations, the church at Sardis had died. Jesus, the Great Physician, slipped into this church, knelt down and felt their pulse. Then, after He looked for vital signs, He notes in His report that this church is dead. It is no longer alive as a functioning body.

The same thing happened in colonial America. Those who came here to escape persecution were so grounded in their faith. They were so fervent in their love for the Lord, but they made what was called the Halfway Covenant, so that the children of believers could join the church in the hope that they too would embrace the ways of God.

Unfortunately, those children became mere church attenders. They went through the motions, they knew the right phrases, they could recite the facts of the gospel and they knew what their parents believed, but the gospel never went the eighteen inches from their heads to their hearts. They knew the facts but never embraced the faith, and by the time of the great revivals, the church was so populated by unbelievers, that Jonathan Edwards called the church a bunch of "sinners in the hands of an angry God," who were going to fall into the chasm of hell because they'd never been regenerated. That is what Jesus said happened to Sardis.

THE PATHWAY THAT LEADS TO DEATH: BEWARE OF EVER BEING LIKE THIS

The problem Jesus found in Sardis wasn't new. Cain grew up nearly in Paradise. He grew up with faithful parents telling him about the true God, but he departed and never looked back. Esau sold an eternally valuable spiritual inheritance for a brief moment of fleshly desire, and because he found no place for repentance, he missed the heavenly city. Balaam wanted to die the death of the righteous and get to heaven, but he lived the life of rebellion and went to hell instead. Judas lived with and walked beside and followed Jesus around for years, but only grew colder and harder by the year. Scripture is full of cautionary tales of those who profess Christ but never possessed Him.

Jesus spent His whole ministry bumping into lifeless religion, and He gave His greatest warnings to religious phonies. Perhaps the strongest warnings ever uttered came from our loving Savior whenever He came across those who only appeared to be righteous, but weren't, and His most graphic illustrations were about these Christian lookalikes. Starting in Matthew 7, Jesus gives seven warnings against ever being like this:

Warning 1: Beware of being a ravenous wolf dressed in sheep's clothing.

Being dressed in sheep's clothing means that on the outside, this person looks like they're listening to Jesus. "My sheep hear my voice," Jesus said, so this person looks like they've built their life on what characterizes a Christian, but they've only embraced those truths on the outside.

Jesus says, "Beware of false prophets, who come to you in sheep's clothing, but inwardly they are ravenous wolves."[170]

On the inside, where only Jesus can see, this is not a person who hungers and thirsts for righteousness. They don't hunger for the Word of God or for Christ. When Jesus looks on the inside, He sees that they are ravenous, driven by their own hungers. They're dressed like a sheep, but inwardly they're a wolf, and Jesus says no matter what they look like on the outside, eventually what is on the inside will come out, and "you will know them by their fruits."

Warning 2: Beware of being a fruitless tree waiting to be cut down and burned in the fire.

Jesus says, "Every tree that does not bear good fruit is cut down and thrown into the fire."[171] Remember who's speaking here? This is Jesus. The kind, compassionate, Jesus. And He's threatening to cut people down and burn them.

A large chunk of Christendom really doesn't like this verse. They don't like to think that Jesus would ever say if there isn't a changed life, then you'll be thrown into the fire. But Jesus says if you don't bear good fruit, that's exactly what happens—you're cut down and burned.

Does that sound positive? Does that sound like you'll make it to heaven as some kind of second-class citizen? Jesus says if you haven't been saved from sin, you haven't been saved from hell either. "Thrown into the fire" is about as blunt as it gets. Jesus says there are two types of trees, bad ones, that get burned, and good ones that bear fruit. Like wolves in sheep's clothing, it's hard to tell by looking at the outside. You can't tell the difference between good trees and bad trees just by what orchard they're in or what the bark looks like or how healthy the leaves appear to be. "You will know them by their fruit." That's the only way to tell. If you don't bear good fruit, you're a bad tree. Period.

---

170 Matthew 7:15–16
171 Matthew 7:19

Warning 3: Beware of being a shocked church worker who never really knew Jesus.

"Many will say to Me in that day, 'Lord, Lord, have we not prophesied in Your name, cast out demons in Your name, and done many wonders in Your name?'" But Jesus says, "Not everyone who says to Me, 'Lord, Lord,' shall enter the kingdom of heaven."[172]

Jesus warns against being someone who identified with the visible work of God on earth, but they never had God do a work in their own hearts. They declared the truths of God in the name of Jesus, but that truth never made it from their head to their heart. Like Sardis, these people have a name that they are alive, but when Jesus sees them standing before Him, He'll declare them dead just as He did in Revelation 3.

Isaiah 29:13 says, "these people draw near with their mouths and honor Me with their lips, but have removed their hearts far from me." That was Israel, that was the Pharisees, that was Sardis, and that's what's present today.

In every generation God has had to pronounce judgment against certain people who have associated closely with Him, but weren't really His. On the day of judgment, many will stand before God who worked in the church, who preached in His name, even those who cast out demons and did miracles. They will call Him, Lord, Lord, but will be shocked to find out that Jesus doesn't recognize them as His.

Warning 4: Beware of being a house built on the sand only to be swept away to destruction.

"Everyone who hears these sayings of Mine, and does not do them, will be like a foolish man who built his house on the sand. The rain descended, the floods came, and the winds blew and beat on that house; and it fell. And great was its fall."[173]

Jesus identifies this person as someone "who hears these sayings of Mine." These are not pagans. These are those who are sitting in church every week, listening to the message, and looking so good for that one hour on Sunday. They can sing, they can teach, they know all the right answers,

---

172 Matthew 7:22, 21
173 Matthew 7:26–27

but they never knew Christ, personally, intimately, savingly. You can hear what He says, but if there's no change in your life, if you can hear and do nothing about it, then Jesus says you're a house built on the sand and you will fall.

Warning 5: Beware of being a weed gathered from a grain field only to be cast into a bonfire.

Jesus says the kingdom of heaven is like grain planted in a grain field. Until the harvest time, you can't tell which plants are the wheat and which plants are the weeds. But when it's harvest time and the fruit is produced, the weeds, the tares, are obvious. And Jesus says, "First gather together the tares and bind them in bundles to burn them, but gather the wheat into my barn."[174]

Beware of growing in a grain field, attending church with all the fruitful grain, and then being thrown into the fire as a weed. Not every plant bears as much fruit; not every believer produces as much fruit, but believers are fruitful. If you don't produce some amount of fruit, you're a weed.

John the Baptist said, "His winnowing fan is in His hand, and He will thoroughly clean out His threshing floor, and gather His wheat into the barn; but He will burn up the chaff with unquenchable fire."[175] This is not good. It's not even "saved yet as though by fire." This is eternal damnation. DO NOT BE LIKE THIS.

Warning 6: Beware of being an outwardly fancy cup but fouled with filth on the inside.

This week, my wife was away, and it's always tough when she's gone, especially when the girls are away too, because the only thing I know how to make for dinner is cereal. So we've pretty much been living off of cereal and coffee. And I got up early in the morning, reached into the dishwasher, and grabbed my favorite coffee mug. It looked clean on the outside, but it was still pretty dark, and I didn't see until I started to pour my coffee in that the inside was completely fouled—no one had turned on the dishwasher. And Jesus says, beware of ever being like this.

---

174 Matthew 13:30
175 Matthew 3:12

"Woe to you, scribes and Pharisees, hypocrites! For you cleanse the outside of the cup and dish, but inside they are full of extortion and self-indulgence."[176] The Pharisees would have made great neighbors. They had perfectly manicured lawns, they spoke nice, smelled nice, never hurt a fly. But notice what Jesus says about them in verse 25: "Inside they are full of extortion and self-indulgence." They were living the American dream. They spent their lives, their time, and their money on what they liked. They took advantage of everyone around them and indulged themselves on whatever they wanted.

It doesn't matter how nice the outside of the cup looks. My mug was all crusty from staying in that humid, warm place where bacteria grows mightily with nothing to stop it, because the dishwasher never got turned on. Jesus doesn't see people's nice-looking outsides. He looks on the inside. And when He looked at the Pharisees, what He saw was fouled. Sin was growing mightily with nothing to stop it.

Warning 7: Beware of being whitewashed on the outside but still a tomb full of rotting corpses.

Some of Jesus' harshest words were for those among His people who were merely pretending. Jesus spared no words to convey His utter contempt for religious charlatans with the false fruits of self-righteousness. Jesus warned that many of those closest to the things of God, like the temple-serving priests, like the Scripture-copying scribes, and like the Bible-teaching Pharisees, would one day find themselves cast into outer darkness.

"Woe to you, scribes and Pharisees, hypocrites! For you are like whitewashed tombs which indeed appear beautiful outwardly, but inside are full of dead men's bones and all uncleanness. Even so you also outwardly appear righteous to men, but inside you are full of hypocrisy and lawlessness."[177]

Jesus calls these phonies *hupo-crites*, which is a word that comes from the stage. In Greek theater, each actor would have two masks stuck up on top of sticks, one with a happy face, and one with a sad face, and when

176 Matthew 23:25
177 Matthew 23:27–28

they'd say their happy lines, they'd hold up the happy face, and when they'd say their sad lines, they'd hold up the sad face. The whole idea was that you'd speak everything through that mask, and you'd portray yourself as what the mask is, not what you really are. *Hupo-crites.*

The Pharisees looked alive, but behind the mask, they were dead. Their words came through the mask as "Lord, Lord," but inside, their hearts were far from Him. You can wear sheep's clothing, you can grow in the grain field, you can be a happy, mask-wearing church worker, but if you only profess Jesus Christ and don't possess Him, like Sardis, you will be declared dead, and those who don't repent will find themselves hearing Christ's strongest condemnation.

God wants us to know the difference between appearance and reality. In every generation, He finds those who merely profess Him, but don't possess Him. Old Testament pretenders like Cain, Esau, and Balaam, New Testament religious leaders like the Pharisees, and first-century churches like Sardis were living lives of hygienically sterile exterior holiness but were rotting with corrupted hearts inside and faced damnation. And Jesus is still bumping into lifeless religion masquerading as His living Church.

For so many dead, liberal, cold, and lifeless churches today, the gospel is in a coffin. These churches have a name, like the first church, or the reorganized church, or the St. Someone church, they have gorgeous facilities, but as the Great Physician kneels to feel their pulse, He pronounces them dead. Yes, there are a few believers in those places, like in Sardis, but those few believers are living in a morgue.

All across our country today, unsaved people are doing church, and they do it well. They're teaching Sunday School, singing on stage, preaching from our pulpits, but there's a warning here for church attenders, those who show up every Sunday and play church, but who are not true followers of Jesus: beware of the dangers of merely professing Jesus and never possessing Him.

Jesus' warning to those in Sardis, and to us today, is that you can live your whole life in the church, attending every service, looking vibrantly alive on the outside, and still be on a pathway that leads to death.

THE FOUR WORST WORDS YOU'LL EVER HEAR

Jesus warned Ephesus He'd remove their lamp, their church, from its lampstand. He told Smyrna the devil would throw them in prison and kill some of them. He told Pergamos He'd come against them Himself and fight against them. And He said He'd kill Jezebel's children with death if they didn't repent. But His most terrifying warning is not against misbehaving believers, but against well-behaved unbelievers. His strongest condemnation comes to Sardis, and to any who profess Him without possessing Him.

We spend so much of our time worrying about being the next terrorist target, being the next Oklahoma City or New York City, or being on a plane that gets hijacked, or having a prowler come in our home and do something terrible to us. But Jesus is the final word on terror and terrorism. He said, "Do not fear those who kill the body but cannot kill the soul. But rather fear Him who is able to destroy both soul and body in hell."

Nothing is worse, more horrifying, than an eternity without God. The most terrifying thing in the world is not a bomb, or a chemical weapon, or a biological attack. The scariest thing on earth is to enter eternity still covered in the phosphorous, burning napalm of sin.

What we need to proclaim in America today isn't that God has a wonderful plan for your life and you should live it to the fullest. What we should say is to fear Him who will cast your body and soul into hell if you're not possessing true life eternal and forgiveness of sins.

"Not everyone who says to Me, 'Lord, Lord' will enter the kingdom of heaven," Jesus says. But do you know who does? "He who does the will of My Father in heaven." Works without faith is useless. But faith without works is impossible.

How do you know if you're saved? This is the hint: Jesus says, "depart from me you who practice lawlessness." If you do the will of the Father in heaven, then you are one of those who were saved (and therefore changed) by grace, and you get in. If you practice lawlessness, you might have been one of those who professed Christ, but you never possessed Him, and Jesus will say His four horrible words of Matthew 7:23, "I never knew you."

Counterfeit Christians can live their whole lives in the church, professing Christ, but they're plowing ahead, practicing lawlessness, unashamed and just putting on a good show on the outside. They're up to their necks in worship, religion, bible, and God, but they never follow the Way, the Truth never gets from their head to their heart, and when Jesus checks for a pulse, He finds no Life in them. And Jesus says beware of ever being like this.

If you got hit by a bus today, or if your town really is the next New York City, or your next plane ride ended by crashing into a building, what would you face when you stand before God? Does Jesus know you? Will He confess to His Father and before His angels, this is so and so, who I bought with my own blood. This one's mine. Or will He say, sorry, I don't know you?

Those Who Profess and Do Not Possess

Jesus tells His disciples a story of ten bridesmaids waiting for the bridegroom to come in Matthew 25. Five were wise and brought oil for their lamps. Five were foolish and forgot. When the bridegroom came, the foolish asked to borrow some oil, but there wasn't enough to share. Salvation is personal and non-transferable. You can't get some of it from your believing spouse or your believing children or your believing friends in church. Jesus doesn't recognize people in groups. He recognizes you personally, or He doesn't recognize you at all.

There are only two ways to face Jesus: prepared and unprepared, and true believers don't just carry a pretty lamp and dress like a bridesmaid and appear to be waiting for the bridegroom. They're the ones actually ready, the ones with oil in their lamps, not just empty words through a mask, but those who possess the power of an endless life.

Jesus' message to Sardis is simple: You can mechanically go through all the motions of Christianity and not have the power of an endless life. You can be like one of those five foolish bridesmaids, unprepared and asleep.

Sardis had a big name but no life. They were as dead as last week's cut flowers, cold and lifeless. They were walking corpses, acting, thinking, and responding just like all those dead-in-their-trespasses-and-sins lost people around them. Like an old campfire that is cold and gray, when Jesus stirred around in the ashes, He found a few embers that still glowed with life, but the rest were dead, cold, and lifeless.

The church was populated by unregenerate, unbelieving, lost people, and they were standing in the most dangerous position on the planet—right inside the sanctuary of the church, thinking their outward religion would save them when all the while they were facing eternal condemnation.

The church can't dispense salvation. The church doesn't save. Being a member of an organization or a denomination doesn't make you a citizen of heaven. Only Jesus can. And while those in Sardis were intimately familiar with the church, they'd never truly met Jesus.

The church can't save, but Jesus can. And it's not too late. So Jesus calls them to repent, and to remember.

What You Received and Heard

"Remember therefore how you have received and heard." Spiritually dead or not, Sardis had received something special. They were right in that area of Asia Minor where over half the New Testament was sent, where every letter was circulated, where God's Word had spread, and they had heard something life-giving.

There's death and there's life. There's darkness and there's light. There's the kingdom of Satan, and there's the kingdom of God. And only Jesus can take you from one to the other. So let's do a self-diagnostic. God commands us, "examine yourselves as to whether you are in the faith. Test yourselves."[178]

Are you dead in your trespasses and sins like most of the so-called believers in Sardis, or alive in Christ? How do you know? Remember what you've received and heard. Sardis had received and heard the same things every other church had been receiving, from Peter, from Paul, from John, and from Jesus Himself: the facts of the gospel.

Jesus lived. That's history. Jesus died. That's theology. But when I believe that Jesus died and took my sins on Himself on the cross, that's salvation. And when what Jesus did for me in the past begins to change me in the present, that's sanctification. Those are the facts. Nonnegotiables.

Hearing the facts, though, isn't good enough. Any Christian look-alike can recite the facts. How many churchgoing lost people have no problem taking you through the Romans Road or a list of verses on salvation?

---

178 2 Corinthians 13:5

Knowing the facts puts you at the same level as the demons who also believe, and tremble.[179]

So Jesus' next instruction to Sardis is "hold fast and repent."

Repentance is a change of mind that leads to a change of behavior. When those facts make it from your head to your heart, when you put your faith, your trust, in Jesus Christ, in what He did on the cross, to save you forever, then in that moment, you are made alive, and your life begins to change.

First the facts, then the faith. Most people assume there will be some sort of feeling afterward. But how many people lie awake at night worried they're not going to heaven because they don't feel saved?

That's the problem with one segment of Christianity that bases everything on feelings. Historically, there are many believers who never felt saved. The facts come first, and faith is based on those facts, but the feelings may or may not come. Jesus doesn't call us to go back to what we felt the day we walked the aisle or the how clean we felt the day we were baptized. He says to go back to what you received and heard, to go back to the facts of the gospel. Have you accepted those facts as true, put your trust in the gospel you've heard? Do you have faith based on those facts? If you do, then Jesus makes you a promise: "I will not blot out [your] name from the Book of Life; but I will confess [your] name before My Father and before His angels."

Our faith isn't in the words we prayed or the certificate of baptism on our wall or the warm fuzzy feelings we have when we're singing on Sunday morning. Our faith is in the fact of Jesus Christ. His death, His burial and resurrection, and that He did it *for me.* All the facts of salvation are right here in God's Word. They've never changed, they're not locked away in Latin or veiled behind metaphoric language. They're very clear, and they're in God's Word that you hold in your hand. We agree with God about our sin, we confess our need of Him, and we cry out to God for salvation.

Faith follows the facts. Feelings don't have to follow faith, but sanctification does. Do you want to know for sure you're saved? Then ask yourself, am I being sanctified? Can you see an increase in your response to Christ's holiness and a decrease in your response to the flesh?

179 James 2:19

Jesus says if you've never been saved from sin, you've never been saved from hell. Not that we don't sin after we're saved, but that we're saved from the utter, dominating, enslaving power of sin in our lives. Jesus says, "Therefore if the Son makes you free, you shall be free indeed."[180]

If Jesus makes us free, we are no longer enslaved to sin. No longer ruled by the lust of the flesh, the lust of the eyes, the pride of life. Still a sinner, but no longer under the power of sin. The devil "does not come except to steal, and to kill, and to destroy. I [Jesus] have come that they may have life, and that they may have it more abundantly."[181]

All the things that used to characterize us before we were saved no longer characterize us. When we were still of our father, the devil, we were murderous, we were lustful, we were a liar. But when we have Jesus, we follow the Way, we know the Truth, we live the Life.

The most important decision you could ever make is to follow Jesus, not just to claim His name and attend His church, but to possess the power of the endless life Jesus offers. And the most important assurance you can have is that you truly belong to Him. Beware of professing Him without ever possessing Him.

A believer in Christ from the Reformation carved this poem into the Lutheran Cathedral in Lubeck, Germany:

> Thus speaketh Christ our Lord to us,
> You call Me master and obey Me not,
> You call Me light and see Me not,
> You call Me the way and walk Me not,
> You call Me life and live Me not,
> You call Me wise and follow Me not,
> You call Me fair and love Me not,
> You call Me rich and ask Me not,
> You call Me eternal and seek Me not,
> If I condemn thee, blame Me not.

---

180 John 8:36
181 John 10:10

RESPOND to Truth

If someone caught a drive-by look at my life, would they call me alive? Would Jesus, who sees into the heart?

Can I recite the facts of the gospel? Have I put my faith in those facts, or in the words of the prayer I prayed and the date I walked the aisle?

Jesus says when I hear His words and don't act on them, I'm like a house built on sand. What have I heard from Jesus in His Word that I'm not acting on?

According to Jesus, what is the proof of salvation? (John 15:1–8)

What does fruit look like? (John 4:35–36; Galatians 5:22–23; Ephesians 5:9; Philippians 1:9–11; Colossians 1:3–12; Hebrews 13:15)

What can I do in my life today to cultivate the fruit of righteousness?

Christ's Call to Every Believer: Stay Awake

15

UN-SCALABLE, UNASSAILABLE, AND OVERCONFIDENT

If you read the John MacArthur Study Bible, he says that the church at Sardis was populated with unbelievers and just a few true believers who "have not defiled their garments." The editors of the ESV Study Bible say Sardis was full of believers, but they were sick, in a coma, near death, but still capable of responding to Christ's call.

So there are two interpretations: unbelievers pretending to be believers, or believers acting like unbelievers. The first one, we already looked at. Those are the wolves in sheep's clothing, tares among wheat. They're clean and pristine on the outside—they look alive—but dirty and filthy on the inside of the cup—Jesus kneels down beside them, checks their pulse and declares them dead.

But the other way to look at this passage is that these are believers who have fallen so far from where they ought to be, who are living so much like the unregenerate unbelievers around them, that for all intents and purposes, they might as well be dead.

These are people who have been brought from darkness to light, from the kingdom of Satan to the kingdom of God. They have been made alive in Christ as Ephesians 2 talks about, bought-and-paid-for saints, slaves of God.

But they're acting in such opposition to God that they look more like His enemies than His slaves, and we've already seen from the church at Thyatira what Jesus does with His people when they begin to act like unbelievers.

But either way you look at it, the message is the same and the warning is clear. Whether these "dead" Sardians were believers or not, there is a message to believers here, and Jesus wants everyone who has an ear to hear it. Wake up.

REVELATION 3:1–6

And to the angel of the church in Sardis write,

"These things says He who has the seven Spirits of God and the seven stars: 'I know your works, that you have a name that you are alive, but you are dead. Be watchful, and strengthen the things which remain, that are ready to die, for I have not found your works perfect before God. Remember therefore how you have received and heard; hold fast and repent. Therefore if you will not watch, I will come upon you as a thief, and you will not know what hour I will come upon you. You have a few names even in Sardis who have not defiled their garments, and they shall walk with me in white, for they are worthy. He who overcomes shall be clothed in white garments, and I will not blot out his name from the Book of Life; but I will confess his name before My Father and before His angels.

"He who has an ear, let him hear what the Spirit says to the churches.'"

Sardis was built up on top of a thousand foot high cliff. It was completely sheer, un-scalable, going straight up like a skyscraper, and the city was built like a castle right into the rock at the top. But Sardis, completely impenetrable, safe behind their unassailable walls, confident on top of their un-scalable cliff, had been defeated twice in history. And both times, they were defeated the exact same way.

History tells us that the enemy was camped across from Sardis, watching the cliff, looking for a way in. A soldier would sit up on top of the wall and keep watch, but one day, he accidentally dropped his helmet, and it bounced all the way down the cliff. So the enemy watched as that soldier walked down a tiny, little, narrow pathway on the face of the cliff, all the way down to the bottom, picked up his helmet, and climbed back up and sat on the wall again.

So all the enemy had to do was wait for dark, climb up the same way that soldier had, up that nearly invisible pathway, and take the city. And when they reached the castle, they found Sardis's soldiers, but they weren't keeping watch up on the wall. They weren't guarding the city. They weren't being vigilant. The enemy found them asleep in the guardhouse.

And Jesus says that Sardis, as a church, has fallen asleep on the job. "I know your works," He says, "that you have a name that you are alive, but you are dead. Be watchful, and strengthen the things which remain, that are ready to die, for I have not found your works perfect before God. Therefore if you will not watch, I will come upon you as a thief, and you will not know what hour I will come upon you."

Both times Sardis was overrun, it was because the guards were asleep on the job, and Jesus warns that it's going to happen again if they don't wake up. This time, He would be the one coming like a thief, and they'd be caught unaware and unprepared, because as a church, they'd become so comfortable and overconfident that they failed to stay awake.

Jesus' Five-Fold Appeal to the Spiritually Lethargic

Jesus' letter to Sardis is a short one, but it has more imperatives in it than any of the other six letters. And in this short letter, Jesus gives a five-fold appeal to the spiritually lethargic of Sardis and to anyone else with an ear to hear.

But these five commands are not given the way you'd give an order to a group. You know when you get a group email, and it's really more for the other people, so you just file it away in your bottomless pit of Google storage space? This is not that.

Jesus doesn't give a general suggestion to the whole church. These are commands, and they're personally addressed. Jesus is singling each person out individually, and each imperative could really be translated with the word "you" in front of it. *You* be watchful. *You* strengthen. *You* remember. The best way to understand how pointed these commands are would be if there was a finger attached to each one, pointing, singling you out from the crowd, kind of like the Uncle Sam Wants You posters. *You* hold fast. *You* repent.

And the first of Jesus' commands to the church at Sardis is you be watchful. This is His most often repeated positive command in all the New Testament, and it's a call to spiritual vigilance. Sardis had the gospels. They had the epistles. They had Christ's call to stay awake repeated over and over, and now He was singling each person out and personally applying His call to each one of them. And by saying, "He who has an ear, let him hear," He's singling out each of us as well.

Christ's next appeal is also in verse 2: "Strengthen the things which remain, that are ready to die, for I have not found your works perfect before God." "Strengthen" is actually a building term. The way they built their aqueducts back then, they'd have the duct for carrying water, then they'd strengthen it from both sides. Even today, you can find aqueducts from the first century that still work, that still carry water, because they were strengthened, reinforced, built up on either side, exactly the way that Jesus uses this word.

Do you know how you can strengthen your spiritual life? To build it up on either side so that it doesn't falter? One two-fold reinforcement is the spiritual discipline of fasting and prayer. Fasting is giving up something I want, something I desire, and putting my body in its place, saying that I am not in control. The other side of that is prayer. Prayer is putting God in His place, saying that He is in control. Putting God in His rightful place on one side, putting my body in its place on the other, like two supports on either side of an aqueduct. That's the word strengthen.

Third: "Remember therefore how you have received and heard."

Did you know there's a striking resemblance between the first-century church of Sardis and the twenty-first-century church today? Sardis was a second-generation church, full of second-generation believers. They'd never met Jesus walking around on earth. They didn't have the apostles filling their pulpits, speaking God's Word and explaining it to them. They had the same thing we have—God's written, inspired Word.

Do you realize that Jesus could have spoken this message to Sardis Himself? Instead of coming to Patmos, He could have walked into Sardis, stood at their pulpit, and spoken to them directly. He could have sent John there personally, had the last of the apostles stand before the congregation and verbally repeat the message Jesus gave him.

But He didn't. Jesus commanded John to write all this down. He doesn't communicate through the spoken word anymore. He is declaring to Sardis, and to us, that this is how we have contact with the Living Word—through the written Word.

That is the most striking truth from any of these seven letters, that God communicates to us through the written Word. We're growing away from that. More and more, people don't memorize the Word of God. They don't study the Word of God. They memorize principles from the Word of God and they study messages about the Word of God, but so many churches no longer even center on the reading and proclamation of the Scripture. That's why the Church is weakening, like Sardis, because we're not filling ourselves with Spiritual nourishment. Man doesn't live by bread alone, but by every word that comes from the mouth of God.

That's why He gives them this command: remember. We don't need some new truth. We don't need a vision or a dream or a new, spoken, inspired word from God because we already have the inspired words of God. Peter says we have all we need for life and godliness. This is the last piece, the Book of the Revelation, finishing God's revelation of Himself through His Word. And what we need isn't some new doctrine or new revelation or new truth. We need to remember the old ones.

So instead of telling Sardis to find some new, revitalizing truth, Jesus tells Sardis to remember. To go back to what they already had, to what they'd already received and heard. Don't go building new structures—strengthen what you already have. Reinforce it, go deeper. Like Jeremiah says, seek the old paths again.[182]

Next, Jesus says, "Hold fast." That's the same word from chapter 1, *tereo*, to guard, to keep. Do you know how people understood "hold fast" in the first century? Like it's used in Acts 12:5, when Peter was "kept" in prison.

---

182 Jeremiah 6:16

He was bound to two soldiers with chains on both his wrists, and when an angel broke the chains and led him out, the soldiers were put to death in his place because they failed to "keep" him, to guard him. When Paul was imprisoned in Philippi, and an earthquake broke open the prison so he could have gotten away, his jailer nearly killed himself because he was afraid of what would happen. He had failed to "keep" them, to hold them fast.[183]

When you hold something fast, you do it like your life depends on it. Jesus tells each person in the church of Sardis individually, *you* hold fast. Like there's an enemy at the gate, ready to pounce if you fall asleep, like Jesus Himself is right at the door, about to open it and you want to be found faithful. Like your life depends on it, because spiritually, it does.

And finally, the last command of Jesus' five-fold appeal to the spiritually lethargic: "repent." Whether you're an unbeliever just pretending or a believer falling asleep on the job, there's only one right response to Christ's message. A change of mind that leads to a change in behavior. Repent.

In these five commands is a diagnostic for Sardian Christians: God hates profession without possession. Are you pretending? A true believer doesn't habitually practice sin. A counterfeit believer can't help but practice sin, because he doesn't have God's new nature within him. But God didn't write these commands so we could check on other people. They were inspired so we may examine ourselves.

Do I have the divine nature inside me or am I merely pretending? If I do have the divine nature, do I cultivate it by daily Bible reading and prayer? Is there an unconfessed sin that's defiling me? Am I willing to confess and forsake it? Do I allow my old nature to control my thoughts and desires or does the divine nature rule me? When temptation comes, do I play with it or do I flee from it?

Jesus doesn't approve of just maintenance. It's life and growth and fruit, or nothing. Are you growing? God wants to see you watching, washed in white, written in eternity, waiting to hear Him call your name. Are you ready?

Repent isn't just Christ's call to Sardis. It was His call to every church on His inspection tour that failed to meet His approval. It's His call to

---

183 Acts 16:23

every church in every century, and it isn't just to a church. It has a finger attached, pointing straight at you. If you, like Sardis, have fallen asleep, it's time to repent.

Asleep on the Wall

The city of Sardis had every strategic advantage against an invading army. They were un-scalable, unassailable, and all they needed to do was to stay awake and they would have never been defeated.

The church in Sardis had every spiritual advantage. They possessed the Spirit, they had access to the power of an endless life, the overflowing of the Spirit available to tap into at any time. All they had to do was stay awake and they would have been as 1 John 2:28 says, confident and unashamed before Him at His coming.

Spiritually un-scalable, unassailable, and overconfident, Sardis had fallen asleep on the wall. And Christ's call to every believer, in Sardis, and in our churches today, is stay awake. "If you will not watch," Jesus says, "I will come upon you as a thief."[184]

Dead-in-their-sins, unregenerate Christian counterfeits are one thing, but to be spiritually sleeping on the job doesn't sound as serious. After all, we're talking about Christians, saved people here. If Jesus had returned, He might have found them inactive, but they were at least written in the book.

More than any other command repeated to His people, Jesus wants His own to keep watch, stay awake, to be vigilant. This isn't just a warning against being in the middle of something unimportant when Jesus comes back. This isn't like being caught off guard by a surprise party you weren't ready for. He is warning us against being caught living in direct disobedience to the Holy Son of God who's coming back. Jesus doesn't equate Sardis's spiritual condition with sleep. He equates it with death.

Sardis was so weak, so sick, so close to being completely dead that they were in spiritual cardiac arrest, spiritually comatose. Whether the church was populated with unbelievers or simply believers who had become characterized by spiritual lethargy, they had become a church whose usefulness to God was one long beep and a flat line across a heart monitor. The church

---

184 Revelation 3:3

Jesus died for, effectively dead. It might not sound serious to us, but it's extremely important to the Savior who died for us, so important it's His most frequent call to believers.

CHRIST'S CALL TO SPIRITUAL VIGILANCE

When Jesus would come into a town, the demon-possessed would be terrified of Him, begging Him not to destroy them because of the power of God that was in Him. The crowds flocked to Him for miracles and they were amazed at the authority of His teaching. The Pharisees couldn't even stone Him because He would just walk away and they were left standing there not knowing what happened.

If anyone should have felt confident and unassailable, it should have been Jesus' disciples. If ever there was a group of people who shouldn't have needed to keep watch, it was the men who lived their lives in the shadow of God Almighty walking on earth.

But Jesus' warning to spiritual vigilance didn't start with Sardis. It started with His disciples, and with that command to stay awake comes three lessons.

Lesson 1: Live for Christ's Coming

In Matthew 24:36–44, Jesus is giving His disciples a seminar on prophecy, and He's describing the day He comes back for His people. No one knows the day or hour He'll come back, Jesus says, and just like in the days of Noah, when people were just merrily going along, living their lives, right up until it was too late, people will be caught unaware when Jesus comes back, too. "Watch therefore," He says, "for you do not know what hour your Lord is coming."

The word is *gregoreo*. Wake up. Keep watch. Stay vigilant. Don't fall asleep or, like a watchman asleep in the guardhouse, you'll be overrun.

This is Jesus' first lesson on watchfulness: Believers are to stay vigilant so that nothing keeps them from living for His coming. "But know this, that if the master of the house had known what hour the thief would come, he would have watched and not allowed his house to be broken into.

Therefore you also be ready, for the Son of Man is coming at an hour you do not expect."

Believers are called to live every day as if it were our last. That doesn't mean we don't plan for the future. It doesn't mean we quit our jobs and spend every moment going door to door evangelizing. It doesn't mean we skip the tedious, menial tasks of taking care of the house or ourselves because who wants to be caught brushing their teeth when Jesus comes? Living like each day is our last is to be actively doing what Jesus left us to do, and that's Jesus' second lesson on spiritual watchfulness.

Lesson 2: Follow the Master's Instructions

Believers are to go through life always awaiting their Master's return, always doing what He left them to do. Mark 13:32–37 says, "But of that day and hour no one knows, not even the angels in heaven, nor the Son, but only the Father. Take heed, watch and pray; for you do not know when the time is. It is like a man going to a far country, who left his house and gave authority to his servants, and to each his work, and commanded the doorkeeper to watch. Watch therefore, for you do not know when the master of the house is coming—in the evening, at midnight, at the crowing of the rooster, or in the morning—lest, coming suddenly, he find you sleeping. And what I say to you, I say to all: Watch!"

Jesus' constant imperative, His command to every believer, is to watch for His return. But not to just passively keep an eye on the sky, but to actively be doing what He left us to do. You see, we aren't left here in the world to have fire insurance from hell and to have a fun life. We were left here as soldiers, as athletes, as farmers, as slaves of God, and we were left here with a job to do. And Jesus says if we don't watch, He will come and shut us down, because we must live out our calling to be effective for Him, and that's what He's left us in this world to do.

That's why Christians have always stuck out in every culture, because the Christians are not in step with everybody else. Everyone who's lost is living for what they can get, what they can experience, what they can eat, and their security. And the Christians aren't in step with that. They say, no, we're farmers and we've been left with a field to tend for God. We're soldiers, and we're left to guard against the wiles of the devil. We are servants, and we're left with specific tasks from God. We're not earth-dwellers. This world is not my home. I'm just passing through.

Lesson 3: Watch Out for Temptation

Jesus is in the garden of Gethsemane, He's about to go to the cross, He's sweating drops of blood in agony over what's about to happen, and He leaves His disciples to pray, and when He goes back to check on them, He finds them asleep. Three times. Three times He tells them to stay awake and pray and avoid temptation, and three times they fall asleep on the job.

Jesus' third lesson on watchfulness is that believers either watch out for the devil's temptations or get devoured by yielding to them. "Watch and pray, lest you enter into temptation. The spirit is willing, but the flesh is weak."

Christians don't have to run headlong into sin. They don't have to want sin and willingly embrace it to fall into it. The spirit is willing, wanting to do what's right, but the flesh is weak, and if we're not purposefully, intentionally, watchfully guarding against it, then sin will come and find us.

Sardis didn't purposefully run headlong off a cliff, they just failed to keep watch, and they'd drifted into a state of uselessness to God that so resembled the lost condition He found them in that when He inspected their church, He called them something usually reserved for unbelievers: dead.

The most disappointing state a believer can be in is being completely useless to the God who bought them. Jesus, who died to make them alive, found a church full of the walking dead. Jesus, who, more than any other command, told His people to stay awake, found Sardis asleep on the wall. Jesus came to give life and give it abundantly, and Sardis was living like they were still dead.

THE ENEMY AT OUR GATES

Spiritual vigilance isn't a quality of top-tier Christians or the exceptionally faithful. It's a command to all of us.

Jesus told Sardis to wake up or He'd return and catch them unawares, but He also warns of another danger. The Bible tells us that we have an

enemy waiting at our gates, watching our walls, and if we become spiritually lethargic, overconfident, and comfortable, the enemy will find a way
in. The devil is like a roaring lion seeking someone to devour and we are
commanded by Jesus Christ Himself to stay awake, to watch, to be vigilant,
so that we will not fall into temptation.

After Peter fell asleep three times when Jesus told him to stay awake,
he learned from his mistake. He understood the seriousness of Christ's
command, and how easy it is to drift into overconfidence and become useless to God. So Peter writes, "Be sober, be vigilant; because your adversary
the devil walks about like a roaring lion, seeking whom he may devour.
Resist him, steadfast in the faith."[185] Peter learned the hard way that if we
don't stay awake, we will be lured into temptation and sin that robs us of
our usefulness, effectiveness, and power.

Spiritual vigilance means we identify the enemy. When Pergamos failed
to do this, they welcomed the lies of Satan with open arms. When Thyatira
failed to identify the enemy, they ended up with a false teacher leading their
church services. Paul said to the elders at Ephesus, "For I know this, that after
my departure savage wolves will come in among you, not sparing the flock.
Also from among yourselves men will rise up, speaking perverse things, to
draw away the disciples after themselves. Therefore watch, and remember that
for three years I did not cease to warn everyone night and day with tears."[186]

We are called to watch out for the permeating evil of false doctrine
and to be on guard against false teaching. The easiest way for the enemy to
defeat us is to go unnoticed among us and destroy us from the inside. The
devil doesn't go around wearing horns and carrying a pitchfork. He dresses
up like an angel of light. And his servants disguise themselves as apostles of Christ. That's why Paul says, "if even we or an angel from heaven"[187]
preaches a different gospel, he is to be accursed.

"Do not be deceived," he says to the Corinthians, "'Evil company corrupts good habits.' Awake to righteousness, and do not sin, for some do not
have the knowledge of God. I speak this to your shame."[188]

---

185 1 Peter 5:8–9
186 Acts 20:29–31
187 Galatians 1:8
188 1 Corinthians 15:33–34

Spiritual vigilance also means we hold our ground. "For you were once darkness, but now you are children of light in the Lord. Walk as children of light, finding out what is acceptable to the Lord. And have no fellowship with the unfruitful works of darkness, but rather expose them. Therefore He says, 'Awake, you who sleep, arise from the dead, and Christ will give you light.'"[189]

We're supposed to find out what's pleasing to God, to have no friendship with the works of darkness. "Watch, stand fast in the faith, be brave, be strong," Paul says.[190] Draw the line, don't let the enemy in. Hold your ground. Protect what you have and hold the line. Don't compromise with sin, don't let it into your house. When you hear a noise in your house, if you're a father, you wake right up. You are on duty. That's what Paul means when he says "awake." You're immediately awake, ready to protect your house. You're not about to let anything dangerous in.

Spiritual vigilance also means we call in reinforcements. When Jesus called His disciples to spiritual vigilance in the garden of Gethsemane, He gave them two commands: "watch and pray." Colossians 4:2 says, "Continue earnestly in prayer, being vigilant in it." Prayer is acknowledging that I can't fight the battle on my own. Only with the power of God in me, the Holy Spirit overflowing me, the promises of Christ behind me can I obey Christ's call to stay awake and guard against temptation.

Both My Armors

One of the sweetest emails I ever received was from a Special Forces unit in Afghanistan. One of the soldiers had heard me preach in California and bought one of my books, and he had taken it with him all the way to Afghanistan, even with the weight limit of what he could carry. And he was living in one of those valley outposts where they get mortared every day, and he sent me a picture of his bunk. His body armor that he wore all the time was there, and propped up against that was my book. It was tattered and torn up from being dragged all over the desert, and there was his Bible propped up against that. And he wrote in his email, "Pray for me, that I will wear both my armors."

189 Ephesians 5:8–14
190 1 Corinthians 16:13

Romans 13:11–14 says, "And do this, knowing the time, that it is high time to awake out of sleep; for now our salvation is nearer than when we first believed. The night is far spent, the day is at hand. Therefore let us cast off the works of darkness, and let us put on the armor of light. Let us walk properly, as in the day, not in revelry and drunkenness, not in lewdness and lust, not in strife and envy. But put on the Lord Jesus Christ, and make no provision for the flesh in regard to its lusts."

Do you know what watchfulness is? Spiritual watchfulness? It's the realization that we are being mortared every day. It's the awareness that we are in a battle, and we need to put on our armor, the armor of light, the armor of God, that we need to put on the Lord Jesus Christ, because our lives depend on it.

Bullets and mortar shells and bombs can kill our earthly bodies, but the Bible says there's a more dangerous enemy out there. Ephesians 6:12–13 says, "We do not wrestle against flesh and blood, but against principalities, against powers, against the rulers of the darkness of this age, against spiritual hosts of wickedness in the heavenly places. Therefore take up the whole armor of God, that you may be able to withstand in the evil day, and having done all, to stand." And then Paul tells us what we are to put on, "truth," "the breastplate of righteousness," "the gospel of peace," the "shield of faith," the "helmet of salvation," and the "sword of the Spirit, which is the Word of God."

What truth are we supposed to put on? Not some new truth. Don't prowl around always looking for some new truth. If it's really new, it's probably not true, because there's nothing new under the sun. The Bible we hold in our hands, that is the forever-settled-in-heaven Book. Jesus said *I* am the truth. That's what we guard ourselves with.

Next, we are to put on righteousness, but not our own righteousness. That's like wearing filthy rags, not very safe in a warzone. First Corinthians 1:30 says Jesus is our righteousness and our sanctification. Because He justified us in the past, we can live sanctified in the present. If we try to manufacture some kind of righteousness of our own, it will fail, because only Jesus can make us holy and righteous. That's why we must put on the Lord Jesus Christ. He is our armor.

Then we put on our feet the gospel of peace, the good news—not the terrible news, that after 10,000 years in purgatory, we still might possibly make it to heaven—but the good news that Jesus gives. He didn't come to steal and kill and destroy. That's the devil's job. Jesus came to give life and life abundant, the life overflowing with the Spirit, the life of the spiritually undefeated.

The shield of faith is next, faith that is based, not on feelings, or on an experience, or on a service, or on the water we were baptized in, but on the facts of the gospel, the good news we've already put on. That's what our faith is in, and with that faith as our shield, Ephesians 6:16 says, we can extinguish the flaming arrows of the evil one.

Did you know that when Roman soldiers were going up against the enemy, they'd soak their wooden shields in water first? That way when the enemy shot flaming arrows at them, the arrows would hit and just fizzle out, because there was nothing there to burn. That is what our faith should be, soaked in the living water that Jesus says He is, the water that never leaves us thirsty, the power of His endless life that is available to us, and when we overflow with the Spirit, the enemy can't destroy our usefulness to God like he was doing in Sardis.

We put on the helmet of salvation, Paul says, the salvation that can never be taken away from us, that we can never lose, a helmet we can't accidentally drop off a cliff. Our salvation is secured by Jesus. He keeps it, He *tereos* it, because our life depends on it. And lastly, we pick up the sword of the spirit, which is the Word of God.

Did you know that's the only offensive weapon in our arsenal? We don't get a whole armory full of RPGs and rocket launchers and everything else. We get one sword, the Word of God that we've hidden in our hearts, that we carry with us, that we have on the tips of our tongues ready to fight against error and falsehood and sin and the devil. And we can either have the couple verses we memorized as a kid like a little thumbtack to fight the devil with, or we can have a Roman broadsword of the Word of God, like the sword of Rome that conquered the world.

Do I seem obsessed with the reading of God's Word? That's because the devil is out there, at my gates, watching my walls, and I want to have the strongest, biggest, undefeatable sword at my disposal, all the Scripture I can possibly carry.

I don't want to be overconfident. I don't want to fall asleep. I want to be ready, doing my job until Jesus comes back and catches me watching for His return, doing what He left me to do.

Throughout Scripture, the call is clear. Jesus called His disciples, His church, His bought-and-paid-for saints at Sardis, and everyone with an ear to hear to spiritual vigilance, a finger pointing right at each one. He calls His people to stay spiritually vigilant so that nothing keeps us from living for His coming, to live every day like it was our last, to go through life always awaiting our master's return, always doing what He asked us to do, to watch out for the devil's temptations or we'll get devoured by yielding to them. He calls us to identify the enemy, to hold our ground, to call in reinforcements through prayer.

And if we as His people stay awake, watching, keeping guard, then we will be found with undefiled garments and one day we will walk with Him in white as He promised the faithful few of Sardis.

Heavenly Father, thank You that we are clothed in Christ's righteousness. Thank You that we are written down, never to be blotted out of Your Book. Thank You that we are going to be confessed before You. And may we go through life realizing this world is not our home and we need to be ready every day for it to be our last day, the day we see You face-to-face. Stir our hearts to that end. In the precious name of Jesus and for His glory alone, we pray. Amen.

RESPOND to Truth

How do I equip myself with the armor of God? (Truth—Philippians 4:8. Righteousness—Matthew 5:6; Philippians 3:9. Gospel—Romans 1:16. Faith—Romans 10:17. Salvation—Galatians 2:20. The Word of God—Psalm 119:11)

What temptations am I susceptible to? How can I arm myself against them?

How can I obey Christ's command to strengthen and deepen my Christian walk?

What can I do today to "hold fast" to what I've received and heard?

What did Jesus leave me here to be? (2 Timothy 2:3–6). What did Jesus leave me here to do?

If Jesus returned today, would He find me living in light of His return, doing what He called me to do, and on guard against the devil? What can I remember, hold fast to, and put into practice today so that He will?

PHILADELPHIA

16 | How to Meet Christ's Absolute Approval

The letter to the church at Philadelphia teaches us perhaps the most astounding truth of all seven letters. That it is possible for an individual, and for an entire church, to go through the scrutinizing, penetrating, omniscient, holy sight of God, and for Him to find nothing wrong.

Think about that. The church in Philadelphia faced the same temptations as every other church Christ wrote to. They were surrounded by immorality like Ephesus. They faced the same fears and persecution as Smyrna. They had to deal with false teaching just like Pergamos did. They, like Thyatira, were living in the midst of an incredibly worldly culture. And they were just as removed from the first-hand teaching of the apostles as Sardis.

But Philadelphia received nothing but approval from Jesus Christ. Every other church has an example of what not to do. Even Christ's command to Smyrna, the church that was faithful in suffering, was a negative: fear not. Don't do this. But Philadelphia, even with all the same temptations, has none of the condemnation.

Philadelphia is the model church, the one that Jesus holds up as an example to us: live like this, be like this church. If you model your life after this church, you'll be doing well. Let's take a look at the church Jesus says is doing exactly what He wants them to do.

Revelation 3:7–13

And to the angel of the church in Philadelphia write,

"These things says He who is holy, He who is true, 'He who has the key of David, He who opens and no one shuts, and shuts and no one opens': 'I know your works. See, I have set before you an open door, and no one can shut it; for you have a little strength, have kept My word, and have not denied My name. Indeed I will make those who are of the synagogue of Satan, who say they are Jews and are not, but lie—indeed I will make them come and worship before your feet, and to know that I have loved you. Because you have kept My command to persevere, I also will keep you from the hour of trial which shall come upon the whole world, to test those who dwell on the earth. Behold, I am coming quickly! Hold fast what you have, that no one may take your crown. He who overcomes, I will make him a pillar in the temple of My God, and he shall go out no more. I will write on him the name of My God and the name of the city of My God, the New Jerusalem, which comes down out of heaven from My God. And I will write on him My new name.

"'He who has an ear, let him hear what the Spirit says to the churches.'"

"I know your works." Period. Do you know what that makes me say? What an amazing church. They weren't given anything extra. They had the same epistles, the same gospels, the same Word of God that every other church had. They had the same temptations, the same struggles, the same pressures, but Jesus says, "I know your works." This church, Jesus does not condemn, He does not correct, He does not rebuke, He does not point out anything they're doing wrong. There isn't a "nevertheless." There's no "but this I have against you." Only approval.

And then Jesus gives Philadelphia a very unique promise. He said He'd make them pillars that would never fall, never fail, never crack, and they'd rest forever in the presence of God. Jesus promises permanence. Rest. Security. Forever. Wow.

This is the most amazing letter of the seven. There are more promises, there are more blessings, and there are more insights about Jesus Christ than in any other letter. Everybody builds their life on something. You can build on a person or a philosophy or a religious system or a political system or you can build it around your career or your plans for the future, but you will build your life on something. And the church at Philadelphia had built their lives on the truths of this letter and built a church that met Jesus' absolute approval.

FOUR TRUTHS FOR A FOREVER-CHANGED LIFE

There aren't many truths that can change your life forever. You can learn a new skill, and it can change how you do things for a while as long as you remember it. You can learn a new fact and it might change how you think about things for a while, but there aren't a lot of things that truly change your life forever.

Jesus lists four. In this incredible letter to Philadelphia Jesus reintroduces Himself. He never just says, "Hi, I'm Jesus." He tells us again, each time, who He is, along with a description of what He does. And in Jesus' simple introduction to the church at Philadelphia we read four truths for a forever-changed life. These are the four truths that Philadelphia built their church and their lives on, and they were never the same.

Truth 1: He Who Is Holy

In the first five letters, Jesus kind of cuts and pastes His titles from chapter 1 to introduce Himself to a church. But for this special letter to Philadelphia, Jesus reaches all the way back to the Old Testament and imports some of the most powerful descriptions of the all-powerful, covenant-keeping God of Heaven, and that's how He introduces Himself.

The first thing He calls Himself is holy. I was in the Holy Land recently, and I was in a little marketplace and I bought this little dish of zatar. It's ground-up hyssop, like the psalm says, "purge me with hyssop and I shall be clean," you put it on your salad, it's biblical, and we were going to have Holy Land meals. But you know what it doesn't have? Preservatives.

I bought that little container of zatar, and someone had hand-written "zatar" on it with a sharpie, and I took it home and put it in my Holy Land tub under the bed and didn't take it out until I was packing for another trip, and when I opened that little dish, I found an entire life cycle of moths.

See, they hadn't just harvested the hyssop, they'd harvested a moth egg, put it all together in the container and called it zatar and sold it to me, and it had gone from egg to worm to cocoon to moth, and then laid more eggs, and there in my little container of zatar was an entire ecosystem of death.

That is not holiness. Holiness is like a Twinkie. You can buy one of those and keep it in a box under the bed for five years and take it out and it's just as fresh and soft and moist as if it just came out of the oven. They're still golden yellow and perfect five years later.

Everything on earth is like my little tub of zatar; it's corrupted. But Jesus says in Hebrews 7:26 He is holy, harmless, undefiled, separate from sinners. When He calls Himself "He who is holy," He is telling the Philadelphians that He is the only source of unpolluted, un-fallen, uncorrupted, un-blighted existence.

This is the only attribute of God that gets the ultimate emphasis. Remember that Jesus never calls Himself love, love, love. He is holy, holy, holy. So this letter is coming from the holy, holy, holy One from the holy, holy, holy place. If you read Revelation 5 and the description of heaven, this is what we'll be saying forever in heaven. This is the name that rings out in the throne room of the universe, the only name to get the ultimate emphasis.

How does this truth make for a forever-changed life? How does Jesus' holiness apply to me? Well, the Philadelphians got it, and they understood what to do with this truth from Peter's letter that was passed around this region. First Peter 1:15–16 says, "But as He who called you is holy, you also be holy in all your conduct, because it is written, 'Be holy, for I am holy.'"

We are called by Someone who is holy—uncorrupted, un-fallen, unpolluted. And that begins to change us, all the way down to our behavior. That word for "conduct" is also translated "behavior," or "way of life." When you believe right, you behave right, and the church at Philadelphia believed in a Jesus Christ who is holy, holy, holy. And that truth changed their behavior, their conduct, their way of life, forever.

Truth 2: He Who Is True

Jesus' most emphasized attribute goes hand in hand with His second title to the church at Philadelphia: He who is true.

In Revelation 6:10, the saints are crying out to the One who is "holy and true." This combination of holy, just or righteous and true is found throughout Revelation. In Revelation 15:3, they "sing the song of Moses, the servant of God, and the song of the Lamb, saying: 'Great and marvelous are Your works, Lord God Almighty! Just and true are Your ways, O King of the saints!'" "Even so, Lord God Almighty, true and righteous are Your judgments."[191] And then in Revelation 19:2, "True and righteous are His judgments."

Once Jesus says He is holy, just, righteous, to say He's true naturally comes next. He who is holy cannot lie. He who is uncorrupted cannot fail. He who is the only source of un-blighted existence is naturally the only source of absolute and unfailing truth in an uncertain world.

The word "true" is *alethinos*, which means it's genuine, the real thing, not counterfeit, like a piece of pure metal that stands the test. When you take a piece of gold jewelry to sell, they warn you before they test it that if it's not real gold, the acid they use will destroy it. You know what Jesus says? I stand the test. He is found to be *alethinos*, genuine, real, trustworthy, unfailing.

The Pharisees were professional talkers, but they never really said anything, and everybody knew it. But when Jesus spoke, Mark 1:22 says, the people were amazed. Why? They were hearing from the One who is true. The genuine article. He spoke as one having authority.

Jesus speaks truth, not as the scribes did, but as the last word. In today's world, there's always someone higher up on the food chain. If you don't like what they tell you in the aisle, you can go to the service desk. You don't like what they say there, you can go to the manager. The manager doesn't say what you like, you can write a letter to the stockholder's board. There's always a higher authority to go to. Not with Jesus. He's the final word.

You want to hear an absolutely life-changing truth? In a world of uncertainty, Jesus introduces Himself as the True One, the final word on everything, the ultimate authority.

---

191 Revelation 16:7

The Philadelphians, whose lives were uncertain, who faced persecution and losing their jobs, who faced lurking disasters, constant unknowns, and endless potential dangers, were built on the foundation of the True One, the Final Word on Everything, and it made them unshakable.

Truth 3: He Who Holds the Key

Here's where we really go back. "The Holy and True One" is all over Scripture, Old and New Testaments, but Jesus' next title is distinctly Old Testament.

Jesus introduces Himself as "He who has the key of David." In Revelation 22:16, He calls Himself the root and offspring of David. In Revelation 5:5, He says He is the root of David. What is that?

If you read carefully the 141 God-inspired chapters devoted to David in the Old Testament, you will see he consistently symbolizes the Person and the office of the Messiah. God made a promise to David that the Messiah would come through him. So when Jesus is called the Son of David, the root of David, the offspring of David, and here He holds the key of David, it all goes back to Him as the Messiah.

Messiah, or *meshiac* in Hebrew, was prophesied to be the embodiment and fulfillment of every promise God ever made. Every promise, kept, in the Person and office of the Messiah. So when Jesus says He's holding the key of David, He's reminding them that He is the Messiah, the promise-keeper, and the Promise kept.

But that's not all. To find the "key of David" we have to go back to Isaiah 22:22, where we meet a man named Shebna, who is introduced as the steward of the king of Judah. Everyone would have known what the king's steward was back then; they all knew what Jesus was talking about, and in the Old Testament times, the steward had three jobs.

Firstly, the steward served the king by dispensing the king's wealth. Investing the king's wealth, paying people, even honoring people with riches on occasion. It's kind of like what we see today with wealthier people. They don't go to the grocery store and buy things for themselves. They have someone else to go shopping for them. So as the steward, Shebna had the key to the king's wealth and he would distribute it as needed.

Secondly, the steward was the only person with access to the king's presence. If you wanted to see the king, you had to go through Shebna, and he'd look at the schedule, and Shebna, as the king's steward, would open the king's presence to you.

Finally, the steward displayed the king's power. This is what Joseph did in Genesis 41 for Pharaoh. He was Pharaoh's steward, his second-in-command. Pharaoh gave him the right to do things in his name, to display his power. This is the person who holds the key, and the steward to the king of Judah holds the key of David.

That's the key Jesus says He holds, the key that opens the treasuries of the King, that grants access to presence of the King, and that displays the King's power.

Shebna could only dispense the king's wealth in one place at one time, to one group of people at a time. But when Jesus says He holds the key to God's wealth, He can distribute it anywhere anytime, to all people at the same time. And God owns the cattle on a thousand hills. His wealth never runs out.

Shebna could only allow a few people at a time into the presence of the king and the king had only so much time. But when Jesus died on the cross, He opened access into the presence of God for everyone who believes, and when He tells the Philadelphians they will be pillars in the temple of God, He says they'll never have to leave. The everlasting presence of God is opened by that key.

Shebna had the power of the great king of Judah, but Jesus holds the power of almighty God. He is the final word. And when He opens a door to God's power, no one can shut it.

Truth 4: He Who Opens and No One Can Shut

Jesus is the fulfillment of all of God's promises, but truth number four is God's most amazing promise. "'He who opens and no one shuts, and shuts and no one opens.' See, I have set before you an open door, and no one can shut it."[192]

When Jesus does something, that's it. It can't be stopped, overturned, ruined, thwarted, or ended. When Jesus opens a door of blessing, it can't be shut. When Jesus opens a door of ministry, it can't be shut. Jesus is the One

192 Revelation 3:7–8

to stay in touch with when you want to see things happen. Jesus says there is a group of people in the city of Philadelphia who say they are Jews, but aren't, and He's going to open their hearts to the truth, and they are going to come and worship God at the feet of the believers in this church. That's one door that no one can shut.

But we also see in the gospels a string of events where we can see Jesus opening a door that no one can shut. But instead of announcing to His disciples, "I'm opening a door here, I'm using My key, no one can shut this door," He just abbreviates the whole thing by saying the word "never."

The first door Jesus opens is the door to eternal satisfaction. We see Jesus using His key and opening this door in John 4:14: "Whoever drinks of the water that I shall give him will never thirst," and again two chapters later in John 6:35. "I am the bread of life. He who comes to Me will never hunger, and He who believes in Me will never thirst." Jesus is the only one who can open the door to eternal satisfaction. He doesn't run out, He doesn't run dry. He fills us and offers eternal satisfaction that no one can take from us.

"Then Jesus spoke to them again, saying, 'I am the light of the world. He who follows Me shall not [same Greek word as "never"] walk in darkness, but have the light of life.'"

When Jesus opens the door to eternal light, no one can shut the door, not me, not somebody else. Do you know what hell is described as? The blackness of darkness forever. But the light Jesus gives can't be extinguished. It can't get snuffed out. You can't wander so far that He can't get you back. When Jesus calls Himself the light of the world and opens the door, we will never walk in darkness.

But the last door is the best one. Jesus opens the door to eternal life, and He says it four different ways. "Most assuredly, I say to you, if anyone keeps My word, he shall never see death." "If anyone keeps My word, he shall never taste death." "And I give them eternal life and they shall never perish." "And whoever lives and believes in Me shall never die."[193]

There is a whole segment of Christianity that believes Jesus can open the door of eternal life and I can shut it, or someone else can shut it on me. But Jesus says when He opens a door, it stays open. The apostle Paul put it

193 John 8:51–52; 10:28; 11:26

this way, "Neither death nor life, nor angels nor principalities nor powers, nor things present nor things to come, nor height nor depth, nor any other created thing, shall be able to separate us from the love of God which is in Christ Jesus our Lord."[194]

This is His most amazing promise. When Jesus opens the door of eternal life to us, no one, including us, can shut it. The devil comes to steal, to kill, and to destroy, but Jesus came, "that they may have life, and that they may have it more abundantly," and when Jesus opens the riches, the presence, and the power of God to us, He gives abundantly and in measures that last forever.

HOW TO BUILD A QUAKE-PROOF LIFE

Jesus says that Philadelphia is faithful because they have, verse 8, "a little strength," or "small faith." This isn't a rebuke. It's not Jesus saying, "o ye of little faith." It's not that their faith is small, just that they have a small basket to put it in, a small church, just a few people. And do you know what a small amount of faith can do? Jesus says in Matthew 17:20, "If you have faith the size of a mustard seed, you will say to this mountain, 'Move from here to there,' and it will move; and nothing will be impossible for you."

Mustard-seed faith has mountain-moving power. A mustard seed is the smallest physical object you can feel between the tips of your fingers, it's just barely enough to hold onto, but it's there. You can touch it. Feel it. And the faith of this tiny church had incredible power because of what they put their little faith in.

Jesus tells us that the church at Philadelphia operated completely according to His plan, according to His Word, following His will, responding to Him faithfully and their lives pleased Him in all that they did.

How do we build an unstoppable, forever-changed life that meets Christ's absolute approval? Jesus says the wise man is the one who builds on a good foundation. "Whoever hears these sayings of Mine, and does them, I will liken him to a wise man who built his house on the rock: and the rain descended, the floods came, and the winds blew and beat on that house; and it did not fall, for it was founded on the rock."[195]

194 Romans 8:38–39
195 Matthew 7:24–25

Living on a Fault Line

The city of Philadelphia wasn't built on a solid foundation. They were built on a fault line, and the believers in Philadelphia lived right in an earthquake zone.

When we used to live in the San Fernando Valley in California, we lived in an area that was vulnerable to earthquakes. And I remember one morning we were having breakfast, and my wife and I started getting dizzy. Now I just thought I was dizzy because I was looking at my wife, but then we realized the whole house was like it was on a tilt table. So we grabbed the kids and went outside so if the house collapsed, it wouldn't fall on anyone, and I'll never forget what we saw.

We lived on a street where every house was identical to the house next to it, same roofline, same everything. And there was a visible ripple just going down the street, lifting up one house, then the next house, then the next. And the house next to ours, with an identical roofline, the edge of the roof rose up about three feet higher than ours, then dipped down like it was in the trough of a wave, then it straightened out again, and the ripple moved on down the street.

In AD 17, the entire city of Philadelphia was absolutely flattened by an earthquake, and the Emperor Tiberius gave the city tax exemption and sent money to completely rebuild the city, so by the time Jesus writes this letter, Philadelphia had been rebuilt, but they were still living on a fault line. They were still built on volcanic soil that was extremely unstable.

There could be no better backdrop than that for the message Jesus gives on how to build a quake-proof life in the midst of uncertainty. Our physical lives are so much like our spiritual lives. Most people go through life uncertain, afraid, and they're shaken whenever the house starts to tilt, but there is a way to live quake-proof lives.

When you live in an earthquake zone, you learn to put lips on all the shelves so your stuff doesn't fall off, to reinforce so everything important makes it through the quake, and Philadelphia had learned to build their lives in such a way that they were unshakable. Philadelphia had found that only Jesus offered quake-proof living, where everything important in life doesn't get smashed and fall apart.

Though they would never escape the tremors, the quakes, the uncertainty that comes from living on a fault line, though they might lose all their physical possessions, Jesus offered treasures that could never be lost. Jesus offered a life that couldn't be destroyed. Only Jesus was certain in an uncertain world. They could face endless calamities and disasters, and though He never promised to take them out of the shake zone, Jesus had given them permanence. And they had taken hold of that.

Philadelphia built quake-proof lives so that no matter what disaster came, they were found unshakable, immovable, faithful, and unashamed before Him at His coming.

Built on the Rock

The four truths of a forever changed life made the tiny church at Philadelphia more powerful than the mega church at Ephesus, more successful than the expanding church at Thyatira, more confident than the church in the impenetrable city of Sardis, and richer than the abundantly wealthy of Laodicea.

When you build your life on Him who is holy, you will have a life that meets Christ's absolute approval. The same Jesus that affirms His holiness as His most repeated attribute in verse 7 examines the church at Philadelphia in verse 8 and finds nothing wrong. They had built their church on the first truth of a forever-changed life and had allowed the holiness of Jesus Christ to permeate their conduct so that Jesus found nothing to condemn. And when I build my life on the holiness of Christ as the only source of un-blighted existence, letting His holiness change me down to my conduct, then Jesus will look at me with eyes of fire and find a life that pleases Him in every way—not perfect, but faithful.

When you build your life on Him who is true, you will have a house built on a foundation that will never crack, that stands every test, that holds up in the wind, the rain, the storms, and no matter what earthquake tries to tear you down, you will have a quake-proof, disaster-proof life built on the Rock, "and he who believes in Him will never be disappointed."

When you build your life on Him who holds the key, who dispenses the riches, the presence, and the power of God, then nothing is impossible for you. When you have a little faith, just enough to feel between your fingers, the size of the mustard seed, and you place that faith in the One with mountain moving power, who grants you access to the presence of God, and who owns the cattle on a thousand hills, then you've built an unstoppable life.

And when you build your life on Him who Opens and No One Can Shut, then your satisfaction is found in Christ. Your light comes from Jesus. And your life is endless. When you build on Jesus, you have the power of an endless life, the assurance of eternal security, and your life will be forever changed.

THE ONLY THING JESUS IS LOOKING FOR

What does a life built on this foundation look like? On Jesus' inspection tour, one church is vibrant, one church is alive, one church is faithful, one church is evangelizing, one church is worshiping, and Jesus says their worship is so good He's going to make them an immovable, unshakable pillar in the temple of God. Jesus comes to each church looking for only one thing, and He found it in Philadelphia.

It is possible to stand before the x-ray vision of Jesus Christ and for Him to find nothing wrong. Why? Because they had built on the right foundation. They believed right, so they behaved right. How? They weren't doing anything wrong? Of course they were. They were doing lots of things wrong, but they were living according to the prescribed plan God set out for them.

We're fallen, we're frail, we're sinners, but when we do what it says in 1 John 1:9 and confess our sin, Jesus doesn't condemn us for our sin. He is faithful to forgive. He wants to cleanse us from all unrighteousness. He wants to give us His grace and power so that we can increasingly say yes to Him and say no to sin. That's living according to Christ's holiness. Not expecting perfection, but increasingly responding to His holiness, His truth, and allowing Him to change us. That's a life that meet's Christ's approval.

My wife and I were standing in line at airport security this week, and it was amazing what people tried to get past the x-ray. There were people with gallon-sized pickle jars, people sneaking in quarts of jelly, and it was just amazing. Did they think they could get that to go through and no one would notice?

But it is possible to go through that security station and have nothing beep. Have nothing that you have to take out of your pockets. That's what Jesus found at Philadelphia. The church at Philadelphia was constantly examining their lives for sin, constantly confessing their sin to Jesus, and forsaking that sin.

They weren't returning to it, they weren't trying to sweep it under the rug or sneak it through security. If Jesus wouldn't like it, they got rid of it as soon as they knew it was there, and when He came looking, He found nothing to condemn.

Jesus isn't looking to find absolute perfection. He isn't inspecting us for sinlessness. He isn't looking for us to be the perfect, thriving, immaculate church we might like to be. He is looking for one thing: faithfulness. And He found it in Philadelphia. This church is the model, not of a perfect life, but of a life that meets Christ's absolute approval. Not sinless, but faithful. And that's what we want to be.

Heavenly Father, thank You for this incredible church. For this example of a group of people who can have a surprise inspection by the One that owns them and have nothing hidden from Your sight, and for You to find nothing to condemn. We will never be perfect in this life, we have not been eradicated from our sin, but, like the Philadelphians, we can be faithful to the Word of God in our lives. We can obey You. We can confess and forsake our sin, however often it's necessary to keep our lives free from the leaven of sin. We are weak and frail and very aware of our fallen humanity, but from this letter we can learn how to live in such a way that's pleasing and holy in Your sight. May the God of Truth and Holiness find nothing to rebuke in our lives, and that is what we desire to hear from You every day. In the name of Jesus, we pray. Amen.

RESPOND to Truth

What is the most recognizable thing about Jesus? (Mark 1:21–24)

When Jesus opens a door, it can't be closed. What does it look like when Jesus closes a door? (Matthew 7:23; Mark 3:29)

What does Jesus say about the uncertainty of earthly possessions? What does He say about heavenly ones? (Matthew 6:19–20)

How do Jesus' titles of Holy, True, He who holds the Key of David, and He who opens and no one can shut all fit together? (John 5:24–29; Revelation 1:18)

What exactly is does the faithfulness Jesus is looking for look like in a person's life? (2 Corinthians 5:9; Colossians 1:10; Hebrews 13:21; 1 John 3:22)

What can I do to be faithful and pleasing to God today?

17 | The Rapture According to Jesus

THE NEXT SEVEN EVENTS ON CHRIST'S CALENDAR

God has given us the greatest book ever written. He watched over every word so that His Word, the Bible, is exactly all and explicitly everything we need to know. It is our guide for how we're to live every day of our lives until He comes or calls.

But the Book of the Revelation is special. God says in Revelation 1:1 that He gave us this book for a purpose, so we as His servants would know His plan for the future. Revelation clearly lays out the next seven events on Christ's calendar, and the first one is found in His letter to Philadelphia.

These seven events are not vague or obscure or clouded. They are very clear. God wrote His plan down for us so that we would know, not so that we could guess or argue or make charts. He wants us to know, and to be ready.

When I'm reading a really intense book—and that's what Revelation is, it's a very graphic description of the worst period of human history—I like to jump to the end of the book to find out how it all turns out. That's Revelation 21–22.

The Last Event on Christ's Calendar: Heaven

"Now I saw a new heaven and a new earth, the tabernacle of God is with men, and He will dwell with them, and they shall be His people. And God will wipe away every tear from their eyes; there shall be no more death, nor sorrow, nor crying. There shall be no more pain, for the former things have passed away."[196]

This is the ending, the last pages of the book, the conclusion of all of human history. When God says "new," He doesn't mean new of a different kind. This is new of the same kind. That means that all the best things on earth, every good thing God ever created will be that much better. No more corruption, no more curse, no more death. All the good things get better, and all the bad things are gone.

"And there shall be no more curse, but the throne of God and of the Lamb shall be in it, and His servants shall serve Him there. And they shall reign forever and ever."[197] Wow. What an ending.

The Sixth Event on Christ's Calendar: The Great White Throne Judgment

If you back up through Revelation, it's like watching a countdown to the return of Christ. From the distant future, eternity, we count down to the present and that's where we find how we should be living today. If you back up a page or two from heaven, you find the sixth event on Christ's calendar. This is what the Bible calls the Great White Throne Judgment.

"Then I saw a great white throne and Him who sat on it, from whose face the earth and the heaven fled away. And I saw the dead, small and great, standing before God, and books were opened. And another book was opened, which is the Book of Life. And the dead were judged according to their works, by the things which were written in the books. Then Death and Hades were cast into the lake of fire. This is the second death. And anyone not found written in the Book of Life was cast into the lake of fire."[198]

Do you notice what gets judged here? Works. When you go to hell, the lake of fire, it is because of your works, your sins. People don't go to hell because God didn't choose them or because they never heard about Jesus. They go because they're sinners, who practice lawlessness. Depart from Me, I never knew you. Revelation 3:5, if your name is written in the

196 Revelation 21:1–4
197 Revelation 22:3, 5
198 Revelation 20:11–15

book, it never gets blotted out, but these are the people who never knew Jesus, whose names were never written in the book at all. And they go into the blackness of darkness forever.

The Fifth Event on Christ's Calendar: The Millennium

The fifth event on the countdown to Christ's coming is what we call the Millennium or the Millennial Kingdom. Revelation 20:1–10 gives us a description of the fifth event on Christ's calendar, and He says six times that it lasts for "a thousand years."

There's a whole group of people who call themselves A-millennialists, meaning they don't believe in a millennium. But if you look at what God says, it's very clear. For a thousand years, Christ reigns on the earth. For a thousand years, His saints reign with Him. For a thousand years, Satan is locked up. After a thousand years, Satan is released to deceive the nations for a short time, then he is thrown into the lake of fire forever. That's the millennium.

You can devise a system for figuring out what the Bible *really* means, or you can simply read what it says. And if you just go with what God says will happen, instead of what you think will happen, Revelation becomes far less confusing. Christ will reign on earth, with His saints, for a thousand years. How does He get there? Jesus comes to earth on a white horse, armies behind Him, and that's what we call the Second Coming.

The Fourth Event on Christ's Calendar: His Second Coming

"The heavens opened, and behold, a white horse. And He who sat on him was called Faithful and True, and in righteousness He judges and makes war."

Satan's global rebellion has reached the apex of its power. He's assembled a great army. The armies of Satan have come to fight against Jesus. "And the armies of heaven, clothed in fine linen, white and clean, followed [Jesus] on white horses. Now out of His mouth goes a sharp sword, that with it He should strike the nations. He Himself treads the winepress of the fierceness and wrath of Almighty God."[199]

If I were Tim LaHaye, writing the Left Behind series, and I came to this part, I'd be all excited to write the greatest battle scene of all time.

---

199 Revelation 19:11, 14–15

This would be the moneymaker, the scene they'd make movies about, the chapters the readers won't be able to stop talking about. Imagine it: God versus Satan, since the Garden of Eden, since Cain and Abel, from Babel to Babylon to Satan's throne in Pergamos and through the centuries since, the battle's getting fiercer and fiercer, all leading to the absolute climax of good versus evil in all of human history—and there's no battle.

All John sees is Jesus with His sword, and then the armies of Satan all lying dead, being eaten by birds.

The Third Event on Christ's Calendar: The Tribulation

Now, if you want a battle scene, you have to go to a time before Jesus' Second Coming, when Satan's not quite so out of his league. The bulk of Revelation, chapters 6–19, is written about what Scripture calls the Abomination of Desolations, or sometimes Jacob's Troubles, or, the most popular name, the Tribulation.

"So I looked, and behold, a pale horse. And the name of him who sat on it was Death, and Hades followed with him. And power was given to them over a fourth of the earth, to kill with the sword, with hunger, with death, and by the beasts of the earth. There was a great earthquake; and the sun became black as sackcloth of hair, and the moon became like blood. And the kings of the earth, the great men, the rich men, the commanders, the mighty men, every slave and every free man, hid themselves in the caves and in the rocks of the mountains, and said to the mountains and rocks, 'Fall on us and hide us from the face of Him who sits on the throne and from the wrath of the Lamb! For the great day of His wrath has come, and who is able to stand?'"[200]

But wait. It gets worse.

As the end of the world approaches, so does earth's darkest hour. All Hell breaks loose—no, really. Hell will open and the pit will vomit out its demons to run wild on the earth. Beasts from the abyss will wreak global destruction and death. Satan himself invades the earth and conquers it at last. And that's when it gets really bad.

On this world that Satan rules, God pours out His wrath. God breaks seven seals, each releasing a terrible judgment. As the last seal breaks, there

200 Revelation 6:8, 12, 15–17

are seven trumpet blasts, each a horrific event, each more intense and more horrible than the last. And at the last trumpet blast, seven bowls of judgment are each sloshed out and dumped on the earth in rapid-fire succession. And that's all just leading up to the great Day of the Lord, when heaven opens and Christ comes as the supreme Judge of all the earth.

The Second Event on Christ's Calendar: The Judgment Seat of Christ

The countdown is getting close now. If you just keep backing up, the second event on Christ's calendar is found in Revelation 4–5, and it's another scene in heaven. If you've been paying close attention when you read Revelation, you'll notice something's missing after Revelation 5. All through the Tribulation, chapters 6–19, there's no mention of the Church. Until Jesus comes with ten thousands of His saints, we're not even mentioned. But here we are, in heaven, in chapters 4–5.

Paul says, "To be absent from the body is to be present with the Lord. Therefore we make it our aim, whether present or absent, to be well pleasing to Him. For we must all appear before the judgment seat of Christ."[201]

The second event on Christ's calendar is the Judgment Seat of Christ, and it takes place in heaven. The good news is that sin never enters into it. Our sin is gone. That was taken care of at the cross. Never to be brought up again.

This is the place where all the good works we were created for, everything done for Christ, stands the test and lasts forever, and everything that wasn't done for Him, everything we wasted our time chasing after, burns up. This is where people like Samson will stand saved yet as though by fire and suffering loss. And this is where those like the faithful Philadelphians will receive a crown. It's not a measure of our justification. This isn't about salvation. It's about sanctification, how much I allowed Christ to control me.

How do we get here? Well, every believer who has died ends up here. But there's a second way to arrive at the Judgment Seat of Christ. And that's number one on the countdown to Christ's return.

---

201 2 Corinthians 5:8–10

The Next Event on Christ's Calendar: The Rapture

No one knows the day or hour, but God has it circled on His calendar. The next event, the one that can happen any day, is what we call the Rapture. If you keep backing through Revelation, you find this event given as a promise in Revelation 3:10. Jesus says to the church at Philadelphia, "I also will keep you from the hour of trial which shall come upon the whole world."

This promise is so important that not only did Jesus teach it when He was on earth, it was also so vital to the apostles and the early church that when Paul only had a few weeks in one of the most sinful cities in the Roman Empire, he filled every page of his letter to the church with the hope-filled expectancy of the any-moment return of Christ.

"We who are alive and remain until the coming of the Lord will by no means precede those who are asleep. For the Lord Himself will descend from heaven with a shout, with the voice of an archangel, and with the trumpet of God. And the dead in Christ will rise first. Then we who are alive and remain shall be caught up together with them in the clouds to meet the Lord in the air. And thus we shall always be with the Lord. Therefore comfort one another with these words."[202]

If you've always wanted to circle the word "rapture" in your Bible, here it is. We who are alive and remain will be "caught up." In Greek, it's *harpadzo,* in Latin, it's *rapturos*—so there it is—and in English, it's "caught up." But it's all the same word. It means to be snatched, grabbed, pulled out. You drop something in the campfire, so you reach in real quick and snatch it out so nothing happens to it. Before it can be harmed, you pull it out. That's *rapturos,* the Rapture.

Do you know that over half of Christendom denies that this ever happens? And the other half, for the most part, is so confused about what actually happens that the book of Revelation gets set aside in most churches because it's all so mysterious we can never understand it.

Where did we get the idea that the prophecies about the End Times are mysterious with no real, literal fulfillment? The early church didn't think that. They heard what Jesus said, they believed it, and they behaved

---

202 1 Thessalonians 4:13–18

according to that belief. But somewhere, we've gotten this idea that God can't possibly mean what He says. There has to be another explanation.

Why? Why would we think that when every prophecy that's already been fulfilled has happened just like God said it would? Some things God says using parables or symbols, and some things He says plainly. If we don't know what every single thing symbolizes, that's one thing. But if we dismiss what He says plainly because we don't like what we read, that's a problem.

Jesus is going to keep His Church from a worldwide trial. That's what He said. You can debate all day what He meant by that, but that's what He said, and I choose to believe He said what He meant and meant what He said. So far, it's very clear.

So far, we know that there is an event, and it's on the books. You don't have to call it the Rapture. In fact, the early church never even heard of the Rapture. That word wasn't used until the Greek New Testament was translated into Latin, but the early church did believe the doctrine, they just called it by a different name. Do you know what they called this teaching? The Blessed Hope. So whether you call it the Blessed Hope, the Rapture in Latin, the Harpadzo in Greek, the Catching Up in English, or something else, it's an event, and it's going to happen, if you believe the Bible.

So what is it? What actually is the Rapture? Now we could take months to study all the theological positions on it. We could make a chart of what everyone from Augustine to Calvin to Dallas Theological Seminary have said about it. Or we can just open our Bibles and study the Rapture according to Jesus.

THE INTENTIONAL RESCUE OF CHRIST'S CHURCH

Jesus defines exactly what the Rapture is in Revelation 3:10, and He describes what it looks like in Matthew 24:40–42. He described it this way: "Two men will be in the field: one will be taken and the other left. Two women will be grinding at the mill: One will be taken and the other left. Watch therefore, for you do not know what hour your Lord is coming."

According to Jesus, people will be going merrily along, eating, drinking, getting married, and living their lives, until one day, in the twinkling of an eye, people will disappear off this planet. One will be taken, the other left, one will be taken, another left, and Jesus tells us who is taken, and why, in Revelation 3:10.

"Because you have kept My command to persevere, I also will keep you from the hour of trial which shall come upon the whole world, to test those who dwell on the earth."

Jesus defines the Rapture as the intentional rescue of His church. The word is *ek tereo*, to "keep from." "Keep from" is not to seal you up in a bunker and protect you through the Tribulation. That would be "keep through." If you accidentally drop your iPhone in the soapy dishwater, you don't hold it under the water and promise to keep it safe through the water. You snatch it out. You grab it immediately to "keep it from" getting damaged. That's the word Jesus uses here.

Look at what else Jesus says. If He had only said He'd keep the church from "the hour of trial," we might think He was talking about some enemy in the first century that was persecuting the tiny church at Philadelphia. But He says, "which shall come upon the whole world, to test those who dwell on the earth."

Did He really mean the whole world? *Did God really say?* Yes. He really said. See, there's two ways to read Scripture. You can let Scripture correct your system, or you can read the Bible through the screen of your system and reinterpret everything the Bible says to make it fit your beliefs. The early church didn't have that problem. They didn't have a thousand years of theological debate to confuse them. They just read God's Word and believed it.

Remember that God gave us Revelation for a reason, so that His servants would know the things that would soon take place. He didn't give it to us to confuse us, to divide us into camps, to spark a debate. And when the first century church first read the written-down Revelation of Jesus Christ, they didn't begin dividing into camps according to their belief system. They simply read the truth of Scripture and took it at face value. "Whole world" meant the whole world. And don't worry. Jesus didn't leave them to wonder what the hour of trial meant either. He described it in graphic detail in Revelation 6–19.

Starting in Revelation 6:8, Jesus says there is a time coming when the whole world will be a graveyard; one-fourth of all the people on earth will die. If you check the world population clock and calculate one fourth, that's at least 1.69 billion graves, if the Rapture happened today and the Tribulation started tomorrow. That's six times the population of America, all dead in one event. That's more than the population of either China or India. There won't even be room to bury them all, because the whole world will be a graveyard.

In chapter 14, the whole world becomes a battlefield. There's always a war going on somewhere, but 95 percent of the world is nowhere near a battlefield. In Revelation 14:20, the whole world becomes a battlefield. Armies from all over the world, blood running so deep in the valley of Jezreel that it reaches the bridles of the horses for miles. And when Jesus comes back, His pure white robe is going to be splattered with the blood of all the killing He'll do when He defeats His enemies.

In the Tribulation, the whole world faces starvation. Right now, all the ads for feeding the poor and saving starving children are all localized. Jesus said we'd always have the poor with us, and people do starve to death, but not on every street, in every country, all over the world. Most of us can't imagine starving to death here in America, but in the Tribulation, the whole world faces starvation.

We used to live in Oklahoma, and they'd have the most peculiar signs along the freeway: "Don't drive into smoke." And if you drove through in the winter, you thought Oklahoma was crazy, but wait until you're there in a grassfire. You can't see the hood of your own car. There is so much smoke when the prairies burn that you just pull over, because otherwise you'll run over someone or a cow or hit a semi. You just pull over. You don't drive through smoke. In Revelation 8:7, the whole world will be on fire. A third of the trees will be burned up, and *all* the prairies, all the grass will burn. Not just die. Burn.

Verse 12, the whole world faces a nuclear winter. Jesus describes a time when the sun and the moon are darkened and nature goes into revolt. Remember how they used to tell us we needed to disarm because there'd be nuclear winter and the whole earth would get dark, and the sun wouldn't penetrate, and it'd get cold and we'd have another ice age? Don't worry. It's going to happen. Jesus said so.

But it gets worse. Out of the smoke locusts come with the power of scorpions, but they don't go after the grass that's growing back. They only go after people, and the whole earth becomes a horror show. Right now, you can go pay ten dollars to be scared to death at horror show and they're advertising it like it's entertaining. In the Tribulation, you don't have to go to the horror show. It comes to every person on earth.

If you add it all up, between chapters 6 and 19, half of the world ends up dead. It's a worldwide nightmare. Nobody escapes. If God didn't shorten the days, no one on earth would survive, and He only shortens it for the sake of those who are coming to Christ during it. Mass devastation, mass death, mass destruction, and nobody gets out unscathed.

Throughout history, there have been plagues. Throughout history, there have been famines. Throughout history, there have been earthquakes, and dictators, and wars, and pillaging, and genocide, and everything. But never is it in the whole world, until "the hour of trial," Revelation 6–19.

When Jesus warned Smyrna of trials, of testing, of tribulation, His message to them was trust Me to the end. He didn't promise to take them out, to keep them from, to pull them out of the fire. He just told them not to fear.

But when He writes to Philadelphia, He makes a very different promise. If you have a red-letter edition of the Bible, these words are in red. Jesus promises to "keep" them "from." Not trials, but an hour of trial which shall come upon the whole world. Not just any test, but a test for all who dwell on the earth. Not just tribulations, but The Tribulation, and He doesn't promise to protect them through. He promises to keep them from.

Jesus taught two different plans, one for His Church, and one for the rest of the world. The Tribulation is God doing two things: pouring out His wrath on an unbelieving world, and completing His plan for the nation Israel.

Remember that Israel is the chosen people of promise from the Old Testament, the people God made so many promises to. But because of their disobedience, He had set them aside. The Tribulation is God going back and picking up the people He temporarily set aside, the ones He never gave up on, never replaced, never forgot. In Revelation 6–19, God renews His covenant with Israel by bringing them back to the forefront of His global plan, the one He never abandoned, that He never changed, that He always intended to complete, just as literally and completely as every other fulfilled prophecy of Scripture.

And Jesus says the Church doesn't need to be there. God's going to finish His plan for Israel, He's going to judge an unbelieving world, but Jesus said "I will keep you from," snatch you out, catch you up, take you home. That was the blessed hope of the early church.

What Happened to the Blessed Hope?

The Rapture is going to happen, if you believe the Bible. It's an intentional rescue, if you believe Jesus. It's going to happen before the Tribulation, if you trust Christ's promise to Philadelphia. But over half of all Christendom denies the doctrine of the Rapture the way Jesus taught it, and the other half is so mixed up they've, for the most part, set aside Revelation altogether, just to avoid confusion.

So what happened? It was so clear originally. In fact, until the fourth century, all of Christendom had only one view of the return of Christ. They believed, universally, that He would come back any moment and snatch them up. It wasn't until Augustine, for political reasons, officially changed the Church's stance on the Rapture that people started getting confused.

See, up until then, believers were living like this life was temporary, like all their treasures on earth wouldn't last, and like their citizenship was in heaven. But in the fourth century, Augustine started promoting the belief that the Church has replaced Israel as the center of God's focus, and that the kingdom of heaven was already here, and instead of living for heaven, we should live for the here and now. He's the one who promoted the idea that all the Revelation stuff is too mysterious, that we can't understand it and shouldn't worry about it, and we should be living for the kingdom, and the kingdom is here.

So instead of living for Christ's return, the Church began living for the here and now, to accumulate treasures on earth, and to build our cathedrals bigger and better so they'd last forever. And ever since, the majority of Christendom has been letting their belief system cloud their perception of the Word of God instead of letting the Word of God correct their system.

God, the Author of the book of Revelation, gave us its divine title, a divine outline, told us exactly why He was giving it to us, and then dictated to John exactly what He wanted us to know.

So John looks, and he sees, and, in perfect chronological order, describes exactly what he's seeing. He's letting us in on God's plan before it happens, just like God told him to. The Church is on earth for chapters 1–3. Then, "after these things," he sees the throne room of the universe in chapters 4–5. "Now I saw" the seals opened and the tribulation begins in chapter 6. Then for thirteen chapters, a very specific succession of horrors is rained on the earth, one after another, listed in sequence, described in detail, with God's purpose explained as He goes along.

"After these things," heaven opens and Jesus returns to make war and conquer His enemies in chapter 19. "Then I saw," the beginning of the thousand years in chapter 20, "then I saw" the great white throne in verse 11. And finally, "now I saw" the new heaven and new earth in chapter 21. And the first event, before anything else can happen, is Christ's explicitly promised, planned out, intentional rescue of His Church.

Jesus is coming back. That's indisputable. The Church is going to be caught up and meet Jesus in the air. That's what God breathed out and the apostle Paul wrote down—very clearly. That's what we call the Rapture, what the early church called the Blessed Hope, and this wasn't thought up by John Walvoord (1910–2002) or John Nelson Darby (1800–1882) or Hal Lindsey (b. 1929). This is not a doctrine that was just invented in the last couple hundred years, or a new belief created by the Dallas Theological Seminary, or a good fiction story dreamed up by Tim LaHaye. It was a doctrine invented, taught, and spread by Jesus Christ.

The Doctrine Jesus Taught

We're not the first generation to be curious about the return of Christ. His disciples asked about it, and I'm so glad they did, because we have a seminar given by Jesus to His disciples on the End Times, and it was not comforting.

Jesus said the world would get progressively worse until something He called the "abomination of desolations" spoken of by Daniel would come. Jesus said if God didn't shorten those days, everyone on earth would die.

Stars falling, plagues, death and destruction everywhere, the world would be overrun with demons so bad that the demons on earth in Jesus day were begging Him not to throw them in the pit where those horrible things were.

And Jesus said, "Let not your hearts be troubled." Why?

When Jesus left His disciples for the last time, He left them with a picture of what the Blessed Hope would look like. "And while they looked steadfastly toward heaven as He went up, behold, two men stood by them in white apparel, who also said, 'Men of Galilee, why do you stand gazing up into heaven? This same Jesus, who was taken up from you into heaven, will so come in like manner as you saw Him go into heaven.'"

Have you ever wondered, as Jesus was standing with His followers, why the Pharisees didn't pop out of the bushes and try to stop Him? Where were the Roman soldiers who were guarding His tomb? Where were Pilate and Herod and the Sanhedrin? Jesus wasn't arrested or attacked, and no one tried to stop Him, because after His resurrection, He was only seen by believing eyes and touched by loving hands.

Jesus' ascension was private. It was only for believers, and it was characterized by Jesus raining down blessings on them. That's the picture Jesus gives of His return. A private rescue mission, just for His Church.

But look what Jesus says about His second coming: "Behold, He is coming with clouds, and every eye will see Him, even they who pierced Him. And all the tribes of the earth will mourn because of Him."[203] This is not the same event.

Jesus will take His Church home. And Jesus will come to reign on the earth. But there are twenty-five incredible comparisons and contrasts between the Rapture and the Second Coming that tell us they are two separate, distinct events on Christ's calendar.

At the Rapture, only believing eyes will see Him, and they will be comforted. At the Second Coming, every eye will see Him and all the earth will mourn. At the Rapture, the saints meet Jesus in the air and He takes them to live in heaven. At the Second Coming, the saints return with Christ to reign on earth. No one knows the day or hour of the Rapture, but the Second Coming has clear, direct, chronological signs leading up to it.

203 Revelation 1:7

Jesus taught a completely different plan for His people than the stated plan for the rest of the world. Over and over, every time the doctrine is taught, by Jesus, by Paul, by Peter, by anyone who spread the word in the first century, the Rapture is presented as a source of comfort for the Church. Jesus taught repeatedly, in Matthew 24, Mark 13, and Luke 21, that His second coming is to judge the ungodly. When Jesus comes for the world, it is terrifying, people are hiding in caves and wishing to die. But when Jesus comes for His Bride, He says to take comfort.

"Let not your heart be troubled; you believe in God, believe also in Me. I go to prepare a place for you. And if I go and prepare a place for you, I will come again and receive you to Myself; that where I am, there you may be also."

Why did Jesus have to say, "let not your hearts be troubled?" Because they were troubled. They were afraid. They had just heard a seminar on the worst period of human history and everything they thought they understood about Jesus conquering the world was not turning out like they thought it would, and they needed to be told that Jesus had a plan. He wasn't going to leave them to suffer the wrath of God poured out on an unbelieving world. That time of testing wasn't for them. He was going to snatch them out.

Peter, writing to the most heavily persecuted believers in the world, said we've been born again to a living hope, and this doctrine is the living hope he taught. Paul said to the church at Thessalonica, "Comfort one another with these words." The *harpadzo, rapturos*, "catching up" should be a reassurance, a comfort, a source of great security. And when Jesus wrote to His faithful church at Philadelphia, He gave them a personal promise that He'd keep them from the hour of trial.

The Rapture, according to Jesus, would be a source of comfort for His people. And every generation of believers, from the disciples who heard it straight from the mouth of Christ, to the apostles who taught it, to the church that believed it, drew, not only great comfort from the teaching, but a hope-filled expectancy as well.

James, Jesus' earthly brother, the pastor of the church in Jerusalem, who wrote the earliest epistle to Christ's Church, said that Jesus was standing right outside the door. The second earliest letter, written by Paul, shines with the any-moment return of Christ from every Rapture-induced, hope-filled, expectant chapter.

When you only have a little over a month to speak at the city one historian called a "cesspool of sin," you are sure to cover only what is most important, and Paul considered the doctrine of the any-moment return of Christ so vitally important for new believers that he didn't just teach it. He taught it in every chapter of his letter to the Thessalonians.

Chapter 1: "Wait for His Son from heaven, whom He raised from the dead, even Jesus who delivers us from the wrath to come." Chapter 2: "For what is our hope, or joy, or crown of rejoicing? Is it not even you in the presence of our Lord Jesus Christ at His coming?" Chapter 3: "May the Lord… establish your hearts blameless in holiness before our God and Father at the coming of our Lord Jesus Christ." Chapter 4: "Then we who are alive and remain will be caught up together with them in the clouds to meet the Lord in the air. And thus we shall always be with the Lord." And chapter 5: "Now may the God of peace Himself sanctify you completely; and may your whole spirit, soul, and body be preserved blameless at the coming of our Lord Jesus Christ. He who calls you is faithful, who also will do it."[204]

The Church today needs a good dose of old-fashioned, first-century living hope. They caught what Jesus taught. And He taught such a comforting, hope-filled message that His disciples went out from there and spread that same hope-filled message everywhere they went.

THE ANY-MOMENT RETURN OF JESUS

Whatever you think of when you think of the early church, their fervor for ministry, their zeal for evangelism, their love for one another so that they shared everything they had, their faithfulness in the face of persecution and death, whatever it is you think of when you think of the early church, that came out of a very specific belief.

If you believe right, you behave right, and the early church believed the doctrine that Jesus invented, that the apostles promoted, and that spread everywhere the gospel spread: the doctrine of the any-moment return of Jesus.

---

204 1 Thessalonians 1:10, 2:19, 3:13, 4:17–18, 5:23–24

The blessed hope of the early church led them to live in light of the any-moment return of Christ. Instead of building grand cathedrals to last for centuries and accumulating wealth on earth, they were living day to day like Jesus could come back at any moment, for the first century. And the second century. And the third century.

But beginning in the fourth century, things subtly shifted. The one book that God specifically gave us so we'd know His plan got set aside as too mysterious to understand. One of the greatest promises ever made to all of Christ's Church was disregarded as unclear and not for us. And the hope-filled expectancy, the living hope that characterized Jesus' faithful church at Philadelphia, was exchanged for the fog of complacency and spiritual lethargy of the church at Sardis.

Jesus started a doctrine that shaped the early church. They lived like everything on earth was temporary and that they could, any moment, stand before God accountable for how they lived their life. The doctrine started by Augustine, picked up by Calvin, and spread through Jonathan Edwards and others has changed the way the Church has chosen to live each day. If you believe right, you'll behave right, and Jesus says there are two ways to live.

Like Sardis, we can grow complacent in our grand castles, our high towers, our immaculate buildings and grand cathedrals, and be soldiers asleep on the wall. Or like Philadelphia, we can be small and poor in the things of this world but incredibly rich because our treasures are in heaven. We can live for the here and now, piling up the riches of this world and be caught unaware when Jesus comes like a thief in the night and finds us for all intents and purposes dead and useless, or we can live for the any-moment return of Christ and be found abundantly alive and faithful.

We could use a good dose of what Philadelphia had. The church at Philadelphia lived like Jesus could come back while they were sitting at work, while they were sitting alone at home, or while they were sitting at school. When I believe that Jesus could come back before I get home today, while I'm on the way out the door, that's living hope. That's the Blessed Hope of the early church.

When the apostles taught the doctrine of the Rapture, it was always coupled with the watchfulness that Jesus always demands from His Church.

Paul trained the believers in holiness and blamelessness expressly so they'd be ready for Christ's return. Peter teaches the same thing and calls for a response: since Jesus' return is imminent, "what manner of persons ought you to be?" James taught that the Church should be careful how they act because Jesus was standing right at the door.

It matters what you believe is standing at the door. If you're expecting the worldwide holocaust, then you will spend your life worried, afraid, and storing up bottled water in bomb shelters that can't save you anyway. If you believe the reign of Christ on earth is already here, then you will spend your life building an earthly kingdom and storing up treasures where moth and rust destroy and thieves break in and steal. If you believe the End Times according to Jesus is so completely allegorical that there is no correlation to actual events at all, then you'll spend your life trying to protect, preserve, and control population on a planet that can't last no matter how many unborn children are killed so they can't mess up the planet for the rest of us.

But if you believe that Jesus is standing right at the door, that changes everything. If you believe that, then our citizenship is in heaven. Our treasures are sent ahead where moth, rust, and thieves can't get at them. Our hope is in Jesus Christ, who can't fail, who is holy, true, who opens to us the riches, presence, and power of God, and who has opened a door that can't be shut. If Jesus is standing right at the door, and can return any moment, and the very next event on His calendar after His return is the Judgment Seat where our works either stand or burn, then holiness matters. Conduct matters. Readiness matters. So Jesus says to Philadelphia, "Behold, I am coming quickly! Hold fast what you have, that no one may take your crown."

Three Ways to Greet the Blessed Hope

John says there are three ways to greet the Blessed Hope. "And now, little children, abide in Him, that when He appears, we may have confidence and not be ashamed before Him at His coming."[205]

I can't imagine many things worse than meeting Jesus Christ with shame. But there's something worse still, and that's to miss His coming

---

205 1 John 2:28

altogether. To be one of those working in the field or grinding at the mill who is left behind.

Something terrible is coming, and the whole world will stop and take notice. Demons loosed, plagues spread, death and destruction by the billions. And at the end, Jesus will come again, this time with His saints behind him, and there will be nothing left of His enemies but food for the birds.

Right now, people are sending lifeboats away from the *Titanic* empty because there's no need to worry. There's still time, and there's a good chance Jesus didn't really mean anything He said literally. Would you bet your life on that? Because Jesus says that His Second Coming won't be missed by anyone, but His coming for His Church is private, only for believers, and if you miss it, you might not get another chance.

But then there's those who, like John says, will be ashamed at His coming. Do you know who those are? It's those who spent their lives living for the wrong thing. It's those who, like Sardis, are asleep on the wall, not living for His any-moment return, not ready, not watching.

This is why Revelation 4–22 matters. This is why God wanted His servants to know what was coming, because there's a lesson in the doctrine of the any-moment return of Jesus the way He taught it. If you live for "the kingdom," the here and now, building grand cathedrals that will burn, then imagine the shame when the here and now melts with fervent heat and the kingdom you've built is carried away by thieves, eaten by moths, and crumbled by rust. If you spend every moment of every day protecting an earth that is wearing out like a garment, that God Himself is going to rip apart, imagine watching the friends and neighbors you could have saved by taking them with you, by witnessing to them, instead get left behind on the earth you could never have saved.

We can get caught up in protecting and saving a planet that was never meant to last, we can get caught up in winning back a godless society that Jesus promised would keep getting worse, we can get caught up in building a kingdom for ourselves on an earth that's going to burn, or, with the same undeniable power the early church possessed, we can live for the day when we'll be caught up by Christ.

Philadelphia shows us how to meet Jesus with confidence. Jesus gave them one of the greatest promises ever made, and they didn't just intellectually believe it. They lived it. Whether Jesus came in their lifetimes or not, they lived ready, prepared, doing what He left them to do, and Jesus looks on this church with absolute approval.

If you don't have a favorite epistle of Jesus, a favorite church, it ought to be this one, because this church is the model of how to meet Christ with confidence. Philadelphia is the example of what it takes to be faithful, what it takes to be obedient, how to serve, how to worship, how to live, not perfectly, but forgiven. Faithful.

"I know your works." This is holiness. Jesus is intimately acquainted with their deeds, and they are pleasing to Him. "I have set before you an open door, and no one can shut it." This is disciple making and evangelism. He opened the door for them, gave them great opportunities, and they fulfilled them. "You have a little strength." This is dependence. Jesus knew they were small and weak, but they were leaning on His power, and that made them strong. "Have kept My word." This is obedience. The Philadelphians devoted themselves to the Word of God, "and have not denied My name." This is commitment. The Philadelphians loved Jesus so much they magnified His name unashamedly.

Paul says he runs the race to win the prize, careful to discipline his body so he won't be disqualified. Hebrews tells us to lay aside every weight so we can run with endurance the race set before us. Jesus tells the Philadelphians to hold on to what they have so no one takes their crown.

Do you know what He's saying? You're in the last lap. You're out in front. Stay in your lane. Don't disqualify yourself. Hold on; you're going to win. Like a coach just before the fourth quarter, Jesus is telling His church at Philadelphia to keep doing exactly what they were doing, and they would win and have everlasting rewards.

"Behold, I am coming quickly," Jesus says. There's no quitting allowed. Philadelphia was a church that was ready to meet Jesus Christ, but what counts isn't how we start, but how we finish. 2 Timothy 4:7–8 says, "Finally there is laid up for me the crown of righteousness, which the Lord, the righteous Judge, will give to me on that Day, and not to me only but also to all who have loved His appearing."

"Hold fast what you have," Jesus says. He doesn't allow coasting. "Be diligent to present yourself approved to God, a worker who does not need to be ashamed."[206] Why? "That no one may take your crown." No overconfidence allowed.

Paul said, "I run thus: not with uncertainty. Thus I fight: not as one who beats the air. But I discipline my body and bring it into subjection, lest, when I have preached to others, I myself should become disqualified."[207]

What is the lesson for us? Don't live for a world that won't last. Don't store up treasures that will burn. Be sure that you are one of those He's coming back to rescue, and live every day like it could happen at any time. When the unstoppable One, the holy, true, invincible Jesus Christ who cannot fail, who cannot lie, who will not disappoint, says He's planned an intentional rescue of His church, then I hope that all of us will say with the apostle John, "Even so, come quickly Lord Jesus."[208] Let us live every day to be confident and unashamed before Him at His coming.

> *Father, thank You. Thank You for the blessings of Your Word, for all the writings from Paul and Peter and from You, Lord Jesus, that tell of what You are saving us from, and what we are to comfort one another with. May all of us today renew that old-fashioned expectant hope that any day, Lord Jesus, You will come back for us. And may we live with the living hope that whatever the newspaper says, whatever riots are going on or whatever the latest occupation is, or whatever the economy does, we will live in hope, because we're not looking for anything but You, any moment, to come and take us home. Let us live, Lord Jesus, not just in hope, but in readiness, knowing that we will stand before the Judgment Seat of Christ, and may we, like the faithful church at Philadelphia, live to meet You with confidence, unashamed before You. In the name of the holy, true, unstoppable Jesus Christ, we pray. Amen.*

206 2 Timothy 2:15
207 1 Corinthians 9:26–27
208 Revelation 22:20

RESPOND to Truth

How literally were the prophecies of Jesus' first coming fulfilled? (Isaiah 7:14/Matthew 1:22–23; Micah 5:2/Matthew 2:5–6; Zechariah 9:9/ Matthew 21:4–5; Matthew 26:24–25; 45–49; Zechariah 13:7/Matthew 26:31, 56; Zechariah 11:12–13/Matthew 26:15; 27:9–10; Psalm 22:1, 7–8, 14–18/ Matthew 27:35, 46; Luke 23:35; Psalm 16:10; 110:1/Acts 2:29–35)

What does God say about the prophecies of Christ's second coming? (Jeremiah 1:12; Matthew 5:18, 24:35)

If we believe in a literal fulfillment of End Times prophecy, what common belief systems no longer work?

When was the doctrine of the Rapture first invented? (see Jude 1:14)

How did the Blessed Hope of the early church cause Paul, Peter, and John to live? (Philippians 3:7–21; Titus 2:11–13; 2 Peter 3:10–14; 1 John 3:2–3)

What Sardis habits have I picked up, and what can I do today to live more like the church at Philadelphia?

PART III

The Seven Bad Habits of Lukewarm Christians

18 | The First Sickening Habit That Makes Christ Vomit

Have you ever been walking into a room to talk to someone who's having a conversation, and you can tell by the tone of their voice or the look on their face that something heated is going on? Then there's a little check in your forward momentum, and you just kind of ease out of there, because you don't want to be there for whatever's going on.

That's what is happening to Laodicea. Jesus is speaking to them, and He is letting us in on the conversation, but something heated is going on. This is not a list of commendations. This is sharp and serious and heated, and commentators agree that in this letter, Jesus is uncharacteristically harsh. This is the most piercing, stinging, scathing letter that Jesus ever wrote, and that's because Laodicea was in the worst condition of any group of believers Jesus visited.

Yes, Ephesus had spiritual heart problems, but Jesus found ten marvelous qualities to commend. Smyrna was facing immense persecution, but Jesus found them holding fast. Pergamos had a spiritually compromised immune system, but they held up under persecution. Thyatira had a problem with sin and worldliness, but Jesus approved of their growing works. Sardis was full of the walking dead, but there were still some who hadn't soiled their garments.

But Laodicea is the first church Jesus visited where He found nothing good to say. This letter is caustic, it's condemning, and unfortunately, it's also the most important letter for the modern church to read, because it's a commentary, not just on the first-century Laodiceans, but on the Church today.

THE LUKEWARM CHURCH

Jesus' Letter to the Modern Church

Revelation 3:14–22 is possibly the most important section of Scripture for the church of modern times. There are 1,189 chapters in the whole Bible, but only two were personally written by Jesus Christ for His Church. And of those two chapters, seven letters to seven churches, only one letter is very specifically targeted at us, the modern, twenty-first-century church.

Jesus doesn't write to every church of the first century. The church at Antioch isn't here. The church of Jerusalem isn't here. Jesus didn't pick the seven biggest or the seven most important or the seven most convenient. He picked the seven churches that are a perfect representation of all His churches, for all time.

Jesus knows that there are seven types of people that make up His church. There are Ephesus-believers, who have lost their first love; there are Pergamos-believers who are compromising with sin; there are Sardis-believers, who are asleep on the job, and so on. And all these types of believers are found in every church, in every century.

But these seven churches also represent seven church ages, from the first century to now. What we call the apostolic era was represented by the church at Ephesus. The gospel spread, and the church had incredible power, but along the way they drifted from their first love. Love cooled for some, others professed Christ falsely, and the clergy began to be exalted higher than they ought to be. That was what the universal church was like, for the most part, during the apostolic age, from AD 30–60.

Smyrna represented the age of the persecuted church, from AD 60–300. There were further departures from the simplicity of the gospel, but for the most part, the church was a sweet savor to God by their faithfulness even unto death.

True faith began to fade from AD 300–500, the Pergamite period. Spirituality gradually formed itself into a system, the church united with the world, and the paganism of Babylon and Romanism entered into the church.

Thyatira represents the Dark Ages for the church, from AD 500–1500, when the truth was hidden in darkness and the church was corrupt, usurping the place of Christ and burning His true followers at the stake.

The age of Sardis was marked by the church having reputation for being alive, starting with the Reformation around AD 1500, all the way to AD 1800. But while it was seen as the age of separation and the return and rule of Christ, it was marked with a deadness of institutionalizing Christianity with all the denominations and was characterized by spiritual lethargy.

For the next two hundred years, the church was Philadelphian, known for fearless evangelism, so that the gospel has reached into every corner of the world and spread like it hasn't spread since Pentecost. But since 1950, we have entered into the age of the lukewarm church, where, like Laodicea, the church is known, not for being on fire for Christ, not for giving a cup of cold water in Jesus' name, but for being nothing at all.

Jesus warned of a day of an unthinking multitude that thinks they are Christians but are not, and of a church that has become dominated by materialism, empty profession, and false peace. Untested, self-sufficient, and comfortable, the bulk of the modern church has become sickening to Christ.

They still have a cross somewhere. They still have a Bible of some form, rarely used. They still have a doctrine, but it's been watered down so it doesn't offend anyone, except God. They are known for their social activism. They are known for their facilities. They are known for their orations and their productions, but there's no power of God. There's no supernatural transformation of sinners from darkness to light, set free from the power of Satan to the power of God, and enjoying the assurance of the forgiveness of sins. And there's certainly no sanctification going on.

Middle of the road, don't rock the boat, don't make waves, friends of everybody, just going to church and avoiding the really bad sins, Laodicean Christians don't bring up anything that might convict or offend, and that sickens Christ. If you think that's not you, that's not your church, then listen to what Jesus says: "He who has an ear, let him hear."

There is a lesson here for us. This is a universally applicable message, for everyone, from the first century to the twenty-first century, for every type of church and every type of believer, there's an application. This is what Jesus sees when He inspects His Church today:

Seven Habits of Highly Defective People

Jesus looks at Laodicea, and in twenty-first-century language, He says perhaps the most unlikely words our Savior could ever say: "You make me sick." That's why I call this series of lessons on Laodicea "The Seven Bad Habits that Sicken Christ and Make Him Vomit," or "The Seven Habits of Highly Defective People," to use the Steven Covey business book title.

The believers at Laodicea were highly defective, and this is why: They had cultivated seven bad habits, seven sickening habits, that made Christ want to vomit them out.

First, they had cultivated the bad habit of spiritual neutrality, being just middle-of-the-road Christians with no real use to Christ. They were spiritually self-sufficient; they had need of nothing, including Christ's power in their lives. They were spiritually insensitive, having every advantage and access to the Scriptures and failing to hear and obey the voice of Jesus in their every day lives. They were spiritually wasteful, piling up treasures on earth instead of investing in heaven, and they were characterized by spiritual neglect, failing to clothe themselves in Christ's righteousness. They had materialism-induced spiritual blindness, and lastly, they were spiritually lax, failing to see the seriousness of sin and the importance of holiness.

A lot of us pay dearly for things, but no one has ever paid more dearly for anything than Christ did for His Church. And His Church, that He purchased with His own blood, had grown so stagnant and useless that He says they make Him sick.

The Laodiceans had picked up seven bad habits that make Christ sick, and those seven habits are found in Revelation 3:14–22. Jesus tells them, one right after the other, seven things they are doing wrong, and doesn't offer a single approval for anything they were doing,

But we can still learn from this church. In the same way that Solomon did with his son, we can learn seven valuable lessons from the sickening church at Laodicea. Solomon would take his son out and say, "Look at what they're doing. That's not what pleases God." So by looking at a disobedience, or a negative, or what's not pleasing, we see a very powerful picture of what does please God: not doing that. And in the letter to Laodicea, that's what I call the Seven Habits of Sanctified Believers.

REVELATION 3:14–22

And to the angel of the church of the Laodiceans write,

"These things says the Amen, the Faithful and True Witness, the Beginning of the creation of God: 'I know your works, that you are neither cold nor hot. I could wish that you were cold or hot. So then, because you are lukewarm, and neither cold nor hot, I will vomit you out of My mouth. Because you say, "I am rich, have become wealthy, and have need of nothing"—and do not know that you are wretched, miserable, poor, blind, and naked—I counsel you to buy from Me gold refined in the fire, that you may be rich; and white garments, that you may be clothed, that the shame of your nakedness may not be revealed; and anoint your eyes with eye salve, that you may see. As many as I love, I chasten. Therefore be zealous and repent. Behold, I stand at the door and knock. If anyone hears My voice and opens the door, I will come in to him and dine with him, and he with Me. To him who overcomes I will grant to sit with Me on My throne, as I also overcame and sat down with My Father on His throne.

"'He who has an ear, let him hear what the Spirit says to the churches.'"

Jesus is immutable. He doesn't change. The lifestyle that pleased Christ in the first century is the same lifestyle that pleases Him in the twenty-first century. And what sickened Him in the first, second, and third centuries still sicken Him in the nineteenth, twentieth, and twenty-first centuries.

We're not passively reading something that is static and in the past. This is applicable in our lives today, not just because Jesus writes to anyone with an ear to hear, but because this is the church that most resembles what Jesus finds when He searches the hearts and minds today, when He walks among His churches in this country, in this century, this is what He sees.

Neither Hot Nor Cold

"I know your works, that you are neither cold nor hot. I could wish you were cold or hot. So then, because you are lukewarm, and neither cold nor hot, I will vomit you out of My mouth."

Jesus couldn't have painted a more vivid picture for the church at Laodicea than this one. Traditionally, people interpret this passage to mean that God would rather have people hot and on fire for Christ or to be cold and nothing. But do you think God would rather us be nothing? No. And when He spoke to the Laodiceans, they understood exactly what He meant.

Laodicea had no water source of their own. Hieropolis, just within walking distance of Laodicea, had beautiful, healthful, therapeutic hot springs. Just breathing in the steam made you healthier. So Laodicea ran a pipeline all the way from Hieropolis into their own city so they could have some hot water.

On the other side, in the mountain town of Colosse, water came up from the ground ice cold and refreshing and perfect, like a really expensive bottle of spring-fed water, and Laodicea had an aqueduct coming from Colosse's mountain springs into town.

But by the time either one, the hot water from Hieropolis or the cold water from Colosse, made it to Laodicea, both of them were lukewarm and nasty. The once-hot water now smelled like rotten eggs and the water that used to be cold was warm and stagnant, and Jesus says Laodicea was as sickening as their water.

Jesus wanted the Laodiceans to either be vibrantly hot for Him or cool and refreshing. They should have been offering the cool, comforting hope of the gospel for those coming in hot from the battle or be hot and therapeutic, ministering the word and warming up those who were coming in from the cold of sin. But they were neither one. They had lost whatever they were originally, whatever use they once had for Christ. They'd lost either their therapeutic heat or their beneficial, refreshing coolness, and because they were lukewarm, He was going to vomit them out of His mouth.

Jesus graphically expresses His outrage and His dismay at their state with an allusion to spewing them away from Him. I remember from the joys of raising eight children, you'd know when they were really sick when they were projectile vomiting. This isn't the quiet kind. It's the spewing-like-a-fire-hose kind. That's exactly the Greek word Jesus uses.

The Lord and Savior of the church has such a revulsion over Laodicea that He wants to projectile-vomit them out. That's an indication of just how greatly their conduct offended Christ.

This is the first sickening habit that makes for a lukewarm church:

THE HABIT OF SPIRITUAL NEUTRALITY

Passively Squeezed

There are two ways to reject Christ: You can outright say, "I don't want anything to do with that," or you can shrug and say you'll think about it and just never make a choice. That's no, too. You can think about it forever, but if you don't repent, receive, believe, that's a rejection too.

Just like with salvation, there are two ways to be a church that's revolting to Christ. You can actively go after sin, invite it into your camp and preach it from your pulpit, or you simply drift, and that's the first sickening habit that Christ finds in His church.

Laodicea was spiritually neutral. They were not doing what they were called to do. They were just drifting. They were going from obedience to being neutral. They didn't oppose Christ, they just were neutral. Neutrality isn't "in Your face, God, I don't want anything to do with You." It's just, "okay, okay, okay, I'll get to that," and then you just go into neutral. You don't engage.

Living the Christian life is constantly resisting the pressure of the world that is squeezing us, and spiritual neutrality is not resisting the world, not disciplining ourselves for godliness. Instead, we just please ourselves, and we begin to embrace the world and everything else that is not focused on glorifying God. When we passively allow it to shape our lives instead of actively resisting it, that's what neutrality looks like.

God said it clearest. "Do not love the world." And then He amplifies it. "Or the things in the world." Anything that does not glorify God pushes us away from His glory. It doesn't have to be evil. It doesn't have to be some horrendous sinful thing. It just has to not bring glory to God, it's something that's of the world. And when we don't aggressively resist the world, then we are passively squeezed into its mold.

The apostle Paul said, "Do not be conformed to the world." The word "conformed" is to be squeezed into the mold of, and it's passive. It isn't an active choice; it's not an intentional thing. You get conformed, squeezed into the mold of, when you stop actively, aggressively resisting the world. You don't have to run after sin. You just have to not flee from it. That's being passively squeezed. And that's spiritual neutrality.

Anyone who's grown up in an alcoholic home has a completely different view of alcohol from everyone else. They're not okay with recreational, responsible, just-once-in-a-while drinking because they've seen just how destructive alcohol can be. Anyone who's been in a terrible car accident, those are the people who tell you not to drive too fast, who tell you to buckle your seat belt every time, who tell you to stop when you get tired, who warn you about the traffic and the weather, because they know how easily an accident can happen. Anyone who's been trapped in a house fire looks for exits everywhere they go. They remember what it was like, and it's always back there in their minds.

And anyone who's truly understood the seriousness and consequences and eternal damnation of their sin, that Jesus took on, that Jesus paid for, that cost Jesus His life in our place, that person has a very different view of sin than the rest of the world. They feel sin closing in on them and look for exits everywhere they go. They know the enslaving addictiveness of sin and they're not okay with recreational, responsible, just-once-in-a-while sin. They know the devastation of a life wrecked by sin, so they put their seat belt on just sitting in the driveway because they're not about to go anywhere without protection.

Spiritual neutrality is when we stop having a serious aversion to sin, when we forget how dangerous it is, and when we start being entertained by it, amused by it, we're comfortable around it and the people who practice it. Spiritual neutrality is when we stop aggressively resisting sin, and are passively squeezed into the mold of the world.

Compartmentalized Christianity

Secondly, spiritual neutrality is when we compartmentalize our life so that not every part has to come under Christ's control. We have our church life, and we know how we're supposed to operate there, and we do pretty well. And we have our business life, and we have our social life, and we have our secret life, and we give Christ control over His part, but not over every part.

"Or do you not know that your body is the temple of the Holy Spirit?" Your body, the whole thing, sitting there reading this book. That whole thing is what belongs to the Holy Spirit. "Therefore glorify God in your body and your spirit, which are God's."

Remember that we are bought with a price. Not just the church part. Jesus didn't buy a time-share when He bought you with His own blood. He bought complete, total, full-time, 24-7-365, 366-on-a-leap-year-ownership, and spiritual neutrality is when we forget that. We drift away from that, and we stop glorifying God in the little things.

"Therefore, whether you eat or drink, or whatever you do, do all to the glory of God."[209] I don't get to do ministry for the glory of God and then do work for the glory of my bank account. I don't get to do church for the glory of God and do my free time for the glory of me, my personal enjoyment, or my agenda, or my goals. We are supposed to bring every part of our lives under Christ's control.

First Corinthians 10:31 is our goal in life. It's not to get more for me. It's to give more to Him. To glorify Him in the little things, and then in the big things. But if we compartmentalize our Christianity, giving Him control over some things and not others, then we stop glorifying Him in the little things, and then in the big things, and we have become, like the Laodiceans, spiritually neutral.

The Weight of Glory

When Paul tells us that our bodies and spirits belong to God, he follows it with the word "therefore." "Therefore" is an explanatory summation particle, a gateway to stand there and look back to see why something is

---

209 1 Corinthians 10:31

necessary. When you find a "therefore," you have to look back to see what it's there for. And at the end of verse 20, "therefore" tells us to look back where Paul says that our bodies are reserved, that we are owned by God, that we are inhabited by the Spirit, that we are no longer ours. We are His.

So, because of all that, because of the purchase of God, because of the moving in of the Spirit, because of His declaration of taking possession, "glorify God."

We don't use "glorify" in every day language. It's only ever used in the Bible and Christian songs and by Christian teachers, so we don't really have a good idea of what it means. "Glory" means "weight," "heaviness." Do you know how to glorify God? It means you feel the weight of Him on every part of your life.

For most Christians, God is weightless. The polls find that there is no quantifiable difference between Christians and unsaved people. Why? Because we don't feel His weight on us. We don't feel His "glory" on us. We don't feel the pressure, the weight, of having to respond to who He is and what He wants from us.

Spiritual neutrality is when we stop feeling the weight of God on our lives. We just drift through life, and if we stop responding to God in one area of our lives, and nothing too bad happens, we stop responding in other areas of our lives. God has no weight, and it's sickening to Christ.

Paul put it this way: "No soldier entangles himself in the affairs of this world that he may please the one who enlisted him." Spiritual neutrality is entangling ourselves in the affairs of this world instead of, drafted by grace into God's army, living every moment to please the One who enlisted us, who owns us.

If this is His body, then would He take His body to this place? Would He put on His body these clothes? Would He place His body in front of that screen, watching those things? Would He, from His body, say those words? Would He starve His body by not feeding it the Word of God?

Sanctified believers feel the weight of His glory on every part of their lives. They feel the ownership of God. And not feeling that ownership is sickening to Christ.

LIVING IN THE SHADOW OF THE CROSS

As Savior and Lord of the Church, Jesus went visiting one of His local churches, looking to see if those He justified were living out being sanctified. That's the bottom line at Laodicea—He was going to see His justified ones to see if they were living sanctified lives. Justification and sanctification go hand and hand, like two sides of the same coin. You can't be sanctified (have a holy life) without being justified. People try, but it's impossible. And you haven't been truly justified unless He's doing a sanctifying work in your life.

The sad news is that He found the Laodiceans neglecting what He died for them to be. He wanted them to live a life that was constantly overshadowed by His work on the cross, but He found instead that the justifying work He'd done in the past was simply ancient history to them that they hadn't given a second thought to since.

Jesus wanted to find the shadow of His cross falling across their path, their every action, their every thought, their every attitude influenced and motivated by the shadow of His justifying work falling across their lives. And instead, He found a group of people stagnating in spiritual neutrality, claiming they were indeed justified, but neglecting to live sanctified. They failed to feel the weight of glory of all the truth that was readily available to them.

Laodicea had neglected the truths of the book of Romans, which most theologians agree is the most important book of the Bible. We know that Laodicea had Romans in their library, on their shelves, in their church, but they had failed to appropriate it into their lives. When Jesus tells Laodicea to "be zealous and repent," He calls them to turn from spiritual neutrality back to the truths that they had neglected for so long, and that foundational truth is laid out for us by the apostle Paul in the first six chapters of the book of Romans.

Justified by Faith

Romans outlines the heart of the gospel. It's the CliffsNotes for all the content Jesus has delivered and taught to all true, Bible-believing churches of the first century. It distills down into a few chapters all that the apostles preached, taught, and what was delivered to all the churches, including Laodicea. It's the foundation they should have built on, and what Jesus found they'd failed to live by.

Paul systematically lays down the foundation of Christ's death as how we are to live our daily lives. Like a lawyer presenting a case, the apostle Paul gives evidence after evidence, truth after truth, and then he brings it to a verdict, a decision, a turning point, and makes a passionate appeal for a changed life, a crucified life, the life Laodicea failed to live.

Most of us can't say enough how thankful we are that Jesus died for us, but like Laodicea, we go on living like we're on our own. Jesus had all of my sins imputed to Him. He had all of my sins credited to His account. He had to suffer in my place, your place, and His justifying death accomplishes salvation. Romans is the foundation for understanding what salvation did to God because of our sins, and to us because we're the sinners.

The first half of chapter one is about the righteous, the justified ones. In the second half, God's wrath is poured out on the unrighteous. In chapter 2, God is the impartial Judge. Whether you have the Law or not, whether or not you grew up under the teaching of the Old Testament, He analyzes what's going on in your life, He judges, and He does it righteously and impartially. And regardless of our past, we are all accountable. You can't be saved unless you're first lost, and in chapter 3, everyone is found guilty and convicted of sin.

There's the righteous, there's the unrighteous, and God judges between them, finding everyone guilty, and chapter three ends with the wonderful conclusion: only the justifying work of Christ can save you. Why? Because God is impartial and righteous, the perfect Judge, and He can't let sin slide. All sin has to be accounted for. Salvation is a judicial accounting concept. All the sin in the universe has to be somewhere, and there's only two places it can be deposited. On Christ, who took my place, paid the penalty, and forever erased the record of it, or on the sinner forever.

The worst thing Jesus ever said to anyone was, "You will die in your sin." Do you know what hell is? It's the wrath of God poured on, day after day, forever burning against sin, and the worst fate in the universe is to die with that sin still on you. Jesus, and only Jesus, offers justification. That's chapter 3.

In chapter 4, we learn that Abraham received justification by faith, not by law-keeping. The fifth chapter, the best one so far, is about the glorious by-products of Christ's justifying death for me. Salvation gives me peace with God, a standing by grace, but now, Romans 6:1–11, the justifying death of Christ opens to me the sanctifying life of Christ.

For five and a half chapters, Paul has lined out the justifying work of Christ systematically, all leading up to chapter 6 verse 11. For those five and a half chapters, God doesn't give a single command. Not a single one. Not until 6:11. That's significant to me. In chapter 6, with all the weight of the first five and a half chapters bearing down on it, Paul calls for a very specific response.

After five solid chapters of so much doctrine, what is so important that God would use His first command, His first imperative in the whole book to communicate with us? Everything is bearing down, the weight of all that theology, all those truths coming down to a point, and we can't just go on. We have to respond.

This is the decision Laodicea failed to make. They shrugged, said they'd think about it, and passively rejected Christ's sanctifying work in their lives. They accepted His justifying work on the cross, said thanks, and stagnated in spiritual neutrality ever since.

Sanctified by His Life

"Reckon yourselves to be dead to sin and alive in Christ Jesus."[210] The imperative is to *logizomai*, to "reckon," or "consider," or "count." *Logizomai* means to operate on what you already know to be true.

What do we know to be true? What did the Laodiceans know that they were failing to do? In Romans 6, Paul gives three incredible truths of what living in the shadow of Christ's cross is all about.

First, Christ's death on the cross has once and for all freed me from sin's hold on my life. "What shall we say then? Shall we who died to sin still live in it?" Paul's first point: Christ's death has freed me from sin's hold.

---

210 Romans 6:11

The One who bought me, who purchased me, who justified me gave me a package deal. We're saved from the penalty of sin at the cross. Penalty gone. And the rest of the package is to unleash into my life His sanctifying work. Jesus living through us frees us from the absolutely dominating power of sin, and that deliverance from sin's power is life long. That's why He purchased me to begin with—so that I can be to the praise of His glory. And when I reach heaven, I won't just be saved from the penalty of sin or freed from the power of sin, but I will be untouched by the presence of sin as well. It's a whole package, and right now, every time I give sin power over me, I'm neglecting sanctification and Jesus who justified me is nauseated by my choices.

Like Solomon with his son, Jesus has pointed out to us, "See that spiritual neutrality? That doesn't please God," and now it's up to us to do the opposite: repent. The first habit of a sanctified believer is to repent of spiritual neutrality, and repentance is a lifelong choice. Any time we find ourselves drifting into spiritual neutrality, as often as we need to, we stop, we repent, and we ask God to help us resist sin.

If the lukewarm believer stops aggressively resisting sin, then the sanctified believer makes a habit of aggressively resisting sin. God doesn't want us to be neutral about sin. We're against it, in any form in our life. We're pursuing holiness.

Like someone who escaped the trap of a house fire, we resist the trap of sin and always know where the exits are, ready to run, to flee from sin when it comes. Like someone who's been in a car wreck, we watch our speed, we strap ourselves in with the Word of God and the armor of God, and we resist the urge to fall asleep, heeding Christ's call to stay awake. And like someone who knows the addictive, destructive power of alcohol, we aren't entertained or amused or comfortable around recreational sin, no matter how responsibly we want to practice it. We resist sin as aggressively humanly possible, only it's not human strength that gives us the power to say no to sin. It's the power of the cross.

Living in the shadow of Christ's cross means, number two, that I am going to be forever impacted by Christ's death in my place. "Or do you not know that as many of us as were baptized into Christ Jesus were baptized into His death?"

When I was obediently baptized as a believer in the name of Jesus, I made a public declaration that Jesus has already done something for me. I have been justified. And beginning at the moment of salvation, Christ's death forever has an impact on my life.

Christ's cross doesn't only have an impact on my standing with God or on my Sunday schedule. It progressively impacts every area of my life until there is no part of my life that's not under Christ's control. That's called progressive sanctification.

Do you know what hinders sanctification? It's when I think there's an area of my life where I think I can do better than what God can do. There are parts of my life I just don't want to let Him loose on, because I just don't want to believe He knows better than me, I'm not sure He can do as good a job as I can do. Sanctification is surrender. When I let Christ's cross impact me, when I give up and say that He knows more, that He owns me, and there's not one part of my life where I'm not willing to give Him free reign.

When I operate on the truth that Christ's death forever has an impact on my life, then I live crucified, giving up my way for His way, in every way. My thoughts, my actions, my attitudes, my agenda, my plans for the future, my home life, my work life, my secret life, all impacted, forever, by Christ's death in my place. That's living in the shadow of Christ's cross.

The third point Paul makes is that I should walk in sanctification because Jesus justified me, and he says it again and again for the next several verses.

"Therefore, we were buried with Him through baptism into death, and that just as Christ was raised from the dead by the glory of the Father, even so we also should walk in newness of life."[211] Christ's death is my justification. Christ's life in me is my sanctification. "For if we have been united together in the likeness of His death, certainly we shall be also in the likeness of His resurrection."[212]

"Knowing this, that our old man was crucified with Him, that the body of sin might be done away with, that we should no longer be slaves of sin.

211 Romans 6:4
212 Romans 6:5

Now if we died with Christ, we believe that we shall also live with Him. For the death that He died, He died to sin once for all; but the life that He lives, He lives to God. Likewise,"[213] and there's that word, "reckon," or "consider," or "count." Operate on what you know to be true.

What do we know? Christ's death on the cross has freed me from the power of sin. Christ's death on the cross forever has an impact on my life. I should walk in sanctification because Christ's death on the cross justified me. That's what I know. Now I have to make a choice. Act, or be spiritually neutral and fail to act.

Jesus' justifying work has weight. It bears down on me. It comes to a point where I have to make a decision, and I should walk in sanctification because I'm justified.

This is what Laodicea had forgotten. Jesus' sacrifice was weightless to them. They weren't aggressively resisting the sin He freed them from. They weren't allowing the impact of what Jesus had done to change every part of their lives. They were drifting, not glorifying God in the small things, then the big things. They didn't feel the seriousness of sin. They didn't feel the urgency for holiness and sanctification in every part of their lives. And they didn't feel the weight of glory.

We have to know what Christ has done before we know what we must do. *Logizomai*, in verse 11, operate on what you know to be true. You and I have a choice today. We have the same five and a half chapters bearing down on us. We have the same weight, the same justifying work of Jesus done in our past, and what He did in the past should effect our present. It should change us, every part of us. Living in the shadow of Christ's cross means that His work colors everything we do. There are no parts of our lives where we don't feel the weight of what He's done.

Spiritually neutrality is when compartmentalized Christians are passively squeezed into the mold of the world because they don't feel the weight of glory. The first habit of a sanctified believer is to repent, and live in the shadow of Christ's cross, daily, aggressively resisting sin, surrendering every part of our lives to the One who died for us, and feeling His weight on us every day.

213 Romans 6:6, 8, 10

Spiritual neutrality isn't a decision. It's an indecision. It's not a choice. It's putting off making a choice. It's not somewhere you decide to go. It's a place you slowly drift to. And Laodicea had, because they weren't actively, intentionally, purposefully living in the shadow of the cross, and it made Jesus sick to His stomach, and wishing He could spew them away from Him as fast as He could.

When Jesus looks at the twenty-first-century church, He sees the same bad habits He saw in Laodicea, but He doesn't have to see them in my life. I can choose to live crucified, to live free from the hold and power of sin, to live impacted by His death, and to live sanctified because I have been justified. I can learn from Laodicea what not to do, so that when Jesus visits me, His justified one, He will find sanctified living. The weight of glory bearing down, Jesus calls for a decision, to live a changed life, a crucified life, a life lived in the shadow of the cross.

Father, I pray that every one of us would cry out to You today and repent of any area of our lives that we have removed from Your control. We don't want that in our lives. And I pray by the power of the cross to crucify and take back that area under Your control again, my eyes, my mind, my tongue, my fears, my habits. And Lord, I pray that we will cultivate the habit of repenting, as often as it takes, every time we drift into spiritual neutrality, and we just go with the flow instead of reconquering by Your grace those areas of our lives that our flesh and the world and the devil want to neutralize. O Lord, we ask that in the precious name of Jesus, and for His glory. Amen.

RESPOND to Truth

How does Jesus feel about middle-of-the-road, don't-rock-the-boat Christians? (Matthew 12:30–37; 25:14–30; Revelation 3:15–16)

How does our modern view of the seriousness of sin and passion for holiness compare with Christ's view? (Hebrews 12:14–17; James 4:4–10)

What does the opposite of spiritual neutrality look like?
(1 Corinthians 6:18–20; 1 Timothy 6:11–14)

Am I entertained by sin, comfortable around it, and close friends with those who practice it? What does Jesus think about that?

What parts of my life have I carved out for myself that should be surrendered back to Jesus?

If Jesus were to follow me around for a week, would He find the weight of glory affecting all of my actions, the shadow of the cross falling across my every step? Or would He find that I thank Him once a week for a past event that has no present effect on me?

19 | Christians Who Have Need of Nothing: The Sickening Habit of Self-Sufficiency

I AM RICH: THE NAUSEATING CONDITION OF LAODICEA

Perhaps the most noticeable parallel between Laodicea and the modern church is what I call the second bad habit of lukewarm Christians, and it's actually considered a virtue here in America. We spend our lives working for it, we base our career choices on it, we look for it in a potential spouse, we drill it into our children, and this is a lifestyle that Jesus finds in Laodicea, and when He points it out, He says, "that makes Me sick."

The second sickening habit that makes Christ want to vomit is spiritual self-sufficiency, and it's when God's people say to themselves, "I am rich, have become wealthy, and have need of nothing."

Making Piles

If you were to walk around first-century Laodicea, you would get the feel of a wealthy financial district. It would be like walking through the global center for banking in London, or the area around Rockefeller center in Manhattan. That was what Laodicea was like. Wealth was evident, banking was concentrated, gold was readily seen, worn by all the people, and available for sale, so much so that if you saw gold anywhere else in the Roman Empire, you'd recognize it immediately as coming from Laodicea.

Laodicea was by far the wealthiest city it the whole region. No city rivaled their riches. It was their defining feature, the most noticeable thing about the city. And that's just secular history. You can read that anywhere.

And when Jesus visits, He overhears the Laodiceans saying, "I am rich." That's what they say to themselves. That's how they see themselves. And that's the impression of everyone who visited the city: They were rich.

Like the modern-day church, the Laodiceans were concerned with financial security. They were building up their investments and accumulating possessions, but what Jesus found is something we often don't realize: our wealth can often be an impediment to needing Jesus. We know Him, but we don't often need Him.

The Laodiceans were sitting back and saying to themselves that they "have become wealthy." The NASB says, "and have become wealthy." In the NIV, "I have acquired wealth." And ESV says, "I have prospered." But the closest to the original Greek meaning is the KJV: "and increased with goods."

Back then, there was no such thing as digital wealth. If you had it, it was sitting there, in barns, in storehouses. You had servants and gold and houses and all this stuff. And when Jesus says they are "increased with goods," He means that they were making piles. Stacking up wealth all around them, completely self-sufficient. And this is what Jesus says to the self-sufficient church:

REVELATION 3:15–19

"I know your works, that you are neither cold nor hot. I could wish you were cold or hot. So then, because you are lukewarm, and neither cold nor hot, I will vomit you out of My mouth. Because you say, 'I am rich, have become wealthy, and have need of nothing'— and do not know that you are wretched, miserable, poor, blind, and naked—I counsel you to buy from Me gold refined in the fire, that you may be rich; and white garments, that you may be clothed, that the shame of your nakedness may not be revealed; and anoint

*your eyes with eye salve, that you may see. As many as I love,
I rebuke and chasten. Therefore be zealous and repent."*

When I speak in third-world places, by and large, I don't even see a cell phone. It's like you're back in the forties. No one's distracted. You know what they say when you come and speak at those places? They have a morning service from eight to noon, a little church dinner, and then they say, "Hey, can you speak again?" And if I don't have another message prepared, that's fine. They have me just speak the same one over again. They're not checking their iPhones and worrying about what time it is. They're not concerned that the game's going to start or the restaurant is going to be full, or needing to update or check in or anything. They have nothing else going in life but Christ.

Laodicea was the exact opposite. They were rich. They had become wealthy, and they had so many gizmos and so many interruptions in their lives that their wealth, by all appearances, had become a hindrance to their spiritual health. They had neglected for so long what was needed for their souls, and while they were rich and increased in goods and had so many materialistic pursuits of pleasure, they had become completely un-needing of Christ.

Remember the rich young ruler that ran to Jesus? He ran up asking how to be saved. Jesus told him about the commands, but he'd already done all that, so Jesus said he needed to sell all his possessions. And instantly, the Bible says, his face fell, he turned, and he walked away.

Like Laodicea, the rich young ruler had great, vast, piled-up stuff. His treasures were supreme over any desire for God or Christ, and he couldn't surrender his stuff to God. He needed the stuff more than he needed Christ. That's what materialism does. Sanctification is God loosening the tug of material things, so often, the more financial resources we have, the harder it is to surrender control of our lives to Christ.

The Pilgrims put it this way: Out of a hundred people, ninety-nine can survive horrific trials, tragedy, sickness, suffering, and disaster and be okay. But only one in a hundred can survive material prosperity.

...And Have Need of Nothing

The same earthquake that destroyed Philadelphia in AD 17 also leveled Laodicea. Philadelphia appealed to the emperor, and he gave them tax exemption and sent money to rebuild, but when he offered the same thing to Laodicea, they said, "keep your money." And they completely rebuilt the city themselves.

Jesus was speaking to the most financially prosperous group of people in the region, and there was not a more defective group of Christians to be found. They were building up bigger barns and piling up treasures around them, living for this world instead of for the next one. Their vast piles had gotten in the way of sanctification, and Jesus was so disgusted by them that He wanted to spew them away from Him as fast as He could. They had abandoned living in the power of the cross.

By all appearances, it was their wealth that was holding them back. Jesus said it. He said they'd confessed it. They didn't need all that spiritual stuff like they used to, or like their parents did. The Laodiceans had heard the gospel, had read the Scriptures, and they thought they had graduated from that. They were doing just fine on their own. And that sickens Christ.

When the emperor offered money to rebuild, the Laodiceans said, "We don't need that. We can do it ourselves," and Jesus said they did the same thing to Him. The God of all the universe offered them unimaginable riches, and they said, "We don't need that. We can do it ourselves." That's spiritual self-sufficiency.

You think no one would do that? That's not you? Oh, but there's a test.

THE TEST FOR SPIRITUAL SELF-SUFFICIENCY

If Laodicea is the example of what not to do, then David would be the example of a life of spiritual dependence on God. He says in Psalm 16, "Preserve me, O God, for in You I put my trust. My goodness is nothing apart from You. O Lord, You are the portion of my inheritance. I will bless the Lord who has given me counsel. I have set the Lord always before me."[214]

That's the exact opposite of spiritual self-sufficiency, and in the last verse, verse 11, David gives three tests, so that we can do a self-diagnostic.

214 Psalm 16:1, 2, 5, 7, 8

Do I Seek God's Guidance?

Sanctification is when God is leading and controlling me. And spiritual self-sufficiency is the opposite of that. That's David's first test, Psalm 16:11: "You will show me the path of life." So I ask myself, do I seek God's guidance? Or am I walking through life self-sufficiently, out in front of God, finding my own way?

There are many pathway divergences in life, and if I don't constantly ask what God wants, what He wants me to do, what His word says, how I can honor Him, I walk through life displeasing to God. That's spiritual self-sufficiency, when instead of seeking God as my guide, I find my own way through life.

This one isn't hard to spot. You see someone out there and the Lord is just trailing them. They're trying every door and bumping and falling into pits and they're tripping and all scraped up in life and the Lord's behind them whispering, "You're supposed to be going that way. You're plowing ahead the wrong way." And they're saying, "I don't need You."

I'm actually old enough to remember having to walk to the outhouse in the middle of the night, and I remember thinking every monster in the world was between the house and the outhouse. And of course no one would go with me, so I made sure to take every light possible. Do you know there are Christians who are out there in the dark, stumbling around, still looking for the outhouse and never finding it because they never think to switch on the light?

Think no one would do that? No? How does God lead us? How does God guide us? "Your word is a lamp to my feet and a light to my path." Seeking God's guidance isn't coming to a crossroads and hoping for some kind of sign. It's turning on the light of God's Word.

David's first test for spiritual self-sufficiency: Do I seek God's guidance? Spiritual self-sufficiency is when I go my own way. I revert to my own self-guidance system, I stop listening to Christ as my guide, and I run out in front. Seeking God's guidance means we go to His Word, our light, our lamp, and let Him guide our way. We read His Word and let Him tell us what He expects from our life, what He wants us to do, what He says pleases Him. God is out in front, and I let Him lead.

So we have to ask ourselves, is He being my guide? Or am I being my own guide? Am I choosing to stay obediently behind Him and follow Him or am I out in front, bumping into things and falling into pits because I don't think to turn on the Light of His Word? Seeking God's guidance is a daily choice. And if we don't make that choice daily, we become, like Laodicea, sickeningly self-sufficient.

Do I Seek God's Presence?

If there's one thing that Christians know about Laodicea, it's that they are the lukewarm church in a city known for its tepid water. But the Laodiceans weren't out there in the middle of the night poisoning their own water. They were just too far from the source. It would come boiling hot from the hot springs at Hieropolis or come ice-cold from the mountain springs of Colosse, but Laodicea was just so far from the water source that by the time the hot water got there, it was tepid, it smelled and tasted like rotten eggs, and no one wanted to drink it. And by the time the cold water got there, it had gotten so stagnant and nasty that it, too, was lukewarm and good for nothing.

That's what happened to the church. The passionate love and fearless evangelism used to characterize Christ's church had gradually cooled, tempered by wealth until it had become lukewarm and nauseating to Christ. The hope-filled expectancy that used to make churches like Laodicea a cool drink of water, refreshing and revitalizing to those around them, had stagnated. They were living for the here and now, building bigger barns and making piles. And it made them as nasty as their water.

Spiritual self-sufficiency is when I drift too far from the source. David says, "In Your presence is fullness of joy," and that's the second test.

Self-sufficiency is when I feel like I can make it on my own. I have what I need. I have my own source of joy, my own strength, my own resources. I have piles and stacks and barns and bigger barns, and I don't need God's presence in my life. I can make it myself.

David says fullness of joy comes from God, from being in His presence. So I have to ask myself, do I seek God's presence? Do I seek to stay in touch with Him? Do I listen to Him through His Word and speak to Him through prayer? Do I long to come into His presence through corporate worship with other believers, or am I doing just fine on my own?

The proof of staying in God's presence is what David calls the spiritual fruit of joy. That's when I am detached from my circumstances and rejoicing in Christ. If my joy, my contentment, is tied to things, to circumstances, then that means I've drifted too far away from the source.

This summer, I started filming what I used to teach at the Master's seminary, historical theology, and history of doctrine, and church history, and I would film it on sight in all these historical places. So whenever we'd go on one of these trips, there'd be one person in our group who held this little personal Wi-Fi thing, and I had to make sure that wherever I was standing, I was always in range of that device, so all the electronics would work, and the filming would work, and I was always checking, constantly making sure that I wasn't out of range.

Do you know that some Christians just slowly drift out of range of God's presence? He's supposed to be our source of joy, being detached from our circumstances, our source of strength, our source of righteousness, our source of hope and peace and security, our resource for everything, and some Christians just drift. They get out of range. They just float out there on their own, making it on their own, not tapping in to the presence of God. Not taking advantage of all the riches freely available to us. Not relying on God for everything. They are self-sufficient, not Christ sufficient.

Remember what living in the shadow of Christ's cross means? I operate on what I know to be true. That word, *logizomai,* speaks of a usable balance. God has credited Christ's righteousness to our account, and we are supposed to be constantly checking what we have in our account and tapping into that. Self-sufficiency is when we don't even check. We have need of nothing, and so instead of operating on Christ's expense account, all of which has been credited to me, with no holds on it, no penalties, no fees, we just drift out of range, never check the balance, and don't seek God's presence. We're just fine on our own.

Is it Christ that suffices me? Or is it self? That's the second test.

Do I Seek God's Influence?

Spiritual self-sufficiency is when I have time for every other influence on my life but God. We are supposed to stay under God's influence, at His right hand, letting Him control our lives, not just to guide us, but to control us day by day, and that's David's third test: "At Your right hand are pleasures forevermore."

Jesus said it like this: "But seek first the kingdom of God and His righteousness, and all these things will be added to you." Spiritual self-sufficiency is when I seek all these other things first, and then hope that I find time for God later.

When Jesus says, "the kingdom of God," that speaks of His rule, His influence, His control. Test number three: Do I seek God's influence? But more than that, do I seek God's influence first, before every other influence on my life? Seeking God's kingdom, His influence, His control, is supposed to be "first." That's first in place, first in time, first in order of importance, and first on our to-do list.

Spiritual self-sufficiency is when I try to make it one day on my own. I don't seek God's guidance. I don't seek His presence. I don't seek His influence.

We abandon God's guidance when we fail to check in with His word. We stumble along according to our self-guidance system. We never bother flipping on the light to guide our steps.

We abandon God's presence when we don't bother to stay in range, we drift away from Him as our source, we get our joy and everything else from somewhere else. We're self-sufficient, not Christ sufficient.

But the most dangerous sign of self-sufficiency is when we stop seeking God's will before our own, and that shows up when we have time for every other influence on our life but Him. Jesus says that's self-sufficiency, and it makes Him sick.

THE CURE FOR SPIRITUAL SELF-SUFFICIENCY: WALKING IN THE POWER OF THE CROSS

How did you do on David's self-diagnostic? Like David, are you living in daily dependence on God's guidance, presence, and influence to make it through each day, or like the Laodiceans, are you rich, increased in goods, and have need of nothing, including God?

Don't worry if you failed the test. There's a cure. And the cure for spiritual self-sufficiency is what I call walking in the power of the cross.

God's Emancipation Proclamation

The cross of Christ, God says, is my source of power to live in a world of sin. Galatians 6:14 says, "But God forbid that I should boast," that's spiritual self-sufficiency, "except in the cross of our Lord Jesus Christ." That's the power of the cross. What does the power of the cross do? Paul applies it in two ways, the external, and the internal. The external is "by whom the world has been crucified to me," and the internal is "and I to the world."

I think about those in today's world who are absolutely enslaved to sin, whether it's sexual sin, with children or with prostitutes or the sin of homosexuality, or it's enslavement to fear or hatred or something else. Before we're saved, we were powerless to get away. We were addicted to sins that we had no power to say no to. They were absolutely dominating, inescapable. We were completely enslaved.

The power of the cross means "the world has been crucified to me." All that's in the domain of Satan, all that pulls me away from God, everything that is not glorifying to God, that used to have a hold on me. But the cross of Christ has broken sin's hold on me.

The prison bars have been broken, the shackles have fallen off, the cell door is swung open, and I have been freed from sin's hold on my life. I do have the power to say no to sin. What used to rule me no longer has absolute, dominating power over me. The pull of those sins may still be strong. But the power has been broken. That's the power of the cross.

The second effect of the cross of Christ is internal: "and I [have been crucified] to the world." That means hunger for sin has been broken. It doesn't matter what sin you hunger for. It can be the lust of the flesh, always craving and never being satisfied. It can be the lust of the eyes, always needing one more this or that. It can be the pride of life, always hungering for more attention, to be the center of any gathering, to always top everybody else. It doesn't matter what sin we hungered for, because now, we have a spiritual appetite suppressant.

I remember when my wife was concerned about how much sugar I was putting in my coffee, so I started drinking coffee without all the sugar in it, and you know what I found out? I don't like coffee. I like sugar. But I kept at it, and after about a month, I realized I wasn't craving sugar anymore. And now, when I put sugar in my coffee, I want to spit it out, because it tastes terrible to me. That's what the cross of Christ does. It changes our spiritual appetites. It makes us hunger and thirst for righteousness, it makes sin taste putrid in our mouths, and it crucifies the hunger that we had for sin.

Do you know what else it does? The cross of Christ makes me allergic to what used to feed me. Personally, I know that if I drink milk or eat any dairy products, it makes my nose run. It doesn't stop me from pouring it on my cereal or having a bowl of ice cream, but every time I have dairy, I know immediately because I have a bad reaction. That's how the cross of Christ works. It doesn't stop me from putting milk on my cereal, but when I do, when I get around sin, when I taste it, when I feed myself with it, I find that I'm allergic to it. I have a bad reaction.

The power of the cross changes my appetite and makes me allergic to the sin that used to feed me. I can still feed my old hunger and resurrect it, but Christ has dealt it a mortal blow. It's so weakened it never has to rise up again.

But do you know what a lot of Christians do? Instead of walking in the power that Christ's cross makes available to us, we say, no thanks. We're doing just fine on our own.

In the 1860s, the United States declared that no person could be owned by another. Those who were once slaves were now free. But do you know that for decades, they never left the plantations? They had freedom; they just didn't know what to do with it.

Galatians 6:14 is God's Emancipation Proclamation. When the apostle Paul was arrested in Philippi in Acts 16, God sent an earthquake to free him. The prison bars were broken, the chains fell off, and the cell door swung open, but Paul didn't leave. He hung around. And there are a lot of Christians who are like the apostle Paul. God has declared them emancipated, free from the hold of sin. They are no longer under the control of their former masters. But they're still living on the plantations. They're still sitting in the prison house of sin. They have freedom, according to Galatians 6:14, they just don't know what to do with it.

Crucified with Christ

God's Emancipation Proclamation tells us that we have the power of the cross at our disposal, but it doesn't tell us how to walk in that power. Galatians 2:20 does. It's Paul's personal salvation testimony, and it is a testimony of one of the most spiritually self-sufficient people in history, and how he learned to walk in the power of the cross.

Paul told the church at Philippi, "If anyone else thinks he may have confidence in the flesh, I more so: circumcised the eighth day, of the stock of Israel, of the tribe of Benjamin, a Hebrew of the Hebrews; concerning the law, a Pharisee; concerning zeal, persecuting the church; concerning the righteousness which is in the law, blameless." He was self-sufficient. He was an expert at the law, he was zealous for what he thought were good works, and his righteousness was unsurpassed.

But then he says, "What things were gain to me, these I have counted loss for Christ." He went from being righteous in his own works to having a righteousness that comes from Christ. He went from boasting in his strength to boasting in his weaknesses so that Christ could be strong. He went from being self-sufficient, to finding His sufficiency in Christ.[215]

How?

"I have been crucified with Christ," Paul says in Galatians 2:20. He was set free, emancipated, and he goes on to describe the exchanged life: "It is no longer I who live, but Christ lives in me."

There are 30,000 religions in the world, and the gospel of Jesus Christ. 30,000 religions begin with "I." I go to confession. I have a membership. I went on a pilgrimage. I did this and I did that. And then there's the gospel of Jesus Christ, and it doesn't start with "I." It starts with, "It is no longer I who live, but Christ lives in me."

Do you know the cure for spiritual self-sufficiency? It is no longer I who live. That is our purpose statement for living. Not I. Christ. Life is not

215 Philippians 3:4–7; 2 Corinthians 12:9–10

about me, what I'm doing, what I'm not doing, what I'm trying to do. It's Christ, living out through me.

But Paul goes on. "And the life which I now live in the flesh…"

Uh-oh. The life I live in the flesh. The flesh is more than just our physical body. The flesh is the enemy of God and a traitor to us. The flesh, behind the scenes, is doing everything it can to distract us away from God, to get us to disobey the Lord, to cause us to not hunger after Him, to cause us to go our own way instead of following Him. Our flesh is traitorous.

We do not get eradicated as some Christians believe. Our sin nature is not wiped out. We still live in a body of sin, as Paul says in Romans. We still have a nature that wants to sin. We still live in a world of sin. The life I live is still, and will be until heaven, in the flesh.

So how do we live this sanctified life? How do we live out this holy calling that we have? "This life I live in the flesh, I live by faith in the Son of God, who loved me and gave Himself for me."

The gospel of Jesus Christ begins and ends with that: "who gave Himself for me." The justifying work of Christ opens to me the sanctifying life of Christ. The same power that saved me from the penalty of sin will enable me to walk off that plantation, to walk out of that prison house, to no longer submit to my old masters, and instead to walk in the power of the cross.

I am dead to sin every moment of life that I choose to be by faith. The essence of daily life boils down to the walking in the power of the cross, and whether I will allow Christ to crucify the world to me and me to the world. Only the cross deals with the hold of sin on my life. Only the cross can break the hold of habits, besetting sins, addictions, enslavements to sin, and persistent areas of defeat. And only the cross can break the hunger of sin in my life, the distractions, the trifles, the wasted time, deadening behavior, lost spiritual appetites, and the unfocused living that our flesh constantly maintains.

Spiritual self-sufficiency is when we say we don't need the power of Christ's cross in our lives. We can do it in our own strength. We don't need His guidance to keep us on the right path. We don't need to stay connected to Him because we have our own source of joy, our own source of strength, our own pile of treasures, and we don't need Him. We don't need

His influence to live in a world of sin, in the flesh. We've got it covered on our own. But Paul says the only way to live in this world of sin is to live crucified—the world to me, and me to the world, and only the power of the cross can do that.

The Prayer of the Spiritually Dependent

The opposite of spiritual self-sufficiency is spiritual dependence, acknowledging that I can't make it on my own. I can't get through one day without Jesus guiding me, without His presence supplying me, without His word influencing me. So when Jesus taught His disciples to pray in Matthew 6, He taught them the prayer of spiritual dependence.

"Our Father in heaven, hallowed be Your name." Do you know what that says? Focus me. I want to start my day focused in on who God is, and I give Him His proper place in my life. Beginning my day by focusing on who God is not only puts Him in His place. It puts me in mine. If He is God, I am not. Any prayer of spiritual dependence has to start with God as its focus.

"Your kingdom come." Again, His kingdom means His rule, His influence, His control. "Your kingdom come" is telling God that I want Him to run my life. It's saying, control me. Don't let me get outside of Your influence. I'm seeking You first.

"Your will be done on earth as it is in heaven." I don't want to be out in front, bumping into things and trying to find my way in the dark. This prayer says lead me. I want Your guidance. I want You to be out in front. And I want Your will to be done, so lead me to do what pleases You.

"Give us this day our daily bread." I don't stand up and say, "I am rich, have become wealthy and have need of nothing." No. I am in desperate need of what only Jesus can provide. I'm not relying on my own strength, my wisdom, my resources. I get supplied by Jesus Christ so that I can do His will, daily. Supply me. Be my source. Keep me in range. Every day.

"And forgive us our debts, as we forgive our debtors." I know that I need the power of the cross to walk in a world of sin. I know I have not been eradicated. I need Jesus to keep me out of the prison house of sin, saying no to its hold and denying its hunger. This prayer says cleanse me, and keep me clean.

"And do not lead us into temptation, but deliver us from the evil one." Protect me. This is me admitting that my own strength isn't enough. I still live in the flesh, in this body of sin, and every temptation that comes, I pray, Lord, protect me. Keep me from evil. Lead me away from that.

"For Yours is the kingdom and the power and the glory forever. Amen." When I say the kingdom, the power, and the glory belongs to Jesus, acknowledging that it all belongs to Him, that He is in control, then I am praying, Lord, empty me. Empty me so that You get all the credit. Like Paul said, "I will rather boast about my weaknesses, so the power of Christ may rest upon me."[216]

That's what the prayer of spiritual dependence comes down to: Empty me so I can be filled with You. It is no longer I but Christ who lives in me, that's Paul's testimony. You will show me the path of life. In your presence is fullness of You. At Your right hand are pleasures forevermore. That's David's testimony. Focus me, control me, lead me, supply me, cleanse me, protect me, and empty me so that I can be filled with You. Let us make that our testimony and our prayer today.

Our Father in heaven, focus me on who You are. Let Your kingdom, Your control, Your influence come and control me. Lead me so that Your will is done in my life. Supply me what I need each day so that I can obey You. Cleanse me every time I sin, every time I fail to surrender every area of my life to You. Protect me, from temptation, from self-sufficiency, from the evil one and all his fiery arrows that only You, Lord Jesus, can protect us from. And Father, we pray, that You would empty us. Everything that we boast in, everything we rely on that isn't You, everything that makes us self-sufficient, self-confident, self-focused, self-involved, everything that has to do with self, Lord, empty us of that. And fill us instead with You. In the name of Jesus, we pray. Amen.

216 2 Corinthians 12:10

RESPOND to Truth

Am I spiritually self-sufficient? (Psalm 16, Matthew 6:33)

What are some of the dangers of spiritual self-sufficiency for believers? For those who just think they're believers? (Proverbs 16:18; Matthew 7:22–23; Luke 12:16–21; Luke 16:19–25; John 15:4–5; 1 Corinthians 10:6–13)

What do I crave more than God's Word? What do I seek before God's Word each day?

What steps can I take today to give God back His rightful place as first, in order of importance, in time, and on my to-do list?

What sins have I given power to in the last seven days? What hungers have I been feeding instead of crucifying?

What commitments did David make to walk daily in the power of the cross? (Psalm 101)

20 | Spiritually Insensitive: Believers Who Don't Have a Clue

Jesus' most caustic letter tells the believers at Laodicea that He wants to spew them out of His mouth. They are spiritually neutral. No longer do they care about the seriousness of sin. They're not consumed by a passion for holiness. And they've compartmentalized their lives so that He no longer has control over every part. They were rich, wealthy, increased with goods, and completely self-sufficient. They no longer sought God's guidance in their every day lives. They didn't crave His presence, and they didn't submit to His influence. The cross of Christ had all but been forgotten, and Jesus is about to tell us why.

Jesus begins the letter to Laodicea with a demand to pay attention. We are immediately faced with who it is that's speaking, the authority with which He speaks, and whether or not we're going to respond.

Imagine the greatest consortium of doctors from John Hopkins and the Mayo Clinic and Boston General and whatever group of hospitals you think are the most prestigious, and they give you a handwritten letter with your medical diagnosis. That's what Jesus does. The opening words introduce Christ and give His credentials.

When the Great Physician gives a diagnosis, it's actual, not hypothetical. He came to their church, walked through their daily lives as believers. He watched them at home, He watched them at work, He watched them in the church service, and He watched them everywhere in between. He came on an unannounced visit to their church, a real, literal place 2,000 years ago, and wrote back a startling letter about their deteriorating spiritual health. And their condition was sickening to Christ.

And this is their medical diagnosis:

REVELATION 3:14, 17, 20

"And to the angel of the church of the Laodiceans write,
> *'These things says the Amen, the Faithful and True Witness, the*
Beginning of the creation of God: "You say, 'I am rich, have become
wealthy, and have need of nothing'—and do not know that you are
wretched, miserable, poor, blind, and naked. Behold, I stand at the
door and knock. If anyone hears My voice and opens the door, I will
come in to him and dine with him, and he with Me.""

LISTENING TO JESUS

Ephesus needed to be reminded that Jesus held the authority to remove their church from it's place, and so Jesus introduced Himself as the One who holds the seven stars and walks among the lampstands. Smyrna needed Someone to hold onto in the midst of terrible sufferings, so Jesus introduced Himself as the First and the Last, the One who was dead and who came back to life. The compromising church needed to see the Jesus with the sword coming out of His mouth. The corrupt church needed to be reminded that He has eyes of fire and feet of brass for judgment. The dead church was so secure in their fortress-like city, Jesus had to introduce Himself as the One who holds their church in His hands and threatened to come like a thief. And to Philadelphia, the quake-prone church that was built on a fault line, He introduced Himself as the solid, immovable source of all that can't be destroyed.

But when He introduces Himself to Laodicea, He introduces Himself as the One they should listen to. Laodicea had become so confident, so secure, so independent, and so insensitive, that Jesus had to remind them who He was just to get them to listen to Him.

The Amen of God

Jesus starts His letter by introducing Himself as the Amen. Most of us read that and think, what's that? Well, I remember when I would preach in Georgia, they'd use that word all the time. I actually had to learn to preach differently. It was almost like a singsong thing. You have to pause after everything you say so that the congregation can say, "aaaaamen." It wasn't just an "amen." It was "aaaaamen." And that meant, "I agree with what you're saying."

Jesus introduces Himself to Laodicea with a title He's never used before, the Amen of God. That means that He's in perfect agreement with God. God says something and Jesus says "aaaaamen." God says something else and Jesus says "aaaaamen." Nobody else ever calls Jesus that. It's unique to Revelation 3. Jesus is the Amen of God.

Isaiah 65:16 says, "He who blesses himself in the earth shall bless himself in the God of truth, and he who swears in the earth shall swear by the God of truth." If you want a Hebrew lesson, here it is. The word that Isaiah wrote down wasn't the English word "truth." It was the Hebrew word *amen*. That means the blessings of God are confirmed with "amen." When you swear by something, you swear by it with the word "amen."

Amen is the seal, the confirmation, and that's what Jesus claims to be. Jesus is calling Himself the "yes" to all of God's promises. In Jesus, because of His work on the cross, those promises are ours. He is the fulfillment, the One who signs it, seals it, and delivers what God has promised to us, His people.

Paul picks up on this in 1 Corinthians 1:20, not the title, but the same idea. "For all the promises of God, in Him [Jesus] are 'yes' and in Him are 'amen.'" That means that all of the promises of God come through the pipeline of Jesus Christ. They are attached to and come through Him.

Every time Jesus says "verily, verily, I say unto thee" or in modern translations, "truly, truly, I say to you," He's really saying, "amen, amen." Whatever He's about to say is true, verified. Absolute. This is something you can trust. So when Jesus introduces Himself as the Amen, He's prefacing this letter, His medical diagnosis, as being verifiably, perfectly true.

This title is only used for Christ in the letter to Laodicea, in the whole Bible. He's never called this anywhere else. Here, and only here, He lifts up this unique title for Himself, and He presents Himself as the God of truth from Isaiah, with all the authority of God, and as the "yes" to God's promises, the One who, when He says He'll do something, has the authority to carry it out.

The Faithful and True Witness

If you ever watch a courtroom scene on TV, you know there are many types of witnesses. There are true witnesses and there are false witnesses. There are expert witnesses, and there are unreliable witnesses. And everybody has a different perspective on what happened. So by the time the trial is over, hopefully the jury has pieced together something close to the truth and made the right verdict.

Jesus isn't like that.

First of all, He is true. You know it. Jesus says it, it's true. Jesus' testimony is always accurate, completely reliable. The only thing out of His mouth is absolute truth, the whole truth, and nothing but the truth. He says in John 14:6: "I am the way, the truth, and the life." Jesus doesn't just tell the truth. He is the truth, the Amen, the verification, the faithful and true witness. He can't lie.

But He's also faithful. He can be trusted. He is reliable. There's no one else like Him. Jesus' testimony is not tainted by an obstructed view or memory that fades with time or with some kind of agenda. Jesus can't be confused. He can't forget. He can't misinterpret something. He is reliable, down to the last detail.

But the last piece of this title, "witness" is perhaps the most important. Jesus has the ultimate perspective. Jesus alone can see and know and testify to what we can't know about. Most of us don't fully realize that Jesus has seen the end of our lives from the beginning. He knows everything about us, and He's speaking to us as a witness to what we haven't yet seen or couldn't possibly comprehend.

So Jesus introduces Himself as the verifier, the witness. What He says is truth. No one can know what He knows, and He verifies what we can't know. *And lastly, He says, I am "the Beginning of the Creation of God."*

The Beginning of the Creation of God

When Jesus calls Himself the "Beginning of the Creation of God," that does not mean He was the first thing created by God. No. Jesus is God. He wasn't created by God. That's what Jehovah's (false) Witnesses believe. That's what Mormons believe. That's not what we believe. Why? Because that's not what it says.

The word Jesus uses here is *arche*. That means Jesus is the origin and source of all creation, the beginning. Not the first thing at the beginning, but the One who actually began everything else. Everything created comes from Him, through Him. He is the origin. The Creator. John 1:3 says, "All things were made through Him, and without Him nothing was made that was made." That's what *arche* means.

Paul explains it this way: "He is the image of the invisible God, the firstborn over all creation." But Paul doesn't leave it at that. He explains what "firstborn over all creation" means. "For by Him all things were created that are in heaven and that are on earth, visible and invisible, whether thrones or dominions or principalities or powers. All things were created through Him and for Him."

So when Jesus calls Himself the *arche* of all creation, He's claiming to be the Creator, the One who made everything. "Firstborn" doesn't mean He was born first. It means He is the first, the supreme, the One who stands at the head of creation.

But there's another piece to that. Hebrews 1:3 says that Jesus is the One who is "upholding all things by the word of His power." And Paul went on in Colossians 1:15–17 to say: "He is before all things, and in Him all things consist," or "hold together."

Do you know that physicists are still trying to figure out what holds atoms together? They should fly apart because like particles repel each other, but something is holding all of creation together, keeping it all from just coming apart. Scientists call them "gluons," key word: glue. But we know what's really holding the world together, and that's Jesus. How do we know that? Because in 2 Peter 3:10 He lets go. "The heavens will pass away with a great noise, and the elements will melt with fervent heat; both the earth and the works that are in it will be burned up."

"Melt with fervent heat." The whole earth. That's what happens when creation is no longer held together by the Beginning of the Creation of God, the arche. Jesus holds everything together by the word of His power, and He was the One who created it in the first place.

But what's so wonderful is that Jesus isn't just out there, in space, holding what He's created together from His far-away throne. Paul said, "He is the image of the invisible God." Hebrews 1:3 calls Him "the brightness of His glory and the express image of His person." W.A. Criswell, the phenomenal Southern Baptist theologian, said that Jesus is the only God we'll ever see. The Father is spirit, and the Spirit is spirit, but Jesus came in human flesh to be seen by us.

"No one has ever seen God at any time; the only begotten God who is in the bosom of the Father, He has explained Him."[217] Jesus came to us, visible, to explain to us the invisible God. The one with supreme power, who stands between earth and utter annihilation, has come to us to make Himself, and His word, and His will, known to us.

So, when the Amen, the Faithful and True Witness, the *arche,* who holds the world together, makes Himself visible, comes to us, and speaks, do we listen?

Laodicea didn't.

WRETCHED, MISERABLE, POOR, BLIND, AND NAKED: JESUS' DIAGNOSIS OF HIS CHURCH

If we were on a bus tour today and went through St. Louis, my kids would have a race to see who could spot the arch first, because when you see the arch, you know you're in St. Louis. If you wanted to risk the traffic on the Washington, D.C., beltway, everyone in the car would be looking to see the 555-foot-tall Washington Monument. There's the Golden Gate Bridge, or Manhattan's Globe, but every city has something that sticks out in people's minds. And Laodicea had three.

If we were part of a first-century caravan and went through Laodicea, three industries would have been evident, so evident that if you were

217 John 1:18

anywhere else in the Roman Empire and saw these three things, you'd know immediately they came from Laodicea.

The first was gold. It was just everywhere, worn, sold, flaunted unashamedly. The second was eye salve, manufactured and distributed from Laodicea's world-famous medical complex. If you were anywhere in the Roman Empire and needed your eyes fixed, you came here. And the third was their luxurious clothing. Wherever you were in the empire, if you saw someone wearing a Laodicea original, you knew it.

So if there were three things every citizen of Laodicea was proud of, it was their wealth, their eyesight, and their clothing. And Jesus, with the authority of the Amen, the perspective of the Faithful and True Witness, and the power of the Beginning of the Creation of God, says, "You are wretched, miserable, poor, blind, and naked."

The medical advice of your friends and acquaintances from work or school is nice. The medical advice from a trusted family member is nicer. But when you get a world-renowned expert, someone who is skilled and qualified, someone who is universally trusted in their field, and when they give a diagnosis, it is almost beyond foolishness to ignore.

Jesus is the highest authority on spiritual wellness in the universe. As the Amen of God, Jesus has absolute authority, the authority of being God and the authority of being the One who dispenses all the riches that belong to God. As the Faithful and True Witness, Jesus has the ultimate perspective. He can see the future that we will never see until it's too late, He understands what we can never understand, and He can see what is true down to the thoughts and intentions of the heart. As the Beginning of the Creation of God, He's not just the doctor who can fix the body when it breaks. He is the creator, who knit the body together in the first place, who holds all things together by the Word of His power, and as the only God we will ever see, what He says to us isn't hypothetical. It's actual. And we should listen.

So when Jesus, the One with absolute authority, the ultimate perspective, and by the word of His power holds together every molecule of the universe gives a diagnosis of His church, it is almost beyond foolishness to ignore.

Jesus called them wretched, but they felt comfortable being neutral. He said they were miserable, pitiable, people you should feel sorry for, but they were confident in their self-sufficiency. Jesus called them poor, but they say, "I am rich." He said they were blind, but they boasted of 20-20 vision. Jesus sees only nakedness, and they see only the sumptuous clothing that made them the envy of everyone in the empire.

Spiritual insensitivity is when we lose our spiritual sight and no longer see ourselves as God's Word explains we are. We no longer see ourselves the way God sees us, and simply stop listening to Jesus. Spiritual insensitivity is when believers are wretched, miserable, poor, blind, and naked, and don't have a clue. And the Laodiceans had grown so insensitive to the voice of Jesus that they'd become like chain smokers who could no longer smell their own smoke. That's why this condition is so sickening to Christ. Because God's people should know better.

Christians Who Should Know Better

Now let's back up a minute. Jesus calls the Laodiceans spiritually insensitive, and tells them it's sickening to the point that He wants to vomit them out. But how do we know they really are insensitive and not just ignorant? Did they really know what He wanted? Or were they just feeling around, hoping to figure out what Jesus expects from His people and just not doing a good job of it?

Here's the thing: Jesus is not being hard on some little fledgling church that barely had access to His Word. They knew exactly what He wanted from them because they had His spelled-out expectations in their hands. By AD 90, when Revelation was written, the other twenty-six books of the New Testament weren't just slowly making the rounds, maybe showing up in pieces here and there. They were readily available to all the Roman Empire churches—we find the fragments, the documents, everywhere. Laodicea had God's Word.

Laodicea had about as much exposure to God's Word as we do, and they had one up on us because they were just two generations removed from actually having the apostles with them. Peter had passed through this area, John had passed through this area, and Paul died and came back to life near here. We know from the book of Colossians that a personally trained apprentice of

Paul's came across the river from Colosse to lead this church. The Laodiceans had everything they could possibly need. They wanted for nothing.

Today, you and I can attend church without being martyred for our faith. Our church buildings, by and large, are air-conditioned, don't leak, and keep us warm in the winter. Our pews are comfortable. We have a copy of the Bible on every electronic device. We have commentaries, Greek dictionaries, Bible Study guides, online resources, and a physical copy of God's Word in every hotel nightstand. We have Christian radio, Christian concerts, Christian books. We want for nothing.

But, like in Laodicea, God's Word gets taken for granted.

Laodicea had God's Word available at their fingertips, and what Jesus was doing on His inspection tour was checking what His churches knew and what they were doing with it. And He judges the modern church the same way He judged Laodicea: for what all we know, and what we aren't doing with it.

Whether in ancient Laodicea or modern-day America, God's people have no excuse for not knowing or obeying His Word. When we stand before God, we don't get to claim ignorance. We don't get to claim, "I never heard, I didn't know." There is no excuse.

If we stand before Christ with a wasted life, a life lived contrary to the principles in His word, not walking in His power or living in the shadow of the cross, then that's not ignorance. It's insensitivity. It's not, "I didn't know." It's "I didn't listen."

The Amen is speaking. The Faithful and True One is bearing witness. And the Beginning of the Creation of God calls for a response. We have His Word. So what are we going to do with it?

MY SHEEP HEAR MY VOICE: HEARING AND RESPONDING TO JESUS

Hearing Jesus Speak

Steve Jobs completely revolutionized the music industry because now, everyone can carry around their 3,000 favorite songs with them everywhere they go. But what's really revolutionary is to realize that you are carrying around your very own personal recording of the voice of God, and you can flip it open, turn it on, and hear it whenever you ask Him to open your eyes and heart to receive it.

The Bible is like computer code, and you need the right operating system in order to open it. That's the Holy Spirit. And when the Holy Spirit opens to you the Scriptures, then you can hear the very voice of God. If spiritual self-sufficiency is trying to make it one day without God, then spiritual insensitivity is when His voice gets pushed into the background by something else so I stop listening to it altogether.

What is the first thing you seek in the morning? Is it your emails? Your text messages? Or do you sleep with your phone beside you so it can zzzz, zzzz, zzzz, and you won't miss anything? If you go on a trip and accidentally leave your phone charger, do you have to go and buy another one, but if you accidentally leave your Bible, you think, oh, I can do without it until I get home?

Do we have to repent of going first to read the email before God's Word? Or do we have to repent of longing for the financial news to know what's going on in the Asian markets instead of longing for God's Word? Or are we just dying to know the sports' standings or even to hear the voice of the weatherman every day instead of listening to the voice of God?

Are the Facebook posts, the Twitter feeds, the social media updates so important that you carry your phone around with you everywhere, to the bathroom, into the kitchen, in the pocket of your bathrobe while you're having coffee, and you have it connected to your car by Bluetooth so you are always in touch with every influence in the world, but when you pick up your Bible Sunday morning to go to church you realize it hasn't moved since you put it there last Sunday after church?

You don't have to carry around a 1,200 page, red-leather bound copy, but you do have to be hearing Him speak from it some way. Memorize it, read it, listen to it, study it, or yes, carry a big one. But it isn't just having it around. It's listening to it, and responding to what it says.

I Stand at the Door and Knock

There are two ways to be spiritually insensitive: not listening to Jesus' voice, and not responding to it when we do hear it. Jesus says that His people, those who are truly His, are characterized by two things.

"My sheep hear my voice," Jesus says, "and I know them." Jesus' true followers, who are really His, that can't get snatched out of His hand, the ones He knows, those are His sheep, and they do two things. First, they "hear my voice." And second, "they follow me."[218]

The Christian life can be summed up in these two things: listening to Jesus speak, and responding to His Word. Hearing isn't enough. Jesus says to Laodicea, "I stand at the door and knock. If anyone" number one, "hears My voice" and number two, "opens the door, I will come in to him and dine with him, and he with Me."[219]

Hearing Jesus knock is about as far as Laodicea got. They'd become so spiritually self-sufficient and passively neutral that they'd tuned out the persistent knocking. They never opened the door. Never appropriated the power of the cross into their lives. Never committed to living every day in the shadow of the cross.

Revelation 1:3 says, "Blessed is he who reads and those who hear the words of this prophecy." It would be nice if it stopped there. If we, the sheep, could push the Shepherd's voice into the background and mosey on to greener pastures all on our own. If we could hear the knocking and still sit comfortably in our armchairs without getting up to open the door. But Jesus says the blessing comes when, after we've read and heard God's Word, we "keep those things which are written in it."

The Mirror of the Word

Spiritual insensitivity is when we become a forgetful hearer instead of a doer of the Word. "But be doers of the word, and not hearers only, deceiving yourselves. For if anyone is a hearer of the word and not a doer, he is like a man observing his natural face in a mirror; for he observes himself, goes away, and immediately forgets what kind of man he was."[220]

The Bible contains what we should look like, and every time we look into it, we see how far short of that we are. Spiritual insensitivity is when we lose touch with the mirror of the Word that shows us what needs changing each day as we wait before the Lord. But it's also when we look into the

218 John 10:27
219 Revelation 3:22
220 James 1:22–24

mirror of the word, say, hmmm, that's not very good, and immediately go on and forget what we look like.

But, "he who looks into the perfect law of liberty and continues in it, and is not a forgetful hearer but a doer of the work, this one will be blessed in what he does."

If you are a person who cares about your appearance, you never leave the house without looking in the mirror, checking and fixing whatever needs fixing so you look just right. If you really care about what other people think, you compare your reflection in the mirror to what they expect and what they desire, and make sure it matches up.

And if you are a person who cares about holiness, you never leave the house without looking in the mirror of the Word, without checking and fixing whatever needs fixing so you properly reflect His holiness. And if you care about what Jesus thinks, you compare the reflection that you see in the Word of God to what He expects and desires, and make sure it matches up.

When Jesus gives us a command, it's like getting an RSVP. Every other piece of mail, you can tear open, skim, and toss, but an RSVP requires a response. His sheep don't just hear Him, they follow Him. His people don't just tune out the knocking. They get up and open the door. Jesus says those who love Him are the ones who hear His commands? No. The ones who keep His commands. And a sanctified believer doesn't make a habit of looking in the mirror and just going on with their day unchanged. A sanctified believer won't go another minute without seeking to make what we see of ourselves in the mirror of God's Word match up with what Jesus expects and desires.

Five disobedient churches for five different reasons, seven bad habits, and many ways each bad habit shows itself, but Jesus says there's one acceptable response: "Therefore be zealous and repent."

Repentance is a change of mind that leads to a change of behavior. The only way our minds can change is if we fill them with the Word of God, when we listen, and when we respond. That's why of all the different commands and warnings Jesus gives to His churches, He only gives one command to all seven: "He who has an ear, let him hear."

Spiritual insensitivity may be the third bad habit of lukewarm Christians, but it's the bad habit that leads to all the others. If we neglect the mirror of the word and become forgetful hearers, life gets compartmentalized, God no longer has the same weight in our lives, and we passively get squeezed into the mold of the world. We stumble through life as our own guide, we become self-sufficient, not Christ-sufficient, and we begin to have time for every other influence in life but Christ. And if we go through life spiritually insensitive, ignoring the voice of God through His Word, then spiritual wastefulness, neglect, blindness, and laxity won't be far behind.

The opposite of spiritual insensitivity is hearing and responding to God's Word, and it should be the first habit that sanctified believers seek to cultivate. When you're in the Word of God and responding to it, you will be living in the shadow of the cross and walking in its power. Hearing and responding to God's Word is how we seek His guidance. It's where we find His presence, and it's where we allow Him to be the supreme influence on our lives instead of us trying to go through life self-sufficiently. It's where we feel God's weight, it's what reminds us of the seriousness of sin, and it compels and constrains us to give every part of our lives to God.

If there is only one habit that we maintain in our lives, the one thing we do daily, the one thing we can't forget, we won't put off, we don't neglect, it should be hearing and responding to God's Word. Whether listening to it, reading it, memorizing it, hearing it taught, or all of the above, hearing and responding to the Word of God is the first habit of a sanctified believer. "My sheep hear My voice, I know them, and they follow Me." Let us make that our prayer today.

Father in heaven, I thank You that we have the inerrant words of God readily available to us. They are infallible. They are flawless. They are like silver refined in a furnace seven times, completely pure. Thank You that we have the complete revelation of everything You want us to know. We don't need anything else to be dug up or discovered to tell us what You want us to hear. We already have it. You've already told us. And I pray that Your Word would be the standard by which we measure our lives, the message that we cling to. It's already here. You've already spoken. And when we look into the mirror of Your Word and see in ourselves one or more of the seven sickening habits that disgust You, Lord Jesus, I pray that we would hear and respond, and that we would repent, because that's the only response You accept. Let us zealously pursue You. Give us ears to hear and hearts to respond. In Your Son's precious name, we pray. Amen.

RESPOND to Truth

How often have I looked into the mirror of God's Word this week?

What is more important than God's Word in my schedule? In my priorities? How does Jesus feel about that? (Matthew 6:33; Matthew 22:37–38; Revelation 2:4–5)

What does Jesus say the Church would be like approaching the End of Days? (2 Timothy 4:3–4) Am I guilty of that? Is there something the Amen, the Faithful and True Witness, the Beginning of the Creation of God has been saying that I've been disregarding or dismissing?

The Laodiceans boasted in riches, eye care, and clothing. Jesus said they were poor, blind, and naked. What do I boast in or see as my greatest strength? Is Jesus my source of that strength or claim to fame, or am I getting my riches, eye care, and clothing from the wrong source?

What is the difference between just reading God's Word, and actually reading and obeying it, according to Jesus? (Matthew 7:24–27)

When I look into the mirror of God's Word, what do I see in my life that doesn't match up? What can I do today to change that?

Spiritual Wastefulness: Abandoning Christ as Our Investment Counselor

21

The New York Times recently published an article on a group of Japanese gypsies who are finding ways around the radiation zone barrier where the reactor spilled out all its radiation, and these people are going in, just for a few minutes at a time, to get what people left behind when the area was evacuated. They'll go in for a half an hour one week, an hour the next week, and what the doctors are finding is that even though they appear to be absolutely healthy on the outside, they're exposing themselves to such high levels of radiation that they're dying from the inside out. The radiation levels, even with that once-in-a-while exposure, is eating away at the marrow of their bones, shriveling them up, and it's just a matter of time before they just die.

When Jesus visited the seventh church, Laodicea, He found an equally dangerous condition. The Laodiceans weren't just going into the radiation zone once a week. They were living there. They were so consumed with the acquisition of stuff, with the piling up of riches, that they were living right in the radiation zone of materialism.

Materialism doesn't sound all that dangerous to us here in America. It's not one of those overtly repulsive sins. It's one of the acceptable ones, and we even treat it as a virtue, both here in America, and they did it back in Laodicea. But Jesus says it's shriveling the marrow and no matter how healthy we look on the outside, anyone who exposes themselves to radioactive material is risking their life. If materialism sounds less serious or less sickening to Christ than spiritual neutrality or spiritual self-sufficiency, think again.

To understand the danger that Jesus saw when He found the Laodiceans living in the radiation zone of materialism, we have to go back to what the world's wisest man said about the dangers of wealth.

THE EIGHT DANGERS OF TOO MUCH STUFF: INVESTMENT ADVICE FROM THE WORLD'S RICHEST MAN

Solomon, more than any other person in history, had the world at his feet. People came from all over the world to see him, to pay homage to him, to give him gifts. He was unsurpassed in education and knowledge. Because the Lord blessed him and gave him his wish for wisdom, nobody compared to the wisdom of Solomon, before him, or since.

Solomon was unstoppable. He was unbridled in his ability and desire to pursue pleasure. If he wanted something, he could have it, and he set out to discover the very best way to live, and in doing so, Solomon found all the wrong ways to live.

He was also at the peak of worldly fame, popularity, and prominence. Ecclesiastes compares him to all the famous people of his day, but nobody compared to Solomon. And he was the possessor of uncountable wealth.

But, if we did take the time to count it, we would find that his father David left him 5,000 tons of gold.[221] That's 160,000,000 ounces. Last I checked, gold was $1,300 an ounce, which means Solomon inherited 280 billion dollars from his dad. Nobody has that kind of wealth today, and that was just Solomon's starting point. And, that was just in gold.

He also inherited $32 billion in loose change, silver. In Solomon's day, the Bible says, silver was so plentiful it was like rocks in the garden. Solomon didn't even bother with it. You know how most people will pick up a quarter off the ground, but a penny might not be worth getting your

221 1 Chronicles 22:14

hands dirty for? That's what silver was to Solomon. Rocks in the garden.[222] Pretty, but not worth bothering with.

So when Solomon writes a treatise on the dangers of wealth, you know he knows what he's talking about. So after spending his whole life chasing wealth, we find Solomon's conclusion in Ecclesiastes 5:10–15.

"He who loves silver will not be satisfied with silver."

When I heard this passage preached a long time ago, I wrote in my Bible "the more you have, the more you want." That's the first danger of too much stuff, according to the richest man in history. And it's true.

It's the John D. Rockefeller syndrome. Just one more dollar. He was the modern world's first billionaire, and when he was interviewed, that's what he said. All I want is one more dollar. That's the best definition of materialism: that insatiable need for just one more dollar. I need just a little more, or a lot more, but more.

The second danger is similar: "He who loves abundance, [is never satisfied] with increase. This also is vanity." The more you have, the less you're satisfied.

Do you know that some of the happiest people in the world are the people who have nothing? Ask anyone who comes back from a mission trip to a third world country, they were always hit by two things: how little those people had, and how happy they were.

But we in America have been schooled in discontent. That's what advertising does. Your teeth aren't white enough. Your skin isn't smooth enough. Your hair, you don't have enough. *Better* Homes and Gardens. It's not enough to have a home, to have a garden. Mine has to be better than yours. Does your car have rubbed walnut with gold flecks in it? Then you need better. Newer. Bigger. More.

We've been told that we won't be satisfied until we have whatever it is they're selling. But Solomon says the more you have, the less you're satisfied, and wealth does more than breed discontentment. It increases insecurity.

"When goods increase, they increase who eat them." Ask anyone who's won the lottery. Relatives they never knew they had suddenly want a piece of what they have. I've talked to doctors who say somebody is always

---

222 1 Kings 10:27

wanting something from them. Everyone assumes because they're doctors that they're rich, but they don't realize with all the malpractice insurance and all the changing regulations and everything that these doctors are barely making it. When goods increase, or even when people think they increase, the more people there are that want them. That's the third danger: the more you have, the more people (including the government) want to take it away.

The next danger is that the more you have, the less you get to use it. "So what profit have the owners except to see them with their eyes?" People can't even park in their garages anymore because of all the stuff, and there's so much stuff, they can't even see what stuff they have, and so they never get to use it. And when the garage is full, you have to go out and get a storage space to hold more stuff.

The more you have, the less you get to use it. You store it, then never see it again. You don't even think about it except for once a month when you write a check to the storage place to keep your stuff for you that you can't see and won't use. And what's really sad is that you hardly get to enjoy what you have because you're always afraid of losing it.

"The sleep of a laboring man is sweet, whether he eats little or much; but the abundance of the rich will not permit him to sleep." The more you have, the more you have to worry about. The more you wonder if someone's breaking into that auxiliary place where you keep your stuff. You can install a better security system, put your valuables in a safe, get insurance on everything they'll sell insurance for, but there's no way to protect your stuff from worry. If you work for your food, eat it, and sleep, you sleep well. But when you have too much stuff, you can't sleep for worrying about it.

Wealth brings discontentment and insecurity, according to Solomon. But it also brings incredible loss. "There is a severe evil which I have seen under the sun," he said. "Riches kept for their owner to his hurt."

I've seen this happen when it's evident to your family that you care about your stuff more than you care about them. You care about the promotion, the better job, the bigger office, the bigger paycheck, and in spending all your time on the acquisition of stuff, and money to buy more stuff, it's evident to everyone but you that your family isn't as important as your stuff. It's like the goal of life is to hold onto it as long as possible. And it never shows up more than on your deathbed when it really hits you what you spent your life for. That's riches kept for their owner to his hurt.

See, what you value is what you spend your time on, because time is the most valuable resource we have. It's the only thing we'll never have more of. And I've seen, again and again, someone come to the end of their life and realize that they traded in their precious, limited time for money, and they could have instead spent that time on their family. That is the sixth danger: The more you have, the more you can hurt yourself with it.

The seventh danger: The more you have, the more you have to lose. Randy Alcorn would lie down outside of abortion clinics to stop people from going in, and the government came after him for racketeering and took everything he had. And he discovered that the more you have, the more you have to lose. But, because he practiced what he preached, he discovered that the opposite is also true.

So now, he's a janitor in a church, and he still preaches and writes bestselling books, but they can't do anything else to him, because he has nothing left to lose. Solomon says, "Those riches perish through misfortune." But Randy Alcorn learned they can't take what you don't have, and he's happier than ever, serving the Lord and continuing his ministry. The more you have, the more you have to lose, and similarly, danger number eight, the more you have, the more you leave behind.

"As he came from his mother's womb, naked shall he return, to go as he came; and he shall take nothing from his labor which he may carry away in his hand."

Of all the funerals I've conducted, of all my years of graveside services, I have never seen a U-Haul driving behind a hearse. You can't take it with you.

I remember once on a family trip, we were driving along this road and you could tell someone had just died, because their kids were dividing up the stuff, and they were making three piles. There was the huge, heaping trash pile right by the road, and there was a trailer where they were piling up the valuable furniture and everything they wanted to keep, and then in the middle of the yard, there were all these tables, where everything they didn't want was being sold.

If you've lived your life for riches, it all gets pried out of your hands in the end, and all you have is loss. If you spend your life making piles, everything you've piled up gets left behind. You either send your treasures ahead to heaven, or they just end up going into someone else's pile. The more you have, the more you leave behind.

The world's richest man, the wisest man ever to live, who had more stuff than anyone alive today, by far, as his starting point, spent his life trying to figure out what made life worthwhile. And do you know what he found? It wasn't stuff. Stuff makes you want more stuff, and makes you more dissatisfied with the stuff you have. The more stuff you have, the more people want to take it, the less you can use it, and the more you have to worry about. Too much stuff is hurtful to its owner, the more you have, the more you have to lose, and it all just gets left behind anyway.

If the richest and wisest man in history says wealth is dangerous, then it's a pretty good idea to listen. But a lot of people have trouble with Ecclesiastes. It kind of comes off like the ramblings of a bitter old man, so is it really relevant to us? Well, yes, because regardless of how bitter Solomon was, regardless of what he spent his life doing, Ecclesiastes is just as inspired by God as every other book of Scripture.

But, if the investment advice from history's richest and wisest man isn't good enough, don't worry. He's not the only one to comment on it. So just to clear up any uncertainty on the subject, let's take a look at the dangers of wealth according to the world's leading authority on everything: Jesus Christ.

THE DANGERS OF WEALTH ACCORDING TO JESUS

Jesus spent much of His earthly ministry speaking on the evils of loving money. In fact, one out of every seven words out of His mouth was about the dangers of wealth, and almost half of His parables have to do with riches. Solomon said it was dangerous to *have* too much stuff. Jesus goes one step further and warns of what happens when we *love* stuff.

So, if like Paul says, "The love of money is a root of all kinds of evil,"[223] then what are those evils? Jesus gives seven warnings about the love of money, and they're not as simple as various levels of discontentment, insecurity, and eventual loss. Here is where things get serious.

Danger #1: Wealth exchanges the eternal for what is only temporary.

"Do not lay up for yourselves treasures on earth, where moth and rust destroy and where thieves break in and steal; but lay up for yourselves treasures in heaven, where neither moth nor rust destroys and where thieves do not break in and steal."[224]

We have a limited number of resources, time being the most important. But whether it's time or money or possessions, we only have so much. And there are two destinations, two treasuries, two places we can store up our treasures. The word "lay up" is the same idea as "increased with goods" from Revelation 3, the idea of making piles.

Making piles isn't the problem. It's where you choose to put those piles. In heaven, where things are eternal, or on earth, where everything is temporary. Piles made on earth only make you want more piles, and be less satisfied with the piles you've already made. Only what will last forever truly satisfies, and the first danger of wealth, according to Jesus, is that you're making piles in the wrong places, exchanging the eternal for what is only temporary.

There was an article recently on someone who went into a major department store and switched all the price tags. They took the 99 cent price tag and put it on a $400 vase, and took the $400 price tag and put it on a 49 cent Disney pen. And people were paying all the wrong prices for everything, and nobody realized what had happened.

And that's exactly what's happened to us. Jesus has treasure—the real stuff. The lasting stuff, and He tells us that's what we should buy, but the devil has gone through this world and switched all the price tags. We're paying so dearly for that 49 cent pen when what Jesus says is valuable would have been ours for the taking.

223 1 Timothy 6:10
224 Matthew 6:19–20

Danger #2: Wealth robs us of faith.

"So why do you worry about clothing? Consider the lilies of the field, how they grow: they neither toil nor spin; and yet I say to you that even Solomon in all his glory was not arrayed like one of these. Now if God so clothes the grass of the field, which today is, and tomorrow is thrown into the oven, will He not much more clothe you, O you of little faith?"[225]

Fear robs you of faith. What do you need faith for when you have vast piles of stuff? Why do you need to trust God for your future when you've already calculated exactly what you need for the rest of your life and you've built your barns big enough and filled them so you're set for life?

Now this isn't saying we should get rid of all our stuff. The Bible says if you don't have food and clothes, you shouldn't be content.[226] And it says if you don't provide for your family, you're worse than an unbeliever.[227] That's not what we're talking about.

We're talking about when you pile up stuff because you can't trust God to take care of you. We don't trust Him with our future, with our family, with our finances, so we turn to ourselves for security. When we trust our bank account, our corporate pension, and instead of trusting God for our daily bread, we give in to worry, and we begin to live in fear instead of faith.

First Timothy 6:17 tells us not to trust in riches. They're uncertain. They can't be counted on. Solomon already warned that the more you have, the more people are after it, the less you get to use it, and the more you have to worry about. Job, who in his day had more riches and possessions than anyone around, said, "If I have put my confidence in gold, and called fine gold my trust, if I have gloated because my wealth was great, and because my hand had secured so much, that too would have been an iniquity calling for judgment, for I would have denied God above."[228] When we trust in our money to protect us instead of God, then we're in the danger zone.

225 Matthew 6:28–30
226 1 Timothy 6:8
227 1 Timothy 5:8
228 Job 31:24–25, 28

Danger #3: Wealth makes death a loss.

Jesus says, "For where your treasure is, there your heart will be also."[229] If your heart is in heaven, then death is gain. Like the apostle Paul said, to live is Christ, to die is gain. But if your heart is here on earth, death is a loss.

Jesus says where your treasure is determines where your heart is. If your treasure is stored up here on earth, you spend your whole life backing away from everything that's important to you. But if you send it all ahead, death is the day you move into your dream house, that you've been sending all your treasures to, that you've been dreaming about and waiting for.

Jesus says, "Where your treasure is, there your heart will be also." Jesus says our view of our treasures is our reference point for life. If our treasures are here, death will be a loss, because we're going to lose all of our stuff. But if we're like Paul, our citizenship is in heaven, and our treasures are with the One we love, and death for us is gain. Either our best days and all our stuff is behind us, or our best days are yet to come. So where is your heart? Is it firmly entrenched here on earth, or is it longing for heaven?

The first three dangers are summed up in this: Do not lay up for yourselves treasures on earth. There are two things done wrong here. Making piles, number one, "for yourself," and number two, "on earth."

Why is that bad? Because it trades what is eternal for what is temporary, what has value forever for what has a little value only for a little while. Making piles "for yourself" "on earth" is bad because you will always be fearful that moth and rust will destroy it, and that thieves will break in and steal it, instead of having faith in the God who can protect you and your treasures by keeping them in a place that has no rust, that has no moths, and where thieves can never get in. And it's bad because it makes death a loss. Making piles doesn't do that. Making piles "for yourself" "on earth" does. It's not money. It's the love of money. That's the root of all kinds of evil.

Danger #4: Wealth chokes God's Word out of your life.

Jesus taught that wealth exchanges the eternal for the temporal, robs you of faith, and makes death a loss, but He didn't stop there. Jesus was teaching a parable about salvation, and He's explaining what the parable means to

---

229 Matthew 6:21

His disciples when He teaches the fourth danger of loving wealth, and this is where He really rocks the boat.

"Now he who received seed among the thorns is he who hears the word, and the cares of this world and the deceitfulness of riches choke the word, and he becomes unfruitful."[230]

We're getting into dangerous territory here. When God's Word gets choked out and there is no fruit, that means the person was never saved. That's a danger in itself. Wealth can keep people from embracing the truth of God. It's a hindrance to salvation. But what about believers? Is this still a danger for us?

Jesus says that even among believers, wealth becomes a distraction that puts a strangle hold on the influence of God's Word in our lives. The truth of God is throttled and choked by the cares of this world because if all our minds are on is the cares of this world, we don't have time for God and His word. If we are pursuing riches, they're so deceitful that while they're giving us whatever benefit we think we're getting, they're choking the Word of God in our life. Jesus said it. And it shocked people.

This warning from Jesus is so important that it's recorded in all three of the synoptic gospels. The crowds of Jesus' day had a similar view of wealth that we have. If you are wealthy, it must be a sign of God's blessing, and if you are poor, there must be something wrong with you. But Jesus saw wealth, not as a sign of blessing, but as a handicap, as something that choked out God's Word and inhibited fruitfulness. If you were in the crowd back then, you would have heard a collective gasp as Jesus said this, but it's true. Jesus saw wealth as a handicap, and this is why:

Danger #5: Wealth is a cruel taskmaster.

Jesus said, "No one can serve two masters; for either he will hate the one and love the other, or else he will be loyal to the one and despise the other. You cannot serve God and mammon [riches]." We live in a society where our possessions first imprison us with debt, then they take over our houses, and finally our stuff begins to occupy our time. We have been conquered by our possessions.

---

230 Matthew 13:22

In trying to possess more and more wealth, it becomes our master and we become its slaves, and we find that our wealth is no longer something we possess. It's something that possesses us. Everything I own actually owns me.

Jesus said you can't serve more than one master, and wealth, by nature, becomes a cruel taskmaster. It demands time, mental energy, and a lifestyle that increasingly leaves God out of it. You can either serve God, or you can serve wealth. But you can't serve both.

Do you know the most enduring title for those who are going to heaven? All throughout Scripture, both Old and New Testaments, the one title that has always described those bound for heaven is "servants of God." If you want to be a servant of God, you can't be a servant of wealth. And if wealth is your master, you can't serve God.

Oh, but it gets worse.

Danger #6: Wealth makes it harder to get to heaven.

Wow. Jesus said that? And you thought Solomon had a harsh view of riches. Look at what Jesus says in Matthew 19:16–24. A rich man runs up to Jesus, wanting to know how to be saved, and Jesus tells him. Now, you and I don't share the gospel this way, but Jesus knew this man's heart. And He knew what was holding him back, and Jesus said, "go, sell what you have and give to the poor, and you will have treasure in heaven; and come, follow Me."

And Matthew records that the rich man's face fell immediately, and he turned and walked away. So Jesus turns to His disciples and this is where He says it: "It is easier for a camel to go through the eye of a needle than for a rich man to enter the kingdom of heaven."

You've heard of the gate in Jerusalem that a camel had to kneel to go through? It's a nice illustration, but that's not what Jesus is talking about. The camel was the largest land animal in the region, and the eye of a needle was the smallest opening it was humanly possible to make. Jesus wasn't illustrating difficulty. He was illustrating absolute impossibility.

Wait. It's impossible for a rich man to get to heaven? I'm so glad the disciples asked that, because Jesus said with men, it's impossible, but with God, all things are possible. But the principle is the same: Wealth makes it harder to get to heaven. You can argue with the world's wisest man if you want to, but this comes from the mouth of Jesus. Jesus said it.

How can money matter that much? Because wealth, as a distraction, begins to choke out the truth of God's Word. Wealth, as a cruel taskmaster, begins to own us, and you can't love God and be consumed by a love of money. Wealth, whether it's having it or loving it, is dangerous. It's radioactive. And overexposure to it is a bone-shriveling, marrow-eating death sentence, however healthy you look.

Me, Myself, and I: Leaving God Out of the Conversation

If wealth is so dangerous, then what do we do? Is Jesus advocating a vow of poverty? Should we all move out of our houses, sell our cars, quit our jobs, and live on food stamps? No. That's not what He's saying. Remember, making piles isn't the problem. The problem is where the piles are stacked, and who they're stacked for.

All of these dangers, warned against by Solomon, by Jesus, and by so many others in Scripture, are for one simple reason:

Danger #7: Wealth leaves God out of the conversation.

Jesus sums up all of His teaching on wealth in one parable, found in Luke 12:15–21. Someone runs up to Jesus out of the crowd and asks Jesus to make his brother share their inheritance with him, and Jesus, instead of addressing the surface problem, goes straight to the heart of the issue.

"Take heed and beware of covetousness," Jesus says, "for one's life does not consist in the abundance of the things he possesses." Do you know what covetousness is? That's the tenth commandment, and it's when we want what someone else has instead of wanting what we have. It's when we go in just for an hour or two, exposing ourselves to deadly radiation, just for a little more. That's what Jesus is warning against. And then He tells them a story:

"The ground of a certain rich man yielded plentifully." No problem so far. This man was a good agricultural businessman. That's fine. "And he thought within himself, saying, 'What shall I do, since I have no room to store my crops?'" So not only was he a good businessman. He was a good manager. He was anticipating the yield, anticipating a need, and he was seeking to increase his storage space. All good stuff. Jesus doesn't condemn any of this so far.

"So he said, 'I will do this: I will pull down my barns and build greater, and there I will store all my crops and my goods.'" Jesus is into all that. He says, yes, everything should be done decently and in order. Don't leave your corn on the ground. Don't let your animals out in the winter, they'll die. Have everything stored neatly and orderly. Jesus approves. Right up until verse 19:

"And I will say to my soul, 'Soul, you have many goods laid up for many years; take your ease; eat, drink, and be merry.'"

Do you notice who is left out of the conversation? This was all me. "what am I going to do with *my* stuff for *me*, and for *my* future and *my* retirement? If you only consult yourself, you end up with the retirement plan for all of western society: take your ease, eat, drink, and be merry. Where did God say to do that in Scripture? If the whole goal of life is that *I* will build a big enough barn for all of *my* stuff so that *I* will have enough to take care of *me* for the rest of *my* life, then look at what God thinks about that:

"But God said to him, 'Fool! This night your soul will be required of you; then whose will those things be which you have provided?'"

Remember, the more you have, the more you have to lose, the more it hurts to leave behind, and the more painful it is when God has to pry it out of your hand. That's what happened to the rich man. So that was the story, but here's the lesson: "So is he who lays up treasure for himself, and is not rich toward God."

Did you catch it? He who lays up treasure for *himself*. There's nothing wrong with treasure. It's who does it belong to. As long as I look on my time, my schedule, my clothes, my money, my job, my future, my goals, my plans, my, my, my, my, me, me, me, me, I, I, I, I...

Wealth leaves God out of the conversation. Making piles is good. Making them for me is bad. Making them on earth is bad. And that's all Jesus found when He visited Laodicea. He saw pile after pile of stuff, all on earth, all for me, for myself, and what I want. They were not rich toward God, and they were living right in the radiation zone of materialism.

OUR SPIRITUAL SHOPPING LIST: WHAT TO BUY FROM JESUS

REVELATION 3:17–18

"Because you say, 'I am rich, have become wealthy, and have need of nothing'—and do not know that you are wretched, miserable, poor, blind, and naked—I counsel you to buy from Me gold refined in the fire."

Laodicea had a self-confessed malady: "I am rich." They were spending their whole lives making piles for themselves, and all their piles were on earth. They'd left God out of the conversation. In their state of being rich, Jesus tells Laodicea that they are sickening and in desperate need of repentance.

Laodicea was known for its gold, its wealth, and its abundant riches, but Jesus says they're poor because they've been getting their riches from the wrong place. They had been deceived by the devil switching all the price tags, and they were buying up everything worthless, when Jesus said He's the One who knows what's valuable. And instead of buying the real stuff, the gold refined in the fire, from Jesus Christ, Laodicea had cultivated the bad habit of spiritual wastefulness.

Spiritual wastefulness is when we abandon Christ as our investment counselor. "I counsel you," Jesus says. He wants to be our investment counselor. He wants to give us riches that can't be touched by moth and rust and thieves. He wants us to invest in what lasts forever. To trade what's temporary for the eternal, to live in faith, not fear, to include Him in the conversation and let Him be our counselor.

But spiritual wastefulness is when we leave God out of the conversation. It's when we think we're responsible for the disposition of our greatest treasure, our time, and of all our other treasures. We think it's ours. It's all about my plans. Spiritual wastefulness is when we start investing our time and money in things that are going to perish on earth instead of investing in what will last forever in heaven, when we start measuring things by their earthly value instead of their heavenly value. Slowly we start to trade our precious time that has been given to us by God for objects that will only rust, burn, rot, or get stolen. Or death will pry them out of our hands. Our regular deposits to the Bank of Heaven are neglected, and we funnel everything that God gives us into treasures on earth.

In abandoning Jesus as their investment counselor, the believers in Laodicea were holding onto radioactive material, allowing it to increase their worry and their fear instead of walking by faith. They were investing their time and money on earth, not on heaven and trading what could have lasted forever for what never could. For them, death would be a loss, because they'd spent their lives laying up the wrong treasures in the wrong places for the wrong reasons.

In trying to serve two masters, Laodicea had really only been serving one, and it wasn't Jesus Christ. His word had been choked out of their lives and throttled by the cares of this world. Their view of Him was obstructed by all their piles, and they were facing the eye of a needle with camel-sized baggage. Their wealth was making it harder to get to heaven, and they were so clueless they didn't even realize it.

Can you see why Jesus was so concerned? Why Laodicea's condition made Him sick? They thought they were perfectly healthy. They felt fine. But they were living in a radiation zone, and Jesus saw down to the shriveling marrow of their bones, and He saw a church that was dying.

Investing in the Riches of the Cross

In Jesus' day, there were three types of people. The beggars (poor), the workers (day laborers living paycheck to paycheck), and the pile-makers (rich). If you don't have a dollar to your name, don't have a job or the means to get one, and your only choice is to beg if you want to eat, then you're off the hook. This lesson isn't for you. If you have to work today in order to eat tonight, and you only have enough money for the food for dinner and maybe tomorrow's breakfast, but no more, then this lesson doesn't apply to you either.

But if you can go more than one day without working and not starve, and if you have enough money in the bank, buried in the backyard, or under your mattress to sustain you for more than three meals at a time, then you are, by Scripture's definition, rich. And you need an investment counselor.

Jesus says to anyone who is "rich," "I counsel you." That word "counsel," is translated "plotted," almost everywhere else it appears in Scripture. It speaks of heavy, thought out, deliberate action.

Think about what that means, plotting to overthrow a government, or plotting to rob a bank, or plotting to take over that company, or plotting to kill this person. A plotting person gets consumed with the plot. It's the only thing on your mind, and Jesus is telling this church to get completely focused on what He called them to do. What did He call us to do?

Jesus told the church at Laodicea to make specific purchases from Him. They'd bought gold from the wrong source, clothes from the wrong source, and they needed to go to Him and buy what He says has value. Invest in what will last forever.

Did you know that when you and I were saved, God opened up an account for us? Right now, we're in a temporary holding pattern. We're just biding our time, but where we're going is so important, that He's set up an account for us there. And we can send riches ahead. He's given us all the deposit slips, and we can send ahead as much as we want, and every deposit we make glorifies Him. Jesus wanted Laodicea, and us today, to be investing in our eternal IRA. So how do we do that?

Paul said to Timothy, "Command those who are rich," that's not the beggars, who can't feed themselves, or the workers, who can only feed themselves today if they work today, but the rich, who have more than they need for the next twenty-four hours. That's us. "Command those who are rich in this present age not to be haughty, nor to trust in uncertain riches, but in the living God, who gives us richly all things to enjoy. Let them" that's the rich," do good, that they be rich in good works, ready to give, willing to share, storing up for themselves a good foundation for the time to come."[231]

How do we invest in heaven? By doing good works, being ready to give, and willing to share. And by doing that, we are storing up for ourselves a good nest egg for our real retirement.

Did you know that every time you invest in someone else's ministry, everything they do for the kingdom gets credited to your account?[232] When

231 1 Timothy 6:17–18
232 Philippians 4:17

you invest in a church, the work the church does gets credited to your account. When you invest your time, that gets credited, when you invest your talents, that gets shipped ahead too. When you choose to use whatever resource it is, time, talents, money, personality, whatever, when you choose to use it for God, it gets credited to your account in heaven.

Jim Elliot is a perfect example of that. He said, "He is no fool who gives up what he cannot keep to gain what he cannot lose." Think about that. What we have on earth, time, money, and possessions, we cannot keep. But we can invest it, trade it in for riches in heaven that we can never lose.

What made Jim Elliot such an incredible witness for Christ was not the day he lost his life as a missionary to the Auca Indians. It was the day when, as a teenager, he realized that all his athletic ability, his mental gifts, and his incredible personality were not resources he could use for himself. They were entrusted to him by God, and he decided to invest them for Christ. The day he died, he didn't lose something. He gained something. That was the day he was reunited with all the treasures he'd been shipping ahead to the Bank of Heaven since he was a teenager.

There are fifteen dangers of too much stuff, eight from Solomon, and seven from Jesus, but there is one very good thing about wealth: The more you have, the more you can send ahead to heaven.

The Bank of Heaven gives a return of 10,000 percent. It is insured by the God of the universe, it never needs a bailout, nothing in it ever loses value, and it's impossible to rob. There is no rust. There are no moths. Thieves can never get in to steal from it. What is put into the Bank of Heaven lasts forever.

It's so easy for us to read about Laodicea's spiritual condition, look at our stuff, read all the warning labels and say these warnings about the dangers of wealth apply to the Ford family or the Warren Buffets of this world or to Ellison of Oracle—but not us. But does it? By Jesus' definition, I am rich. Have I also been living in the radiation zone of materialism for so long that I'm shriveling up on the inside?

The first symptom of being poisoned by radioactive materialism is discontentment. The more you have, the more you want, and the less you're satisfied. Do you find yourself needing just one more dollar? Just a little more this or a lot more that before you can be content?

The next symptom is insecurity. Are you finding more and more people after your money, after your stuff, you can't use it because you have to hide it away or store it somewhere, and you can't sleep for worrying about it? That's a sure sign you're being poisoned from the inside out.

But you know you're at end stage radiation poisoning when death starts to look like a loss. So ask yourself, is your dream house at the beach, or is it the one Jesus is building for you? Are you piling your stuff into a retirement account, a 401K, or are you investing in the 10,000H—the heavenly retirement account with a 10,000 percent return? Are you backing away from your treasures, or getting closer to them every day you're alive? If any of these three symptoms is you, then there's a lesson here in Jesus' words to Laodicea.

Peter said that life is camping. Heaven is home. When you're camping, not motor home camping, but real, in-a-tent, sleep-on-the-ground, eaten-by-bugs camping, it may be fun for a little while, but after a few days, you just can't wait to get home. You're tired of waking up freezing cold, going to sleep on rocks, being bit by every mosquito that buzzes by. And you just can't wait to be home, in a real bed, clean, with running water.

Life is supposed to be like camping. Heaven is supposed to be our real home. Is that true for you? Are you living like this life is temporary? Are you, every day, more tired of waking up cold and laying on rocks, and eaten by bugs, and ready, more and more each day, to be home? Where all your treasures are? If Jesus came and said, it's time to go, are you ready to toss it all in the truck and finally go home? Or are your tent pegs pounded in so tightly you don't want to leave?

The goal isn't to have nothing, but to own nothing. We don't have to get rid of all our stuff, but our goal today should be to give the ownership of it back to God. The danger of stuff is that we leave God out of the conversation, abandon Christ as our investment counselor, and make piles "for yourself" "on earth." But when we systematically hand over the ownership of everything back to God, then we are investing, not in the moth-ridden, rust-encrusted, thief-prone banks of this earth, but in the Bank of Heaven.

The words of this old hymn are our words of surrender: "All I have belongs to You, for all I have has come from You. Nothing I own, nothing

I possess, is by my own hand, but by Your faithfulness. So please take this offering from a heart of thanksgiving, for You've given all I have."

Let us make those words our prayer today.

Father, I pray in the name of Jesus, with Your Word open before us, with hearing Your Word in our ears, that we would hear with our hearts. That we would hear the message, that we wouldn't deflect the message thinking it's for someone else, someone with more than I have. We are in the danger zone. We are exposed to one of the deadliest of all temptations, the covetousness of materialism, the longing and pursuit with our lives for more stuff. And Lord, I pray, that in any way that we need to be stirred and convicted by Your word, that we would have ears to hear. Open our eyes to the truth of what response You want from us. In Jesus' name. Amen.

RESPOND to Truth

How does God say we are to treat our wealth?
(Matthew 25:14–30; Luke 12:35–48)

If I saw my stuff as potentially radioactive like Jesus does, what would I get rid of?

What portion of my resources (time, money, possessions) have I budgeted to invest in myself this week? How could I invest it in heaven instead?

How does God feel about spiritual wastefulness? (Isaiah 55:1–2)
What kind of life does satisfy? (Isaiah 55)

How has materialism stifled my ability to live for God only?
What steps can I take not to be controlled by material things?

What is "gold refined in the fire" according to Peter? (1 Peter 1:6–7)

Getting Dressed for Christ: The Righteous Acts of the Saints | 22

In American history, there was one man who dominated the news industry. William Randolph Hearst owned so many newspapers that if he wanted something to be news, all he had to do was put it in his newspapers, and it became news. And he was very wealthy.

He had so much money, he didn't know what to do with it, so after World War I, he went to Europe, and bought all these castles that hadn't been destroyed, and he had his engineers cut them and ship them all the way down the rivers around to California and he reassembled a mega-castle, made of components of all the best of Europe's castles.

And then he filled it with the finest of Italian, German, British, and low country art he could find, cleaning out the art market, and he filled his castle with it so that the Hearst castle became a Mecca. Everybody wanted to go there. Then he built this road up the mountain to the castle, lined it with torches, and he would take his invited guests in these open touring cars up the serpentine drive all the way to the castle, and they would be let out in front of his mansion in the dark, and led inside to their own private room.

And when they got there, they'd find clothes, in their size, laid out for them. And the staff would say, "By the way, you're invited in an hour to dinner with Mr. Hearst, and he wants you to wear those clothes."

Do you know in the history that he did this, only maybe two people ever dared to come wearing their own clothes? They weren't invited back.

Do you know that someone much greater than William Randolph Hearst has left us some outfits? We have been invited to dinner, and Jesus has laid out for us clothes that are just our size, that He has picked, and He says, "I counsel you to buy from me white garments."

The believers at Laodicea dared to come wearing their own clothes. They had neglected what Jesus said He wanted to see them wearing, and that's the fifth sickening habit that makes Christ want to vomit.

SPIRITUAL NEGLECT: NAKED AND ASHAMED

If you were touring Laodicea in the first century, you would have noticed the people wearing, and the shops that dotted the city selling, something that was very distinctively Laodicean. If you saw it anywhere else in the Roman Empire, you'd stop and ask where they got that from, because only Laodicea produced and sold this luxurious, exquisite black wool.

Now you can get wool anywhere you have a sheep. Just shear it and comb it and make something, but this wool was like silk. And it was known and exported and worn and talked about around the Roman Empire, because there was nothing softer, nothing more luxurious. And everyone knew this was Laodicea's trademark. It was sheared right from Laodicea's own special flocks, processed, and sold only here.

So Jesus comes to Laodicea, sees them dressed in the finest clothes to be found, and this is what He says: "I counsel you to buy from Me white garments, that you may be clothed, that the shame of your nakedness may not be revealed."[233]

Jesus looks, He sees what they're clothing themselves with, and says they're naked. And He says, "buy from Me white garments." What color were the clothes in Laodicea? They had bought clothes from the wrong source. They were wearing the wrong garments, and Jesus said they will be found to be naked and ashamed.

The Laodiceans had traded the eternal for the temporal. They'd swapped the celestial for the mundane. They'd spent their lives accumulating trinkets and trash instead of treasures in heaven. And they had put on

233 Revelation 3:18

the black garments that would be useless in heaven instead of buying from Christ the white garments He says they need.

Spiritual neglect is when we fail to get dressed for Christ each day by putting on His power, His armor, His character. Clothing ourselves for Christ gets neglected, and then forgotten. We become more concerned with what we look like to men rather than to God. We impress people outwardly instead of pleasing God inwardly. And Jesus says what is needed for them, and for us, is to repent and put on Christ daily.

When you're picking out a wedding present, a gift to present to someone you love, you could guess what they want, just do your best to pick out what you think they could use. But if you do that, you risk getting them something they really don't like and would feel bad to return, and when it comes to the wedding supper of the Lamb, it's really not the thought that counts. Every pagan religion in the world is filled with people who have good intentions. And so many standing naked and ashamed before Christ will be like the Laodiceans, clueless and saying, "I wish You would have told me."

Well, He did. Jesus left us a gift registry. Scripture is filled with what pleases our bridegroom, what He considers beautiful, what He wants to see His bride wearing on her wedding day.

Paul says that, every day, we are to put on the Lord Jesus Christ, like putting on a suit of armor or an overcoat so we don't get soaked when it rains. Colossians 3 says we are to clothe ourselves in Christ's virtues. Sanctification is always portrayed as putting on Christ, the armor of Christ, the righteousness of Christ, the virtues and characteristics of Christ. That's what God calls being dressed in Christ daily.

"The night is far spent, the day is at hand. Therefore let us cast off the works of darkness, and let us put on the armor of light. Let us walk properly, as in the day, not in revelry and drunkenness, not in lewdness and lust, not in strife and envy. But put on the Lord Jesus Christ, and make no provision for the flesh, to fulfill its lusts."[234]

Do you notice something? Before we can put on the armor of light, before we can put on the Lord Jesus Christ, we have to put off our old, black wool garments. Paul says to put off revelry, meaning sensual pursuits;

234 Romans 13:12–14

drunkenness, being overcome by substances; lewdness, mocking at sin with conversation or conduct; lust, the insatiable desire for gratification; strife, never getting along with people; and envy, internally wanting what everyone else has.

And then, after we've taken all that off, we are to put on the Lord Jesus Christ.

How do we know if we are, every day, putting on the Lord Jesus Christ? How do we know if we're clothing ourselves daily in the righteous acts of the saints? There's a simple test to find out. Remember how God's Word is a mirror, James 1:22–25? And when we look in that mirror, we can see what we're wearing, by comparing what we see in our own lives to what the mirror of God's Word says we should look like.

Paul gives one list of "put offs" and "put ons" in Galatians 5:19–23. "Now the works of the flesh are evident, which are: adultery, fornication, uncleanness, lewdness, idolatry, sorcery, hatred, contentions, jealousies, outbursts of wrath, selfish ambitions, dissensions, heresies, envy, murders, drunkenness, revelries, and the like. But the fruit of the Spirit is love, joy, peace, longsuffering, kindness, goodness, faithfulness, gentleness, self-control."

If my life is decreasingly characterized by contentions, jealousies, outbursts of wrath, envy, and all the other works of the flesh, then I am daily putting off those old black garments. And if my life is increasingly characterized by love, joy, peace, and the fruit of the Spirit, then I am daily putting on the Lord Jesus Christ.

Let's look in the mirror of God's Word and compare. Love is the absence of selfishness. Is the product of the Holy Spirit present in our lives? Can others trace my progress in expressing God's love? Am I less selfish and less self-seeking than I was last month?

Joy is the spiritual quality that releases us from our circumstances. Do those that see me and watch me characterize me as a joyful person?

Peace is the internal serenity that only God can give. Troubles are not absent, rather God is present. Has peace become more and more a way of life for me this year?

Longsuffering is the absence of irritation at the actions of others. Am I more patient than I was three months ago? Or less? Am I yielding to the

Holy Spirit in my dealings with people, or showing irritation that reveals a lack of surrender?

Kindness is a beautiful reflection of God in my life. Is my manner of dealing with people abrasive or am I reflecting grace in my dealings with others? Does Christ's kindness soften any word or action of mine that might hurt someone else? Is my character showing an increase in personal kindness in my way with others?

Goodness is being God-like, the opposite of fallen humanity. Am I a visibly better person than last year? Do people see me doing good to all those around me?

Faithfulness is a trustworthy and dependable life. Am I the kind of person who keeps my own life in order so I can be counted on by others? Am I making strides in reliability and dependability?

Gentleness is the opposite of asserting yourself. Servants of God must not strive. They must resist selfish ambition because it's a reflection of Satan, not God. Jesus Himself was described as meek and lowly. What shape is my personal agenda in? Is it intact and my personal rights being defended? Or is my personal agenda in hopeless shape, crucified with Christ and fading daily?

Self-control is defined in the Greek dictionary as "a virtue which consists in the mastery of appetites and passions, especially sensual ones." Am I yielded to the Holy Spirit so that I become a vessel of worship, or am I holding myself out as an instrument of sin? Do others see me graciously under the control of the Spirit?

There will come a day when you and I will be revealed, in front of everybody, for what we've done on this earth. And do you know what's sad? When He hands us our life's accomplishments, woven together into a garment, many believers are going to be ashamed because of how little they have to put on.

Revelation 21:4 says He wipes away all tears. I believe it's because so many believers will be naked and ashamed that they'll just break down crying, looking back over their wasted life and saying, "I wish You would have told me. I wish You would have told me what to live for."

But Jesus did. He told the Laodiceans, and He's telling us. We can be naked and ashamed, or we can weave together with our choices a garment to the glory of God to wear for our bridegroom at the wedding feast.

Revelation 19:7 says, "And His wife has made herself ready." I tell you what: you can't get ready for heaven in heaven. We're talking about today. We're talking about choices you're going to make once you put this book down. Choices you'll make this week, choices you made last week, last year. If you're the wife-to-be of Jesus Christ you're going to be shown for what you did to get ready in this moment.

You can't get ready in heaven. It's already too late then. The party will have already started. We have to get ready here on earth. And that's why Jesus tells the Laodiceans, "I counsel you to buy from Me white garments, that the shame of your nakedness may not be revealed."

This is something we should be consumed with doing. Plotting how we can buy from Jesus these garments. Plotting how we can send those garments ahead to heaven for the wedding feast. Plotting how we can be getting ready, making ourselves ready as a bride for her husband. Plotting what to put in our hope chest for that day. When Jesus says, "I counsel you to buy from Me," He's asking us to plot out what we're going to wear. He's asking for deliberate, thought-out, planned daily decisions to put on the Lord Jesus Christ.

THE MARRIAGE SUPPER OF THE LAMB

Our invitation to this dinner with Christ is recorded in Matthew 22. "The kingdom of heaven is like a certain king who arranged a marriage for his son, and sent out his servants to call those who were invited to the wedding; and they were not willing to come. Again, he sent out other servants, saying, 'Tell those who are invited, "See, I have prepared my dinner; my oxen and fatted cattle are killed, and all things are ready. Come to the wedding"' But they made light of it and went their ways, one to his own farm, another to his business. And the rest seized his servants, treated them spitefully, and killed them. But when the king heard about it, he was furious. And he sent out his armies, destroyed those murderers, and burned up their city. Then he said to his servants, 'The wedding is ready, but those who were invited were not worthy. Therefore go into the highways, and as many as you find, invite to the wedding.' So those servants went out into the highways and gathered together all whom they found, both bad and good. And the wedding hall was filled with guests.

"But when the king came in to see the guests, he saw a man there who did not have on a wedding garment. So he said to him, 'Friend, how did you come in here without a wedding garment?' And he was speechless. Then the king said to the servants, 'Bind him hand and foot, take him away, and cast him into outer darkness; there will be weeping and gnashing of teeth.'

"For many are called, but few are chosen."[235]

Does that seem like a harsh reaction? Not if you understand the glorious reality of the wedding feast as the Bible describes it and the incredible price Jesus paid to invite us.

The picture Jesus paints is of the Hebrew wedding celebration that would have been immediately recognizable to everyone who heard this parable. In ancient days, the wedding feast was inseparable from the wedding itself. The wedding feast involved a weeklong series of meals and festivities, it was the highlight of all the social activities of the ancient world, and for a royal wedding, such as the one Jesus mentions here, this celebration would last for several weeks. Guests were invited to stay at the house of the groom's parents for the whole time. The father would make an elaborate provision, as much as he could afford, and in a royal wedding, it would be held in the palace, and the king could afford anything he desired.

A wedding feast prepared by a king for his son would be a feast of all feasts, and Jesus described the most elaborate banquet imaginable. It's the most unimaginable party thrown by God for the bride that is uniting with His Son. What a picture. And in this event, we find all of God's promises completed.

The greatest party of all time is approaching as the King of kings, the Lord of the Universe, is preparing a wedding feast like none other. In the most breathtaking location imaginable, He is spreading an immense table. The greatest names of all time will be present and seated. At dinner, the invited guests will be rubbing shoulders with Adam and his lovely wife, Eve. One of their twin sons Abel will be sitting with them as well with Seth and his wife. Not too far away will be the great preacher, the earliest known

235 Matthew 22:2–14

prophet, Enoch, and his family. The great-grandson, Noah, and his family will be nearby.

On down the long table, lavishly set, will be the likes of Job and his clan, Abraham, Isaac, Jacob, with their various family members. What reunions as Moses and Elijah walk around talking with guests and visiting with old friends. Further on, Jeremiah sits in rapt attention with Daniel and Isaiah as Ezekiel points out again the wonders they see about the banquet hall as angelic creatures move about, as choirs of angels sing, and as the glories of the galaxies radiating the glory of God shine down upon the gathered saints.

Interspersed with all these Old Testament saints will be multitudes of beaming faces well-known to us. Matthew and the rest of the twelve will be at the entrances. There will be twelve gates as the guests stream through on their way to sit. Paul, at one gate, is weeping for joy as he finally sees so many of his spiritual children and grandchildren. Because he died before many of them had grown up, it's a precious reunion. At one gate, John also weeps for joy as he returns to this place he saw from the isle of Patmos.

Saints of all the ages are taking their places, a name card with a special name, only theirs, and only known by them and their Savior, marks each seat. And then the party begins, with glorious enraptured souls, the hallelujahs begin to echo down the aisles of the marriage supper of the Lamb. Expectantly, each guest, invited personally only by Jesus looks up and then they see Jesus. Glorious and majestic, He comes to each, and calling them by name, and extending His nail-scarred hands and touching them with His love.

Throughout Scripture, believers, saints, both Old and New Testament, are described as a bride. Isaiah 54:5 says, "Your maker is your husband, the Lord of hosts is His name." In Jeremiah 3:14, God pleads with Israel, saying, "Return, O backsliding children, for I am married to you." He says in Hosea 2:19, "I will betroth you to Me forever."

Jesus continues this beautiful picture in the gospels, describing the marriage banquet in Matthew 22 as a picture of salvation. In Matthew 25, He describes the virgins waiting for the bridegroom and the necessity of being ready. And in Mark 2:19 and John 3:29, He calls Himself the bridegroom. Second Corinthians 11:2 says we are engaged to one husband, and in Ephesians 5:23, every husband and wife is a picture of Christ and His Church.

Just as marriage demands absolute loyalty and faithfulness here on earth, so Jesus demands absolute loyalty and faithfulness from His bride. Being married to Christ mirrors the highest relationship we know on this planet, and until that wedding feast, you and I are betrothed to Christ.

We are coming to the culmination of all the hearts of all the saints of all time. It is the wedding banquet. It is the marriage supper of the Lamb. And it is the scene of Revelation 19, when those who love Him and waited all their life for Him, honor Jesus.

"And I heard, as it were, the voice of a great multitude, as the sound of many waters and as the sound of mighty thunderings, saying, 'Alleluia! For the Lord God Omnipotent Reigns! Let us be glad and rejoice and give Him glory, for the marriage of the Lamb has come, and His wife has made herself ready.' And to her it was granted to be arrayed in fine linen, clean and bright, for the fine linen is the righteous acts of the saints."[236]

Jesus says if you're coming to the culmination of your heart, and the hearts of all the saints of all times, if you're coming to the wedding banquet, if it is a marriage supper of you and me to Him, and if we're going to meet Him who loved us, and if we've waited all of our life for Him, what are you bringing?

You and I have been called to a great wedding feast. The King is making it ready for His Son, and we are invited to the feast. But we have to be clothed, first in the righteousness of Christ, which we can't earn, which we can't buy, which is put on at salvation, which is only by grace, and then in the white linen garments Jesus commands believers to put on after they're saved. These are the good works, the ones we were created for, the whole purpose we were saved. The catastrophic problem of today is that people have detached a transformed life from salvation. But Jesus' bride has a transformed life. That's the message of Revelation.

DRESSING FOR THE WEDDING

Christ's righteousness gets us into the wedding feast, but once we're there, we are presented with a garment made of our good works that we were

236 Revelation 19:6–8

created for. And you and I, today, get to weave together with our choices to the glory of God and by His grace a garment. We will be clothed with that garment made from our righteous acts that, starting now, we offer to God.

Jesus' gift registry includes a list of ten things that will be rewarded in heaven, the good works He's looking for, the righteous acts that get woven together into a garment. These are the ten things He'll be looking for us to put on and be wearing at the wedding feast. And the first one is found in Matthew 5:11–12.

Number 1: A Christlike disposition in adversity

Jesus said if you have a Christlike disposition in adversity, you will be blessed. "Blessed are you when they revile and persecute you, and say all kinds of evil against you falsely for My sake. Rejoice and be exceedingly glad, for great is your reward in heaven."

When we are attacked, maligned, defrauded, whatever, remember what Stephen experienced. He looked and saw Jesus as he was being attacked and Jesus stood, because Jesus honors those who are attacked and maligned and persecuted for His name's sake.

Number 2: A Christlike secrecy in spiritual disciplines

Secondly, Jesus rewards a Christlike secrecy in spiritual disciplines. Jesus says in Matthew 6:3–18, when you do your good works, don't let your left hand know what your right hand is doing. Jesus talks about prayer and fasting and giving alms.

Did you know Jesus loves us to do secret things? When we don't even blow the trumpet a little bit for ourselves. He loves us to do sacrificial things and be so excited to do them that nobody finds out. When you do things in secret, your father will see it and will reward you someday openly.

Number 3: A Christlike attitude toward possessions

Jesus also rewards a Christlike attitude toward our possessions. Matthew 6:19 warns us not to lay up for ourselves treasures on earth. The moths and rust will steal and destroy and ruin them, but we are to instead lay up treasures with Jesus in heaven.

Take some of your stacked possessions and overnight them to the Bank of Heaven. Give and you'll have them forever. Keep and you'll lose them forever. The question that matters at the end of your life isn't how much did you keep to the bitter end. It's how much did you send ahead.

Number 4: A Christlike love of the unlovable

Luke 6:35 says, "love your enemies. Do good, and lend, hoping for nothing in return; and your reward will be great." That's what transformed the world in Jesus' day. But we have trouble loving other Christians. Find an enemy. We all have them. And love them and lend to them and even outright give stuff to them. Blow them away. Blow you and me away too, because we don't do that very often. It's amazing. We have neighbors, coworkers, relatives that are unpleasant to us. Give them something in the name of Jesus, and He'll reward you for that.

Number 5: A Christlike serving of the unfortunate

Jesus says when you give a feast, Luke 14:13–14, invite the poor, the maimed, the lame, the blind, and you will be rewarded because they can't repay you. Do you know what that says to me? Pick a new social set. Pick the handicapped, pick the poor, pick the informally educated. We call those illiterate. They're informally educated. Pick the non-financially successful people. Pick other ethnic groups. That's an expression of the body of Christ. It's unshockable, it's accepting, it's color-blind, and it's incredibly generous.

We should make plans right now to use our house, our car, our money and use it for the very least people who don't have a place to invite you back to. Who won't give your kids great gifts when they graduate or get married, because they have nothing. And Jesus says when we give to people who can never return the favor, then you get rewarded in heaven.

You know the whole social circuit, I invite you to my big gala and you invite me back to yours, and we all impress each other? That's not part of God's plan for heavenly treasure. It's fine, it's fun, but that's not God's plan. His plan is when we have a party, we invite the blind, the lame, the handicapped, the poor, and the people that are not really desirable on this planet. And Jesus said when you invite them, you're inviting Jesus Himself to your party.

Number 6: A Christlike investment in people

People last forever. Things don't. That's why people can never be an interruption. Things can, but people can't. And 1 Corinthians 3:8 says if you plant and water you will receive your reward according to your own labor.

Jesus rewards investment in people. Jesus counts souls invested in. He counts lives touched by the gospel. He counts those that we touch by prayer and by our deeds of kindness.

What have we done this week that's counted? I bet the businesses that we're all a part of have tallied up the week's sales and profit. Have you counted up this week's investment in people? Have you prayed for souls, have you given the gospel? Have you tried to share? I went out to lunch with someone this week and I noticed that right away they got a gospel tract and they had it on the table, and they were just itching to give it to the waiter. Christ counted that for His kingdom.

Number 7: A Christlike devotion to God's will

Colossians 3:23–24 says this: "Whatever you do, do it heartily, as to the Lord and not to men, knowing that from the Lord you will receive the reward."

Jesus says that we are called to do something for Him this week. When you go to school, then act like you are a Rhodes scholar for Jesus. If you work for your company, be the most productive person there like Jesus Himself is your boss. Are you home rearing children? Raise them like you're Mary raising Jesus. Just elevate whatever you do to doing it for Christ. There are rewards for how you work at work, how you study at school, and for everything you do, if you do it for Christ.

Number 8: A Christloving expectancy for His return

2 Timothy 4:8 "Finally, there is laid up for me," Paul said, "a crown of righteousness, which the Lord, the righteous Judge, will give to me on that Day, and not to me only but also to all who have loved His appearing."

Now let me ask you this: Does someone who's engaged need to be told to be on the lookout for the return of the love of their life? Does a newlywed have to be told to be in love? No.

I think the only part of me that's still young is how I feel about my wife. We were shopping the other day and scratching off these stickers to get discounts, and I was having so much fun. I was just looking over her shoulder and putting my arm around her, and just following her around the store buying socks for the kids, and the cashier and her friend were talking together, and when we came up to the counter, they asked us, "Did you just get married?" And I said, "Yes. Eight children ago."

That's what Jesus says we are to Him. We are to act like we're newlyweds with Him. He wants us to long for Him, to love Him. You know how people just slip off to spend time together? They just love each other so much they can't wait to get alone. Jesus wants us to intimately long for Him, in prayer, in worship.

See, no one has to tell me to love my wife. When you love someone, you do whatever you have to do to spend time with them. You just can't get enough of being with them. And that's what Jesus says we are to Him. We are engaged to Him, and no one who's engaged has to be told to watch for their beloved to come and get them. They just do. And that's something Jesus rewards.

Number 9: A Christlike endurance in trials

First Peter 1:7 says, "The genuineness of your faith, being much more precious than gold that perishes, though it is tested by fire, may be found to praise, honor, and glory at the revelation of Jesus Christ."

Whatever you're struggling with, if it's health, you can be rewarded for your attitude in your health problems. If it's adversaries, you can be rewarded for your answers to them. If it's more than that, if it's emotional distress or whatever, we will be rewarded if the response we have is Christlike. That is beautiful to Him. It honors Him. It praises Him. It glorifies Him. It doesn't matter what we struggle with. If we struggle with it with the attitude of Christ, He rewards it.

Number 10: A Christlike focus on the Word

Second John 5–8 "And now I plead with you, lady, not as though I wrote a new commandment to you, but that which we have had from the beginning: that we love one another. This is love, that we walk according to His commandments. This is the commandment, that as you have heard from the beginning, you should walk in it. For many deceivers have gone out into the world who do not confess Jesus Christ as coming in the flesh. This is a deceiver and an antichrist. Look to yourselves, that we do not lose those things we worked for, but that we may receive a full reward."

Jesus rewards those who love Him so much they get His Word into their lives. They love Him so much they're filled with His Word and are not deceived by the world. Are you overflowing with the world this week or with the Word?

I was sitting waiting for someone this week, I came ten minutes early so no one knew I was there and I'd get extra time to read. So I was sitting in my car and I was so excited and I was writing in my Bible, and I had my pen out, and I couldn't believe I was finding stuff I'd never seen before, and all of a sudden, I got this feeling someone was watching me, and there was this face right against my window, looking at me. This person I was meeting for lunch had found me in the car and they said, "That was so precious to see you reading your Bible."

Do you long for God's Word? I actually can't wait until someone misses a meeting so I get an extra half hour to read His letters to me. Are you excited to immediately read what your beloved wrote to you? Or do you just have God's Word tucked under your arm as you go on with your day?

The ninety-six days leading up to my wedding to my lovely wife, I was in forty-two countries. I was in Egypt, India, China, all over the world. And I missed my bride-to-be so much, but everywhere I went, I'd check into the hotel, go to the counter, and give them my name, and they'd look at me, and at my name, and back at me, and they'd crawl behind the counter, and pull out a letter, and say, "We have a letter for you, sir."

She had found me. She found me in the most remote parts of the world, and sent me letters. And I tell you what, my bags dropped to the floor, and I sat down wherever I was, and that letter got torn open, and It didn't matter to me whether I found my room or not. I read the letter from the one I loved.

Do you know that you have a letter waiting for you every day from your beloved one? Have you dropped your bags lately? Most of us get the letter from the Lord, we tuck it under our arm, and we carry our bags. Have we dropped everything because we long to hear from the One we love?

As a godly marriage grows in love here on earth, so our love for Jesus grows every day. That's what God says He wants to have with us. He uses the closest human relationship we'll ever know to describe what He wants to have with us, only even more glorious. As the intimacy of marriage is the deepest and closest sharing we can know on earth, so the relationship we have with the Lord is to be the closest and deepest relationship we'll ever have. And as marriage brings the deepest and truest joys we know humanly speaking, so does a genuine relationship with Jesus, and it just gets sweeter as the days go by. It begins now, but one day, we will no longer be watching for our bridegroom to come get us. The feast will be ready, and you and I will see Him face-to-face.

Jesus wants us to be constantly repenting of spiritual neglect. He wants us getting dressed daily in a series of outfits He's designed for us. And every day we have a choice, to either obey or disobey. To either wear what He's picked out for us, or to neglect what He's told us to do. There will be a lot of people ashamed on that day because they neglected what Jesus commanded them to be doing, but that doesn't have to be us. Jesus didn't leave us to guess what makes for white garments. Throughout the Scriptures, Jesus very specifically lays out what He thinks is beautiful, what He likes, what He wants to see us wearing on our wedding day.

What can I lay away in my hope chest or overnight to heaven so it's there, in my room, just my size, ready to wear to the wedding feast? What one thing can I buy from Jesus, for Jesus, off His registry so that I can dress in what pleases Him for my wedding day? Is it a Christlike love of the unlovable? A hope-filled expectancy for His return? Maybe I'm going through a trial right now and I can put on a Christlike attitude.

I can show up naked and ashamed, wearing the wrong clothes, the black wool instead of the fine, white linen, or I can show up in white garments as a bride made ready for her husband. We can't get ready at the feast. We have to get ready now. Let's make that our prayer today.

Father, to think that You loved us so much that not only did You make a plan, and send Your Son, and allow Him the most cruel and ignominious death imaginable, but You also planned a celebration for us who caused His death, who caused His pain. He had to bear stripes to heal our sin-sick souls. Not only are we going to be able to get to heaven, but You are preparing a banquet for us to celebrate with the One who loved us and gave Himself for us. And You are going to allow us to be married to our Savior forever. We don't understand that. We don't understand the concept of spiritual union with You, the God of the universe, but Your Word tells us something, and what we can understand is that it's going to be glorious. And what we can understand is that there's something we need to do here to get ready, get ready for our wedding. To make sure we have dressed appropriate for our wedding. And if nothing else, I pray that Your Spirit would touch our hearts with the fact that every day that goes by we're getting closer, and it's such a special day that we ought to be sure that we're getting ready. I pray that You would bless our hearts through Your Word. May Christ be exalted, O Father, and may Your saints be edified. And I pray if any reading this are going to try to sneak into the wedding banquet without a wedding garment, that they'll see it's hopeless, and that it's too late if they're not ready for heaven here on earth by calling out to Jesus for salvation. You have a message for all, and I pray that we would respond. In the name of Jesus, we pray. Amen.

RESPOND to Truth

How do I show love in my closest human relationship? Do I show the same love to Christ?

Is my love for Jesus as evident to the cashiers who cross my path as newlyweds' love is for each other? How can I be more visible about my love for Christ?

Am I more concerned about how I look to other people, or how I look to God? Am I pleasing men outwardly, or pleasing God inwardly?

If I could see what God sees instead of what man sees, would I see myself clothed in white when I look in the mirror? Or would I see someone who is naked and ashamed?

What one piece of old clothing am I still wearing? (Romans 13:13; Galatians 5:19–21) What can I do to put it off today?

What item of white clothing is lacking in my hope chest? (Galatians 5:22–23; Matthew 5:11–12; 6:3–18; 6:19; Luke 6:35; 14:13–14; 1 Corinthians 3:8; Colossians 3:23–24; 2 Timothy 4:8; 1 Peter 1:7; 2 John 5–8) What can I do to put that one thing on today?

23 | Self-Induced Spiritual Blindness

L aodicea's sixth bad habit is spiritual blindness, but what's so bad about it is it's a condition that Jesus already cured. When Jesus described salvation to the apostle Paul, He said that the very first thing salvation does for us is open our eyes. So to say that spiritual blindness makes Jesus sick would be an understatement. To open our eyes was the entire reason He came to earth in the first place.

THE CHRISTMAS STORY
AS YOU'VE NEVER HEARD IT BEFORE

Let me tell you a story.

Everybody on earth was blind. In total darkness. They couldn't see, didn't know what was going on, and everybody, still blind, was crawling along toward this precipice, this deep chasm, and it drops down to a bottomless pit, into the blackness of darkness forever, where the wrath of God eternally burns against sin. So, all these blind, sin-darkened people were crawling toward the abyss, and they didn't even know it. They were lovers of the darkness, haters of God, and they've never seen the light. Headed toward destruction, and nobody knows, because nobody can see. That's how the story starts.

But the story continues. The sun comes up. The Sunrise from on high lit up the world and suddenly, some of those crawling toward the edge had their eyes opened. They saw the Dayspring, the Sunrise, the Light, and for the first time in their lives, they started seeing the edge they were headed toward. They saw the domain of Satan, the world and the flesh, they saw God, His word, His truth, His kingdom, His purposes, and for the first time in their lives, they saw the difference. And in that moment, they turned. From loving the darkness, to loving the light. From the kingdom of Satan to the kingdom of God.

Sound familiar? That's the Christmas story. Now it's not the way Charlie Brown tells it. But Luke did. If you read Luke 1:78–79, you'll find the Christmas story, summed up like you've never heard it before. "Through the tender mercy of our God, with which the Dayspring from on high has visited us; to give light to those who sit in darkness and the shadow of death."

The Christmas story is about people sitting in darkness and the shadow of death, and Jesus Christ, the Dayspring, comes and visits them, giving them light.

In the book of Acts, the sequel to the gospel of Luke, the apostle Paul is describing the moment of his salvation. Now he was the supreme example of spiritual blindness. He was so convinced he was doing God's work that he was willing to kill and torture and arrest and throw into prison as many of Jesus' followers as he could get his hands on.

I can just see him, proudly marching along the Damascus road, feeling his pockets for the arrest warrants, plotting out exactly where he would go first, how he would root out these Christians, planning what he'd do with them once he found them, and he was so certain that God was with him, wanting him to exterminate these "followers of the Way."

And then, in that moment, a searchlight-bright light stopped him dead in his tracks, knocked him over, and as he was lying on the ground wondering what in the world just happened, he heard a voice speaking.

"But rise and stand on your feet, for I have appeared to you for this purpose, to make you a minister and a witness both of the things which you have seen and of the things which I will yet reveal to you." And the voice of Jesus, right there on the road to Damascus, describes to Paul what the gospel of Jesus Christ is going to do. There are seven miraculous elements of salvation, as Jesus described it to Paul, and the very first one is "to open their eyes."[237]

237 Acts 26:16–18

Salvation, according to Jesus, does seven things. But the first, before anything else can happen, our eyes are opened. We go from blindness to seeing. But then, something else happens. Once our eyes are opened, we, for the first time, realize we're sitting in darkness, realize we're crawling toward the edge. We see clearly the difference between the death and destruction and darkness we're headed toward, and we do something. That's the second thing: "to turn them from darkness to light." We don't just sit there, looking around and seeing the condition we're in. We turn. We go from loving the darkness to loving the light, and instead of crawling toward the precipice, we turn and start going the other way.

Do you know why the world doesn't mind the baby in the manger? Because He doesn't offend. Oh, Jesus came, that's nice. But what people leave out is that He came to do this. He came to open our eyes, to turn us from darkness to light. Can you imagine if that was the Christmas story that people read and acted out and put on television specials? That we are sinners lost in darkness and Jesus came, not just to be this sweet, inoffensive baby in the manger, but to be the Dayspring, the Sunrise, to shine a light across our path and turn us around, to completely change us, from darkness to light, from the kingdom of Satan to the kingdom of God? That offends. But that's the Christmas story, according to Luke 1:78–79.

So Jesus told Paul that's what his message would do. Open their eyes, turn them from darkness to light. And it did. And through Paul's ministry, the gospel made its way across Asia Minor and into the city of Laodicea. And to those Laodiceans, sitting in darkness, headed toward the chasm of hell, the Dayspring rose and opened their eyes.

So now, the Dayspring is back for a visit. He's returned, after His death, after His resurrection, after His ascension, He's back. He's walking among His churches. The local assemblies of believers that He calls lamps in lampstands, that are supposed to not only be seeing, but also be spreading that light to others who are still sitting in darkness. So the Dayspring comes to all those whose eyes He'd opened…

And He found them crawling along, bumping into things, eyes tightly closed to the things of God.

Get Your Eyes Fixed Here

REVELATION 3:17–18

"Because you say, 'I am rich, have become wealthy, and have need of nothing'—and do not know that you are wretched, miserable, poor, blind, and naked—I counsel you to buy from Me gold refined in the fire, that you may be rich; and white garments, that you may be clothed, that the shame of your nakedness may not be revealed; and anoint your eyes with eye salve, that you may see."

The first thing you would have seen coming up over the hill into Laodicea would have been the sprawling medical complex. Today, you go down to Texas if you have cancer, and to the Mayo if you don't know what it is, and to Boston General for your heart. And just like hospitals today are specializing, there was a specialty in Laodicea. They had one of the premier medical treatment centers of the ancient world, specifically, for eye care.

In the ancient world's filthiness and the travel with all the dust the chariots kicked up, there was constant contagion in the eyes. People often lost their sight from infections. But people from Laodicea had developed, compounded, and carefully guarded a secret eye salve recipe. So if you had any money at all and had problems with your eyes, you would go for treatment to this city.

So, visiting Laodicea, you would have noticed the incredible medical school, the sprawling campus, the hospital, and the specialty eye care salve. Get your eyes fixed here. But just like He did with their luxurious clothing and abundant riches, Jesus said they'd gotten their eye care from the wrong source, and they did not have, as they boasted, 20-20 vision. At any hint of infection, they'd salve their physical eyes, but they were blind spiritually and didn't even know it.

The Blind Leading the Blind

The Laodiceans were spiritually blind because they couldn't recognize their own condition. Jesus told the Pharisees in John 9:39–41, "'For judgment

I came into this world, that those who do not see may see, and those who see may be made blind.'" Then some of the Pharisees who were with Him heard these words, and said to Him, 'Are we blind also?'" And Jesus answered, "'If you were blind, you would have no sin; but now you say, 'We see.' Therefore your sin remains."

These were the Ivy League, seminary-trained, professional clerics. They made bigger tassels on their robes so everyone knew they were extra religious. You could see them in their gardens, counting the seeds with tweezers, picking one out of every ten to give to the Lord. They would sound the trumpets when they gave big bags of money and prayed loudly so everyone could hear them. They were the Pharisees, the Bible teachers, the religious leaders of the day, who, more than anyone, should know and see God clearly.

Some of the most spiritually blinded people in the world are in the work of the ministry. I know. I have their books. I collect theology books written by people who know Greek and Hebrew and Aramaic and all these other obscure, dead languages better than anybody, and they've studied the Bible for years, but they are so blind. They don't believe in the resurrection of Christ. They don't believe in the deity of Christ. They don't believe in the miracles of Christ. They don't believe in the inspiration of Scripture. They don't believe in salvation by grace alone through faith in Christ. That's exactly who Jesus is addressing here: "Let them alone. They are blind leaders of the blind. And if a blind man leads a blind man, they will both fall into a ditch."

A few years ago, I was asked to do a funeral at a mainline denomination church, and they were very concerned about me being from a Bible church, but I told them I had all the books written by the founder of their denomination, and I could just read one of his funeral sermons and preach that, and they were so relieved.

So I was going to preach that mainline denomination funeral. And I took a sermon out of the founder's book, and I simply laid out the gospel, exactly like he did, how God opens our eyes and we go from darkness to light. And do you know what happened? It was a packed out, standing-room-only funeral, and afterwards, about sixty people waited in line to shake my hand. My hand. I wasn't the one who died. But they were amazed because they'd never heard what I'd preached before. They had no idea that's what their denomination was founded on. And I wondered what they'd been hearing in church every Sunday. That's what Jesus meant by the blind leading the blind.

But Jesus didn't just issue this indictment against the Pharisees or against the Laodiceans or against somebody else's denomination. I see this all the time. When someone first gets saved, they're so excited. That first thing the gospel does, the first miraculous element of salvation, you can actually see it happen.

If you've never had the opportunity to lead someone to Christ, it's the most amazing thing. You can pinpoint the exact moment they go from blindness to seeing. Everything that made no sense at all before suddenly all makes sense. And they understand, for the first time, the truth of the gospel, and the truth of Scripture. And they're so excited. What God says they should do, they do immediately. If God says do this, they do it. If He says do that, they're going to do that too. They don't want to be in disobedience to God for another moment longer.

But you know what happens after a while? The dust of this world gets in and they just can't see it anymore. What used to be so clear isn't so clear anymore. What used to make sense isn't quite as easy to see, isn't quite as sure, and so they're not sure exactly what it means. Maybe it doesn't mean that. Maybe God was talking about something else. And they don't know what God wants from them or what He's trying to say, and it isn't, "This is the way, walk in it."[238] It's "I don't really know what the way is, and I just hope I get to heaven."

Spiritual blindness is just that: blindness to the things of God. We no longer see Him in His Word. We stop noticing His hand in our lives. We don't reach up and grasp His hand extended to us every day to hold onto us so we can follow Him through life. We begin to stumble along. We act more and more like lost people, who do not know, who cannot see, and who do not follow the Lord. That's what spiritual blindness is. We revert back to acting like unsaved people. That's what had happened to Laodicea.

Jesus said the believers at Laodicea lacked three things for a life pleasing to God. The first was gold, not the gold they'd been piling up on earth,

238 Isaiah 30:21

but gold refined in the fire they could only buy from Jesus. The second was white garments, the exact opposite of the black wool garments that Laodicea was known for, also only available through Jesus. And the third was eye salve. Laodicea was known for healthy eyes, perfect eyesight, and the medication that the rest of the known world sought after when they had eye problems. But Jesus says they have the greatest eye problem: utter blindness to the things of God.

LIFELONG SPIRITUAL EYE CARE

When you go for years without seeing an eye doctor, you can get so used to seeing the world unclearly that you begin to think the world is just like that. But when you finally give in and see the doctor and walk out with new glasses, all of a sudden the world is clear. You can see, not just trees, but the individual leaves on the trees, and you just had no idea your eyesight was that bad.

Many Christians have gotten so used to fumbling along, looking at the world through blurred vision, that they think the world is just like that. The Bible is just always hard to understand. God's will is always going to be mysterious. His purpose for my life is something I can never really know. And we have no idea that it's not God or His Word that's blurry. It's just our spiritual eyesight.

You've all seen the poster on the wall at the eye doctor's office. Line 1 is a great, big, giant "E," and then the letters get smaller the further you go down the chart. If you can read the whole poster from across the room, your eyesight is great. But if you can't even read the "E," you're in trouble. So if we were to go to Jesus as our Great Physician, and on His wall was a spiritual eye chart, how far down could you read?

The Test for Spiritual Sight
Line 1: Do you have a confidence that you are saved?
First of all, if you don't feel saved, then do like 2 Corinthians 13:5 says and examine yourself to see if you're really in the faith. Check against God's Word. But if you know God's Word, and He says you're saved but you just

have no confidence, no assurance, no certainty, then it could be that your spiritual sight has been clouded.

The Bible says, "The Spirit Himself bears witness with our spirit that we are children of God."[239] Part of seeing clearly is that the Holy Spirit inside you bears witness, testifies, telling you that you are saved, and you see clearly that you are. But many believers struggle for years with wondering whether they're saved or not. They know the facts of the gospel, but they can't see with clarity that they themselves are children of God. If that's you, then that's a sign you may need, like the Laodiceans, to buy eye salve from Jesus.

Line 2: Can you see God at work in your life?

Those who see God clearly see Him everywhere. His work in creation, His hand in their lives, and when they come to a crossroads, God is so present to them that He's the first Person they consult on which direction to go.

Joseph's brothers sold him into slavery. He was abandoned by his family, falsely imprisoned, and completely forgotten, but when he looked at his life, all he saw was that God meant it all for good. When David looked at the sky, he said, "The heavens declare the glory of God; and the firmament shows His handiwork."[240]

Do you look at God's creation and worship Him? Or do you just notice the temperature so you know which coat to wear? Do you notice God at work, or do you just see coincidence and luck? That could be a sign of failing eyesight.

Line 3: Does God's Word make sense?

One of the most common complaints of unbelievers is that the Bible just doesn't make sense. They just can't understand any of it. Do you know why? Because Paul says the natural man can't understand the things of God. It's foolishness to him. They're not supposed to be able to understand, because their spiritual eyes are closed. But we, as believers, should not only under-stand God's Word, but it should be a great attraction for us.

You don't need a doctorate in theology to understand God's Word. You need the Holy Spirit. But when the Spirit is grieved and quenched, our spir-itual sight is dimmed, and God's Word, that used to be so clear, is harder to

239 Romans 8:16
240 Psalm 19:1

understand, harder to make sense of, and we start thinking it can't mean what it says, and there's really no way to know for sure.

God's Word is not supposed to be confusing. The devil is the author of confusion, not God. God gave us His Word, and specifically what most people believe is the most confusing book of the Bible, Revelation, so that we would *know*, not guess, not hope, not reinterpret or chart or rearrange or extrapolate, but that we would know what He says, what He wants, who He is, and what He's going to do. If God's Word is just a big blur, you can maybe make out John 3:16 and some of Romans, but not much more, then you need eye salve.

Line 4: Can you see God in His Word?

The test for our spiritual sight is how hungrily we long for God in His Word. When was the last time something jumped out at you that you'd never noticed before? When was the last time you appreciated your Savior in a whole new light? When was the last time you were anxious to get alone with God's Word so He could reveal Himself to you? Do you know what 20-20 spiritual vision looks like? Job described it this way: "I have heard of You by the hearing of the ear, but now my eye sees you."

Many Christians go through their entire lives hearing about God, but never seeing Him for themselves. They hear a pastor describe Him and explain the Scripture, but they can't go to God's Word themselves because their eyes are so clouded over they won't be able to see anything anyway. Matthew 5:8 says, "Blessed are the pure in heart, for they will see God." To render that literally, from Greek, it would read, "Blessed are the pure in heart, for only they will continually see God for themselves."

When Moses caught a glimpse of God, in Exodus 33:18, He said, "Please, show me Your glory." Those who see God want to see God more. Is that you? If not, it's time to salve your eyes.

Line 5: Do you know what God's will is?

One of the most common prayer requests, especially for younger people, is that they can find God's will for their lives. Did you know that in five different places in Scripture it says, "This is the will of God"? Do you know what

His will is? He's said it. Are you praying that you'll know how to please God? Great. But have you read in His Word what He says pleases Him? What He says doesn't? Those who see God clearly read in His Word what His will is, and they follow it.

Jesus gave us at the moment of salvation a perfect set of spiritual eyes. I remember when our oldest son was only about a week old. We took him to church and one of the sweet elderly ladies who had obviously never had children of her own asked, "Are his eyes open yet?" And my wife said, "Well, he's not a kitten."

You and I are not like kittens. We don't get saved, and then gradually our eyes get opened. We are like my son, born eyes-wide-open and screaming. Our eyes are opened immediately at salvation, and we have perfect sight, perfect eyes. It's only afterward that the dust of the chariots and the filthiness of this world get in and we get infected, and blurred, and contaminated.

Jesus gave us those perfect eyes, but He leaves the maintenance of those eyes to us. We are responsible to keep the corrosive, blinding, dimming elements of this world from contaminating and destroying our spiritual eyesight. So what is it that clouds over the eyes? What causes spiritual cataracts?

The answer is found in Matthew 5:8.

Dust from the Chariots: Double-Minded and Un-Surrendered

This is the beginning of Jesus' longest recorded sermon. He's describing what happens after our eyes are opened, and He makes a startling statement: Only the pure in heart can see God.

Matthew 5:8 says, "Blessed are the pure in heart, for they shall see God." We all know that verse. It's one of the beatitudes. It's beautiful. We have it on our walls and stitched on pillows, but it's not just a nice verse. It's a profound truth. If only the pure of heart can see God, then Jesus is telling us here, and in Revelation 3:18, that impurity of heart blinds the eyes. If you don't keep your heart pure, you will see less and less of God.

Spiritual purity maintains spiritual sight. The word "pure" is *katharos*, meaning to make pure by cleansing from dirt, from filth, or from contamination. Again, rendered literally, "Blessed are the cleansed from dirt, filth, and contamination, for they shall see God."

Outside the beatitudes, the word *katharos* was often used in the world of the Bible, especially in industry, and particularly in metalworking. It spoke of metals that were refined until they were unmixed, unadulterated, and unalloyed with other things. You didn't want them mixed. You didn't want them having impurities. You wanted to start out with the pure metal. Pure gold, pure silver, pure copper. That's the idea of this word.

So, when we apply that back into our lives, that means that only those who are unalloyed, unmixed, unadulterated, and free from contamination get to see God. Later in the same sermon, Jesus explained it another way: "No one can serve two masters; for either he will hate the one and love the other, or else he will be loyal to the one and despise the other. You cannot serve God and mammon."[241]

Jesus says you can't serve two masters. You can't have a divided heart. You can't partition your hard drive. You know how you can divide your hard drive if it's big enough? You can have half be for this and half be for that, but the problem is, if one half breaks down, both halves break down. They're tied together. And Jesus says your heart is tied together, and if you partition it and let this half get polluted, it pollutes the whole thing. You can't have two masters.

Jesus' oldest brother, James, wrote an entire epistle on the dangers of having a divided heart. In chapter 1, he describes a "double-minded man" as "unstable in all his ways."[242] Those who are double-minded, who have their Sunday mind, and their real mind they use for the rest of their life, they're unstable, because they're constantly going between allegiance to one master and allegiance to their real master. They say, yeah, that's important… only during that one hour I'm at church or Bible study or with those people.

In chapter 4, James says you can't be friends with God and friends with the world at the same time. Do you know what he called that? Adultery. Here's God, who you're supposed to belong to, and you're over here giving yourself to someone else. That's what it means to be mixed, alloyed, adulterated. That's double-mindedness. That's being un-surrendered. And Jesus says it causes spiritual blindness.

---

241 Matthew 6:24
242 James 1:8

Peter also warns against having an un-surrendered life. He says, "Giving all diligence, add to your faith virtue, to virtue knowledge, to knowledge self-control, to self-control perseverance, to perseverance godliness, to godliness brotherly kindness, and to brotherly kindness love." That's a surrendered life. When every part is being brought into subjection to Christ. Surrendering one area of our life after another until the whole thing belongs to Christ. That's sanctification, that's surrender. But this is what happens in a double-minded or un-surrendered life: "For he who lacks these things is shortsighted, even to blindness, and has forgotten that he was cleansed from his old sins."

Jesus says you can't see God clearly unless you have a pure heart. The only ones who see God are the ones who have pure motives, who are single-minded for Him, who offer Him undivided devotion as their only Master, who walk in spiritual integrity. We are to bring everything under a central command. Not compartmentalized, not double-minded. Surrendered. When every part is increasingly under Christ's control, we will see God clearly.

Blessed are the Pure in Heart

When we are first saved, we are given the gift of sight. We can hear God's voice in His Word. We can see Him clearly in His Word. We can worship Him in His creation. We can feel His Spirit at work within us. All that is a part of spiritual sight.

So the more confusing life is, the more unclear it is what we're supposed to do, where we're supposed to be, how we're supposed to act, what God expects from us, the more that we have trouble seeing clearly in life, the more we need to apply the spiritual eye salve that Jesus is talking about.

Jesus counsels the blind Laodiceans in lifelong vision care. It starts with the healthy eyes He gave us at salvation, and it is maintained by what I call practical purity.

Jesus said only the "pure in heart" get to see God, but there are five different purities talked about in the Bible. The first is the purity of God. That's just who He is, His character. Holiness, like a consuming fire, evident throughout Scripture, and His only name that gets said in triplicate.

That's not what He's talking about in Matthew 5:8.

The second purity is the purity of creation. When God originally created, the universe, the angels, and humanity were all completely pure, undefiled. But after the fall, it was all polluted. The universe groans under the curse. A third of the angels fell in Satan's rebellion. And each one of us is a sinner by nature, by choice and by decree. We were born sinners, we choose sin, and God declared us to be sinners ever since Adam fell. But, originally, everything was pure from God's hands.

That's not the purity we're talking about either.

The third purity is called positional purity, and it's what God offers to every believer. It means that Christ's righteousness was credited to my account, just as my sin was credited to His. When God looks at me, He sees me as if I'd never sinned, covered in the righteousness of Christ. And no, that's not what Matthew 5:8 is talking about.

Well then, there's the purity we'll have when we're glorified. When Jesus comes to take us home or calls us to meet Him in the clouds, we will be glorified, finally free from that sin nature we were born with, finally unable to choose sin, finally, truly pure. And that's when we will forever be in God's presence seeing Him. And that's still not the purity of Matthew 5:8.

Matthew 5:8 purity is called practical purity.

Positional purity at salvation is a gift. Practical purity is the hard part. It requires supreme effort. It comes from God but it demands our participation in a way that other kinds of purity do not. We can't participate in the purity of God. He just is. We can't do anything about the original purity that we lost at the fall. I don't have to do anything for the purity that saves me. Jesus imputes that to my account, and the purity I'll have in heaven is a gift too. But the other kind, the practical kind, requires something of me. It's the only one I have a responsibility to participate in.

See, we weren't saved just to be pure in God's sight, but also to be pure in practice, in conduct. And we weren't just saved for future, heavenly purity, but also for present, earthly purity.

We were saved to reflect Christ's holiness by walking in practical purity moment by moment. That's why Paul says, "Let us cleanse ourselves from all filthiness of the flesh and spirit, perfecting holiness in the fear of

God."[243] That's why Peter says, "as He who calls you is holy, you also be holy in all your conduct, because it is written, 'Be holy, for I am holy.'"[244]

Practical purity is possible. Whatever God desires from us, He provides the way for us to obey. The key to practical purity is confessing we have no power on our own to make it for even one moment. Like John 15:5 says, "Without Me you can do nothing." At best we will be iron mixed with clay, but God wants us, today, to be as pure as we can be. Because only by living in purity can we truly see God.

CHRIST YOUR EYES WITH EYE SALVE: THE PRACTICAL PURITY OF THOSE WHO SEE GOD

Here's the good news: Spiritual blindness is preventable. It's treatable. It does not have to persist. Jesus wants to promote healthy eyes. Why? He wants us to see Him clearly. He wants us to understand and see His will clearly in His Word. And He wants us looking with those spiritual eyes to see life clearly. So we need to be regularly applying the eye salve that Jesus says preserves spiritual sight.

That word "anoint" is actually a play on words. In Greek, it comes from the same word for Christ. "Christ" means the "Anointed One." So when something is anointed, it's literally Christ-ed.

Jesus is saying in Revelation 3:18, Christ your eyes with eye salve. He's the One who gave us the eyes. He's the only One who can keep them healthy. He's the only source of the eye salve that preserves spiritual sight, and in Matthew 5:8, He tells us what that is: a lifestyle of practical purity.

There is nothing more prevalent in the epistles than a lifestyle of practical purity. It makes up the bulk of everything Scripture talks about from 1 Corinthians on. But it wasn't new to Jesus' ministry or the teachings of the apostles. Practical purity is taught throughout Scripture.

Neither Jesus nor the apostles had the New Testament Scriptures to teach from. They were living it. They were writing it. So what they had to teach from was the Old Testament, and one of Jesus' favorite books was

243 2 Corinthians 7:1
244 1 Peter 1:15–16

Isaiah. In fact, when Jesus said, "Blessed are the pure in heart, for they will see God," He may very well have been alluding to Isaiah 33:14–17.

Isaiah begins by asking a question. "Who among us shall dwell with the devouring fire? Who among us shall dwell with everlasting burnings?" Do you know what he's asking? Who can dwell in God's presence? Who can approach His throne of fire and the all-consuming holiness that God said was so dangerous He wouldn't even let Moses see His face, only His back? Who can see God?

So God inspired Isaiah to write down what I call six choices that preserve spiritual sight. If you want to see God, these are the six things that keep the contaminants out, that protect you from the dust. If you are spiritually blind, if you can't read the eye chart and you know that you're like the Laodiceans and need the same eye salve they did, this is the salve.

Six Choices that Preserve Spiritual Sight

Who can see God? Number one, "He who walks righteously." Do you know the difference between a good driver and a bad driver? The good driver is constantly making tiny course corrections to stay on the road. That doesn't mean they're perfect. They might miss a sign every once in a while. They might drift into the rumble strip, but they immediately turn the wheel to get back on course. The bad drivers are the ones who are consistently in the ditch.

The one with a lifestyle of practical purity, who walks righteously, that's who can dwell in God's presence. That's who can see Him. This is a person who says, whoops, I can't do that. Oops. I can't go that way. It's a lifestyle of making constant course adjustments, in my appetites, in places that I go, in what I allow into my mind to hear and see. Maintaining a lifestyle of practical purity pleases God and preserves spiritual sight. Not perfect, but committed to staying on the road. That's number one.

Number two: "and speaks uprightly." This is a person whose speech is under control. Remember, "Out of the abundance of the heart the mouth speaks."[245] If our heart is correct, our speech is under control. Do you know how you can tell? When someone loses their temper, do they just say things that they wish they could take back? That's speech not under control. That

245 Matthew 12:34

clouds over the eyes. But someone whose heart is pure has their speech reined in, and they preserve their spiritual sight.

Thirdly, "he who despises the gain of oppressions." That's someone who is compassionate. You hate to hear of someone else being oppressed or who's struggling. An others-focused heart of compassion preserves spiritual sight. It keeps you seeing God clearly.

Fourthly, "who gestures with his hands, refusing bribes." That's honesty. You say it doesn't matter, I'm not for sale. I remember when I was a salesman years ago, all the salesmen would "fudge" their numbers. That's what they called it. And our division wanted to win, to beat the other divisions in sales, and the manager came to me and said my sales numbers weren't good enough and I needed to change them. I told him those numbers were exactly what I sold, and he asked me to just fudge it a little bit. But I said no because it's dishonest, and that causes spiritual cataracts. This goes back to the integrity Jesus calls us to. Not trying to serve two masters.

Number five: "Who stops his ears from hearing of bloodshed." Do you know what that is? That's pure audio input. Do you want to know what glazes over the eyes real fast? Listening to the music of people who are God's avowed enemies, and knowing every word by heart. Listening to drug-induced lyrics that displease God.

All our devices, our TVs and computers, have two input jacks, audio input, and video input. So do we. What are we supposed to let in? Things that are true, honest, just, pure, lovely, of good report, virtue, and praise. That's Philippians 4:8. That's what God wants. If we plug into our audio input jack things that are true, lovely, pure, excellent, and praiseworthy, then our spiritual sight gets clearer and clearer.

Number six: "and shuts his eyes from seeing evil." That's pure video input. What about our entertainment? We are living in an age when we let anybody be entertained by evil. You want a society study? Go to a movie. Watch the previews. What are they about? The occult, murder, adultery, fornication. And we have degrees of fornication. It can be a PG fornication, or a PG-13 fornication. I don't even know all the ratings. R, or N, whatever. We're entertained by evil. God says we're not even supposed to have a hint of evil. We are to have pure video input. The more you fill your eyes with what displeases God, the less you see what does please Him. But when you fix your eyes on what is pure, then that is a choice that preserves spiritual sight.

The Indescribable Joys of Seeing God

There is a captivating beauty to God, and there are six indescribable joys of seeing God listed just in Isaiah 33. First, the person who protects their spiritual eyes by a lifestyle of practical purity will, "dwell on high."

Do you know what drug addicts call being on drugs? Being high. Beyond description, in a different place. And the Lord says, you'll dwell on high. I remember when my wife and I used to eat at the The Original Pantry in downtown Los Angeles, the waiter was a coke addict. And he used to look at us reading our Bibles on the way to work every morning, and after about three months, he said, "what drug are you guys on? You're high every morning." So those with clear spiritual sight will dwell "on high."

Next, "his place of defense will be the fortress of rocks." That's true security. Third, "Bread will be given him." That's true satisfaction. Our longings are satisfied when we see God. Fourth, "His water will be sure." We're never-endingly refreshed. And the last two are the greatest attraction for us and a heavenward gaze: "Your eyes will see the King in His beauty. You will see the land that is very far off."

If you spend twelve hours driving, looking way down the road at things that are "very far off," you find when you get home in the garage, everything close up is hard to focus on. You can't get your eyes to focus on anything that's not miles down the road. But if you spend hours staring at a book or looking at your iPhone screen, then when you look up, your eyes can't focus on anything further than a foot in front of your face. It all looks blurry, it's hard to see, so you just give up and look back down at your book or electronic device.

Our spiritual sight is the same way. The longer we stare at the things of this world, the dimmer and blurrier and less clear the things of heaven will be. But the longer we look for heaven, for the things of God, as Colossians 3:2 says, for "the things above, not on things on the earth," then it's the world that gets out of focus. Helen Lemmel wrote in her great hymn, "Turn your eyes upon Jesus. Look full in His wonderful face, and the things of earth will grow strangely dim."

Are the things of this world progressively growing dimmer and dimmer, or is it Jesus who's becoming more and more unclear as the days go by? Have you Christ-ed your eyes with eye salve this week? Like the psalmist, let us make this our prayer: "Open my eyes that I may see wonderful things."[246]

Spiritual blindness is preventable, treatable, and it doesn't have to persist one moment longer. Christ your eyes with the eye salve of practical purity. It takes participation and deliberate effort on our part, but it's not impossible. Jesus counsels us in lifelong spiritual eye care because He wants us to see life clearly, to see Him clearly. The joys of seeing God, continually, for ourselves, are indescribable. Let us take up the challenge today.

Father in heaven, we have sought to give our attention to Your Word, and now we bow before You and ask You to help us zealously respond and to repent of any area of our life that is destroying our spiritual eyesight, that is clouding over the clarity of seeing You in Your Word. Only the pure in heart see You, and the ones who are continuously seeing You, Lord Jesus, are the ones who have a heart cleansed and kept clean by persistent confession and repentance. Father, I pray that we would be vigilant in anointing, in Christ-ing our eyes. They belong to You. We pray that You would open them, that You would heal them, that You would do whatever needs to be done that we might see You clearly. In the name of Jesus, we ask for this and for Your glory, we pray. Amen.

RESPOND to Truth

What are the signs of spiritual blindness? (Matthew 23:24–26; John 3:19–20; Romans 2:19–24; 2 Timothy 3:1–7; Hebrews 3:12–13; 2 Peter 1:5–9; Revelation 3:17)

246 Psalm 119:18

Why is spiritual sight so vitally important? (Matthew 6:22)

How does the view we have of God now compare with how we'll see Him in heaven? (1 Corinthians 13:12)

How does our view of God affect our everyday lives? (2 Corinthians 3:18)

What does clear spiritual sight look like? (Romans 8:16; 2 Kings 6:14–17; Psalm 119; Psalm 42:1; Isaiah 30:21) How well does that describe me?

What choices can I make today to, as Isaiah 33:15 says, walk righteously in practical purity? (John 14:21; John 15:3; Galatians 5:16; 1 Thessalonians 5:17 with Jeremiah 33:3 and Psalm 51:10; 1 John 1:9)

Living Crucified: Therefore Be Zealous and Repent | 24

For five verses, Jesus has been pounding Laodicea with a list of their sins. He has been, in no uncertain terms, saying exactly what He thinks about the state of His church. And now in verse 19, He comes to the seventh bad habit. Spiritual laxity may be last, but it is not least. In fact, it is the one bad habit that encompasses all the others. This is the reason Laodicea had felt they could get away with spiritual neutrality for so long. This is why spiritual self-sufficiency didn't seem like such a problem, why abandoning Christ as their investment counselor was no big deal, and why clothing themselves for Christ's sake daily was not a high priority. Because of their spiritual blindness and spiritual insensitivity to the things of God, Laodicea had drifted into a state of spiritual laxity, their last bad habit, and their worst. And this is what Jesus says to them, "Those whom I love, I rebuke and chasten. Therefore, be zealous and repent."

Repentance has most often been described as doing a 180. You're going down the road in one direction, when God gets a hold of you, and you turn completely to go in the other direction. Like the apostle Paul on the road to Damascus, something stops you in your tracks, you see for the first time what you have been doing and where you have been going, and you turn around and go in the other direction.

The problem with repentance is that it requires a standard. A standard to compare your life to so that you see what you are doing wrong, and repentance means returning to that standard. That's why there's so little repentance going on today, because we have no standard, and we do like they did in the book of Judges, when "everyone does what is right in his own eyes."[247]

It is a decreasing event in churches across America that you're even asked to open a Bible, that it's even referred to, let alone read from. We have more access to God's Word than any generation in history and less of it implanted in our souls than any generation before us.

There is no perfect church, no perfect pastor, no perfect denomination of any kind, but there is a perfect revelation of God. It is complete. We don't need anything else. If God didn't say it, we don't need to worry about it. And if God did want us to know something, it's written down for us, all in one handy, travel-sized Book.

What God wrote down, He wrote down perfectly. There are no errors in it, not one cultural error, not one scientific error, not one historical error, not one moral error, not one doctrinal error, not one theological error. The Bible is objective, propositional truth. Not just a truth, but the Truth. And all of it, every word on every page, is inspired by God.

"All Scripture is given by inspiration of God, and is profitable for doctrine, for reproof, for correction, for instruction in righteousness, that the man of God may be complete, thoroughly equipped for every good work."[248]

Do you know what this verse says God's Word is good for? Doctrine is when God tells us what is right. Reproof is when God tells us what is wrong. Correction is God telling us how to get right, and instruction in righteousness is how to stay right.

God's Word is the standard that tells us what is wrong with our direction, tells us what direction we should be going, and gets us back on the path that God has for us. So to see what Jesus was asking Laodicea to repent from, we need to see the standard that they had ignored, the path that they had wandered from, and that is what God calls in the book of Acts "The Way."

247 Judges 17:6
248 2 Timothy 3:16–17

FOLLOWERS OF THE WAY

The Christian life is a lot like keeping a car on the road. If I was trying to pantomime "car," "driver," or "steering wheel," I'd put my hands at ten and two, and move them back and forth just a little, and for the vast majority of adults, that would immediately get "car," "driver," or "steering wheel." Driving down a road, no matter how straight it is, isn't just putting on the cruise control, locking the wheel in place, and taking a nap in the front seat. It is made of constant, incremental course adjustments to stay on the road.

That's what the Christian life is like. And you could take the metaphor even further. The gas you feed the car with is the Word of God, the steering wheel is our will, our choices whether to follow the road or not. The rumble strip is the conviction of the Holy Spirit, and when we get off in the ditch, that's when God in His mercy has to come and pull us out.

And repentance is when, after seeing in God's Word all the "wrong way" signs, we stop in our tracks, and make a U-turn at the earliest possible moment.

Jesus described salvation as a narrow gate, "for wide is the gate and broad is the way that leads to destruction, and there are many who go in by it. Because narrow is the gate and difficult is the way which leads to life, and there are few who find it."[249] And when He introduced Himself to the world, He called Himself "the Way, the Truth, and the Life."

Believers are not simply people who have checked a box, saying "I've done that." True followers of Jesus know the Truth, they live the life, and they follow the Way. The believers at Laodicea wouldn't hesitate to check the box saying, "I've done that." But they neglected doctrine, what God's Word says is right. And this way of life is found in the book of Acts, where no less than seven times, the Church of Jesus Christ is referred to as "the Way."

The first time this comes up is in Acts chapter 9. Stephen has just been martyred, and Saul, "still breathing threats and murder against the disciples of the Lord, went to the high priest and asked letters from him to the synagogues of Damascus, so that if he found any who were of the Way,

249 Matthew 7:13–14

whether men or women, he might bring them bound to Jerusalem."[250] Later, he's retelling the story and says, "I persecuted this Way to the death, binding and delivering into prisons both men and women."[251]

How do you think Saul recognized those who were "of the Way"? Did he go to Damascus, find the house church and read a list of names off some registry? No. This Way wasn't just the way to heaven. It's a way of life. These were people who had a different lifestyle. Who were living, walking, talking, and thinking differently. That's who he was looking for. Not names on a roster. People who were living the life.

Followers of the Way stand out. They're recognizable, and they stand out most clearly to the enemies of God. In Acts 19, Paul is preaching in Ephesus, but the Jews living there start speaking evil of "the Way." Later in the same chapter, a commotion arises because of "the Way." In Acts 24, when Paul says he lives according to "the Way," even unsaved governor Felix recognizes immediately what Paul is talking about.

Now if these Way-followers had been living the same way as every other good Jew in Ephesus, there wouldn't have been a commotion. But because these people were an anomaly in their own culture, people noticed, and they tried to get rid of them. If Paul had been a good law-abiding Roman citizen who worshiped the emperor like everybody else, he would never have been dragged before Felix, and Felix would never have heard of these people.

But the Way stands out most clearly when confronted with a demon-possessed fortune-teller in Acts 16:17. "This girl followed Paul and us, and cried out, saying, 'These men are the servants of the Most High God, who proclaim to us the way of salvation.'"

Is that the first thing an enemy of God would recognize about you? Would the intelligent, centuries-old demons immediately identify you as a servant of the Most High God, who is on the Way, and who proclaims the way of salvation?

See, it's not just the way of salvation. It's a way of life. It's not something I did. It's who I am.

---

250 Acts 9:1–2
251 Acts 22:4

Have you ever gotten onto an elevator and noticed that everybody turns around and faces the same direction? Sometimes, just to remind myself what it's like to be a Christian, I get onto the elevator and stand there facing the people. It's uncomfortable. And everyone starts wondering what's wrong with me. But eventually, they start looking to see what I'm staring at, why I'm facing that way. That's the power the early church had. It's not that they beat everyone around them over the head with a Bible saying, "you're going the wrong way. You're going to hell." They just lived the Life, according to the Truth, and followed the Way, and people began to be curious. They wanted to know what was going on with these weird Way-followers, and God's Word spread.

It's a lifestyle, a present way of life that Paul describes as a struggle, a constant commitment to personal discipline. "Do you not know that those who run in a race all run, but one receives the prize? Run in such a way that you may obtain it. And everyone who competes for the prize is temperate in all things. Now they do it to obtain a perishable crown, but we for an imperishable crown. Therefore I run thus; not with uncertainty. Thus I fight: not as one who beats the air. But I discipline my body and bring it into subjection, lest, when I have preached to others, I myself become disqualified."[252]

As followers of the Way, we are called to increasing levels of surrender. Don't fall asleep at the wheel. Don't drift into the ditch. Don't run out of gas. Constantly, incrementally, course correct. Yes, salvation was something that happened in the past, but it has so completely changed me that I live a life of surrender, increasingly giving over areas of my life to Christ's control.

Paul describes it this way: "I beseech you therefore, brethren, by the mercies of God, that you present your bodies a living sacrifice, holy, acceptable to God, which is your reasonable service of worship. And do not be conformed to this world, but be transformed by the renewing of your mind, that you may prove what is that good and acceptable and perfect will of God."[253]

"Do not be conformed to the world." Don't go the same way the world is going. They're going the wrong way. Do you feel like an outsider? Like

252 1 Corinthians 9:24–27
253 Romans 12:1–3

you're weird, out of step with the rest of the world? Good. Then you are one of the few who are going the right direction. Jesus says the Way is a narrow road, and few find it. The road to destruction is wide and many there are that find it. If you feel like you're staring at the people on the elevator and they're all squirming wondering what's wrong with you, then you're one of those really strange people, one of those Way-followers.

Citizens of Heaven

Salvation is not a decision. It's a direction. It's not a past event. It's a present reality. And it is not now, nor has it ever been membership in a church. Salvation is having your citizenship in heaven.

Unless you or someone you love came to this country as an immigrant and worked and studied and earned your citizenship, you probably don't fully realize how important citizenship is. But if you lived in the Roman Empire in the first century, you understood just what being a Roman citizen meant.

Every Roman citizen understood and spoke the same language, had the same law, and had the same culture. They all knew the *Lex Juris*, the jurisprudence of Rome. Being a Roman citizen was so important that people would pay large sums of money to become one, and whether you were a citizen or not could actually be the difference between life and death.

When Paul was preaching in Jerusalem in Acts 22, he preached the gospel with such boldness that the crowd said, "Away with such a fellow from the earth, for he is not fit to live." He was dragged away and tied up, about to be scourged, but Paul just pulls out that Roman citizenship and the soldiers just gasped and pulled back, because they had violated his rights as a citizen.

Do you know we have an even more valuable citizenship? Paul, who understood better than anybody the value of his earthly citizenship, said, "But what things were gain to me, these I have counted loss for Christ. Yet indeed I also count all things loss for the excellence of the knowledge of Christ Jesus my Lord." "For our citizenship is in heaven."[254]

For over two hundred years, the most sold, read, and studied book in the world, next to the Bible, was a book called *Pilgrim's Progress*. And it

254 Philippians 3:7–8, 20

described the Christian life, not as a decision we made in the past, but as a journey that we're on in the present, from the City of Destruction, where all of us started, to the Celestial City, our ultimate destination, the place of our citizenship.

John Bunyan understood something that many Christians in the twenty-first century have forgotten. We are not defined as people who have their names on a membership roster somewhere. We're not simply described as people who made a decision in the past. In fact, we no longer belong here on this earth at all.

The Old Testament saints understood the same thing Paul did, the same thing John Bunyan described in *Pilgrim's Progress*, that we are "strangers and pilgrims on the earth." Hebrews 11:13–16 says, "For those who say such things declare plainly that they seek a homeland. And truly if they had called to mind that country from which they had come out, they would have had opportunity to return. But now they desire a better, that is, a heavenly country. Therefore God is not ashamed to be called their God, for He has prepared a city for them."

When you're following the Way, God is not ashamed to call you His, because you're living for the city He's prepared. That's why Peter calls us "sojourners and pilgrims," and the writer of Hebrews says, "Here we have no continuing city, but we seek the one to come."[255]

Paul compares being a believer to being a soldier, far from home. Second Timothy 2:3–7 says, "No one engaged in warfare entangles himself with the affairs of this life, that he may please him who enlisted him as a soldier." And when Paul came to the end of his life, he described it like the end of his tour of duty. "The time of my departure is at hand. I have fought the good fight, I have finished the race, I have kept the faith."

Paul uses the word for a Roman soldier finally packing up his tent and going home after a long tour of duty. He's been far from home, fighting, longing to return to his own country, and at last, it was time for his "departure," to roll up his sleeping bag, pull up his tent pegs, and go home to his family, his people, the place where he belonged. That's what it means to be a citizen of heaven.

---

255 1 Peter 2:11; Hebrews 13:14

THE BAD HABIT THAT SUMS UP ALL THE OTHERS

God's Word, according to 2 Timothy 3:16, is good for four things. It tells us what's right. Laodicea knew what was right: living as followers of the Way, citizens of heaven, called to increasing levels of surrender, but they weren't obeying it, and so for five verses, Jesus has been telling Laodicea what's wrong. They were spiritually neutral, self-sufficient, insensitive, and wasteful. They're characterized by spiritual neglect and spiritual blindness, and now, in Revelation 3:19, Jesus sums up their condition with this command: "Therefore, be zealous and repent."

Spiritual laxity is the bad habit that sums up all the others. Jesus' last command begins with that summary explanatory particle, "therefore," our gateway to stand in, to pause, and to look back to see why verse 19 is necessary. Jesus says repent. Why? Because of the sickening neutrality of verse 15. Because of the heart-breaking self-sufficiency He found in verse 17, and because of every other bad habit He had to point out to His people.

Jesus commands His people to be "zealous," to have a continuous, constant attitude of enthusiasm, eagerness. Spiritual laxity is when we find one, two, or all six of the other bad habits in our own life, and, instead of being zealous, eager, and enthusiastic about complete, immediate repentance, we simply shrug it off. Instead of horror over what sickens Christ, we're unconcerned. What insults Him doesn't bother us, what breaks His heart doesn't shatter ours. What He died for, we don't spend our lives living for, and we neglect what He is consumed with.

A Way-follower isn't just someone who knows the Truth. A Way-follower is someone who lives the Life, and that's what made the Way-followers of the book of Acts so recognizable to everyone around them. They were zealous, on fire for Christ. They refreshed everyone around them like a cool drink of water.

"Zealous," in verse 19 is the exact opposite of "lukewarm" in verse 16, and the Laodiceans had begun to drift. They had lost their distinctiveness, their heat, their fervor, their cool refreshment. They had become neutral. Instead of standing against the crowd, zealous for good works and recognizable to the enemies of God as a force to be reckoned with, they had lost their power. Not hot, not cold, just the same temperature as the world around them, and there was nothing remotely dangerous about them anymore.

Spiritual laxity means that all the incremental course corrections necessary to keep the car on the road start to get neglected. Confident we're going the right way, we stop listening to the voice of Jesus trailing behind us saying, "You're supposed to be going that way. You're plowing ahead the wrong way." We stop seeking His guidance, we stop needing His presence, and we start ignoring His influence. After a while, we're tired of hearing the GPS tell us how often we're off route, and just turn the voice off. Self-sufficient, we are sickening to Christ, and unconcerned about it.

Instead of standing against the crowd, going the opposite direction, standing out as different, instead of orienting ourselves to God and His Word, the voices of the world start crowding Him out. Jesus says His sheep simply will not listen to the voice of strangers. But spiritual laxity listens to both: this is what God says. This is what the world says. Let's see what happens. Instead of hearing and responding to Jesus, we drift. We start to feel silly standing there in the elevator facing the opposite direction, and all those other voices start to sound reasonable. Slowly, our ears are tuned to the world and the voice of Jesus is dulled, and we become spiritually insensitive.

Laodicea had become a group of past tense Christians. The past event of Christ's death was having no present impact. Had they lost their salvation? Of course not. No matter what His people do, Jesus is not a past tense Savior. But instead of letting their past, the moment of their salvation, impact their present, and instead of living in the present for the future return of Christ, they were living in the here and now. Spiritually lax toward the things of God, their piles were getting higher, their barns were getting bigger, and their lives were being wasted. You could probably find their names on a roster somewhere, but you couldn't pick them out of a crowd. Paul, back when he was breathing threats and murder against the Way, and Satan, waging war against the people of God, probably wouldn't have bothered.

Spiritual laxity means I sit back and hope I somehow magically conform to Christ's image. I'm not consumed with the plot. I'm off in the corner sharing a blueberry muffin recipe. My nice, black wool garments are fine. If I collect some white garments along the way, that's fine, but it's an awful lot of work to put on the Lord Jesus Christ. That's not the first thing I think about in the morning, the last thing I think about at night, and the thing that colors everything else I do. I get consumed by a lot of things, by work, by my plans, by my agenda, my goals, my life, my friends, my free time, and Christ is a casualty of spiritual neglect.

Spiritual laxity is being content to be a member of a church without acting like a citizen of heaven. I don't speak a different language, walk a different path, face a different direction. My eyes aren't on my home. They're focused here, like everybody else's. I've made myself at home in a foreign country, forgetting that this world is not my home. And on the day I die, because I got too comfortable, because my tent pegs were pounded in too firmly, because I wasn't ready to throw it all in the truck and go home, Jesus will have to pry this world out of my hands. I've turned my eyes away from Jesus, and the things of this world have made Him strangely dim.

Lord, I Broke a Glass

Today, if you want to post a notice, you take it to the nearest Starbucks and post it on the bulletin board, and everyone waiting in line for coffee will see it. The Starbucks of 1517 was the big, wooden church doors, and in 1517, if you wanted your whole community to see something, you posted a notice on those doors.

On that October 31st, if you had watched Martin Luther pick up his hammer and a nail, and pound his ninety-five theses into the church doors, looking over his shoulder, this is the first thing you would have read:

"When our Lord and Master, Jesus Christ, said 'Repent,' He called for the entire life of believers to be one of repentance."

That moment sparked the Protestant Reformation, when Martin Luther protested the corruption of the Roman church that had distorted the truth of God. So when Jesus says, "Repent," to the church of Laodicea, He is calling each of them, individually, and us today, to our own personal reformation. He's calling for the entire life of each believer to be one of repentance.

Repentance means confessing our sin, and forsaking it. Confession is agreeing with God about what we have done that displeases Him. The second half of repentance, forsaking it, means that we change our mind about the sin and declaring that anything God is against, we are against too.

I remember when we had just moved into our brand-new Tulsa-style house, and it had all this tile, which was great until one of our eight children dropped a glass. I can still remember it like it was in slow motion, and there was this beautiful explosion of glass, and pieces of it went ten feet in all directions.

Now, I could have said, "Okay, kids, everyone's wearing boots from now on," and we could all go crunching around and get it ground into the carpet in every corner of the house, and then the kids would tromp upstairs, and whenever they took off their slippers, it would get in their feet, and into their beds. Or we could do something about it and correct it right there. So immediately I said, "Everybody freeze," and we got the dustpan, and picked up all the big pieces, and then we got the sweeper, and then we got on patrol and checked under every piece of furniture until all those glistening shards were gone.

Repentance is much like what I had to do with the explosion of glass. Do you know what Jesus says? Repent of not being so concerned about cleaning up all the explosions that sin causes. It happens in our relationships. We have an explosion in a relationship with someone, and instead of cleaning it up, we just act like it didn't happen, and it's like tracking glass around and it just cuts and continues to do damage.

Sweeping the glass under the rug or leaving it under the furniture isn't good enough. Proverbs 28:13 says, "He who covers his sins will not prosper, but whoever confesses and forsakes them will have mercy." Confession is saying, "Lord, I broke a glass and it smashed everywhere." Forsaking sin is sweeping into every corner, under every couch, cleaning out every last sliver of that sin from your life and guarding against it in the future.

Spiritual laxity is when we drop our guard about un-confessed sin in our lives. We forget how horrible sin always is to Christ. Our sin cost Jesus His very life. It separated Him from His intimate fellowship with the Father, and it made Jesus feel the wrath of God in our place. Do you know what Jesus said to do about sin? Get rid of it. Don't sweep it under the rug, don't pack it into the hidden rooms of your life. It stinks. It makes Him sick. Sin makes Christ sick, but if it doesn't bother me, that's spiritual laxity.

You and I know what's right. We have God's Word, the absolute standard, inerrant, breathed-out, complete. It is our absolute authority, and we don't need anything else. If God said it, we need to hear it, and if He didn't say it, we don't need to worry about it. We have no excuse. We know what's right.

And we know what's wrong. It's not what I think is sin, or what society decides is sin, or what Paul thought was sinful way back in the first century. It's what God Himself declares is sin in the forever-settled-in-heaven Word of God, that goes beyond culture or century, and that is still true today. We have no excuse. We know what's wrong.

And in verse 19 of Revelation 3, Jesus tells us how to get right. We see what our life is supposed to look like, we see where it falls short, maybe in one way, maybe in all seven, but Jesus says there's one way to get right: repentance.

Lord, I broke a glass. Please help me sweep it up.

WHEN JESUS TRAINS YOU FOR RIGHTEOUSNESS

The entire Word of God, but especially the epistles, can be summed up as God telling us what's right, what's wrong, how to get right, and how to stay right. We see the truth of God (doctrine), where we've failed to meet that standard (reproof), how to return to that standard (correction), and how to stay on the road (training in righteousness). Laodicea was exposed to doctrine when the book of Acts circulated through and they saw what followers of the Way are supposed to look like. They are reproved when Jesus writes them a scathing letter exposing their spiritual laxity, and are corrected when Jesus calls for repentance.

But repentance is just the beginning. Repentance is how we get right after we sin, but the only way to stay right in a world of sin is to allow the Holy Spirit to begin systematically, continuously training us for righteousness.

Step 1: Operate on what you know to be true
(living in the shadow of the cross)
Jesus' righteousness training program is found in Romans chapter 6. For five and a half chapters, Paul had been outlining doctrine, giving reproof, and

providing correction where needed. But beginning in Romans 6:11, with the very first imperative in the whole epistle, God begins our righteousness training program, and it starts with this command: "Likewise, you also, reckon yourself to be dead indeed to sin, but alive to God in Christ Jesus our Lord." The word "reckon," or "consider," or "count," means that we take what we know, and we start operating on it. If you want to break the habit of spiritual laxity, it starts with repentance, a change in direction. And the first step in that new direction is to operate on what you know to be true.

Every imperative in God's Word is like an RSVP that Jesus personally addresses to us. Most mail, you can read, and then toss. But an RSVP is special. It requires a response. You can't just read it, say, oh, that's nice, and throw it away. You have to do something with it.

Spiritual neutrality is reading it, saying, oh, that's nice, and throwing it away. But Jesus calls for a response, to repent of lukewarm neutrality and be zealous about living life the way He instructed us to. Remember, followers of the Way know the Truth. And because they operate on that truth, they live the Life.

Way-followers live in the shadow of the cross. They reckon themselves to be dead to sin and alive to God. They stop living like the past event of His death on the cross has no present effect on their lives. Way followers allow the truth of Jesus' justifying death to open to them His sanctifying life. Way followers train for righteousness by responding to Christ's first RSVP. They operate on what they know to be true. They live in the shadow of the cross.

Step 2: Say "no" to sin (walking in the power of the cross)

Way-followers who are training for righteousness don't just live in the shadow of the cross. They are empowered by it. With the power that makes demons cry out in fear, Way-followers say "no" to sin.

The second step in Jesus' righteousness training program is the second command in Romans 6: "Therefore do not let sin reign in your mortal body, that you should obey it in its lusts."[256]

256 Romans 6:12

Flesh can't defeat flesh. Saying no to sin in my own strength is useless. In my own power, by my own strength, finding my sufficiency in self, saying no to sin is impossible. But with Christ, all things are possible. Sin's hold has been broken, the hunger for sin has been defeated because I have been crucified to the world and the world has been crucified to me. I walk in the power of the cross, no longer self-sufficient, but Christ-sufficient.

One of the most incredible things to witness is when someone goes from being utterly enslaved to sin to habitually saying no to that sin. If you've never said no to sin, actually said it, then you'd be amazed at how powerful it can be. Many people think that sin is just always going to win. They're always going to give in to those temptations, they'll never defeat that habit, get rid of that appetite. But sin has already been defeated. Operate on that truth. Say "no" to sin. That's walking in the power of the cross.

Step 3: Break the old patterns
(hearing and responding to Jesus)

Growing up, I lived at the end of a quarter mile path through a thirty-acre wheat field, and when it would rain, we'd make ruts in the mud. And when it would freeze, those ruts would freeze solid, so my parents would always say, "straddle the ruts." If you dropped into the ruts, it would ruin the underside of the car, and you'd get stuck, so you had to be very careful not to fall in. So I learned very quickly to hold tightly to the wheel so that I wouldn't slide in. And if you do slide in, you get right back out. You straddle the ruts.

Like Laodicea, we get into habits. If this happens, and this happens, we explode. This happens and this happens, and we get depressed. If this happens and this happens, we give in to our lusts. The third step in Jesus' righteousness training program is to straddle the ruts. Break the old habits.

"And do not go on presenting the members of your body to sin as instruments of unrighteousness."[257]

Jesus is telling us to stop holding out our bodies as tools for the devil to use. We have the truth and we're operating on it. We have the power to say no to sin, and we're walking in it. But we were living like the old man for so long, those habits are frozen into the mud, and they seem impossible to avoid.

257 Romans 6:13 NASB

But Jesus doesn't just say, "Stop doing that" and not tell us how. So how do we anticipate the ruts, hold tight to the wheel, and stay out of the ditch?

By being "renewed in the spirit of your mind."[258] When Paul told the Ephesians to put off the old man, to discontinue their former conduct, he told them the only way to put on the new man and make new habits was by the renewing of their minds. And only one thing does that.

God's Word renews our minds and carves new paths in the road. When our minds are renewed by the Word of God, by hearing Jesus speak and responding to Him, those old ruts are worn away, and we are conformed to the image of Christ.

Step 4: Follow Me (investing in the bank of heaven)

Step 4 in righteousness training is to start following Jesus as a daily choice. We're operating on the truth, we're saying no to sin, and we're refusing to make those old choices that left us in the ditch, but now we need to start making new choices, choices to follow Jesus daily.

The first command Jesus gave to His disciples was "follow Me." And they dropped their nets, and followed Him. And that's the same thing He calls us to in Romans 6:13. "But present yourselves to God as being alive from the dead, and your members as instruments of righteousness to God."

Jesus reduced all that He wanted from His disciples down to those two words: follow Me. It was the first thing He ever said to them. And it's a daily choice for us, to stop holding out our bodies as tools for sin, but to, daily, present ourselves to God as instruments of righteousness. It's a choice. A plan. An RSVP that needs a response. I want to be accomplishing with this body what is righteous.

What does it mean to make a choice daily? To follow Him? We ask ourselves, would He go there, would He do this, is this what pleases Him? Asking Him, Lord, how would You want me to live this day? The Laodiceans had abandoned Christ as their investment counselor. They'd stopped following His plan daily, stopped making those daily choices. But Way-followers follow Christ's plan, His advice, His counsel. And when He counsels us on how to live this day, on how to use our resources, how to

---

258 Ephesians 4:23

spend our time, how to please Him, instead of shrugging off His counsel as a nice piece of advice, we say, "yes, that belongs to You." That's what it means to follow God daily as a choice. Daily surrendering my habits, my agenda, my plans, my resources, my time, my money, my goals back to God.

Step 5: Enlist with God (dressing for Christ daily)

"Do you not know that to whom you present yourselves as slaves to obey, you are that one's slaves whom you obey, whether of sin leading to death, or of obedience leading to righteousness?"[259]

The RSVP in this verse is the word "present." And you can present yourself as a slave of sin, or a slave of righteousness. You can present yourself to sin, or present yourself to God. This is beyond just following Jesus. This is being His slave.

When Jesus calls us to present ourselves to God, it is a call to arms, a call to enlist as a soldier, to present our bodies to Him for His use. Salvation is not a ticket from the fire. It's enlisting as a soldier, and it has a dress code. Christ's righteousness has saved us, but we are called to daily re-up with God, daily plotting to put on our armor, the breastplate of righteousness, to put on the helmet of salvation, to wear Christ's character every day, dressing for work.

Jesus' call to zeal and repentance in Revelation 3 should cause us to rush and enlist as God's slave each day. We once held out our bodies as tools for unrighteousness to use, but now we are consumed with presenting ourselves to God. We put on the character of Christ daily like armor, ready to go to war, diligent to present ourselves dressed and ready for service each day.

Step 6: Pursue a passion for holiness (living a lifestyle of practical purity)

The sixth imperative, the last step in Christ's righteousness training program, is to pursue a passion for holiness. "So now present your members as slaves of righteousness for holiness."[260]

259 Romans 6:16
260 Romans 6:19

Seek to be holy even as God is holy. That is what He is asking for. This isn't the holiness I was handed positionally when Jesus died in my place and exchanged my sin for His righteousness. This is a lifestyle of holiness, and we are called and empowered by Christ to be enslaved by His righteousness unto holiness.

Paul says, "The love of Christ compels us," it "constrains us"[261] to present each member of our bodies as slaves of righteousness. Enslaved feet walk in purity and righteousness. Enslaved lips have their speech under control. Enslaved hearts show compassion, and enslaved hands refuse bribes because they are honest. Enslaved ears only listen to what is pure. Enslaved eyes only look at pure video input, and those who are enslaved by a passion for holiness are those who will continually see God for themselves.

Jesus concludes His letter to Laodicea the same way He did every letter: "He who has an ear, let him hear what the Spirit says to the churches." Can you hear His call? God's Word is living and active, sharper than any two-edged sword, it cuts deep, and in it we see what is right, and what is wrong. This side of heaven, you and I will always fall short of God's perfect standard, but no matter how far off track we find ourselves, God tells us how to get right. Repentance. And if you see in yourself any one of the seven bad habits Jesus found in Laodicea, then let us choose to get right and begin training for righteousness today.

Lord, I broke a glass. Please help me clean it up. Like the apostle Paul, the good that we want to do, we don't do, and the thing we don't want to do, we find ourselves doing repeatedly, falling into those old ruts. Let our whole life be one of repentance, and every time we find ourselves falling into those old patterns, let us confess, and forsake, and in repentance, draw closer to You. Train us in righteousness, we pray. Let us know the truth and operate on it. Give us the power to say no to sin as often as necessary. Use your perfect, complete, inerrant word to renew our minds and pave over the ruts so that we do not go on presenting ourselves as instruments

---

261 2 Corinthians 5:14

of unrighteousness. When You call us to follow You, let us be like Peter and Andrew and James and John and drop our nets immediately, making it a daily choice to follow You, Lord Jesus. We are Your slaves. Enslave us with a passion for holiness. And in Your name, we pray. Amen.

RESPOND to Truth

Do I cause a commotion with those around me because I stand out as a follower of the Way? Or does anyone even notice?

How did Abraham live out his heavenly citizenship? (Hebrews 11:8–10)

What bad habits have I been dismissing as not that serious?

How does God feel about sin? (Genesis 6:5–6; Deuteronomy 29:25–28; Proverbs 11:20; Isaiah 5:24–25; 53:5; Luke 13:34) Do I feel the same way?

What bad habits do I fall into? What steps can I take today to allow God to pave over those ruts?

What one doctrine (what's right) in God's Word do I not line up with (what's wrong)? Am I willing to repent of that today (how to get right)? How can I get in step with Jesus' righteousness training program today (how to stay right)?

25 | Life as God Designed It to Be

One of the most significant moments in all seven letters is the moment when, in Revelation 3:20, Jesus' tone of voice changes. He goes from the harshest, most pointed rebuke, saying "you make Me sick," to, in verse 20, saying "I stand at the door and knock." But not just that He's knocking. He's always been there knocking, pleading with them to open the door and let Him in.

At the end of every letter, no matter how harsh, no matter how displeasing they are, even if Jesus can find nothing positive to say, He ends every letter with a promise. This promise comes from the Amen of God, the Faithful and True Witness, the First and the Last, who was dead and who came to life, from the One who knows our works, our failures, and who seals the promise Himself. And each of these promises is given to him "who overcomes."

HE WHO OVERCOMES

The first thing we should ask ourselves is "who are the overcomers?" It's a fair question. When Jesus says that overcomers' names will never be blotted out, that overcomers will one day rule, who exactly is He talking about? Are these the super-saints, the mega-Christians? We're all the foot soldiers and these are the Special Forces believers?

The good news is that I don't have to figure that out myself. God already defined who the overcomers are when John, who wrote down Revelation, wrote the epistle of 1 John. And in that little epistle, he defines exactly who these overcomers are. "For whatever is born of God overcomes the world."[262]

The promises given to overcomers are incredible, unimaginable, and when Jesus makes a promise, He is the Amen. He keeps it. And John says everyone "born of God" is an overcomer. Everyone born of God is a recipient of the promises of Revelation 2–3.

But it's more than that. You're actually familiar with the Greek word for "overcomer" already. It's all over our clothing and written across our shoes. It's the word *nike*. Actually, *nikao*, but it's the same word. It means to conquer. It speaks of an armed struggle against.

I remember when I was a truck driver years ago, I'd go into the break room to get coffee, and all the other truck drivers would be there talking about which girl they were with and what they did the night before, and I remember I had to get out of there as fast as I could, because I didn't want to let that lewd conversation in. And so finally one day, they said, "what's wrong with you?" And I told them that their conversation offended God. So then, every time I came in, they stopped talking and said, "Here comes the deacon."

But that's what it means to struggle against. To stand against sin and the flesh and the world and the devil. And believers' lives are characterized by standing against, by the armed struggle against the world.

But not just that. "This is the victory that has overcome the world—our faith. Who is it that overcomes the world, but he who believes that Jesus is the Son of God?"[263]

See, it's not just someone who "has faith," who "believes" in anything and everything. An overcomer is "he who believes that Jesus is the Son of God."

So an overcomer believes, not just in belief, but that Jesus is the Son of God. And an overcomer "struggles against." This is just like how Paul describes the Christian life, as a struggle, a race, or a boxing match. That's what every overcomer does. And an overcomer is anyone who is "born of God."

---

262 1 John 5:4
263 1 John 5:4–5

See, this isn't the top tier of believers. All believers are "born of God," all believers believe "that Jesus is the Son of God," and whether we do it well or not, whether we win the prize or are disqualified, all believers "struggle," and because of Jesus Christ, all believers "overcome."

If it seems like Jesus has done nothing but focus on the negative for two chapters now, that's because we've been skipping the best part. This is the part in every letter when, no matter what condition the believers of that church may be in, Jesus makes all of them a promise, to everyone who is born of God, to everyone who struggles against, to everyone who believes that Jesus is the Son of God, He makes an incredible promise.

If you've been waiting for a happy ending to this book, this is it. This is life as God designed it to be.

THE VICTORIOUS LIFE OF OVERCOMERS

Number 1: Overcomers Receive Abundant Life

Remember the Ephesians? They were a great church for the most part, but they had left their first love. They were no longer doing things solely to the glory of God, and Jesus had some pretty harsh words to say to them. But regardless of their condition, Jesus ends the letter with this: "To him who overcomes I will give to eat from the tree of life, which is in the midst of the Paradise of God."[264]

The first gift that God offers to overcomers is life: endless, overflowing, and abundant. What is the first verse most believers memorize? A lot of people know Psalm 23, most probably know the Lord's Prayer, but the one verse everybody can recite is John 3:16. "For God so loved the world that He gave His only begotten Son, that whoever believes in Him should not perish but have" what? What does God promise to everyone who believes in Him? "Everlasting life."

When Jesus promises overcomers an abundant life, He's speaking of life that never ends. Life that's eternal. But that's not all. The gospel of John describes in detail the kind of life that believers are promised. First, it's eternal, everlasting, never-ending. But second, it's overflowing.

---

264 Revelation 2:7

Every fall in first-century Jerusalem, they'd have an annual reenactment of Moses striking the rock and the water coming out. Every year, hundreds of thousands of Jews would gather around this tall platform, and the high priest would climb up there and take a ceremonial pitcher of water, and he'd pour it forty feet down, and everyone would hear it splat on the ground. So, every year, the parents would teach their kids to be completely quiet so they'd hear the water fall, and it was this huge event commemorating God bringing water in the wilderness.

So Jesus shows up, "on the last day, that great day of the feast." It would have been at this moment, hundreds of thousands of people there, all waiting, all holding their breath for the moment of the water, every eye would be on the runner who's coming from the Pool of Siloam, with the ceremonial pitcher full of water, that had come from the spring of Gihon, through Hezekiah's tunnel, and everyone was watching as he climbed up and gave the pitcher to the priest, and then, right as every child had learned to hold their breath to hear, "Jesus stood and cried out, saying, 'if anyone thirsts, let him come to Me and drink.'"[265]

When John says He cried out, it means He screamed it, with a loud voice. And everyone would have heard what He said next. "'He who believes in Me, as the Scripture has said, out of his heart will flow rivers of living water.'"[266]

This is not a little trickle of water. These are gushing-like-a-fire-hose rivers. Jesus, standing by a well, says to the woman standing there, "Whoever drinks of this water will thirst again, but whoever drinks of the water that I shall give him will become in him a fountain of water springing up into everlasting life."[267]

Jesus offered to anyone who believed in Him a life overflowing with the Spirit. Abundantly alive. Vibrantly alive. That's the kind of life Jesus is promising.

When He says we will eat from the tree of life, He's speaking of life abundant. "I have come that they may have life, and that they may have it more abundantly." The word is *parissos,* and it's like bread rising in an oven, just expanding and expanding until it's overflowing the pan. It's like water

265 John 7:37
266 John 7:38
267 John 4:13–14

rising in a stopped-up sink, you can see it rising and you can't do anything to stop it, and it just overflows up out of the sink. That's *parissos*. That's life abundant.

My dad worked for General Motors for forty years, and he made more money every year in retirement than he made any year he was actually working. Each year he worked, he got more money, and each year he was retired, the money just kept growing and growing and growing. That's what Jesus means when He offers "more abundantly." The life we have just keeps getting more and more and better and better every year. It's life that overflows with the Spirit, and life that never ends. That's Jesus' first promise to His Church.

Number 2: Overcomers Receive an Indestructible Life

Secondly, God describes overcomers as possessing an indestructible life. He says to the saints at Smyrna, "He who overcomes shall not be hurt by the second death."[268]

Did you know that "eternal life" isn't something we *will* have, or *will* get someday? It's present tense, not something we will have but something we have—right now. John 3:36 says, "He who believes in the Son *has* everlasting life."

This is something I like to ask people. After church on Sunday, when people are leaving, I like to ask if the entryway ceiling collapsed in on us right then—and they kind of step back, and look up at the ceiling—if it collapsed, do they know that they have, right now, life? That's the kind of life Jesus offers. Not a someday life, but a present-day, right now life everlasting.

Our life is presently, right now, indestructible. Romans tells us that "for whom He foreknew, He predestined to be conformed to the image of His Son. Moreover whom He predestined, these He also called; whom He called, these He also justified; and whom He justified, these He also glorified." And "if God is for us, who can be against us?"[269]

What God started, He will finish. He won't give up on you, and if He's not finished with you, nothing can stop what He has promised to finish.

268 Revelation 2:11; see Revelation 21:8 on "second death"
269 Romans 8:29–31

That's why my friend, John MacArthur, when he gets on an airplane, tells the person next to him that the plane can't crash because God's not through with him yet.

Now remember who Jesus was originally talking to when He made this promise. These were the suffering Smyrnans. They were being thrown into prison and persecuted and even killed. But Jesus says their life is indestructible because all they can do to you is kill your body. And your life is so much more than that.

John 10:27–28 describes our lives as secure in God's hands. "My sheep hear My voice, and I know them, and they follow Me." That's a description of a believer, and overcomer, and this is the promise: "And I give them eternal life, and they shall never perish; neither shall anyone snatch them out of My hand."

Do you know what this indestructible life means to believers? We never need to fear a bad ending. "Most assuredly, I say to you, he who hears My word and believes in Him who sent Me has everlasting life, and shall not come into judgment, but has passed from death into life."[270]

There is no bad ending for believers. We have, right now, life, it is secure in God's hands, and we cannot and never will be hurt by the second death. We will never be hurt by hell. The life Jesus gives is indestructible.

Number 3: Overcomers Receive an Inexhaustible Supply

Thirdly, true believers, overcomers, according to Jesus, get an inexhaustible supply. "To him who overcomes I will give some of the hidden manna to eat. And I will give him a white stone, and on the stone a new name written which no one knows except him who receives it."[271]

Now, what does that mean? Jesus says that you and I have every spiritual need met. He offered this same promise in John 6 just after feeding five thousand men plus their families. They were fully aware of their physical need. They'd been following Him for a while now, and hadn't brought food. But Jesus, meeting their physical need, said they have a greater need. And He's the only One who can meet it.

---

270 John 5:24
271 Revelation 2:17

"And Jesus said to them, 'I am the bread of life. He who comes to Me shall never hunger, and he who believes in Me shall never thirst.'"[272]

Overcomers live a fully satisfied life. Why? Because true believers live a life that feeds on Christ. "Most assuredly, I say to you, unless you eat the flesh of the Son of Man and drink His blood, you have no life in you."[273]

This verse makes a lot of people uncomfortable today, and it certainly did in Jesus' day. And a lot of people stopped following Him after this. But Jesus is saying that only in Him can we be fully satisfied. The life that has an inexhaustible supply is the life that feeds on Christ.

This is the American dream, to be fully satisfied. To make enough money now that when we're in retirement, we have plenty to live on and be satisfied to the end. Jesus says the only true satisfaction comes from Him. In Him, every spiritual need is met.

Number 4: Overcomers Receive an Inexpressible Future

You and I have a future that is inexpressible. Jesus makes Thyatira this promise in Revelation 2:26–28: "And he who overcomes, and keeps My works until the end, to him I will give power over the nations—'He shall rule them with a rod of iron; they shall be dashed to pieces like the potter's vessels'—as I also have received from My Father; and I will give him the morning star."

Did you know we'll be given a position in heaven? We're not going to be sitting around on clouds playing a harp and wearing a halo. We will be ruling. I don't know exactly what our position will be in heaven, but it's one of authority.

We have these friends in Pakistan who translate our books into their own language, and they told us that every time we send a check to pay them for the translation, the bank manager, who's a Muslim, tells their landlord, who is also a Muslim, exactly how much they made, and the landlord comes and says that's how much their rent is. They only survive because people from the church bring them food. They will always live in poverty, they'll never get ahead, they will always be living like that as Christians in

272 John 6:35
273 John 6:53

a Muslim country, but do you know what? They can live like that because they know they've been promised an inexpressible future.

In that future, there are unbelievable pleasures. When Paul described heaven, he said, "He was caught up into Paradise and heard inexpressible words, which it is not lawful for a man to utter."[274] Mark 10:29–30 describes immeasurable treasures waiting for us in heaven: "Assuredly, I say to you, there is no one who has left house or brothers or sisters or father or mother or wife or children or lands, for My sake and the gospel's who shall not receive a hundredfold now in this time, and in the age to come, eternal life."

We have a bright and glorious future. Consider these promises: Jesus is described as the "Dayspring from on high," and salvation is described as when "the day dawns and the morning star rises in their hearts."[275] We can never lose Jesus' life, light, and hope in the doom and gloom of this world. What a glorious future awaits us. "There shall be no night there: they need no lamp there nor the light of the sun, for the Lord God gives them light, and they shall reign forever and ever."[276]

Revelation 21:7 says, "He who overcomes shall inherit all things, and I will be his God and he shall be My son." But do you know what's incredible? This bright and glorious future starts now. Jesus says, "I am the light of the world. He who follows Me shall not walk in darkness, but have the light of life. Therefore if the Son makes you free, you shall be free indeed."[277]

Our future, beginning now, is bright and glorious. And we're just getting started.

Number 5: Overcomers Receive Complete Security

We have, fifthly, complete security. "He who overcomes shall be clothed in white garments, and I will not blot out his name from the Book of Life; but I will confess his name before My Father and before His angels."[278]

Does that sound like security, complete assurance that you can never lose your salvation? It does if you remember who Jesus says overcomers are.

274 2 Corinthians 12:4
275 Luke 1:78; 2 Peter 1:19
276 Revelation 22:5
277 John 8:12, 36
278 Revelation 3:5

This promise was made to the dead church, Sardis, and the king of Sardis could, in fact, erase names out of the roles if he didn't like you. But to the one who overcomes, Jesus promises complete security.

First, He describes overcomers clothed in white garments. Do you know what makes garments white? "Then one of the elders answered, saying to me, 'Who are these arrayed in white robes, and where did they come from?'" These are the ones who "washed their robes and made them white in the blood of the Lamb."[279]

We are washed in the blood of Christ, and Christ is our garment. His righteousness covers us. We can never be cast out of the wedding feast for being improperly dressed. We can never be blotted out of the Book of Life, because we are clothed in white garments, washed in the blood of Christ, completely secure.

You know how insurance salesmen will try to sell you an umbrella policy to give you better coverage? You and I have the best coverage imaginable. No matter what happens, no matter what we do, Christ's righteousness covers us.

But this also means that Christ is our advocate.

Remember our Great High Priest from Revelation 1? "But He, because He continues forever, has an unchangeable priesthood. Therefore He is also able to save to the uttermost those who come to God through Him, since He always lives to make intercession for them."[280] This is what Jesus is doing right now, interceding, advocating, protecting the name He's written down in the Book of Life and that was inscribed on the palms of His hands. There is no better security than that.

And last, in this promise to Sardis, we are reminded that we have been adopted into God's family, and we will be presented to God by Jesus Himself. Did you know that when you arrive in heaven, you won't have to stand around hoping someone will notice you? Jesus doesn't say, "Oh, good, you made it," and skip off to do something else. He is going to personally, individually, take each one of us by the hand and lead us to the throne of God, and before God and the holy angels, Jesus Christ is going to introduce each of us to His Father.

---

279 Revelation 7:13–14
280 Hebrews 7:24–25

Can you even imagine that moment? Jesus, with nail-scarred hands outstretched, welcomes us through the doorway of death, walks us through the valley of the shadow, and welcomes us to glory. He walks us down the golden streets, He walks us up the broad mains street by the river of the water of life. All around us the saints of all the ages look on in wonder as again Jesus leads one of His precious, blood-bought brothers and sisters up to meet their Father in heaven.

Then, on the throne blazing with light, with a river of fire flowing out before Him, and billions of angels standing around Him, the Ancient of Days looks upon His beloved Son walking toward Him. And there, holding the hand of Jesus, we will hear Him call us by our new name, the one He gave us. And God will hear Jesus present us, by name, as His precious, chosen, and beloved one.

Number 6: Overcomers Receive the Ultimate Destination Trip

You've heard of destination weddings or people who are planning a vacation to some exotic destination? You and I have reservations for the ultimate destination. "He who overcomes, I will make him a pillar in the temple of My God, and he shall go out no more. I will write on him the name of My God and the name of the city of My God, the New Jerusalem, which comes down out of heaven from My God. And I will write on him My new name."[281]

Remember the Philadelphians living on a fault line? This was Jesus' promise to them. Permanence. Tranquility. Pasting on them a mailing label so they'll get to where they're supposed to go.

Jesus promises permanence to every believer in John 14:1–3. "Let not your heart be troubled; you believe in God, believe also in Me. In My Father's house are many mansions; if it were not so, I would have told you. I go to prepare a place for you. And if I go and prepare a place for you, I will come again and receive you to Myself; that where I am, there you may be also."

The tranquility of heaven is described in John 17:24. "Father, I desire that they also whom You gave Me may be with Me where I am, that they may behold My glory which You have given Me." Can you imagine that? Being where Jesus is? Permanent. No hurry, no rush, no worry, no struggles, no sin. Just peace and tranquility forever, with Jesus, seeing His glory.

281 Revelation 3:12

During the bombing of London during World War II, many children were sent to the countryside so that they'd be away from the bombs, and their parents would put a tag on their clothes, writing on them the address in the country so that no matter what happened, they'd make it where they were going. They couldn't get there on their own, but if they're addressed properly, they get there.

Do you know that Jesus has written on us the name of the recipient, God, and the address, the name of the city of God, on us as His people? We are assured that no matter what happens, we are sealed, labeled with God's mailing address and we are headed toward the ultimate destination. There is no dead letter office in heaven. If you're addressed by Jesus Christ, you will arrive at your destination. That's God's promise to overcomers in Revelation 3.

Number 7: Overcomers Receive Genuine Intimacy

This week I did something that I don't think I've ever done before in my life. I decided that I was going to sit down and watch a football game on TV. And I announced it to my family, and they just about fainted. But I got the television out and got it turned on, and moved my chair and got all set, and turned it on right at eight o'clock. You know what? Games don't start when they say. There were a bunch of people in suits talking about the game. And they were betting on whether this player would make twenty-seven points or whether he wouldn't make it past the first whatever. And I asked my kids, where's the game? And they said it's coming, so I waited. And finally, the game came on.

So, I was watching, and I saw the clock and it was at ten or eleven or twelve minutes, and I thought, oh good. This'll be easy. It'll be over just like that. Are you kidding? Ten minutes takes an hour. They stop it constantly. And they kept throwing in advertisements. One of them was about cars, and I tell you, I hardly wanted to drive my car this morning. It didn't do anything the cars on television do. It was agonizing. And I'll never do that again.

But right in the middle, I saw something so refreshing. One of the players has this habit of taking a severely handicapped person, or someone dying of cancer, or in this case it was somebody who'd had seventy-three surgeries. And he flies them to the game, takes them to a hotel, takes them out to dinner and eats with them face-to-face, gives them a special seat in the game, and after the game he spends more time with them. And at the very end of the game, he got up and named the needy person's name on national TV. And that person was so honored and so shocked and said it was the best day of his life, mentioned on national TV and getting to spend time face-to-face with this football player.

To think that someone of national stature would come down to an unknown person, and make sure they get fed and chauffeured and ushered and ticketed into the right spots, and then in front of the whole world, show up and have time with them face to face. That was moving. And that is the same promise that Jesus makes to us.

We've come full circle, back to Laodicea, the most disobedient church, so displeasing Jesus had nothing good to say, but look what He says to them: "To him who overcomes I will grant him to sit with Me on My throne, as I also overcame and sat down with My Father on His throne."

Jesus is promising to us an eternity of genuine intimacy with Him. We will sit with Him forever. There are two lessons we can learn from this last promise to overcomers. First, intimacy is a Person. "And this is eternal life." You want to know what eternal life is? According to Jesus? How He describes it? "That they may know You, the only true God, and Jesus Christ whom You have sent."[282]

Eternal life is knowing Jesus, personally, intimately. And the second lesson is this: intimacy is permanent. "He who overcomes shall inherit all things, and I will be his God and he shall be My son."[283]

We are invited to personal face-to-face time with Jesus Himself, permanently. That's an incredible promise.

SAVING THE BEST FOR LAST

The victorious life of the overcomer is life as God designed it to be. It's the life that every Christian is meant to be living, not just in heaven, but right now, abundant, indestructible, satisfied, and secure, looking

282 John 17:3
283 Revelation 21:7

forward to the most indescribable future of intimacy with God in heaven, the ultimate destination. This is the life that Jesus invites us to start living today.

The Greatest Invitation Jesus Ever Gave

God has a history of incredible invitations. In Isaiah 55:1, God says, "Ho! Everyone who thirsts, come to the waters; and you who have no money, come, buy and eat. Yes, come, buy wine and milk without money and without price."" What a great invitation. God invites a world dying of thirst to come to Him and drink.

A few chapters earlier, we find the invitation that Charles Haddon Spurgeon heard when he was a teenager walking the streets of London in the middle of winter a hundred and fifty years ago. He went into a primitive Methodist chapel, and a factory worker got up and read this verse: "Look to Me, and be saved, all you ends of the earth! For I am God, and there is no other."[284] And Spurgeon heard that verse, was convicted, and went forward and became one of the greatest proclaimers of the gospel.

Jeremiah 33:3 has another great promise that so many in the modern missions movement from the nineteenth and twentieth centuries used as their marching orders. "Call to Me, and I will answer you, and show you great and mighty things, which you do not know." And they said, God do something through me that I could never do so You get all the glory.

Probably Christ's greatest gospel call is in Matthew 11:28–30, where He says, "Come to Me, all you who labor and are heavy laden, and I will give you rest. Take My yoke upon you and learn from Me, for I am gentle and lowly in heart, and you will find rest for your souls. For My yoke is easy and My burden is light." Jesus, saying He wants to go through life with us, yoked together. Incredible.

John 7:17, "If anyone wills to do His will, he shall know concerning the doctrine, whether it is from God." In other words, anybody, the searchers in this world, anyone who doesn't know if the Bible is true, all you have to do is say, "God, I want to do Your will." In fact, in January of 1978, my dear wife was sitting alone in a snowstorm and had a little Gideon New

284 Isaiah 45:22

Testament, and she prayed that. She wanted to know if God was true, and prayed that if He was, He'd show Himself to her.

Jesus defines what He does in salvation in John 7:37–38. "If anyone thirsts, let him come to Me and drink. He who believes in Me, as the Scripture has said, out of his heart will flow rivers of living water." The Lord doesn't want us to be like a squirt gun that's out of water. He wants us to be a fire hose of abundant life. That's an invitation He makes. That's what He does at salvation.

There are many other invitations in Scripture, and we could take time to unpack each one of them and study them all, but none of them is on the same level as Revelation 3:20. All the others are one time, one offer for something specific. But Revelation 3:20 is Jesus offering a lifetime of the most inexpressible time with Him.

The last in a long line of great invitations is Revelation 3:20, and God saved the best for last. "Behold, I stand at the door and knock. If anyone hears My voice and opens the door, I will come in to him and dine with him, and he with Me."

Jesus has, as piercingly, as pointedly, in as blunt a way as possible, been rebuking His church for six verses. In modern language, saying, "you make Me sick." But now, in verse 20, His tone changes completely. Now, He is earnestly pleading, extending the greatest invitation He's ever given to any believer—ever.

This invitation is personal. Jesus had been addressing the Church as a whole, but now, He's zeroing in. This invitation is personal, it's intimate. That's why He says, "If any*one* hears My voice." Our church doesn't open the door to Jesus. Our parents or our spouse or our kids don't open the door. Jesus is knocking at my heart's door, and I have to be the one to open it.

Getting Ready for the Best Part of the Day

When I was young, my parents had this system for Christmas presents. First, I'd open up the socks I knew I was getting, and then the clothes I really needed, but at the end, they saved for last the very best present, the one thing I really wanted. And that's what Jesus does in Revelation chapters 1–3.

Do you remember what the wedding guests said in John 2, when Jesus turned the water into wine? Everybody else puts out the good wine first. Let the guests get drunk, and then put out the cheap stuff and by then, nobody can tell the difference. But Jesus, when He turned the water into wine, they said that He had saved the best for last.

You and I are asked to, today, be getting ready for what Jesus calls the best part of the day. In the Hebrew culture of Jesus' day, there were three meals. The first one, *akratisara*, was their breakfast. It was hard, dry, crusty bread that they soaked in a wine-and-water mixture so it would be soft enough to eat, and you'd eat it on the way out the door. The second, *ariston*, was a packed lunch. You'd carry it in a basket and eat it while you worked. You wouldn't even get to sit down for lunch. It was eaten at work, in the middle of whatever you were doing. So breakfast was hurried, lunch was labored, but neither one of those is the meal Jesus is inviting us to.

Jesus invites us to *deipnon*, the supper. In the ancient world, this was the best part of the day. Whether you were rich and dinner was this lavish banquet, or you were poor and it was the one time you got to feel rich, it was an unhurried, unrushed, relaxing time of food and family.

And Jesus said He wanted to insert Himself into the best part of the day. All the glorious, beautiful, wonderful things of this world are just a preview of what's to come. The intimacy, the abundance, the satisfaction, the indestructible life that God says overcomers presently possess, Jesus says, its just a taste. We get a taste of it as we're in a hurry out the door, we get it in a small measure, working in between bites as we go about our work, but soon, the day will be over, the sun will set, and by candlelight, for the first relaxing moment of the day, you and I will sit down to dinner with Jesus, and for the first time, every tiny glimpse of the glories of heaven will be ours in full measure, forever.

I Stand at the Door and Knock

The nineteenth-century painter Holman Hunt painted this scene of Jesus standing at this big, wooden door, knocking, and he entitled it *The Light of the World*. But when he displayed it for all his friends on a big easel, they came by, and looked at it, and said, "Holman, there's something missing. You forgot to paint the door handle on the door."

But Holman Hunt painted it right. Jesus is knocking on our heart's door, but the handle to open the door is on the inside. Jesus will move heaven and hell to get to the door, but when He stands there knocking, He is waiting for us to hear His voice, and to make the conscious choice to open the door.

When Jesus says, "I stand at the door and knock," He isn't like the UPS man, who comes up, knocks, and then he's gone by the time you get there, on to the next place. "Stand," here, means "planted." Jesus has planted Himself on the front porch, and He is persistently knocking.

Have you ever had someone come to your door, and they knock, then they ring the doorbell, then they peer inside and call out, "I know you're in there"? Notice what Revelation 3:20 says, "whoever hears My voice." Jesus is calling out. He's planted there, knocking, calling out, and He requires a response.

Just like in Holman Hunt's famous painting, the handle is on the inside. When Jesus knocks at the heart of an unsaved person, the handle of salvation is on our side of the door. And when Jesus knocks at the heart's door of a believer, the handle of fellowship is on our side of the door, too.

Jesus invites you and me to live an abundant, indestructible, victorious life as an overcomer right now. He invites us to dinner with Him, to intimacy, to a taste of what's to come, and we can sit in our houses, ignoring Him, leaving Him out on the porch, or we can hear His voice, open the door, and He will come in and dine with us, and we with Him.

Spiritual neutrality hinders intimacy with God. Spiritual self-sufficiency hinders intimacy with God. Spiritual insensitivity hinders intimacy with God. And every other bad habit that sickens Jesus prevents us from living life victoriously, intimately having fellowship with Jesus Christ.

To dine with Christ, we need to be zealous and repent of our spiritual neutrality. To dine with Christ we need to be dependent on Him. To dine with Christ we need to be in His word, hearing His voice. We need to stop wasting our lives chasing after worthless things and get investing with Him. We need to stop neglecting our spiritual garments, and we need to protect our spiritual eyes so we can see Him clearly.

The seven bad habits of lukewarm Christians keep us from seeing Christ clearly, and distract us from hearing Him knocking. Jesus says to avoid all that, and open the door to Him. No other religion in the world portrays God seeking out man. Every other religion has man seeking God, but Jesus Christ comes to us. He knocks, He calls out, and we either ignore Him or open the door.

Revelation 3:20 should be burned into our minds as a picture of Christ standing on the doorstep of our house, seeking but not demanding admission, knocking on the front door. As a lost sinner, have you acknowledged His knocking, your lost-ness and your need? As a saved believer, how many days of this past month have you opened the door to Christ by opening His word and spending time with the greatest Person in the universe, face-to-face, one-on-one, a little foretaste of eternity? Will you open the door today?

Father in heaven, I thank You for this beautiful picture of Jesus. Right now, outside of every lost person's heart, You're knocking. And You say when we hear His voice not to harden our heart because at a time only You know, You will stop and never come back. And for us as believers, You will never leave the doorstep of our life. You will never stop knocking, and every day we leave You outside is our great loss. I pray that Your Church would decide today that there is room in our life, in our schedule, in our time, and will open the door of our lives to You, and to hear You in Your Word. In the name of Jesus Christ and for His glory, we pray. Amen.

RESPOND to Truth

Would you describe your life as abundant? Is there something in your life you need to struggle against that is keeping you from life abundant?

How does knowing you have an indestructible life change your response to suffering? To sickness? What would trust in God look like in those circumstances?

How often do you feel spiritually hungry or thirsty? How often do you feast on Christ? Is it a full, sit-down dinner, or fast food you consume on the way to something more important?

When Jesus knocks on your door, what is the thing that most often keeps you from inviting Him in?

Which bad habit is preventing you from taking full advantage of the riches that are yours in Christ?

What does inviting Jesus inside look like for you? What does enjoying Him look like? How often is that a part of your day? The best part of your day?

26 | *Fruitful and Pleasing to God: Maintaining a Spiritually Healthy Lifestyle*

A DAILY CHECKUP WITH THE GREAT PHYSICIAN

There are few words we could ever say that would equal the importance of our last words on this earth. People are fascinated with the last words of people they've looked up to. And no one forgets the last words a loved one speaks to them on their deathbed. But in the history of this planet, no last words are more important than the last words of Christ, and His last spoken communication to His Church is found in Revelation 1–3.

He didn't speak these words to us so that we could scan the newspapers looking to see who the false prophet will be, the beast, who the antichrist is, and how it's all going to line up. These last words are about, as the world gets darker, God's people doing the good works that He's preparing for us to do. That's what God calls bearing fruit. And Jesus wrote these last words to His church, not so that we could have an intellectual debate about it, but so that we could be fruitful and pleasing to God.

In Revelation 1, Jesus Christ introduces Himself to His Church as the Great Physician, and in chapters 2–3, He systematically diagnoses His

Church. And now, at the end of every letter, He applies the same health warnings to us today.

"He who has an ear, let him hear what the Spirit says to the churches."[285]

If you were to visit the Great Physician today for a checkup, there are three things He would be concerned about. First, God is vitally concerned about our diet. "Man shall not live by bread alone, but by every word that proceeds from the mouth of God."[286] As important as a good diet is to your physical health, a healthy diet of God's Word is essential to your spiritual health, and God is vitally concerned about what we feed ourselves with.

You've heard of the South Beach Diet or the Atkins Diet, or whatever. Well, this verse, Matthew 4:4, is the Jesus Diet. We eat the Word to live. And Jesus says if you want to be healthy, eat the Word to live. Look on it as diligently as you look on your physical diet. The Bible keeps us from sin, but sin also keeps us from the Bible. Anything that impedes or erodes your time with the Lord, you should be suspicious of that. God wants our souls fed regularly with the healthy nourishment of His Word. And one of the clearest indicators of our spiritual health is our diet.

Are we getting a full, balanced meal? *Every* word of God? Now we all have our favorite parts of the Bible, and in fact, my Bible will open to the parts that have been most poured over, but we should be serving the whole Scripture. And because we understand that God speaks to us through His word, we should be looking forward to, and longing for, and anticipating those times with Him.

Has the Word of God been neglected, ignored, dreaded? Or has it been longed for, anticipated? That's how you measure your spiritual health. The first sign something's wrong with your dog or cat is when they stop eating. Have you stopped eating the Word? Do you no longer have an appetite for the things of God? Or are you so full of everything else you're filling yourself with that there's no room left for Him?

God is also concerned about our exercise. And when you go to the doctor with heart problems or health problems, the doctor always wants to look at your diet, and then at your exercise. And God does the same thing.

---

285 Revelation 2:7, 11, 17, 29; 3:6, 13, 22
286 Matthew 4:4

James is probably the first New Testament book to be circulated, and in just 108 verses, there are 54 imperatives, commands, RSVPs for God's people to act on. He didn't leave anything to wonder about. This is what the Lord wants. This is what the Lord wants. This is what the Lord wants. So, God doesn't just want us to listen to what the Word proclaims, eating what we need to live, but He wants us to exercise ourselves to do it.

This is the first exercise: "Therefore, lay aside all filthiness and overflow of wickedness, and receive with meekness the implanted word, which is able to save your souls."[287] The only way to overcome sin is not through hard resolve and determination to do it and do better next time. It's when we receive the Word implanted in our souls, and we say to God, "I believe You, and I want You to do that in my life. I want You to take the Sword of the Spirit and cut away the parts of my life that aren't pleasing to You and I want to, verse 21, lay aside all that."

And that implanted Word is able to save our souls.

Verse 22 is the big one. "But be doers of the word, and not hearers only." That's the exercise. First Timothy 4:7, "exercise yourself toward godliness." James 1:22 is how we do that. By taking the diet of the word, implanted in our souls, and acting on it. Every one of those fifty-four imperatives in James is a different exercise, a command to act on. Those RSVPs in Romans 6, Jesus' righteousness training program. These are the exercises that Jesus says keeps us healthy.

And, after the Great Physician has asked about our diet and exercise, the last thing He wants to check is in Hebrews 12:1: "Therefore we also, since we are surrounded by so great a cloud of witnesses, let us lay aside every weight, and the sin which so easily ensnares us, and let us run with endurance the race that is set before us."

God is vitally concerned about your weight. Have you ever thought about that? I have an app on my iPhone, and it says if you download it, you start losing weight. It hasn't worked yet, but I'm still hoping. People are constantly concerned about their physical weight, but we are supposed to be regularly examining our lifestyle for any buildup of sins that are impeding our spiritual life.

---

287 James 1:21

When I pastored in Rhode Island, it was a big yachting place, and they'd regularly bring the yachts out of the water and have people chip off the barnacles that had excreted this coral-like stuff and crusted over the bottoms of the yachts. And it was like trying to drive with the parking break, dragging all this extra weight through the water, so they'd have to regularly pull the yachts out of the water and scrape off all the extra weight that would drag on them.

That's what we're supposed to do with sin. We're supposed to be constantly examining our lives for extra weight. Sin, that's dragging us down, that's holding back our spiritual growth like a parking break, and lay it aside, scrape it off, so that we can run, like the apostle Paul says, the race set before us.

When we are saved, we get all of God. He doesn't give His Spirit by measure, in little bits and pieces. We got all of Him. But He doesn't have all of us. And we are, like Psalm 92 says, supposed to be more and more fruitful and pleasing to God the older we get as we give more and more of our lives over to Him.

It would be nice if our physical health was like those shots you get as a kid. You take one shot, and you're immune to whatever it was for life. But our physical health isn't like that. It's a constant lifestyle of healthy choices, making sure our diet is healthy and balanced, keeping up regular exercise, and watching our weight. And our spiritual health, us giving control of our lives over to God, isn't a onetime shot that makes us totally fruitful and pleasing to God. It's a lifestyle, a regular, daily, three-part workout, feeding ourselves with the Word of God, exercising ourselves for godliness, and laying aside every weight and the sin that so easily ensnares us.

Each believer is responsible for what's in the Word of God. You and I are responsible for what's in God's Word. Your Sunday school teacher isn't responsible for your spiritual health. Your pastor isn't responsible. Your husband or wife or parents or teachers aren't responsible. They will be responsible to God for what He entrusted to them. But you are responsible to know God's Word and to respond to it.

Sanctification is like remodeling a house. If you try to remodel the whole house at once, it's a big mess and nothing works. But if you work on one thing at a time, one room at a time, then eventually, the whole house is transformed into what you wanted it to be. Going to church isn't the meal. It's the menu. You see, from your pastor or teacher or Bible study leader or in a book like this one, what God's Word says. And you are responsible to find that one thing off the menu that you can work on.

If, when you look in God's Word at the seven churches, or the seven bad habits of lukewarm Christians, you think, wow, I'm never going to be fruitful and pleasing to God, then think again. Jesus is a Master Physician, and He always finishes the work He started. So focus on one thing that the Holy Spirit is impressing on you that you can change, and work on that. Make one choice, the stairs instead of the elevator, carrots instead of potato chips, and start making those decisions that lead to a spiritually healthy lifestyle.

JESUS' CHALLENGES TO EVERY BELIEVER: HE WHO HAS AN EAR TO HEAR

When the Great Physician did His medical inspection tour of the seven churches, He found more than just unhealthy lifestyles in His people. He found cancers. Heart disease. Infections. But no matter the diagnosis, Jesus always provided the cure. And the first is to love Jesus most.

Love Jesus Most

Do you seek the approval of God, or the approval of men? If no one ever saw you serving, would you still serve? If no one ever thanked you for your works, would you still do them? Do you love God when and how it's convenient, or do you love Him unconditionally? Sacrificially?

If Christ kept track of your spending habits, your hobbies, and listened in on your conversations for one week, what would He assume your priorities are? If you talked Jesus through your daily schedule, what activities would you be making excuses for? How quickly would He discover seventy-two hours of wasted time you could have used to read His word all the way through? Does your calendar, your schedule, your agenda show evidence of an all-consuming love for Christ? If you took Jesus through your house, what drawers would you quickly close? What rooms would you keep locked? What magazines or DVDs would you hide away? Does your home show a love for what God loves and a hatred for what God hates? Whether it's sin or just a time-consuming distraction, anything that makes you not want God, God hates.

Believers with spiritual heart disease look perfectly healthy on the outside, but with divided hearts and wandering eyes, they ask their jealous husband, who bought them with His own blood, to share. In the words of Jesus, "These people draw near to Me with their mouth, and honor Me with their lips, but their heart is far from Me."[288]

So what is the cure for spiritual heart disease? How do I unclog my spiritual arteries so my heart beats solely for Jesus Christ? "Repent and do the first works."

When the hearts of believers love Jesus most, God's people are consecrated. They don't let sin into their homes, they are not entertained by it, and when they find it in their own homes, they don't close it all up in a drawer. They drag it all out onto their front lawns and set it on fire.

Ephesians 4:22 says, "Put off, concerning your former conduct, the old man which grows corrupt according to the deceitful lusts." You want a heart-healthy workout? Strip off the extra weight. Whether it's sin or the distractions of this world, lay aside the old man, put off the former conduct, because only when God's people are consecrated can they love God with an undivided heart.

Secondly, in a heart that loves Jesus most, God's Word prevails. Reading the Bible expectantly and asking God to speak to us through His Spirit in His Word is an imperative. There are so many things that crowd in and demand our attention, but God's Word can't prevail from the bottom of the pile on our nightstand. It can't prevail sitting on our shelves gathering dust. "And be renewed in the spirit of your mind," Paul says.[289] Putting off the weight isn't enough. You need a healthy, steady, daily diet of God's Word to sustain you and renew your mind.

And thirdly, in hearts that love Jesus most, God's Son is magnified. God looks for men and women willing to work unhindered by the sacrifice, laboring with an undivided heart, proclaiming an undiluted message,

---

288 Matthew 15:8
289 Ephesians 4:23

investing in a humble occupation—all to make the gospel of Christ known. "Put on the new man which was created according to God, in true righteousness and holiness."[290]

This isn't a onetime thing. It is a daily exercise, exercising for godliness, putting on true righteousness and holiness, and it's absolutely necessary to maintain a healthy heart.

When God's Word is treasured, kept, held on to like our lives depend on it, the things of this world grow strangely dim. When God's Son is magnified, what He hates becomes detestable to us and we, whether literally or figuratively, push it out of our lives and set it on fire. And when God's people are consecrated, then there is nothing left to rob God of His first place in our lives. When God's people are consecrated, God's Word prevails, and God's Son is magnified, the sum total, the bottom line, is a heart that loves God most, the only healthy way to live.

Trust Jesus to the End

Do you hesitate to share Christ because of the way people might react? Do you avoid the truth because it might offend? Do you downplay holiness because it will make you an outsider at your school, with your coworkers? Do you live according to common sense rather than the commands of God because it's easier to walk by sight than by faith? If so, as was the danger in Smyrna, you have developed a spiritual anxiety disorder. "Do not fear," Jesus says.[291] Why? Because His people tend to be afraid.

God doesn't give us a spirit of fear. The world does. Our flesh does. Satan does. But God doesn't. His message to the spiritually anxious of Smyrna, and to us, no matter what we're facing in our daily lives, our health, our careers, our finances, the message is simply fear not. The Church shines brightest for Christ when we fear not, even in the face of persecution and martyrdom. The cure for a spiritual anxiety disorder? "Be faithful until death."[292]

Believers who trust Jesus to the end choose to live godly lives whatever the cost. Whether it's their life or their social status, their freedom or the opinion of their coworkers, they know that they are called to share in the

---

290 Ephesians 4:24
291 Revelation 2:10
292 Revelation 2:10

suffering of Christ. Knowing that all who desire to live godly in Christ Jesus will inevitably suffer persecution, they live in obedience, walking by faith, not by sight. Why?

Because a believer who trusts Jesus to the end lives for the heavenly reward, not the earthly distractions. Knowing that God uses persecution for His purposes and that God promises treasures to those who suffer for Christ, they tally their sorrows in the plus column, knowing the best is yet to come. Waiting for their heavenly home, they live like they're camping, ready to pack up at every moment. Nothing is so important to them that they can't just pull it up or leave it behind at a moment's notice. They die triumphantly because they die for Christ.

Does that seem far removed? A death died for Christ comes from a life lived for Christ, and "he who is faithful in what is least is faithful also in much,"[293] so instead of wondering if you'd be faithful to Christ if the cost was your life, be faithful to Christ when the cost is an interruption in your daily schedule or the possibility of someone rolling their eyes at you.

A believer who trusts Jesus to the end is faithful in the small things. They're willing to be an outsider at work because they choose to be pure in their conversation. They stand up for Christ at school even if their grades suffer for it. They speak the gospel of Jesus Christ with their neighbors even if it hurts their social status. They're willing to give up convenience to please Jesus. Willing to give up what entertains them because it offends Christ. Willing to give up a sport or hobby because it prevents them from gathering with Christ's body too often. They consider all things as loss for the sake of Christ and because they claim He's worth dying for, they make daily choices to act like He's worth living for.

Separate from Sin

Do you spend your time around the enemies of God? Do you find yourself listening to their opinions and considering their viewpoints? Have you started wondering if God really says what He means and means what He says? Instead of enforcing the old-fashioned standards of a fire and brimstone God, are you coming to God your way, on your terms, because that's

---

293 Luke 16:10

what works for you? Are you having difficulty discerning between God's truth and Satan's many counterfeits? Or maybe we can't even know for sure what God's truth is.

Are you decreasingly uncomfortable around sin? What used to repulse you doesn't bother you as much anymore? What used to horrify you is so commonplace that you don't even blink? Has your conversation begun to sound like the world? Do your habits reflect society's expectations or God's? When you draw the line between what's right and wrong, between what you should set before your eyes, what your mind should think on, and what you shouldn't, is your line in the same place God draws it? Does that seem like an unrealistic, naïve thing to aim for?

That isn't maturity or strength or a healthy attitude. That's a serious deficiency in your spiritual immune system. And Jesus says the only cure is to separate from sin. "Repent," He says, "or else."[294]

How do we separate from sin? First, know the truth. Know where the lines are, know what God says is sin, what He says is right and good. There are scientific reasons to trust the Bible, historic reasons, prophetic reasons, but the only reason you need to trust the Bible is because Jesus did. Every page, every chapter, every word. You want to recognize the counterfeits? Know the real thing so well you need duct tape to hold your Bible together. Want to spot the lies? So consume the truth that it's on the tip of your tongue the moment you hear something questionable. When you have a constant diet of God's Word, everything less starts to have a bad taste.

Second, compare what you hear to what you know. Pergamos fell because they couldn't distinguish between truth and lies, and Satan's alternative just walked over that blurred line, applied for membership, and joined the church. When you hear something new, check it against God's Word. Just because a pastor says it, because a prophet says it, because it came out of a cave in the Middle East and looks really old, doesn't make it Truth.

And third, draw the line and stand firm on God's side of it. Stop listening to false teachers. Stop compromising what you believe. Stop compromising how you behave. Flee immorality like it's after you. Sin is too dangerous a thing to toy with. Don't see how close you can get to the edge

294 Revelation 2:16

without going over, and don't look for what little bits of Scripture you can compromise for the sake of harmony with society. Sin is toxic, and it'll erode your immunity until you have an infection.

Un-Friend Worldliness

By the time Jesus gets to Thyatira, the Great Physician has His work cut out for Him. Thyatira had a raging infection of sin. The two things that God specifically told them to avoid, they had jumped into with both feet. If the Great Physician checked your temperature today, would He find the same raging infection in you?

Have you started qualifying how much sin totally offends God, but doesn't offend you? Do you have a certain level of immorality you're comfortable with, PG, or PG-13 is totally fine with you, even though any level of immorality offends a holy God? Are you completely intolerant with the sins of everybody else, but very tolerant of your own? Do you have reasons why God's laws don't apply to you, or why such and such is an exception, at least for you? Are you comfortable that you said the right words when you walked the aisle, secure with your fire insurance and the future promise of heaven, but live in the present however you want?

Do you accept what you hear because it's eloquent and sounds really nice, or because it matches up with God's Word? Do you even check? Has the line between sin and righteousness become so blurred that you're on the wrong side and don't even know it?

Thyatira went astray because of a false teacher, an eloquent woman named Jezebel, who called herself a prophetess. But that didn't excuse those who blindly followed her. We each have a responsibility to know what's in God's Word and to act on it. If you go ninety-five down the highway, it doesn't matter if you never saw a speed limit sign. You're still getting a ticket because you were responsible, the moment you got behind the wheel, to know the rules of the road. Sheep who follow wolves are still in trouble, because Jesus' sheep are supposed to know His voice and follow Him only.

Right now, there are six or seven hundred million people available to be your friend online through social media. Six or seven hundred million. They send a request, and you either confirm it or ignore it. And if somehow you get overwhelmed with friends, you can click "un-friend," and you are no longer exposed to everything going on in their lives. And God says that the believers in Thyatira had done what we are so prone to do today. They had become friends with the world.

"Adulterers and adulteresses! Do you not know that friendship with the world is enmity with God? Whoever therefore wants to be a friend of the world makes himself an enemy of God."[295] And God is saying, do you not know that in the Facebook of your life, friend-ing with the world, in any form it comes in, is enmity with God.

Boy, is that a strong word. Enmity. I don't think people realize what the last part of verse 4 really means, to make yourself an enemy of God. The same God that loves us, and in His mercy and grace pours out the riches of Christ that we could never comprehend, that same God is also quite good at making our lives absolutely miserable. That's what it means to make a enemy of God. It's a military term. It means God is constantly looking for ways to thwart and block me. I try to do this, God steps in to block me. God? My biggest fan? Wants to thwart me? Yes. If I'm a friend of the world.

What does it mean to be a friend of the world? Well, John defines it in 1 John 2:15–16. "Do not love the world," he says. What's the world? "For all that is in the world—the lust of the flesh, the lust of the eyes, and the pride of life—is not of the Father but is of the world."[296]

I'm old enough to remember when we only had three TV channels, and they were only on for part of the day. But there were only three. And John says that there are only three channels for sin. Three channels. Three places our immune system is weak, where infection can get in. The lust of the flesh. The lust of the eyes. And the pride of life. And if the devil can't get us in the lust of the flesh, he'll get us in the lust of the eyes, and if he can't get us there, he'll come through the pride of life.

We are tempted by the flesh to chase pleasure. This equals the cravings of the body. These are all the sensual temptations, whether it's food or pleasure or fun, our bodies are built to crave, and God says don't allow your flesh to control your craving. That is worldly. And God is against that lust,

---

295 James 4:4–5
296 1 John 2:15–16

in any form, in our lives. Being dominated by sensual pleasures. Most of us go, oh, those pedophiles, those sodomites, oh, that's so terrible.

Well, you're not into that? Okay, what about the lust of the eyes? This is the lust for things. And the things may be as large as a house—and every time I hear someone talk about building their dream house, I think about my dream house. You know where it is? It's not here, where tornados and termites and floods can get it. It's a house not made with hands, eternal in the heavens—but the things can be as old and dusty as an antique dresser, it can be the car. But lest we think this is not as bad as the lust of the flesh, remember that covetousness, the insatiable longing for things, is idolatry. The lust for possessions is as wicked as the lust for immoral things. Beware of both.

Or, the final one, the last channel, if it's not the lust of the flesh or the lust of the eyes, it's the pride of life. This equals the boasting of the mouth. The constant one-upping, I can always outdo you. People always boasting. This can show up as selfishness because we think we're important. We become irritable when life doesn't revolve around us. It can lead to untruthfulness because we have to protect our image. It can lead to laziness because we think that our comfort is more important than anything else. But it's all produced by pride. Pride also shows up as a lust for status, fame, fortune, power, authority, wanting a title to make people's heads turn. In the Scriptures, that was Satan's sin. He wasn't into gross immoral behavior. He wasn't into stuff. He was into status.

Any form of lust, God hates. And the desire He has for us is that we love Jesus more than anything else, that we trust Him to the end, that we separate from sin, and when we find ourselves feeding on the lust of the flesh, the lust of the eyes, or the pride of life, we cut off that feed as immediately and completely as possible.

Don't feed yourself with what God says makes you sick. If the movies you watch feed the lust of the flesh with all the blatant sensuality and sexual humor, then cut off the feed. If the advertisements you hear on the radio make you dissatisfied with what you have and want something you don't need and don't have room for, but you just have to have more and bigger and better, turn it off. Cut the feed. Change the channel. And in today's society, we are taught to feed the pride of life. To boost our self-esteem.

Do you know who God says we're supposed to esteem. Others. As more important than ourselves.[297]

Don't feed self. All these lusts, the flesh, the eyes, the pride of life, are reptilian. Do you know what that means? They grow bigger and bigger every year. As long as you feed it, and don't allow God's Word to impede its growth, that lust will keep growing until it consumes you.

When you're friends with someone online, their attitudes, opinions, priorities, likes, and dislikes are always before your eyes. Christ's call to holiness prompts us to ask who we're friends with. When you're a friend of the world, the feed that's constantly coming in is those three things, lust of the flesh, lust of the eyes, pride of life. Do you know what else friends of the world do? They follow people that are not friends of God.

Who are you following? Who do you let set the trends in your life? Whose lives do you seek to emulate? Whose name do we associate with? Whose name are we known by? You can't serve two masters. You either follow Christ, or the world. Followers of the world can't be followers of Christ, because Christ and the world are going in opposite directions. Have you decided, like the song says, "to follow Jesus. No turning back"? Or are you like Lot's wife, constantly checking over your shoulder to see the world she was supposed to have left behind?

What do you post a thumbs up for? What do you like? Is it all the same things the world likes? Or do you love what God loves? Do you hate what God hates? Or have you so fed yourself with the constant feed of the world that you don't even know what God thinks about the things we approve? Do you like what the world likes? God says only the wicked approve of what He hates.

How do you un-friend worldliness? By loving what God loves and hating what He hates. By following Jesus and listening to His voice only. And by choosing to feed yourself with God and His word, not with the world.

Stay Awake

Have you fallen asleep on the wall? If Jesus returned today, would you find yourself totally unprepared? Are you so comfortable you've become

---

297 Philippians 2:3

overconfident? Unaware of the danger around you? Are you drifting into a spiritual coma, slowly becoming useless to Christ and unconcerned about it?

If you are in spiritual cardiac arrest, flat-lining in your Christian walk, and like He said to Sardis, Jesus says to you, "You have a name that you are alive but you are dead,"[298] then it's time to wake up.

Jesus prescribes three treatments for spiritual cardiac arrest. First, live for Christ's coming. Live like He could come back any moment and catch you doing whatever you're doing, like any moment you'll be asked to give an account. Second, follow the Master's instructions. Jesus left us with marching orders to follow until His return. Are you following them? Will you be found faithful in the little things, and the big? And third, watch out for temptation. Satan isn't a figment of the imagination or the mythological embodiment of evil. He's dangerous, he's prowling, and he can't kill what Christ made alive, but putting you to sleep is almost as good.

"Be watchful," Jesus says. Don't underestimate the devil prowling around like a roaring lion, and don't stop looking for the any-moment return of Christ. "Strengthen the things which remain," reinforcing them from both sides. Build up your spiritual arsenal of God's Word, bolster your life with prayer. "Remember therefore how you received and heard," preaching the gospel to yourself and keeping the commands of God ever before your eyes. "Hold fast," and keep God's commands like your life depends on it. Don't let them slip through your fingers. And "repent."[299] Change your mind about your comfort level with spiritual lethargy. Change your behavior by systematically putting on the armor of God, that when Jesus comes like a thief in the night, you will be found with unsoiled garments, confident and unashamed before Him at His coming.

Please God in Every Way

Can you go through the scrutinizing, penetrating, omniscient, holy sight of God and He find nothing wrong? Are you constantly ridding yourself of anything God wouldn't approve of? Are you standing strong and secure despite the earthquakes of life?

298 Revelation 3:1
299 Revelation 3:2–3

It is possible. "I know your works,"[300] Jesus says to Philadelphia. No condemnation, no rebuke. Only approval. Diagnosis: clean bill of health. How is that kind of life maintained?

1. Build your life on the One who is holy, allowing His holiness to prompt a passion for holiness in you.
2. Build your life on the One who is true. He who is holy cannot lie. He who is uncorrupted cannot fail. And He who is the only source of un-blighted existence is naturally the only source of absolute and unfailing truth in an uncertain world.
3. Build your life on the One who holds the key, who embodies and fulfills every promise God ever made, the One who dispenses to us God's wealth, who opens to us God's presence, and who displays to us God's power.
4. Build your life on the One who opens and no one can shut, who shuts and no one can open, who opens the door to eternal satisfaction, light that can't be extinguished, and everlasting life.

When you build your life on Him who is holy, you will have a life that meets Christ's absolute approval. When you build your life on Him who is true, you will have a house built on a rock that withstands any storm. When you build your life on Him who holds the key, who dispenses the riches, presence, and power of God, then nothing is impossible for you. And when you build your life on Him who opens and no one can shut, then your satisfaction is found in Christ, your light comes from Jesus, and your life is endless. When you build on Jesus, you have the power of an endless life, the assurance of eternal security, and your life will be forever changed.

THE SEVEN HABITS OF SANCTIFIED BELIEVERS

Living in the Shadow of the Cross

Jesus warned of a day of an unthinking multitude that thinks they are Christians but are not, and of a church dominated by materialism, empty

---

300 Revelation 3:8

profession, and false peace. Untested, self-sufficient, and comfortable, the bulk of the modern church has become sickening to Christ.

Are you a middle-of-the-road Christian? You don't rock the boat? Don't make waves? You're a friend of everybody, just going to church and avoiding the really bad sins? You don't bring up anything that might convict or offend?

Are you the same temperature as the world around you? Have you forgotten to aggressively resist the world, passively squeezed into its mold? Have you compartmentalized your life so that Christ is neglected in the little things, then the big things? How long has it been since you felt the weight of glory on your life?

Diagnosis: spiritual neutrality. And it's Jesus who gets sick from this one. He is so disgusted with the lukewarm neutrality of His people, Jesus wants to vomit them out of His mouth.

The cure? Living in the shadow of the cross. Operate on the truths of a sanctified life: Christ's death on the cross has once and for all freed me from sin's hold on my life. Penalty, gone. Power, defeated. And one day I will be untouched even by its presence. I am going to be forever impacted by Christ's death in my place. And because I have been justified, I will choose to live sanctified. That's living in the shadow of the cross.

Walking in the Power of the Cross

Increased with goods, making piles for yourself, have you become un-needing of Christ? Are you consumed with the materialistic pursuits of pleasure? Do all your gadgets and online media accounts and piles of possessions distract you from God and His Word?

Do you fail to seek God's guidance, letting Him trail after you as you plow ahead, deaf to His voice? Have you gone days or weeks without seeking His presence, finding your satisfaction elsewhere? Do you have time for every other influence on your life but God?

Don't worry if you failed the test. The cure for spiritual self-sufficiency is walking in the power of the cross. "I have been crucified with Christ; it is no longer I who live, but Christ lives in me; and the life which I now live in the flesh I live by faith in the Son of God, who loved me and gave Himself for me."[301]

The prayer of the spiritually dependent asks God to focus me on who He is, giving Him His proper place in my life. It seeks His kingdom, His rule, His influence, asking God to control me. And then to lead me, to let God be out in front and I willingly follow. Supply me. I am not rich and wealthy, and I don't have need of nothing like the Laodiceans. Cleanse me because I live in a world of sin. Protect me because my own strength is not enough. Empty me so that I can be filled with You. Amen.

Hearing and Responding to Jesus

Do you no longer see yourself as God's Word explains you are? Have you simply stopped listening to Jesus? Is He on your porch, knocking at your door, and you're comfortable tuning Him out?

What is the first thing you seek in the morning? Is it your emails? Your text messages? If you go on a trip and accidentally leave your phone charger, do you have to go and buy a new one, but if you leave your Bible, you think, oh, I can do without it until I get home? Are the Facebook posts, the Twitter feeds, the social media updates so important that you carry your phone around with you everywhere, but when you pick up your Bible Sunday morning to go to church, you realize it hasn't moved since you put it there last Sunday after church?

Have you become a forgetful hearer instead of a doer of the word? Do you read the RSVP of Christ's commands to you, say, oh, that's nice, and throw them in the trash like any other piece of mail without ever responding to Christ?

That's spiritual insensitivity, and there's no excuse for it. Jesus said, "My sheep hear My voice, and I know them, and they follow Me."[302] The cure for spiritual insensitivity? READ GOD'S WORD. Dive into it daily. Love it more than your necessary food. Cling to it like a life raft. And DO WHAT IT SAYS. Make the daily commitment to live according to what you read in God's Word, to not become a forgetful hearer, but to be a doer of the word.

---

301 Galatians 2:20
302 John 10:27

Hearing and responding to Jesus is an absolutely crucial habit for anyone who wants to be fruitful and pleasing to God.

Investing in the Bank of Heaven

Do you find that the more you have, the more you want? Are you less and less satisfied with what you have? Are you increasingly concerned with all the people who are trying to get their hands on your stuff? Are you beset with discontentment, and insecurity? Hanging onto your possessions so tightly that death looks like a loss?

Have you exchanged the eternal for the temporal? Allowed confidence in your wealth to rob you of your faith? Is God's Word getting choked out of your life by your stuff? Are you finding your stuff to be a cruel taskmaster, enslaving you? Are you less and less excited about heaven, knowing all the stuff you'll have to leave behind? When it comes to money, do you have the tendency to leave God out of the conversation?

Spiritual wastefulness is like living in a radiation zone, and even a little exposure is marrow-shriveling and deadly. Instead, get busy investing in the bank of heaven. How? By, 1 Timothy 6:18, doing good works, being ready to give, and being willing to share. That's really storing up for yourself a nest egg for your retirement.

The bank of heaven gives a return of 10,000 percent, it is insured by the God of the universe, it never needs a bailout, nothing in it ever loses value, and it's impossible to rob. "But lay up for yourselves treasures in heaven, where neither moth nor rust destroy and where thieves do not break in and steal." Why? Because "where your treasure is, there your heart will be also."[303]

Dressing for Christ Daily

What are you focused on? What is all-consuming to you? What is on your mind while you brush your teeth, drive to work, mow your lawn? What spills out into every other activity? What pops out of your mouth when you're talking to people, regardless of what the conversation is? Is it getting dressed for Christ daily?

303 Matthew 6:20–21

"I counsel you to buy from Me white garments, that you may be clothed,"[304] Jesus says to Laodicea. There will come a day when you and I will be revealed in front of everybody for what we've done on this earth. And you know what's sad? When He hands us our life's accomplishments, woven together into a garment, many believers are going to be ashamed because of how little they have to put on.

Spiritual neglect sickens Jesus, but there's a cure. To get consumed with plotting to put on Jesus Christ daily. His character, His armor, white garments fit for a bride.

How do I know if I'm wearing the right clothes? If my life is decreasingly characterized by contentions, jealousies, outbursts of wrath, envy, and all the other works of the flesh, then I am daily putting off those old black garments. And if my life is increasingly characterized by tender mercies, kindness, humility, meekness, and longsuffering, then I am daily putting on the Lord Jesus Christ.

"Let us be glad and rejoice and give Him glory, for the marriage of the Lamb has come," Revelation 19:7–8 says. "And His wife has made herself ready." I tell you what: you can't get ready for heaven in heaven. We're talking about today, the choices you'll make this week, the ones you made last week, last year. And if those choices are to put on Jesus Christ, "to her it was granted to be arrayed in fine linen, clean and bright, for the fine linen is the righteous acts of the saints."

A Lifestyle of Practical Purity

Are you unsure whether you're saved? Do you have trouble seeing God at work in your life? Does God's Word just not make sense any more? Do you have trouble seeing God in His Word? Do you have no idea what God's will is for your life?

Do you have a split focus? Parts of your life that are un-surrendered? Does living in practical purity seem impossible? Have you been looking full in the face of the world for so long that the things of God have grown strangely dim?

Spiritual blindness is preventable. It's treatable. It does not have to persist. Jesus wants to promote healthy eyes. He wants us to see Him clearly. He wants

---

304 Revelation 3:18

us to understand and see His will clearly in His Word. And He wants us looking with those spiritual eyes to see life clearly. So we need to be regularly applying the eye salve that Jesus says preserves spiritual sight. "Anoint (literally "Christ") your eyes with eye salve, that you may see."[305] And, "blessed are the pure in heart, for they shall see God" continually, for themselves.[306]

Six choices that preserve spiritual sight: who can see God? 1. He who walks righteously (a lifestyle of practical purity). 2. And speaks uprightly (speech that is under control). 3. He who despises the gain of oppressors (compassion). 4. Who gestures with his hands, refusing bribes (honesty). 5. Who stops his ears from hearing about bloodshed (pure audio input). 6. And shuts his eyes from seeing evil (pure video input).[307]

What are the indescribable joys of continually seeing God for yourself? You will dwell on high. You will find true security, true satisfaction. You will be never-endingly refreshed. You will see God in all His beauty, and as Helen Lemmel said, "Turn your eyes upon Jesus, look full in His wonderful face, and the things of this world will grow strangely dim in the light of His glory and grace."

Living Crucified

Are you living as a follower of the Way? Do you feel constantly out of step with the world around you? Do you stand out to the people around you as weird, different, going in the opposite direction? Are you living like a stranger in this world with only a temporary visa, knowing that your citizenship is in heaven? Is it heaven's laws you know? Heaven's language that you speak? Heaven's citizenship you prize? Are you rising to increasing levels of surrender? Living a life of personal discipline? A soldier, athlete, farmer working toward a goal that is not of this world?

Or have you forgotten how horrible sin always is to Christ? Do your sins just get swept under the rug? Does the sin that sickens, offends, and cost Christ His life entertain you? Amuse you? Enslave you, but you're not all that worried about it? Are you a past-tense Christian? Counting on a decision you made or an aisle you walked, knowing the Truth, but not

305 Revelation 3:18 paraphrased
306 Matthew 5:8
307 Isaiah 33:15–16

living the Life? If followers of the Way were rounded up and put in jail, would the soldiers simply pass on by your house without bothering you? Has Satan moved on to bigger targets because you're harmless?

If paragraph two is true of you but paragraph one is not, then you've just been diagnosed with a common condition among God's people: spiritual laxity. It's an all-encompassing general condition that leads to and makes the believer susceptible to every other spiritual malady Jesus warns about. The good news is that the remedy is the only cure-all this world will ever know. "Therefore, be zealous and repent."[308]

When you've seen what's right in God's Word (doctrine), and you've been convicted of what's wrong in your own life (reproof), then get zealous and repent. Accept God's correction. Change your mind and your direction and get enrolled in Jesus' righteousness training program. Your gym membership has already been paid for by the blood of Christ. Your personal trainer, the Holy Spirit, is available to you 24-7, living right in your house and with you constantly. And the first six steps of the righteousness training program are clearly lined out in Romans 6 of your training manual. Operate on what you know to be true. Say "no" to sin. Break the old patterns. Follow Jesus. Enlist with God daily. And pursue a passion for holiness.

Jesus was crucified to open the way for us to be His obedient, consecrated servants. So that we could be crucified to the power of sin, the lust of the world, and the bondage of self. To please God, we must live crucified lives.

Crucified living is surrendered living. We give up. We abdicate the throne of our lives to Christ. "I beseech you therefore, brethren, by the mercies of God, that you present your bodies a living sacrifice, holy, acceptable to God."[309] That's our offering of worship, bodies that are harnessed under His control.

Crucified living is exchanged living. "I have been crucified with Christ; it is no longer I who live, but Christ lives in me."[310] I've exchanged me as the chief owner/operator of this rig, and Christ becomes the owner/operator. And Jesus doesn't want to fight me for control. Crucified living is me willingly pulling over and handing over the keys, handing over control of my life to Christ.

308 Revelation 3:19
309 Romans 12:1
310 Galatians 2:20

Crucified living means we never get out of sight of the cross. "But God forbid that I should boast except in the cross of our Lord Jesus Christ, by whom the world has been crucified to me, and I to the world."[311] Crucified hands are tied down. They can't go after the things that displease God. The love of Christ constrains us. If we are crucified to the world, we don't go and do and think and act the way we used to. And the world is crucified to me. It doesn't taste as good anymore.

"I have been crucified with..." that's one word in Greek. *Sustaruo.* And it has three truths. It's indicative, which means it's a fact. It happened. Not hypothetical. Not possibly. Actually. Really. And it's passive, which means it was done to me. I didn't crucify myself. God did it. And it's perfect tense, which means it has been completed. I am not constantly being crucified with Christ. I have been. In the past. But the past event has a continuing impact on my present. This fact, of what was done to me, means that my life is to be a surrendered life where I give up the throne, an exchanged life, where I no longer live but Christ lives in me, a life where I never get out of sight of the cross. Jesus died in my place, and I died with Him. Because of that, I have died to sin.

We are dead to sin so we no longer want to continue in sin. We're not only dead to sin. We're alive in Christ. It's an exchanged life, a grace-energized life. It's Christ defeating sin, not me. Martin Luther used to say, "When the devil knocks, I send Jesus to answer the door." That's how we're supposed to live. Fruitful and pleasing to God.

"As many as I love, I rebuke and chasten."[312] Everything Jesus does is prompted by love. And this isn't *agape* commanded love. This is love of choice. Jesus is our friend, He loves spending time with us, and this is why He's doing all this. He rebukes, and He chastens, because He loves. "Therefore be zealous and repent."[313]

No matter how far you've wandered from God, it's always only one step back. Repentance is the first step in a life that is pleasing to God. And that is Christ's last word to His Church.

---

311 Galatians 6:14
312 Revelation 3:19
313 Revelation 3:19

RESPOND to Truth

If your spiritual life were like a house that needed remodeling, what room is in most desperate need of repair? What one problem can you focus in on to fix starting today?

Knowing what it is you want to fix, what portions of God's Word contain the nutrients you're most deficient in? How can you make absolutely sure you're getting a balanced diet of God's Word?

What exercise regimen does God prescribe for your spiritual condition? Where can you start on that? How can you carve out time for that every day?

What weight is dragging you down like an anchor? How can you lay it aside? What are you feeding yourself with that you should cut from your diet? What lazy habits can you change into areas of spiritual discipline?

Where do you see yourself in the portrait God's Word paints of these seven churches? If Jesus wrote you a letter, what would it say?

Do you want to please God in every way? What one thing can you change to model yourself after the church at Philadelphia?

Index

 **Discover The Book Ministries**
A Nonprofit 501C3 Bible Teaching Ministry

To support DTBM or to view additional books, ebooks, and MP3s written by Dr. Barnett please visit:
www.discoverthebook.org

For online video training,
visit the DTBM YouTube channel at
**https://www.youtube.com/channel/
UCVK6dN-9kLDnQhYBFuESO9A/about**

Discover The Book Ministries
8500 North 128th East Avenue | OWASSO, OK 74055-6242